Osborne William Tancock

An English Grammar and Reading Book for Lower Forms in Classical Schools

Second Edition

Osborne William Tancock

An English Grammar and Reading Book for Lower Forms in Classical Schools
Second Edition

ISBN/EAN: 9783337178253

Printed in Europe, USA, Canada, Australia, Japan

Cover: Foto ©Paul-Georg Meister /pixelio.de

More available books at **www.hansebooks.com**

Clarendon Press Series

AN ENGLISH GRAMMAR

AND

READING BOOK

FOR LOWER FORMS IN CLASSICAL SCHOOLS

BY THE

REV. O. W. TANCOCK, M.A.

Assistant Master of Sherborne School

SECOND EDITION, REVISED AND ENLARGED

Oxford
AT THE CLARENDON PRESS
M DCCC LXXIV

PREFACE.

THIS little book is intended to help those who are trying to solve the problem of teaching English systematically in classical schools. My object has been to supply an English grammar for lower forms which shall teach a boy to apply grammatical terms and explanations to his own language, and which may be learnt by the side of his Latin grammar with little additional trouble; and to supply a reading book which shall be to the study of English what a Latin Delectus is to the study of Latin. The Glossary explains the meaning and derivation of every word in the Extracts. I believe that a boy who has worked fairly through the book will have laid the foundation of an accurate knowledge of the structure of his mother tongue, and its relation to kindred languages, and will have learned to distinguish between its two great divisions of words—the words of Teutonic, and those of Latin origin. I have not attempted to teach everything, or to supply the place of advanced grammars; but I have great hope that those who use it will have nothing to unlearn when they come to use larger grammars, and to extend their study of English to the earlier stages of the language.

In the Introductory Chapter I have given—for teachers rather than for boys—a sketch of the growth of the language, with some notice of the laws of that growth, and of the changes which have taken place. Much of what I have said is, of course, derived from Mr. Freeman's writings, in whose steps all must follow who deal with the times of our early forefathers. The chapter was written before Mr. Earle's 'The Philology of the English Tongue' was published, but I have been happy to be able to add a few references to his pages as giving support to what I had written.

In the Grammar in some places rather more of the form and nomenclature of Latin grammar is kept than is entirely pleasing to myself, but I have been obliged to bear in mind that the book is for boys who have their Latin grammars in their hands, and to whom no stumbling-block is greater than a variety of grammatical terms.

I have to acknowledge the courtesy of the owners of the copyrights of many of the Extracts, who have in all cases most kindly given their consent to the use of their works. If by mistake I have in any case made use of a copyright without obtaining permission, I hope the oversight will be excused.

I owe thanks to many friends for much advice and help, to the Rev. C. W. Boase, M.A., of Exeter College, Oxford; and especially to A. M. Curteis, Esq., M.A., Assistant-Master of Sherborne School, who has kindly read and corrected my proof-sheets, and assisted me much in every part of my work.

I gladly take the opportunity of a second edition to thank the Rev. W. W. Skeat for most kindly sending me many valuable criticisms and corrections.

March, 1874.

CONTENTS.

	PAGE
INTRODUCTORY CHAPTER	1
GRAMMAR	33
EXTRACTS	107
GLOSSARY	227

INTRODUCTORY CHAPTER.

English is a Teutonic language of the Low-German branch.

§ 1. THE English language which is spoken by most persons in England, Scotland, Wales, Ireland, and in the many colonies founded or occupied by settlers from these lands, is a language of the Low-German branch of the Teutonic family.

Differences between related languages.

§ 2. When people of common origin separate into tribes and pass to various places, small changes and differences grow in their language. As time goes on, the differences become more numerous and more marked, so that the modes of speech of two tribes can be distinguished according to rules or laws. Such modes of speech are called dialects when the differences which mark them one from another are not great, or distinct languages when the differences have become very important.

When we inquire into the dialects or languages spoken by various peoples or nations, we find that some are very near akin, some have more distant relationship, while others appear at first sight to have no relationship one to another. Accordingly languages are divided into classes called families, each containing a group of languages which are near akin or like one to another, as the Teutonic, Celtic, Italic families of languages.

Tests of relationship.

§ 3. This kinship or likeness of languages and dialects is to be looked for—(1) in *pronunciation*, or the ways of speaking the same words by different peoples; (2) in the *vocabulary*, or the use of the same words to express the same ideas in different languages; (3) in *grammatical structure*, or the ways in which words are put together to make sentences. So that in two dialects of the same language we shall find that letters and words are pronounced rather differently, but that the words used are mostly the same, and that there is not much difference in the grammar—this is, in their ways of showing genders, numbers, and cases of nouns, or voices, moods, tenses, numbers, and persons of verbs, and of linking and arranging words and sentences. Thus, if we take dialects of English as showing difference at its least and likeness at its greatest,

> Stay me weth flagons, cumfurt me weth apples; for I'm sick of love.
> (Cornwall.)
> Stay me wi' vlagons, comfort me wi' yapples, vor I be zeek o' love.
> (Somerset.)
> Stay me wud drinkin pots, comfort me wud appuls, for I be sick wud love.
> (Sussex.)
> Stop ma wid flagons, comfort ma wid apples, for aa's seek o' leuvv.
> (Mid-Cumberland.)
> Stay mah wih flaggons, cumfurt mah wih apples, for a' seek uv luv.
> (Durham.)[1]

the differences are mostly of pronunciation.

Between two languages of the same family the likeness will still be strong even when they have been separated for a very long time; as between English, of the Low-German branch, and modern German, of the High-German branch,

---

[1] Song of Solomon, ii. 5, Bonaparte Collection. Latham, English Language, pp. 350, 346, 357, 362, 378.

of the Teutonic family. But if two languages do not belong to the same family we find not only different pronunciations of the same words when they occur in both, but also usually different words to express the same ideas, and what is of still more importance, great differences of grammatical structure. And this last is the best test of kinship, for one language very frequently and very easily borrows words from another, but it cannot give up its own grammar and take the grammar of another. Thus with specimens of English, German, and Latin, we are struck at once by the small differences between the two languages of the Teutonic family, and the great differences between them and the language of the Italic family, in all our three points:

And John was clad with camel's hair and with a leathern girdle about his loins; and he ate locusts and wild honey.

Johannes aber war bekleidet mit Cameel's haaren und mit einem ledernen Gürtel um seine Lenden, und ass Heuschrecken und wilden Honig.

Et erat Johannes vestitus pilis cameli et zona pellicea circa lumbos eius, et locustas et mel sylvestre edebat. (St. Mark i. 6.)

By the use of these rules of relationship it has been shewn that the likenesses between several languages bring them under the Teutonic family, distributed into groups still more nearly akin.

TEUTONIC FAMILY.

Mœso-Gothic.	*Scandinavian.*	*Low-German.*	*High-German.*
	Iceland,	Old Saxon,	German of the
	Norway,	German of the North,	east and
	Sweden,	Holland,	south districts
	Denmark.	Friesland and islands,	of Germany.
		England.	

In like manner, further inquiries show that distant relationship can be traced by the same rules between various families of languages, thus uniting many under one stock.

A statement of Grimm's Law, which explains and illustrates these relationships, is to be found at the end of this chapter, p. 32.

Origin of the English.

§ 4. In a part of the duchy of Schleswig, south of Denmark, and on the northern coast of Germany, is a little district which bears the name Angeln, of the Angles. From this district we have received the name Angle or Engle, and then our words England, English; for from this and many neighbouring parts came our English-speaking forefathers. The various invaders of Britain, who are commonly grouped under the names Jutes, Saxons, Angles, by degrees settled on the southern and eastern coasts of the island during the fourth, fifth, and sixth centuries of the Christian era[1], bringing with them their language called English. All that we know of the bands, or tribes as they are called, of invaders leads us to suppose that they spoke one language. Nothing that is known of the Jutes marks them off distinctly from the others, and they are sometimes called Engle, as if they were not different from the Angles. In like manner we find that the British had one name for all the invaders, calling Jutes, Saxons, and Angles all alike Saxons, or Sassenach; while not only the Angles of the north, but also the men of Wessex, or the West Saxon kingdom of the south, called their tongue English, as king Alfred writes, 'Ic hie ón Englisc awende[2],' 'I translated it into English,' that is, into the tongue of his own people. We therefore consider that the many sets of invaders who formed these settlements in

---

[1] Freeman, History of the Norman Conquest, i. p. 12.

[2] King Alfred's Gregory's Pastoral Care, p. 6 (Early English Text Society). Compare Mr. Freeman's Lectures on the Origin of the English People, in Macmillan's Magazine, March, April, and May, 1870.

Britain were all alike of the Angle or English race, and that the speech of all alike is to be called English. There were, naturally, many differences of dialect among them—men who came from one place in the fifth century differing from men who came from a neighbouring district in the sixth century. So in the present day, 'the Frisian, which is spoken on a small area... between the Scheldt and Jutland, and on the islands near the shore... is broken up into endless local dialects[1].' Thus the settlers in Thanet might be distinguished from the settlers on the Colne, and both of these from the settlers on the Humber, by their pronunciation or use of certain words, just as a Cumberland man, a Sussex man, and a Dorsetshire man may now be distinguished. But with these differences the language was one, as it is one now, and it has kept its old name.

Settlement of English in Britain.

§ 5. The bodies of English invaders landed on the coasts of Britain, at first, as mere rovers looking for plunder, and a stronghold on land for the winter, or as helpers in the wars of the British chiefs. After a time they made good their footing as settlers on lands better and more pleasant than those they had left behind them. They found Britain inhabited by people very unlike themselves; unlike in language, for the British spoke a language of the Celtic family to which the English gave the name Welsh, that is, foreign or strange; unlike in religion, for the British were Christians while the English were heathen; and unlike in manners and customs, for the British had learnt some of the Roman civilisation from their old rulers whom the English did not know.

---

[1] Max Müller, Lectures on the Science of Language, i. p. 53.

Influence of Celtic upon English.

§ 6. Between the British and the English, who gradually settled in the land and founded communities and kingdoms, there was long and bitter war. By degrees the English pushed the older race back to the western mountain lands, Cumberland, Wales, and the moorland parts of Somerset, Devon, and Cornwall. So that 'during the last years of the sixth century, a line drawn from Abercorn southward to Weymouth would not have unfairly represented the two great divisions of the island[1];' with Christian British on the west of the line and heathen English on the east. How far the two races may have mingled is not certain; probably scarcely at all at first, and little at any time except on the borders of the hilly lands. At any rate the languages did not mix. This we might expect, because in the other countries where a Celtic language has met with another tongue, the Celtic has usually given way before it, as in Gaul before the Latin, without influencing it much. Accordingly we find that very pure English continued to be spoken in Dorset and Somerset quite up to the rivers Parret and Axe, which were at different times long the frontier line between the Celts and the English. In like manner 'the broadest and purest Lowland Scots is spoken on the edge of the Highland line,' for 'it was the nature of the language [of these invaders of the Teutonic race] obstinately to resist all admixture with the Gaelic[2].' Whatever influence Celtic had upon English was entirely confined to the vocabulary, and did not affect the grammatical structure of the language in any degree. The

---

[1] Hist. Eccl. Baedae, Moberly; Introduction, p. i.
[2] Burton, History of Scotland, i. p. 207.

new words introduced were not very many, and they fall under the following heads or classes:—

1. The names of natural objects in the land, as mountains, or rivers, or headlands, &c.; as *Ben*, *Pen*, *Pen*rith; *Avon*, *Axe*, *Exe*, *Ox*, *Ouse*, *Usk*, *Derwent*, *Thames*; *Dover*, *Kent*. A new comer would naturally take many such names from the old inhabitants, as Englishmen have taken *Mississippi*, *Ontario*, in America; *Taranaki*, *Akaroa*, in New Zealand; *Wooloomooloo*, in Australia.

2. The names of some common objects of daily use and industry. These are not many, and were adopted from the talk of the Celtic agricultural serfs and house slave-women, without changing the language, just as the foreign names of common objects are often now adopted into modern English without changing our language; as the American *moccasin*, *yam*; New Zealand *pah*; Australian *kangaroo*, *boomerang*. Thus among words of Celtic origin are *basket*, *bran*, *cart*, *coat*, *gruel*, *park*, *rug*, *wicket*, *willow*[1].

3. The names of some towns or stations, showing in their Latin origin, or Latinised form, a trace of that Roman influence on the Britons of which we have spoken, § 5; as *Lincoln*, colonia; *Doncaster*, *Dorchester*, *Gloucester*, *Exeter*, castra; *Leicester*, legionis castra; *Stratton*, *Stretton*, strata; *Portsmouth*, portus. We might compare the traces of Dutch near New York in the names *Orange*, *Staaten*; or of French in Canada in the names *Montreal*, *Quebec*. It is likely that the fortified posts, *castra*, and roads, *strata*, and ramparts, *vallum*, of the Romans in Britain were altogether new to the English, and made a great impression on them.

---

[1] Compare Latham, English Language, p. 412; Earle, Philology of the English Tongue, p. 20.

English has changed.

§ 7. From about the end of the sixth century the English were settled in the land as though it were their own home. They were broken up into many communities or kingdoms, speaking several dialects, but the same English language. We find, however, that the early written specimens of this language are very different from what we now call English. Thus—

Her cuom Ælla on Bretonlond and his iii suna mid iii scipum, on þa stowe þe is nemned Cymenesora, and þær ofslogon monige Wealas and sume on fleame bedrifon on þone wudu þe is genemned Andredesleage.	This year came Ælla to the land of Britain and his three sons with three ships, to the station that is named Cymenesora, and there slew many Welsh, and some in flight they drove to that wood that is named Andred's-lea[1].

So different indeed that people often talk as if it were quite another language, and call it Anglo-Saxon, to distinguish it from English, speaking of our English as a language descended from Anglo-Saxon. But the name, though in some ways convenient, is apt to mislead, because it is one which the people did not use, and because it may lead us to suppose that the changes in our language have been so unusual as to amount to an absolute break in its history instead of a very regular and natural development.

In order to show clearly the relation of our present English to the English of those early times, it is needful to explain of what kind the changes in the language have been, and how they have come about.

---

[1] Earle, Saxon Chronicles, p. 12.

How languages change.

§ 8. First it must be understood that a language never remains long the same. Change is in fact always going on, so that the speech of each generation differs somewhat from that of the last. The change is of various kinds, and especially in those three points which have been already laid down as points of difference between languages. Thus in the specimen in § 7 we have changes of pronunciation, as *monige*, now *many*; of vocabulary, as *mid*, now *with*; *slowe* has given place to *station*, a word borrowed from Latin; of grammar, as *suna*, marking its plural by *a*, has changed into *sons*, marking its plural by *s*; *Bretonlond* has become *the land of Britain*, marking relation by a preposition for greater clearness. Such changes go on in almost all languages, though with more or less quickness and regularity according as the language is little or much disturbed by the influence of people speaking a different tongue.

Change from Synthetical to Analytical.

§ 9. The most important change has been the change in the grammar of the language from the synthetic to the analytic condition, that is, from a grammar which expresses the relations of ideas and so of words in a sentence by inflexions, as case-endings, tense-endings, and person-endings, to one which expresses them by prepositions, auxiliaries, and pronouns. A tendency to this change is natural to all modern European languages. Thus modern Greek is analytical compared with ancient Greek, and French is analytical compared with Latin. All languages of the Teutonic family have changed or are changing in the same manner as English, but not all to the same extent, so that among them the law is of universal application, 'The earlier the stage, the fuller the inflection; and as languages become modern, they lose their inflections[1].' This tendency is always aided and hastened by any admixture of a foreign language, or any fresh mingling of dialects, causes which have been at work upon English[2].

Scandinavian invasions and influence.

§ 10. The English became Christians during the seventh century, taught in part by missionaries from Rome, who landed in Kent, in part by Scottish missionaries from Iona, who converted the northern kingdoms. In the ninth a new wave of invaders poured down from Northern Europe. They were of the Scandinavian race, and, starting from Norway and Sweden and Denmark, they wasted those parts of the coast of Neustria which were afterwards called Normandy, and the coasts of England, Scotland, and Ireland. The Danes settled on the eastern coast, radiating from the Humber; the Norwegians settled on the western coast, radiating from Morecambe Bay. These new-comers wrought the first great disturbance upon English speech. Their tongue was of the Scandinavian branch (§ 3) of the Teutonic family, and so nearly akin to English that it was rather a new dialect than a new language. By and by they made good their footing in the north and east of the land. Then by degrees they and their language coalesced with the northern English; and this all the more easily since they were of

---

[1] Latham, English Language, p. 269.

[2] Inflexions are lost, because to the uneducated and to foreigners the idea in the word is the main thing, and therefore they lay stress on the root syllables, not on the inflexions, and hence the consonants of the flexion syllables drop off, and the full-toned vowels weaken to the vague *e*, which soon becomes mute.

much the same habits as the English had been. They followed the same course, landing as plunderers, fighting for a home, settling as tillers of the soil, adopting Christianity. They became, one might say, another tribe of Englishmen, just like the Saxons and Angles. They were a people that readily accepted a higher civilisation wherever they found it, even giving up their own language, as in Neustria, where they learned to speak French; or as on the west coast of Scotland, where 'group after group of Norse invaders were absorbed into the Irish-speaking population,' and where, though the 'Norsemen were conquerors,' 'all spoke Irish together[1].' So, while they changed English much, yet in the end they gave up most of their own tongue for the English.

Though, from their roving habits, and from a Danish king, Cnut, having ruled all the land for a time, with his home at Winchester among the West-Saxons, here and there a trace of Danish influence might be found all over the country, yet for a rough division we place Danes in the Angle lands, Northumbria, East Anglia, and the larger half of Mercia, north-east of Watling Street, 'from the Firth of Forth to the heart of Mercia,' and the English in the Saxon lands of Wessex and its subject kingdoms. Accordingly, close likeness to Scandinavian dialects is to be found in northern English, close likeness to Frisian dialects in southern English. On the borders of these, that is, in central England, where Danes and English met, the speech differed from both, and yet was somewhat like both. It kept middle English forms, not like the softer forms of Wessex, and yet less hard than those of the north. But the great distinction was between the south and the

---

[1] Burton, History of Scotland, i. p. 215.

north, just as we read that it was at a much later time: 'Men of the est with men of the west .... acordeth more in sounynge of speche than men of the north with men of the south: therfore hyt ys that Mercii, that buth men of myddel Engelond, as hyt were parteners of the endes, undurstondeth betre the syde longages, Northeron and Southeron, than Northern and Southern undurstondeth oyther other. Al the longage of the Northhumbres and specialych at Yorke, ys so scharp, slyttynge and frotynge, and unschape, that we Southeron men may that longage unnethe undurstonde[1].' The result of the 'commyxtion and mellynge with Danes' was to make the northern tongue harder and harsher than the more southern dialects, as is seen in later writers, and as it has remained always.

1. Some common forms or words which are now of daily use throughout the country are traced to the very early influence of the Scandinavian dialects, or to that of these various settlers, on the northern speech; as the plural form *are* (*aron*) of the auxiliary verb, which expelled the English plural *sindon*; the use of *she*, the demonstrative pronoun, as the feminine of the 3rd personal pronoun; and the word *egg*. And many more are to be found which did not spread far beyond those districts in which the Danes settled, as *bairn* (child), *foss* or *force* (a waterfall), *gill* or *ghyll* (a ravine), *quern* (a handmill), *greet* (to weep): and terminations of proper names, as patronymics in -*son*, Nelson, Swainson: local terminations, -*thwaite*, Crossthwaite; -*beck*, Troutbeck, in the Norwegian settlements in Cumberland and Westmoreland; -*thorpe*, Althorpe; -*by*, Derby, Grimsby, in the Danish settlements of Yorkshire, Derbyshire, Lincolnshire, and Leicestershire.

---

[1] Trevisa, Translation of Higden's Polychronicon, A.D. 1387.

2. The northern dialects began more quickly and readily to develope into an analytical form of speech. Thus in the tenth century, that is, before any other foreign influence was at work, the distinctive termination of the infinitive mood of verbs, *an* or *en*, as sing*en*, was falling into disuse in the north. And in the latest portion of the English Chronicle, which was written at Peterborough in the reign of King Stephen, *ge*, the augment of the past participle, as *ge*nemned, is dropped; and all inflexion of the definite article *the* has ceased. In the same way the disuse of inflexions, which had thus begun, is in later time, the thirteenth, fourteenth and fifteenth centuries, a sign of a northern as against a southern home of a writer or a manuscript; as the disuse of (1) *en*, as an inflexion of the plural number of past tense of verbs; (2) *eth*, as an inflexion of the imperative mood; (3) the prefix *ge*, or *y*, or *i*, of the past participle; (4) final *e*, an inflexion of verbs, or substantives, or adjectives. And to these may be added the fact that the northern dialects earlier lost forms which seemed to be irregular, as the plurals of nouns in *en*, which are even to the present day common in Dorset[1]. This early loss of inflexion in the north is the more to be remarked, since the influence of Norman-French was far less exercised upon the northern dialects of England than upon the southern (§ 17). Such was the Danish or Scandinavian influence which gave great impulse to the development of the language, so as to make it lose 'the fulness and purity of its ancient inflexions and to change it into the analytic language which we use'—a development which advanced steadily in all dialects, in all alike in kind, though not in all at the same rate.

---

[1] Compare Morris, Specimens of Early English, p. xiii.

Influence of Latin civilisation.

§ 11. A modification far more marked in its effect has been produced by the influence of the Latin tongue upon English. Almost all the civilisation of western Europe had its origin in Rome, and was spread by men of the Latin race, or at least by men who had learnt to speak Latin in some form. In some countries, as in Gaul and Spain, Latin civilisation followed upon conquest, and meant the introduction of new manners, customs, law, government, and even of a new language. Into England it did not come so; but first, peacefully, brought by Christian missionaries from Rome; secondly, introduced not by Latins at all, but by Normans and Frenchmen who had learnt their civilisation and language from Latins, but had altered them in the learning. We shall, therefore, speak of the influence of the Latin language upon English under these two heads, adding a third for the influence of Latin classical literature during the sixteenth century.

Early Latin Missionaries, and their influence.

§ 12. The Roman missionaries began their work in Kent in the year A.D. 597. As would be natural, from their small numbers they did not alter the spoken language much. But as their teaching spread among a people ready to learn, many words which they were accustomed to use, either of genuine Latin or of Latinised Greek, belonging to religion and religious offices and observances, gradually became current in English; as *apostóle*, apostle (apostolus); *biscop*, bishop (episcopus); *clustre*, cloister (clausterium); *elmesse*, alms (eleemosyna); *mæsse*, mass (missa); *mynstre*, minster (monasterium); *munuc*, monk (monachus); *preost*, priest (presby-

MEANING OF 'NORMAN CONQUEST.' 15

ter); *seint*, saint (sanctus); *tempel*, temple (templum). These words soon passed into the spoken language and took forms differing much from Latin, and were formed into compounds as ordinary English words; as biscop*rice*, biscep*dome*, biscep*hade*, Læden*spræce* (Latin speech), Læden*getheode* (the Latin language). Through the intercourse thus opened foreign novelties came in which had no English names, and so kept their Latin names; as *candel* (candela), *rose* (rosa), *lilie* (lilia), and the *pepper* (piper) which Baeda had in his capsella. The clergy were educators also, and hence in time many an English monk, like Baeda, would be wont to write in Latin while he would sing his hymns in his own English tongue [1]. Latin was also the language of legal documents, and on this account too a few phrases or words became current. To sum up, Latin being thus the literary language as well as the language of the service books of the churches, gave many new words. But that the language was unchanged by this introduction of Latin words King Alfred shows, for though he uses most of these words, yet in speaking of those who could understand the Latin of the service books he says, 'Swæ feawe hiora wæron ðaette ic furðum anne ánlepne ne mæg geðencean besuðan Temese ða ða ic to rice feng.' 'So few of them there were that I cannot think of a single one south of the Thames when I came to the kingdom [2].'

Meaning of the 'Norman Conquest.'

§ 13. The Norman Conquest was the beginning of the second wave of Latin influence. It has been said (§ 10)

---

[1] Hist. Eccl. Baedae, Moberly; Introduction, pp. xvi, xvii.
[2] King Alfred's Gregory's Pastoral Care, p. 2 (Early English Text Society).

that some of the Danes and Northmen had settled in western Neustria (hence Normannia, Normandy, the land of the Northman), and had adopted that form of the Latin language which we call French. In the eleventh century these French-speaking Normans overcame England, and thus the Latin tongue, starting from a new home, again influenced English. We speak of the Norman Conquest because we thereby get a well-known date for our starting-point; but we mean the influence of French upon English from the eleventh to the fifteenth century. For these Normans spoke a dialect of French, and by the writers of the time are usually called French as opposed to the English. Moreover the invaders were not all Normans, but there were volunteers from Picardy also, and from the royal dominions of the Ile de France, and from Burgundy[1]; in fact, representatives of the 'four principal dialects of the Langue d'Oil, Norman, Picard, Burgundian, and French of the Ile de France[2].' In the thirteenth still another dialect, the southern tongue of Langue d'Oc, had its influence, for after the marriage of Henry III with Eleanor of Provence, we read that a great cry arose that England was being handed over to the many adventurers who flocked from Provence. And during a still later period almost all the new words which were introduced came from the French of the Ile de France, which gradually rose to be the received French language of the educated classes of all parts of the country.

---

[1] Freeman, History of the Norman Conquest, iii. p. 305.
[2] Brachet, Historical French Grammar, p. 18.

Settlement of the Normans and French in England.

§ 14. The Normans spread throughout England as a superior caste; and there were now two languages in all parts, languages which could not unite. The English of the old inhabitant and the French of the new-comer contended during the eleventh, twelfth, thirteenth, and fourteenth centuries. The invaders were systematic in subduing every part of the land. William the Conqueror had castles in Exeter, Carlisle, and Newcastle, as well as in London and Winchester. A Norman baron, Montgomery, fixed himself on the Welsh border; and by and by Norman barons, Brus and Baliol, Sayncler, Fryser, Græme [1], settled beyond the Scottish border. The English gradually but surely were ousted from lands and offices. Almost everywhere were new foreign bishops, like Roger of Salisbury in the reign of Henry I, Henry of Winchester in the reign of Stephen, or Hugh of Lincoln in the reign of Henry II, 'a foreigner with no knowledge of the English tongue,' who never learnt it. During these centuries came also crowds of French-speaking monks, so that a very large number of monasteries of Norman foundation arose in the land, 'garrisoning it, as it were, against the Church of the land as the Normans in their castles against the independent spirit of the English.'

The Normans learnt English and became Englishmen.

§ 15. The history of the language during these centuries would be the story of the way in which the speech of the home-dwellers swallowed up that of the new-comers. The tongue of the lower classes, the majority, prevailed against

---

[1] Burton, History of Scotland, ii. p. 85.

that of the upper, the minority; the outlying districts prevailed against the centres, the villages against the castles, the old monasteries against the large rich new foundations. The Northmen, who had become Frenchmen in France, became Englishmen in England. Some common events of history will illustrate this. At Duke William's coronation at Westminster, at Christmas 1066, the English archbishop Ealdred of York first demanded in English whether the crowd would have him for king, and then the Norman Geoffrey bishop of Coutances asked the same of the Normans in French[1]. In the next generation soldiers of the conquered English race served with honour in the army of William II. Henry I did his best towards uniting the two races by marrying an Englishwoman of the old English line of kings, daughter of Edgar the Atheling's sister. King John's loss of Normandy, which was joined to the dominions of the French king, warned the Normans in England that they must altogether throw in their lot with their new country. In the reign of Henry III the great rebellion of the barons under Montfort, Earl of Leicester, was based on the cry of 'England for the English;' both Norman and Englishman finding a common cause in resisting the king's constant encouragement of foreign adventurers. And presently a king bears the old English name Edward, and calls himself an Englishman.

The widespread use of French in England.

§ 16. The French language, however, spread in the land more than we should have expected from the mere numbers of the Normans; for the usage of the court and the example of the upper classes made it fashionable and a mark of

---

[1] Freeman, History of the Norman Conquest, iii. p. 559.

education and good breeding. Thus, to take the evidence of the end of the fourteenth century, 'Gentilmen children buth ytaught for to speke Freynsch fram tyme that a buth yrokked in here cradel.' 'Uplondysche men wol lykne hamsylf to gentile men and fondeth (try) with gret bysynes for to speke Freynsch for to be more y-told of.' (Trevisa's Higden, A.D. 1387.) The proverb, 'Jack would be a gentleman if he could speak French,' shows how very general it was among the upper classes. In Piers the Plowman, Avarice is represented as supposing *restitucioun* to be French for *robbery*:

'I wende ryflynge were restitucioun;'

and as excusing his ignorance,

'I lerned never rede on boke,
And I can no Frenche in feith but of the ferthest ende of Norfolke [1].'

Chaucer's Prioresse, who was a woman of fashion, spoke French which had not been learned in France,

'And Frensch sche spak ful faire and fetysly
After the scole (i. e. manner) of Stratford atte Bowe [2].'

Yet English was about this time fully recovering its place, for though under Edward I French superseded Latin as the language of the lawyers, yet 'the yer of oure Lord, a thousond thre hondred foure score and fyve of the secunde kyng Richard after the conquest nyne, in al the gramer scoles of Engelond children leveth Freynsch and construeth and lurneth an Englysch.' (Trevisa's Higden.)

---

[1] Piers the Plowman (Clarendon Press ed.), v. 231-239. See note. Compare Earle, Philology of the English Tongue, p. 65.
[2] Chaucer, Canterbury Tales, Prologue 124.

Influence of French on the English language.

§ 17. The English language was changed much in this long struggle and mingling of races. In grammatical structure the change was not great, for the syntax was almost unaffected, no French syntax finding an abiding home in English; just as the result of the great German invasion of Gaul was that 'this invasion touched the vocabulary only; there are no traces of German influence on French syntax [1].'

i. *Influence on the Grammar.* Some effect, however, on the grammar may be traced, for the change of which we have spoken in § 9 from synthetic to analytic was hastened. As the foreigners learnt English, and learnt it from conversation and not from grammars and exercise-books, they could not master all its distinctions of inflexions, as of gender and case, or of person, but confused them. Their own French language was passing through the same development and loss of inflexions. French had already reduced its cases to two, subjective and objective, and was reducing these two to one—it had reduced its genders to two by dropping the neuter of Latin; and it was bringing its modes of forming the plural of nouns to one uniform method. French influence therefore helped the great change working in English, and we may see that it moulded that change specially in one or two instances. Chaucer may be counted as the earliest well-known writer of the English upon which this French influence had done its work. If we study his language to find the effect produced, we see that substantives have little more inflexion than in our own modern English.

---

[1] Brachet, Historical French Grammar, p. 11.

The nominative plural is mostly in *es* or *s*. All distinction of form between the nominative and objective cases of substantives has been lost, and scarcely any other case-form remains: old distinctions of gender are found no longer [1]. The adjective has lost all inflexions of gender and case, and though the definite form is often distinguished from the indefinite by the final *e*, this too is going, for 'words of more than one syllable nearly always omit the final *e* [2].' So too the *e* of plural adjectives is often omitted. Verbs also were losing their inflexions—*eth* of the plural indicative and imperative; the infinitive ending *en*, often weakened to *e*; and the distinctive form of the gerund. The old termination *ende* of the present participle was giving place to *ing*, and the participle was becoming confused with the verbal substantive; the prefix *ge* or *y* or *i* of the past participle was disappearing, and its suffix *en* was dropping off from many verbs. An illustration of the power and weakness of French influence in assisting or guiding such changes may be seen in the history of the plural inflexion *s*. In our earliest written form of English the forms of the plural were several. One declension formed its plural nominative and accusative in *as*, and later this *as* is represented by *es* or *s*; and to this one form the other declensions seem to have been gradually yielding. It happened that this plural form was like the regular plural form of French nouns, while the other English forms were unlike; for exactly the same change had taken place in French nouns. The several plural forms of the early French, as of the Latin, objective case had all ended in *s* (neuter nouns becoming masculine, or in a few instances

---

[1] Here and there we find an oblique case, or a feminine genitive, with the inflexion *e*, and *sun* is still feminine and *moon* masculine.

[2] Chaucer, Prologue, &c. (Clarendon Press Series), Introduction, p. xxviii.

feminine), and when the French subjective case became in time merged in the objective, the *s* of the objective case became for all words the sign of the plural[1]. The French form being the same as that English form which was gaining the mastery, all French substantives adopted into English assisted the natural process. But the power of French was limited. For, on the other hand, English adjectives had a plural inflexion, not *s*, but *an* or *en*, which became weakened into *e* in later time. Now French adjectives, like substantives, had the usual French plural form *s*, but this being a strange form could not be naturalised in English. So that the few foreign forms, 'verbs actyves personalles,' 'cardinales vertues,' which are sometimes found in writers of about Chaucer's date, gained no place in the language.

Some modes of forming derived or compounded words passed from French into English. Words adapted themselves to English rules of inflexion, as the verbs which readily fell under the rules of the weak conjugation, or the nouns which formed a new possessive in *s* like English nouns. And several French suffixes became naturalised, as -*age* (Latin -*aticum*, -*agium*), as in *viage, fromage, message*, which was in time added to true English roots, as *bondage, baggage, package, steerage*: so we have -*ance* (Latin -*antiam*), as *repugnance*, added to an English root in *dalliance, hindrance;* just as in modern English -*tion* (Latin -*tionem*) is sometimes added to English roots, as in the very modern word *starvation*. Some French suffixes also became confused with English when they were somewhat alike, as is seen in the following example. In English -*er* was a mascu-

---

[1] *s, x, z*, regarded as orthographic signs, are equivalents in Old French; *voix* was written indifferently *voix, vois*, or *voiz*. Brachet, Historical French Grammar, p. 94, note 1.

line suffix, as hunt*er*, having in very many instances a corresponding feminine form in -*ster*, as brew*er*, brew*ster*; spin*ner*, spin*ster*; hawk*er*, huck*ster*; so that -*ster* was often a feminine suffix. In French, besides the masculines in *r* (*or*, *our*, *eur*, *er*, *re*), with feminine forms in -*ess*, doct*or*, fait*our*, scol*er*, carpent*ere*, many masculine nouns ended in *stre*, as mai*stre*, mini*stre*, ance*stre*, mon*stre*, having often feminine forms in *stresse*, mai*stresse*, ance*stresse*. Whence -*stre* became in English a well-known masculine termination of words introduced from French, as canoni*stre*, dyvyni*stre*, for*ster*, legi*stre*. Hence the French masculine -*stre* overcame these English feminines in -*ster*, making the ending appear masculine, as it now almost always is, and giving a new feminine ending in -*ess*, -*stress*, as songstr*ess*, seamstr*ess*.

To French influence also is often attributed the simplifying of the order of words in a sentence. It is, however, nothing but one of the effects of the passage of the language into its analytic stage. A synthetic language has a large number of words whose form shows their relation one to another, and accordingly, since the sense is made plain by other means, the order of the words is not of the first importance. But when words do not by their form show these relations, the sense of the sentence depends more upon the position of the words. They will then fall into the logical order of thought, subject with its explanatory words and phrases, and predicate with its explanatory words and phrases, as nearly as possible in the order of their connection.

ii. *Influence on the Vocabulary.* On the vocabulary of the language the influence of French can be much more easily traced. Here we come to the introduction of French words into the speech of the people. New words are always taking a place in every language; for every nation has some intercourse with foreigners, and adopts some of their terms. The importance in this case lies in the immense number of words so introduced. It was natural, because the French in England were a large body of the foremost men in the kingdom, who set the fashion, and whom many would copy. The words introduced were especially those which belonged to the life, habits, tastes, possessions, and ideas of the ruling and refined classes of society. They were words connected with war, government, religion, architecture, literature, science, and the like, rather than with the more homely business or relations of life, as *bataille, chivalry, habergeon, siege, squire; parlement, chancellor, judge; pilgrim, preacher; abbey, castle, chapel, conduit; chilindre, machine, philosophre, science;* with a very large number of abstract terms, as *colour, delite, excellence, felicité, humilité, iniquité, justice, restitucioun.* Of these,—

1. Some supplied names for new things introduced by the French, and for which the English had no names, as they had not the things, as *castle, cherry, forest, olive, palace, palmer.*

2. Some words expressed the same ideas as some English words. This class has helped to make English a language rich in synonyms or words of kindred meaning, and to give it so great a power of discriminating minute shades of difference, as *carpenter*, wright; *county*, shire; *dame*, lady; *deliver*, free; *humility*, lowliness; *iniquity*, wickedness; *jollity*, mirth; *nature*, kind; *route*, road; *sage*, wise; *strange*, uncouth; *succour*, help; *trespass*, sin; *venery*, hunting. As many of the new words could not keep their footing, so on the other hand some of them drove out their English equivalents and rendered them obsolete, as *second*, other, that other, the tother; *cross*, rood; *temptation*, fondinge.

3. The French language contained some hundreds of Teutonic words borrowed from the German conquerors of the Roman province of Gaul. Many of these passed into

English in a form which they would not have had if they had come direct from a German-speaking people, as *bivouac, fief, habergeon, guardian, gage, marshal, seneschal, vassal.*

iii. *Influence on Pronunciation.* Besides these new French words a great change in the form of many English words was made, because Frenchmen could not pronounce some English sounds, and so adapted them to their own familiar French sounds. The harder and harsher letters and combinations became weakened and softened, especially in the southern and midland districts, in which the influence of the French was greatest, and where it would seem that a tendency in the same direction was already in some slight degree showing itself. The changes were losses or alterations or additions of letters or sounds.

1. Letters and sounds which did not exist in French, or could not be easily pronounced by the French were lost. The strong English aspirates and gutturals almost disappeared. The aspirated interrogative or relative forms, *hwa, hwæt, hwelc, hwæther, hwile,* became softened into *who, what, which, whether, while,* and the words *hlaf, hlaford, hlædere, hræthe,* became *loaf, lord, ladder, rathe.* Gutturals ceased to be gutturals, c being sometimes lost, as from *Ic,* which was weakened into *I*: GH gradually passed through various softer forms, K, F, P, a simple breathing, as in *hough, laugh, hiccough, thorough,* to entire silence in *though, night, weight*: hard c (K), G were softened in various ways, as *ceorl,* churl; *Cissanceaster,* Chichester; *poke,* pouch; *sack,* satchel; *spræce,* speech; *Sandwic,* Sandwich; *Swanwic,* Swanage; *Englisc,* English; *buggen,* buy; *wecg,* wedge: or they became mute, as in *cneow,* knee; *cniht,* knight; *gnaw*; *gnash*: CC often changed into the palatal *tch,* as *streccan* to stretch; sc into *sh,* as *scyld,* shield. Possibly the loss of the letters Ð, Þ,

representing the sound *dh* (and perhaps *th*,) may also be assigned to the same influence, for in French and Latin these sounds were usually represented by D or T, or even dropped, as Northman was written Nordmannus, or Nortmannus, or Normannus. From these and kindred changes arise many of the double forms of words in English, the hard forms having often maintained themselves alongside of the new softer forms, the older and more English by the newer and less natural, as *dyke* and *ditch;* *seek* and *beseech;* *wake* and *watch;* *wile* and *guile;* *wise* and *guise.*

2. Vowel-sounds were changed and confused. No two nations have their vowel-sounds exactly alike, and English contained a very large variety of such sounds; so that some confusion naturally arose as soon as men accustomed to French vowel-sounds began to talk English. The distinct pronunciation of vowel-sounds was of very great importance in English, since many inflexions, as those of number, comparison, and more especially those of the strong conjugation of verbs, were formed according to regular laws of the modification or change of vowel-sounds. Under the influence of French the pronunciation of vowels was so confused that the inflexion of these verbs became irregular, and could no longer be explained by the old laws of vowel-change.

3. A few new sounds were added to the language, as J in *jest, journey, joy, jury, justice;* aspirated s (*sh*) and z (*zh*), as in *censure, azure;* and the sound of U, as in *pure, duke, jury,*—the results of English attempts to utter the sounds which the letters had in French.

XXX *Formation of a common literary dialect of English.*

§ 18. The result may be summed up by saying that a new literary dialect of English was produced. Not that no such literary dialect would have otherwise arisen. But in early times English literature was local, and written in dialects full of marked differences and local peculiarities. These dialects, though still used by some writers, ceased to be the vehicles of the real literature of the land, while French and Latin held sway; and when English became again the language of the court and upper classes, as well as of the lower, it was an English differing from all those local dialects. It was, of course, founded mainly upon one of them, that of London and the neighbouring counties, the East-Midland. But it was also the court dialect of the south, or English as spoken by the court, the clergy, the lawyers, the gentlemen, altered by the French element, and by the great mingling of people from various parts which took place in the fifteenth century, during the great Wars of the Roses and the disturbances which preceded and accompanied them. 'Practically we know that the fifteenth century was a period of great change in the whole character of our language; the last remnants of our inflectional system were abandoned, the sharp distinction between "the gentilmans" French and the "uplondischemens" English disappeared, and a "common dialect" was acknowledged by all writers[1].' The other dialects lived, as they still live, the homes of old forms; and the influence of one or another of them may sometimes be traced in this or that writer, but they were no longer used by the best writers.

---

[1] Ellis, Early English Pronunciation, p. 242.

Influence of Classical Latin at 'the Revival of Letters.'

§ 19. Once more a distinct influence was exercised by Latin upon English. During the period which followed the 'Revival of Letters,' or rediscovery of the Latin classical authors, the study of classical Latin much affected the style and language of English writers. The influence of the writers of this period was great because the invention of printing had caused a largely increased circulation of books. And when, about the time of the Reformation, religious controversy occupied men's minds very greatly, much study was given to those writers whose very subjects would naturally tempt them both to follow classical models, and to adopt many technical Latin terms. Passing by the question of style, which did not permanently affect the language, we find that these writers influenced the vocabulary in a twofold manner.

1. A very large number of Latin words, many of which were already current in English in an older and modified form, came in in a purely classical form also. Thus we may compare some of the older words derived from the Latin-speaking missionaries, or through French, with the later classical words, as *bishop, blame, caitiff, channel, conduit, delytable, estate, fashion, feat, lesson, priest, ransom, trump*, with *episcopal, blaspheme, captive, canal, conduct, delectable, state, faction, fact, prelection, presbyter, redemption, triumph*.

2. The knowledge of the correct classical forms of words often induced writers to alter the shape of the words already in the language, so as to give them a more classical appearance. And these modified words, when not used in a new sense, have usually driven out the old forms. Thus Chaucer's *aventure, paraventure, Alisaundre, sawtrie, chilindre, vitaille, subjettes*, have all been restored to more classical forms,

adventure, peradventure, Alexandria, psaltery, cylinder, victual, subjects.

This influence of Latin altered the literary rather than the spoken language, just as from that time Latin words have been mostly introduced into the writings of historians, theologians, and scientific men, rather than into the common talk of the people, so that 'the more familiar, idiomatic, and simple the style, the fewer the foreign words in it[1].'

Ordinary Laws of Change.

§ 20. It remains to point to the simple laws of change which are always at work, and may be traced in their working at all times, and not only in those periods of which we have spoken particularly :—

1. A still continuing development of the analytic stage, so often mentioned. This can be traced in our later English in the growing disuse of the possessive case-ending, which now expresses possession only, one of several relations of the earlier genitive; in the disuse of the second person singular of verbs because of its harsh inflexion, scarcely any one ever using now such a form as *thou wroughtest;* and in the gradual loss of the subjunctive, now almost gone.

2. The change in the vocabulary, made by the introduction of foreign words from every language with which Englishmen come into contact, as names of new things; or by new-formed words, as *telegram;* or by fashion, which revives old-fashioned words and drops others.

3. The constant changes in the meanings of words, so that words have their signification narrowed to a special use; as *fowl, sue, plaintiff;* or retain a metaphorical sense only, as

---

[1] Compare Brachet, Historical French Grammar, p. 2.

integrity; or pass from a lower to a more dignified meaning, as *knight,* which, once meaning a servant, passed into a title of honour; or from a better to a worse meaning, as *villain,* from villager into criminal, or *knave,* from servant into rascal, or *silly,* from blessed into foolish. All the classical words gradually get further away from their classical meaning, and all compounds gradually lose the force of their simple parts and gain a new force.

4. A tendency to change forms which are not understood, or seem to have no meaning, into other shapes which shall convey a meaning, a fruitful source of mistake; as *chaussée* into *cause-way;* *écrevisse* into *cray-fish;* *pentice* into *pent-house;* and the provincial *ill-convenient* for *in-convenient.*

5. The law that a language always works towards uniformity and regularity, so that forms which are or seem to be irregular are made regular or thrust out of use; on the principle that 'things give way on the basis of least resistance.' We see this in the usual belief that all plural forms of nouns are irregularities, except those ending in *s,* though the plurals *oxen, men, teeth,* are in reality as much governed by rule as the commoner form. It is seen also in the way in which verbs of the strong conjugation are accounted irregular, and are being gradually forced into the more usual weak conjugation. This tendency leads by mistaken analogy to many false formations. Thus we have *pea,* as a singular of *peas,* which is itself singular, though mistaken for a plural; and *eave* from *eaves* by a like mistake; and an *l* has been introduced into *could* to make it uniform with *should* and *would.*

The changes in English have been summed up as the result of the practical character of the nation, acting on these principles—(1) 'of two ways to the same end it prefers the shorter and easier to the longer and harder;' thus, making all things without life neuter saves the trouble of remembering what things without life are masculine and what feminine—a main difficulty in learning Latin or French or German: (2) 'of two forms which serve the same object it prefers that which best corresponds to that object;' thus English has gradually come to take the mere root as singular, and to make the plural in only one way by adding *s*; and distinguishes subject from object by position alone, not by both form and position.

In no one thing, probably, has this tendency towards uniformity shown itself more strongly than in the history of the spelling and pronunciation of English. From an absolute carelessness about spelling, so long as it represented fairly the sound of the word intended to be written, we have come to an absolute rigidity of rule, which no longer makes attempt to represent sound. And in like manner, as the mingling of the people and the continual development of the language made a literary dialect uniform in its idioms, grammatical forms, and vocabulary, from which to depart is to be provincial or vulgar, so it has been with pronunciation. 'In the thirteenth, fourteenth, and fifteenth centuries it is almost a straining of the meaning of words to talk of a general English pronunciation.' Great changes took place at the end of the fifteenth century, and again during the sixteenth century. A series of minglings of the people of various parts of the country, a continual change and development, have produced uniformity. So that 'in the present day we may recognize a received pronunciation all over the country, not widely differing in any particular locality[1].'

---

[1] Ellis, Early English Pronunciation, p. 23.

Note on § 3.

The best illustration of the use of the different pronunciation of the same words in different dialects or languages as a test of relationship, is the law of the change or variation of consonants, called **Grimm's Law**. By it the relationship of (i) Sanscrit, Greek, and Latin; (ii) Low-German dialects, as English; (iii) High-German, may be traced thus:—mute consonants are divided into (1) **Lip-letters**, (2) **Throat-letters**, (3) **Tooth-letters**; and in each of these classes are three letters, (1) *Thin*, P, K (C, hard), T; (2) *Middle*, B, G, D; (3) *Aspirate*, PH (F or V), CH (GH), TH. See § 22.

If we call the pronunciation found in Sanscrit, Greek, and Latin the original or first stage, we find that by the third century A.D., in the Low-German (and Gothic) dialects these consonants had become changed from their original pronunciation to a second stage. And we find that by the seventh century, among the High-Germans these consonants had become again changed into a third stage. Each stage, as it were, moved the letters one place onwards, and gave the words in which they occur an altered pronunciation.

First Stage. Greek and Latin.	Second Stage. English. Low-German.			Third Stage. High-German.
Middle B. G. D.	Thin P. C. T.			Aspirate PH. CH. TH.
Thin P. C. T.	Aspirate F (V). CH, (H,GH.) TH.			Middle B. G. D.
Aspirate F. CH, H. TH.	Middle B. G. D.			Thin P. K.
	OLD ENGLISH.	MODERN ENGLISH.	LOW-GERMAN.	
*e*go	i*c*	I	i*k*	i*ch*
*d*uo	*t*wa	*t*wo	*t*wei	ʒwei
se*p*tem	seo*f*on	se*v*en	se*v*en	sie*b*en
o*c*to	ea*h*ta	ei*gh*t	a*ch*t	a*ch*t
*t*res	*th*ri	*th*ree	*d*rei	*d*rei
*f*ra*t*er	bro*th*or	bro*th*er	bro*d*er	[*pruodar*]
*h*esternus	*g*ystran	*y*esterday	*g*estern	[*këstre*]
θυγάτηρ	*d*ohtor	*d*aughter	*d*ochter	*t*ochter

The changes are well illustrated by the various forms of the name of the German race: (1) *T*eutones, in Roman times before the Christian era; (2) *Th*iuda, 'the people,' Gothic, after the third century, *Th*eód, oldest English; (3) *D*eutsch, in modern High-German. The exceptions which may be noted usually arise from some words having escaped the influence of the general law and having remained unchanged.

GRAMMAR.

THE ALPHABET.

§ 21. An **Alphabet** is a collection of letters or signs used to represent sounds, so that letters combined into syllables and words convey through the eye the same ideas as are conveyed through the ear by sounds.

A perfect alphabet would neither have more than one letter for any one sound, nor express more sounds than one by one letter. But alphabets commonly have more letters than one for some of the sounds in the language, that is, they are redundant: (1) because some new letter has been introduced from another language using a different sign for the sound, as in English K has been introduced expressing the same sound as C (hard), and has taken its place in many words, *knight* (*cniht*); (2) or because pronunciation has changed and assimilated sounds of letters which once were different, as the pronunciation of C before E and I, which was hard, has been assimilated to S, or the soft C of the French language. On the other hand, alphabets commonly express more sounds than one by one letter, that is, they are deficient: (1) because small varieties of sound are too many to be distinguished at the early stage of a language when writing is first used in a nation, as of vowel-sounds, *ache, hat; being, bed; white, whit; brute, but*: (2) or because intercourse with other nations brings in new sounds without new signs for them, as *ch* in *cherry*, *z* in *azure*, *u* in *pure*: (3) or because such intercourse lessens the distinction between two sounds, so that one sign is lost and the remaining one serves for both, as in English *th* stands for *dh* in *this*, and for *th* in *thing*.

The English alphabet of twenty-six letters, now used, is the common Latin alphabet (which was spread by the Romans over Western Europe), with one letter, w, from low or mediaeval Latin, added.

The letters have two forms:—

The capital—A, B, C, D, E, F, G, H, I, J, K, L, M, N, O, P, Q, R, S, T, U, V, W, X, Y, Z.

The small—a, b, c, d, e, f, g, h, i, j, k, l, m, n, o, p, q, r, s, t, u, v, w, x, y, z.

§ 22. Letters are **Vowels**, expressing sound by themselves, A, E, I, O, U; a, e, i, o, u:

Or **Consonants**, requiring a vowel to be sounded with them; as, B (be), L (el).

Consonants may be divided into—
    Liquids, L, M, N, R.
    Spirants, F, H, J, S, V.
    Mutes, B, C, D, G, K, P, Q, T.
    Double, X (= CS, KS, GS), Z (= DS, TS).

Y is sometimes a vowel; as, sto*ry*, *y*-clept, h*y*ssop: sometimes combined with a vowel to make an improper diphthong; as, da*y*, b*uy*: sometimes a consonant; as, *y*ard, *y*oung.

W is sometimes combined with a vowel to make an improper diphthong; as, blo*w*, dra*w*: and sometimes it 'is a consonant; as, *w*ard, *w*ood.

It is never really a vowel, but in such words as *draw* is like *y* in *day*, little more than a breathing, a slight remnant of a guttural or hard consonant, which was at one time distinctly pronounced. This may be seen by comparison of the forms draw, dra*g*; day, dae*g*. In some dialects w was written instead of the vowel U, as in Scottish—' It is he onlie that taks on *ws* cure.'

Consonants may be arranged according to the organs of speech.

Labial, or lip-letters.	P	B	F [PH] [V]	
Guttural, or throat-letters.	C (hard) K [Q]	G	CH (*loch*), GH (*hough*)	X
Dental, or tooth-letters.	T	D	TH (*thing*) [=DH *the*]	Z

THE ALPHABET.

C is hard, = K, before A, O, U; as *cat, cot, cut*: but soft, = S, before E, I, Y; as *cent, city, cypress*.

CH is guttural in a few words, as *mechanics, ache*; but is soft, sometimes = the palatal *tch*, and sometimes = the sibilant *sh*, in words introduced from French, as *chapel, cherry, chandler*, and *chandelier, machine*; and in some words of English origin which French has influenced, as *churl, child, speech, teach*; in a few words it is mute, as *drachm, schism*.

G is hard before A, O, U, and in most English words before E, I, as *game, get, gild, got, gut*; but soft, = J, before E, I, Y in words introduced from French, as *gentle, gin, gypsy*; and in a few words of English origin influenced by French, as *gibe*[1].

Almost all trace of aspirated guttural sounds has been lost from English, as for instance the old sound of GH, as *lough*, which has been weakened till in some words it has no sound,—*hough* = *hock*; *cough* = *f*; *hiccough* = *p*; *thorough*, = a very slight aspirate or breathing; *light*, in which all trace is lost. And the other gutturals also are often almost or quite mute, G in *gnaw*, K in *knee*.

Q is always followed by U; its sound then is the same as that of *cw* or *kw*, as *quite*; in some words it is almost = *k*, as *conqueror*.

X has two sounds, *cs* in *axe*, *gs* in *exact*.

S has two sounds, sharp as in *so, this*; flat, and like Z, in *his, flies*: accordingly in many words S or Z may be used, as *civilise, civilize*. In a few words it is = SH, as *censure*.

Z is in some words introduced from French = ZH, as *azure*, an Italian word brought into English through French.

Four letters, 3, Ð, Þ, p, of the earlier English alphabet are not now used, having fallen into disuse chiefly because they were not in the Latin or the Norman-French alphabet, and represented sounds difficult of pronunciation to the Norman-French invaders of the eleventh century, who exercised much influence on the English language and literature:—

3 was a guttural, and was equivalent to an initial G or sometimes Y (itself near akin to G), and to GH at the end of a word, or before T, as ʒive, ʒoure, kniʒtes, = give, your, knights.

Ð ð, Þ þ, were dentals, equivalent to *dh*, and later to *th*: they were used indifferently in different dialects and at different times. At last they passed from use, and are now represented by TH, which has two sounds *dh* and *th*, as *this, thing*.

p was used till the end of the thirteenth century, and then supplanted by the low Latin w.

---

[1] In one word, *gaol* (French *geôle*), and its derivative *gaoler*, G before A has the soft J sound. The words are often spelt *jail, jailer*—an instance at once of the power of French influence, and of the truth of the rule that G is hard before A in English.

§ 23. A **diphthong** is the combined sound of two different vowels, as *ae, ai:* Æthelstan, nail.

A **syllable** is one or more letters, one at least being a vowel, sounded continuously, as *a, man, sword, stretch, al-so.*

A **word** is one or more syllables having a meaning, as *a, man, extraordinary.*

A word of one syllable is a monosyllable; of two, is a disyllable; of three, is a trisyllable; of more than three, is a polysyllable.

THE PARTS OF SPEECH.

§ 24. Words are called in Grammar Parts of Speech, and are of four kinds:—

i. **Nouns.**   ii. **Pronouns.**   iii. **Verbs.**   iv. **Particles.**

i. **Noun** is the name of anything.

Nouns are—

(1) **Substantive**, the name of a thing existing or conceived by the mind; as *man, grass, virtue, length, whiteness.*

(2) **Adjective**, the name of a quality conceived as belonging to the thing of which a substantive is the name; as '*long* grass,' '*remarkable* virtue.'

ii. A **Pronoun** is a word used as either a substantive or an adjective; as *he, my, who, that.*

iii. A **Verb** is a word which expresses some judgment about a noun (its subject), and makes a sentence; as, Grass *grows,* Light *shines.*

iv. **Particles** are words which help to define the relations of nouns and verbs in sentences, or of sentences one to another. These are :—

(1) **Adverb,** which qualifies a verb, or sometimes other words, as adjective, substantive, or another adverb; as, He writes *badly*.

(2) **Preposition,** which defines the relation of a noun to some other word or words in the sentence; as, They lived *on* land.

(3) **Conjunction,** which connects words, clauses, and sentences; as, Yesterday *and* to-day.

(4) **Interjection,** which is an exclamation, expressing feeling, but not grammatically part of a sentence; as, *ah! fie!*

Of these parts of speech—

Noun { Substantive, Adjective, }
Pronoun,
Verb,
 have inflexion.

Particles { Adverb, Preposition, Conjunction, Interjection, }
 have no inflexion.

Inflexion is a series of changes made in the form of a word to express changes in its meaning in relation to other words in a sentence.

The part of a word on which the inflexions are based is the **Stem**.

Those letters in a word which are common to it and all kindred words are the **Root**.

Nouns and Pronouns substantive have inflexion to mark Gender, Number, Case. This inflexion is called **Declension**; so we speak of declining a substantive.

Nouns adjective have inflexion to mark Degree. This is called **Comparison**; so we speak of comparing an adjective.

Verbs have inflexion to mark Voice, Mood, Tense, Number, Person. This is called **Conjugation**; so we speak of conjugating a verb.

NOUN SUBSTANTIVE.

§ 25. **Substantives** are divided into **Common, Proper,** and **Abstract.**

A **Common noun** is the name of a thing, which may be used as the name of a class and also of each particular member of the class; as *man, dog, city.*

A *Collective noun* is (a common noun) the name of a thing composed of many individuals; as *army* (of many soldiers), *fleet* (of many ships).

A **Proper noun** is the name of a thing, which cannot also be used as the name of a class containing it and other like things: as *Europe, John, London.*

An **Abstract noun** is the name of a quality, or attribute, that is thought of, though it cannot exist, apart from the thing to which it belongs; as *whiteness, length.*

INFLEXION OF THE SUBSTANTIVE.

§ 26. The **Substantive** is inflected so as to mark **Gender, Number,** and **Case.**

GENDERS.

§ 27. **Genders** are three — **Masculine, Feminine, Neuter.**

Gender depends on the natural distinction of sex in the thing of which the noun is the name; so that a noun signifying a thing of the male sex may be considered masculine, a noun signifying a thing of the female sex feminine, a noun signifying a thing without sex, that is, an inanimate object, neuter—that is, neither masculine nor feminine. Nouns signifying things of which the sex is not apparent, or in which the idea of sex is not made prominent, are commonly treated as neuter, and accordingly may have the neuter pronoun *it* used with them, as—

It is a fine *bird.*

Take this *child* away and nurse *it* for me.

But as modern English has, except in few instances, ceased to show gender by the form of the noun, we may say that in general English nouns have *no* genders.

SUBSTANTIVES.

Many nouns signifying things of both sexes are called common, that is, are considered to be either masculine or feminine; thus of most animals the usual masculine name may be used to include the feminine, as *man, horse, dog*; or the usual feminine name may sometimes be used to include the masculine, as *goose, duck*. Inanimate things are sometimes personified, that is, are spoken of as if they were persons, and therefore of the masculine or feminine gender; and especially things of familiar life are spoken of as if of the feminine gender, as—

Charity seeketh not *her* own.

A brave vessel
Who had, no doubt, some noble creature in *her*,
Dashed all to pieces.

In Early English the laws of gender were different; and the gender of a noun was shown sometimes by its form, and sometimes only by its meaning, as in Latin, and in German, and most languages. Thus nouns signifying things of the female sex might be of the neuter gender, as *wif*, a wife; and nouns signifying things without sex might be masculine, or feminine, or neuter; as *dream, star*, masc.; *soul, heart, tongue, door*, fem.; *eye, house*, neut. So also nouns ending in *-dom* were masculine; nouns ending in *-nes* were feminine, whatever their meaning[1]. The modern law of want of gender came into general use during the fourteenth century, and is in great measure due to the inability of the Norman-French lords to master the laws of gender of the speech of their English subjects.

The **Gender of Nouns**, when shown in their form, is expressed—

i. By the **ending**, or **termination**, when the noun has both a masculine and feminine form.

(1) Masculines ending in **-er** in one or two instances have a feminine form in **-ster**, as spinn*er*, spin*ster*.

In modern English **-ster** has become in many words a masculine ending, as malt*ster*, tap*ster*; and in some it implies some little contempt, as game*ster*, old*ster*, young*ster*, pun*ster*. See § 17.

The word *widow* was formerly common; but a masc. *widower* has been formed by adding the masculine termination **-er** to it.

(2) Masculine nouns ending in **-dor, -tor, -or, -er**, when derived from Latin, have usually a feminine form in **-dress, -tress, (-trix), -ess**; as

---

[1] Vernon, Anglo-Saxon Guide, pp. 8, 9.

ambassa*dor*, ambassa*dress*; ac*tor*, ac*tress*; execu*tor*, execu*trix*; govern*or*, govern*ess*.

Hence **-ess** has become a received feminine ending, and is added to many masculine nouns, even to some of English origin, with or without modifying the final syllable of the masculine; as, lion, lion*ess*; negro, negr*ess*; duke, duch*ess*; so, god, godd*ess*; sempstr*ess*, songstr*ess*, murder*ess*.

(3) The ending **-ine** has been adopted for a few feminines; as, hero, hero*ine*.

The word *vixen*, feminine of *fox*, formed by modifying the stem-vowel and adding the feminine ending -en, is one remaining instance of an old formation once very common.

ii. By adding a **prefix** signifying sex, as—

he-goat,   *she*-goat.
cock-sparrow,   *hen*-sparrow.
man-servant,   *maid*-servant.
man,   *wo*man (= *wife*man).

iii. By the use of **distinct words, correlative** one to another, as—

husband,   wife. | brother,   sister.
cock,   hen. | uncle,   aunt.
father,   mother. | bull,   cow.

NUMBERS.

§ 28. Nouns (and Pronouns) substantive usually have one form to shew that one thing denoted by the word is spoken of, and another form to shew that more things than one are spoken of. These forms are called **Numbers, Singular** and **Plural**. The singular number speaks of one thing, as *man, dog, he.* The plural number speaks of more than one, as *men, dogs, they*.

There are three modes of forming the plural number of nouns, and some nouns have the same form in singular and plural; making four divisions or declensions of substantives.

SUBSTANTIVES.

i. Nouns forming the plural by **adding the syllable -en**; as, ox, *oxen*.

This form is rare in modern English, but was common in earlier English, as *hosen, housen, eyen, eyne, sisteren, sustrin, shoon*; and is still common in some provincial dialects.

ii. Nouns forming the plural by **a change or modification of the stem-vowel**; as, man, *men*; goose, *geese*; mouse, *mice*.

Some words bear traces of both these modes; as, brother (old plural *brether*), *bretheren, brethren*: *children* contains a trace of an older formation, child (old plural *childer*, once *cildru*), *childeren, children*: cow (*cú*, old plural *cy*), *kine*.

iii. Nouns which have their **singular and plural alike**; as, deer, grouse, sheep, swine.

In old English such nouns are mostly neuter, as *deer, sheep, swine*; so too *hors*, see § 31, the modern *horses* is a double plural.

iv. Nouns forming the plural by **adding the syllable -es**, which in many words coalesces with the final syllable of the singular, and appears as merely **-s**:—

(1) Nouns ending in *ch* (soft), *sh, ss, x, o*; nouns which change *f* or *ff* into *v*, or *x* into *c*; nouns ending in *y* following a consonant and changing into *i*,— mostly retain **-es**; as, church, *churches*; dish, *dishes*; kiss, *kisses*; box, *boxes*; negro, *negroes*; thief, *thieves*; staff, *staves*; appendix, *appendices*; story, *stories*.

(2) Other nouns merely add **-s** to the singular; as, loch, *lochs*; noun, *nouns*; chief, *chiefs*; valley, *valleys*.

(3) A few nouns have plurals irregular in spelling, which really belong to this declension; as, die, *dice*; penny, *pence*. In these words **-ce** misrepresents an earlier plural in **s**, as *dys, dees, pens*, just as *once* is a misspelling for *ones*.

Almost all nouns now belong to this division; for though it was originally only one form among several, yet since words from foreign tongues, as Latin and French, adapted themselves to it more easily than to the others, it encroached upon the others and became the commonest form. Then the usual law, that languages throw off all formations which seem irregularities, has worked so as to make the other forms of the plural disappear, except in the case of a few words in very common use. Thus all new words now adopted into the language in time fall under this declension. See § 20, 5.

Foreign words used in English commonly retain at first the plural formation of their own language, but gradually conform to the usual English mode of forming the plural in **es** or **s**, as *banditti, cherubim, memoranda, fungi*; *bandits, cherubs, memorandums, funguses.*

1. Many nouns are used in the singular number only, as proper names, many abstract nouns, names of materials, which have plural forms exceptionally only, to mark special distinctions or varieties; as *London, Cicero, knowledge, strength, gold.*

2. Many nouns are used in the plural number only; as *scissors, shears, pincers, trousers, obsequies, aborigines, victuals, entrails, politics, ethics. Means,* which was plural, is now used as singular; so *news* also, which originally a genitive singular, 'hwœt *neowes*' = *of new,* became a plural noun in Shakespeare, 'I tell *these news* to thee.'

3. Some nouns change their meaning in the plural; as *iron, irons; baggage, baggages; compass, compasses; spectacle, spectacles.*

4. Some nouns have two plural forms (these often, but not always, differ in meaning, and cannot be interchanged in their use); as—

brother,	*brethren,* and	*brothers.*
die,	*dice,*	*dies.*
staff,	*staves,*	*staffs.*
index,	*indices,*	*indexes.*

5. A few words really singular have, on account of their form, come to be used as plurals:—*alms,* a shortened form of *ælmesse; eaves, peas* (from which, by mistake, new singular forms *eave, pea,* have been formed), *riches.* Of *eave, peas,* and *riches* plural forms *eueses, peses, pesen, richessis,* were once in use.

6. Compounded substantives take the inflexion at the end of the word; as *handfuls, pailfuls, forget-me-nots:* but if the parts retain their distinctive forces the simple substantive claims the inflexion; as *courts* martial, *sons*-in-law.

SUBSTANTIVES.

CASES.

§ 29. **Cases**, or **Case-forms**, are the forms of a noun (or pronoun) which shew its relation to some other word in a sentence.

The cases are three, **Nominative, Objective** (or **Accusative**), **Possessive** (or **Genitive**).

In nouns substantive the objective case is always like the nominative; in pronouns substantive it is usually unlike.

The possessive case is formed, in the singular and plural alike, by the addition of **s** to the nominative.

This **s** is the remnant of a syllable -es (later -is), one of several modes of forming the case in earlier English, and is now usually distinguished from the nominative plural by an apostrophe, as, the *boy's* hat, the *men's* hats.

Plural nouns ending in **s**, and nouns of more than one syllable ending in **s** or having the sound of a final **s** in the nominative singular, commonly drop the **s** of the possessive case, and the apostrophe only is marked; as, the *boys'* hats, *Jesus'* words, for *conscience'* sake.

The full syllable of the earlier form is seen in the word Wednesday, the day of Woden, and is heard in the sound of many words; as, the *horse's* mane; sitting on an *ass's* colt; St. *James's* Epistle; the *Princess's* theatre.

When the origin of the inflexion of the possessive case was forgotten an idea obtained that it was an ellipse of the possessive pronoun *his*; hence it became a custom of writers, especially of the sixteenth and seventeenth centuries, to write thus—

'*Sansfoy his* shield is hangd with bloudy hew.'

'For Jesus *Christ his* sake.'

It is obvious that this is wrong, for it would not account for the forms *hers, ours*, &c.; and whatever explanation accounts for the form *his* from *he* accounts also for the ordinary possessive form.[1]

In earlier English the inflexion **es, is**, was not the only form in use. The old inflexion of the possessive cases of the personal pronouns *mine, thine*, formerly *mín, thín*, see § 40, shews another form. A large class of feminine nouns used another inflexion **e**, of which an instance remains in *Ladyday* (*Ladyeday*), the day of our Lady.

---

[1] For a full account of this error, see Specimens of Early English, Part II, Morris and Skeat, p. 337.

Besides these three case-forms, two more, a dative and an ablative or instrumental case, once existed in English. The dative case lost its distinctive case-ending, and either became, as in the case of nouns, for all purposes of grammar merged in the objective; or, as in many of the pronouns, as *him, them, whom,* displaced the real objective form and remained in use in its stead. Its most usual termination was *m*, and the two adverbs, seldo*m*, whilo*m*, retain the case-form of the plural dative which ended in *-um*. A trace of the ablative, or instrumental case, is to be found in the expression—
The more he has, *the* more he wants,
of which older forms were *thi, thy*; and in the adverb *why.*

All relations marked by case-endings (or inseparable suffixes) can be more accurately defined by prepositions (or separable prefixes); and languages usually cease by degrees to use case-endings, and employ prepositions in their place, as has happened in the modern Greek and French languages as well as in the English.

TABLE OF NOUNS OF THE FOUR DECLENSIONS.

§ 30.

DECLENSION I.

	Sing.	Plur.	Sing.	Plur.
Nom.	ox	oxen	shoe	shoon [or shoes]
Obj.	ox	oxen	shoe	shoon [shoes]
Poss.	ox's	oxen's	shoe's	. . [shoes']

DECLENSION II.

Nom.	man	men	goose	geese
Obj.	man	men	goose	geese
Poss.	man's	men's	goose's	geese's

DECLENSION III.

Nom.	sheep	sheep
Obj.	sheep	sheep
Poss.	sheep's	sheep's

DECLENSION IV.

Nom.	ass	asses	negro	negroes
Obj.	ass	asses	negro	negroes
Poss.	ass's	asses'	negro's	negroes'
Nom.	thief	thieves	lady	ladies
Obj.	thief	thieves	lady	ladies
Poss.	thief's	thieves'	lady's	ladies'
Nom.	girl	girls	boy	boys
Obj.	girl	girls	boy	boys
Poss.	girl's	girls'	boy's	boys'

SUBSTANTIVES. 45

COMPARATIVE TABLE OF INFLEXIONS.

§ 31.

		ENGLISH of the 10th and 11th cent.[1]	ENGLISH of the 13th and 14th cent.[2]	MODERN ENGLISH.
SING.	Nom.	eage	eye	eye
	Obj.	eage	eye	eye
	Poss.	eagan	eye	eye's
	Dat.	eagan	eye	
PLUR.	Nom.	eagan	eyen	eyes
	Obj.	eagan	eyen	eyes
	Poss.	eagena	eyene	eyes'
	Dat.	eagum	eyen	
SING.	Nom.	hors	hors	horse
	Obj.	hors	hors	horse
	Poss.	horses	horses	horse's
	Dat.	horse	horse	
PLUR.	Nom.	hors	hors	horses
	Obj.	hors	hors	horses
	Poss.	horsa	horse	horses'
	Dat.	horsum	horse	
SING.	Nom.	feld	feld	field
	Obj.	feld	feld	field
	Poss.	feldes	feldes	field's
	Dat.	felda	felde	
PLUR.	Nom.	feldas	feldes	fields
	Obj.	feldas	feldes	fields
	Poss.	felda	feldene	fields'
	Dat.	feldum	feldes	

---

[1] Vernon, Anglo-Saxon Guide, pp. 13-15.
[2] Morris, Specimens of Early English, pp. xvii, xix.

ADJECTIVES.

§ 32. **Adjectives** are words joined to substantives to denote some quality or attribute belonging to the thing of which the substantive is the name. They are also called **Epithets**, and sometimes also **Attributes**.

Adjectives (except pronouns adjective) have no inflexion of **gender, number,** and **case**; as—

> A *good* man. The woman is *good*.
> It is a *good* thing. They are *good* men.
> He likes a *good* horse. That is a *good* man's action.

Adjectives are often used in a sentence as substantives, and then, like substantives, have inflexion of number and case; as—

> The *goods* the gods provide us.
> And for it came up four notable *ones* toward the four winds of heaven.
> Form *fours*.
> I will not do it for *forty's* sake.
> I will not destroy it for *ten's* sake.

<small>In Early English adjectives had inflexions to mark gender, number, and case; and also different inflexions to distinguish an adjective used definitely, that is, with the definite article, or with a demonstrative or a possessive pronoun, from the same adjective used indefinitely. The inflexion of number, marking the plural by final e, remained some time after the other inflexions had been lost.</small>

ADJECTIVES.

COMPARATIVE TABLE OF INFLEXIONS.

Definite Form.

§ 33.

	ENGLISH of the 10th and 11th cent.[1]			ENGLISH of the 13th and 14th cent.[2]	MODERN ENGLISH.
	Sing.			*Sing.*	
	M.	*F.*	*N.*	*M. F. N.*	
Nom.	góda,	góde,	góde.	gode.	good.
Obj.	gódan,	gódan,	góde.	goden (gode).	
Poss.		gódan.		goden „	[of both definite
Dat. *Abl.* }		gódan.		goden „	and indefinite forms, of all
	Plur.			*Plur.*	genders, numbers, and cases.]
	M. F. N.			*M. F. N.*	
Nom.	gódan.			goden (gode).	
Obj.	gódan.			goden (gode).	
Poss.	gódena.			godene (gode).	
Dat. *Abl.* }	gódum.			goden (gode).	

Indefinite Form.

	10th and 11th cent.			13th and 14th cent.		
	Sing.			*Sing.*		
	M.	*F.*	*N.*	*M.*	*F.*	*N.*
Nom.	gód,	gód,	gód.	god,	god,	god.
Obj.	godne,	góde,	gód.	godne,	gode,	god.
Poss.	gódes,	gódre,	gódes.	godes,	godre,	godes.
Dat. *Abl.* }	gódum,	gódre,	gódum.	gode,	godre,	gode.
	Plur.			*Plur.*		
	M. F. N.			*M. F. N.*		
Nom.	góde.			gode.		
Obj.	góde.			gode.		
Poss.	gódra.			godre.		
Dat. *Abl.* }	gódum.			gode.		

---

[1] Vernon, Anglo-Saxon Guide, pp. 21, 22.
[2] Morris, Specimens of Early English, p. xxiii.

Comparison of Adjectives.

§ 34. The adjective has three degrees of comparison:—

Positive, speaking of the quality of a thing or class without relation to any other thing; as—

 A *long* stick.

Comparative, speaking of the quality of a thing or class as compared with one other thing or group of things; as—

 A *longer* stick.
 These are *larger* than those.

Superlative, speaking of the quality of a thing or class as compared with all other things of the same class; as—

 This is the *longest* stick.

Adjectives are compared by inflexion.

i. **The Comparative** is now formed by **adding -er,** and the **Superlative** by **adding -est,** to the Positive—

 great, greater, greatest.
 gay, gayer, gayest.

The inflexion sometimes modifies the termination of the positive, or stem. According to the ordinary rules of composition—

(1) Final mute E is elided—

 white, whiter, whitest.

(2) Y following a consonant becomes I—

 tidy, tidier, tidiest.
 silly, sillier, silliest.
But *shy, shyer, shyest.*

ADJECTIVES.

(3) In monosyllables, and a few other words, a single final consonant following a short vowel is doubled—

sad,   sadder,   saddest.
thin,   thinner,   thinnest.
hopeful, hopefuller, hopefullest.

ii. A mode of inflexion by **modification of the vowel** of the positive has almost disappeared; a few instances only remain in use—

old,   elder,   eldest.
nigh,   [near,]   next.
[be]neath, nether.

iii. Some words, mostly adverbs or prepositions, have a comparative and superlative ending in **-more** and **-most** added to the positive or to the comparative—

fore,   [former],   foremost.
[further],   furthermore,   furthermost.
in,   inner,   inmost, innermost.
out,   outer,   outmost, outermost.
[ut],   utter,   utmost, uttermost.
up,   upper,   uppermost.
under, ...   undermost.
hind,   hinder,   hindmost, hindermost.
mid, ...   midmost,
[be]neath, nether,   nethermost.
top, ...   topmost.

In some of these instances we have a real superlative inflexion **-ost** or **-est** added to a termination **-me**, which was itself a superlative form, and was thus again compared, as in *foremost*, of which the old forms were *fore, for-me, fyr-m-est*; but in others we have a later formation, compounded, according to a false analogy, of the adverbs *more, most,* as *rear-most.*

E

Comparison formed by inflexion is less common now than in the earlier stages of the language: many words are seldom inflected, many never; some because of their form, some because of usage merely.

> Words of English origin, and monosyllables generally, can almost always form comparison by inflexion; while words of Latin origin usually are not inflected.

> Disyllables, especially words ending in a vowel, may often form comparison by inflexion; while words of more than two syllables are not commonly inflected.

Adjectives which do not use inflexion, and some also which have inflected forms, express comparison by means of the adverbs *more* and *most*; as—

> *beautiful, more beautiful, most beautiful.*

A degree of quality more than ordinary, expressed without relation to another thing or class, may be called the **Absolute Comparative**; and in like manner a degree of quality the utmost conceivable may be called the **Absolute Superlative**. These used sometimes to be expressed by the inflected forms, as in Spenser's Faerie Queene—

'Help thy *weaker* novice'; i.e. thy novice who is *too weak*.

'And spake reprochfull shame of *highest* God'; i.e. of *most high* God.

Modern English, however, does not allow this use of the inflected forms, but employs adverbs; as—

somewhat long; *too* long; *very* long; a *most* beautiful woman.

Some irregular formations are found, of which the following are the most important:—

ADJECTIVES.

1. [good],   [bet], better,   best.
   [bad], [evil], [ill], worse,   worst.
                          ere, [or],   erst.
   far, [fer],   farther,   farthest, first.
   fore,   former,   foremost.
   forth, [furth],   further,   furthest.
   late,   later, latter,   latest, last.
   little,   less, lesser,   least.
   [mid], [middle], ...   midst.
   much (many),   [mo], more,   most.
   nigh,   nigher, [near,]   nighest, next.
   old,   older, elder,   oldest, eldest.
   [rathe],   rather,   [rathest].

2. The origin of the comparative and its force, in a few words of irregular form, have been forgotten, and the words have been inflected a second time; as *bet, better; less, lesser; mo, more; near, nearer, nearest; worse, worser.* With such double comparatives may be compared the expressions *more better, more fairer, most highest, chiefest* and *most principal.*

3. Some Latin comparatives, adopted into English, retain their proper form and force; as *exterior, interior, major, prior, superior. Extreme,* having taken an English shape, forms a new superlative *extremest.*

NUMERALS.

§ 35. i. **Cardinal** numerals are adjectives answering the question 'how many?'—*one, two, three, four, five, six, seven, eight, nine, ten, eleven, twelve, hundred, thousand.*

Some are to be regarded also as collective substantives; as, a *hundred,* a *thousand,* &c.; and to these may be added, a *pair,* a *couple,* a *leash,* a *dozen,* a *score.*

For numbers from thirteen to twenty, and for all decades, compounds of the first ten are used; for other numbers the different numerals are combined, as *twenty-five*, or *five and twenty*. *Million, billion,* &c., are of Latin origin.

From *one* is formed *none* (*ne*, not, *one*), both singular and plural.

ii. **Ordinal** numerals are adjectives answering the question 'which in order of number?'—*first, second, third, fourth, fifth, sixth,* &c.

First is a superlative form of *far*, and has taken the place of *that one, the tone, the one*, which was once used as the first ordinal.

Second is borrowed from Latin (secundus, following), and has taken the place of *that other, the tother, the other*.

Other ordinals are formed by adding *th* to the cardinals; four, four*th*; thousand*th*; million*th*. From *three* was formed *thridde*, final *th* being weakened into *d* to avoid a second aspirate in the same syllable, then *thridde, thrid*, by metathesis became *third*, as *brid* became *bird*.

Complex ordinals above *twentieth* are expressed by using the cardinal form for all except the last number, and the ordinal form for the last; as—

In his *twenty-fourth* year.
In his *four and twentieth* year.
In the *one thousand eight hundred and seventieth* year.

iii. **Three numeral adverbs,** *once* (ones), *twice* (twies), *thrice* (thries), answering the question 'how many times?' are possessive cases of the first three cardinals, which alone were inflected.

iv. **Multiplicatives** answering the question 'how many fold?' are compounded of cardinal numerals and the word 'fold': *twofold, threefold, hundredfold,* &c.

Single (Latin singuli) supplies the place of a compound of *one*; and like forms from the Latin numerals are used, as *double, triple, treble, quadruple,* &c.

PRONOUNS.

§ 36. **Pronouns** are **Substantive** or **Adjective**, according as they may stand as substantives or adjectives in a sentence.

§ 37. i. The **Substantive Pronouns** are—1. **Personal**, 2. **Reflexive**, 3. the **Relative That**.

1. **Personal**:—

		First Person. (*Speaking.*)	Second Person. (*Spoken to.*)	Third Person. (*Spoken of.*)		
				M.	F.	N.
Sing.	*Nom.*	I,	thou,	he,	she,	it.
	Obj.	me,	thee,	him,	her,	it.
	Poss.	mine, my,	thine, thy,	his,	hers, her,	its.
				M. F. N.		
Plur.	*Nom.*	we,	ye, you,	they.		
	Obj.	us,	you,	them.		
	Poss.	ours, our,	yours, your,	theirs, their.		

In the pronouns of the first and second persons gender is not marked, because the speaker and hearer being (usually) present to each other the distinction of sex in conversation was not necessary.

Of the first person the objective and possessive forms are not from the same root as the nominative.

The forms *my, thy* are weakened forms of *mine, thine,* as *a* is a weakened form of *an*. *Mine, thine, ours, yours, hers, theirs* are the predicative forms, This is *my* hat; This hat is *mine*. See § 38.

In earlier English *ye* was always nominative, *you* always objective, and both forms were of the plural number only, as is the usage in the Authorised Version of the Bible. But this distinction of the cases was lost, and *ye* treated as a weakened form of *you*, so that the forms become interchangeable, as in Spenser and Shakespeare. The plural form *you* gradually came to be used as a more polite and less familiar mode of address than *thou*, which passed from use except in very familiar conversation, and in very solemn or antiquated forms of speech. In the present day *ye* is not used as the objective, and while the plural *you* is used also instead of the singular *thou* in speaking to a person, *ye* is always nominative and always plural.

Of the pronoun of the third person the older feminine was written *heo*, which has been driven out by *she*, the feminine of a demonstrative pronoun *se*, but it survives in the provincial nominative *her*. The plural forms have been borrowed from the demonstrative pronoun adjective *the*, *that*. An earlier form of *it* was *hit*, making the neuter of the possessive case *his* and sometimes *it*: the form *its* is of late date, and does not occur in the Authorised Version of the Bible, 1611, and is seldom found in Shakespeare or Milton.

2. **Reflexive**:—

(1) **Simple**; the objective cases of the personal pronouns.

Sing. me, thee, him, her, it.
Plur. us, you, them.

(2) **Compound**; cases of the personal pronouns compounded with the word *self*, *selves*.

Sing. myself, thyself, himself, herself, itself.
Plur. ourselves, yourselves, themselves.

These forms appear as *self*, *selves*, compounded with the possessive case of the first and second persons, and with the objective case of the third person. In the earlier language *self* was an adjective, and was joined to any case of these pronouns, even to the nominative, as *I self*; but now some uses only remain, others have become obsolete. Practically the construction is that of a substantive with an adjective pronoun in agreement, *my self*, or, of a substantive in apposition to a substantive pronoun, *him self*: accordingly *self* forms a plural *selves* like a substantive, *ourselves*, *themselves*.

3. **Relative**:—

That.

The relative pronoun *that* was originally demonstrative; it is not inflected, is never joined with a substantive, and never follows a preposition; thus we say, He is the man *of whom* I spoke; but, He is the man *that* I spoke *of*. It is more definite and limiting than the other relatives *who*, *which*, as though it kept some of its demonstrative force. In some sentences the word *that* has the combined force of demonstrative and relative, antecedent and relative having coalesced—

We speak *that* we do know.
To do always *that* is righteous in thy sight.

§ 38. ii. The **Adjective Pronouns** are—1. **Possessive**, 2. **Demonstrative**, 3. **Interrogative**, 4. **Relative**, 5. **Indefinite**, 6. **Distributive**.

1. **Possessive** :—

mine, my,	thine, thy,	his.
ours, our,	yours, your,	hers, her.
		its.
		theirs, their.

Whose may be reckoned a possessive pronoun.

The possessive pronouns are the possessive case-forms of the personal pronouns, and cannot now be distinguished from them, although it is usually more convenient to treat them as real possessive pronouns, that is, as adjectives qualifying their substantives. *Ours, yours, hers, theirs* are predicative forms only, and are never used as attributes. They were originally mere dialectic variations of the Northern dialect, as *ouren, youren* were of the Midland. *Mine, thine* are also predicative forms, but were commonly, and are still sometimes, used also in preference to the weaker forms as attributes before words beginning with a vowel or H, as—

Open thou *mine* eyes.
I will wash *mine* hands in innocency.

2. **Demonstrative** :—

Sing.	the,	this,	that,	yon.
Plur.	the,	these,	those,	yon.

The is now the definite article; see § 39.

The demonstrative pronouns have no inflexion to mark gender or case. They show or point out the persons about whom the speaker is speaking. *The* defines the person without reference to his position; *this* points to the person near me as I speak; *that* to the person near you or near some one else away from the speaker; *yon* points to a person at a distance.

In Early English the plural nominative of *this* was (*thás*) *those*, and of *that* was (*thá*) *they*, still used in Dorset as an adjective pronoun, as '*they* sticks'; later *they* became the plural of *he, she, it,* and *those* was used as the plural of *that,* and for *this* a new plural (*thise,*) *these* was formed.

3. **Interrogative :—**

(1) SINGULAR AND PLURAL.

	Masc.	Fem.	Neut.
Nom.	who,	who,	what.
Obj.	whom,	whom,	what.
Poss.	whose,	whose,	whose.

(2) Which.   (3) Whether.

Who, whom, masculine and feminine, are always used substantively, and cannot be joined as attributes to a substantive, therefore *what* supplies their place as an attribute, as '*What* man did you see?' and so is used as an interrogative pronoun adjective of all genders.

Which is a compound form equivalent to *who-like, what-like, whom-like*, the old form being *hwelc*, = *hwa-lic*, the later Northern form *whilk* (compare *each, ilk,* and *such, swilk, swa-lic*). Accordingly it is of both numbers, of all genders, and of both nominative and objective cases. In modern usage it implies one of a definite number known to the person who asks the question.

Whether means 'which of two': it is nearly obsolete.

4. **Relative :—**

Who and *which*, the interrogative pronouns, have become relatives. The three relatives *that, who (what), which,* can generally be used interchangeably, though slight distinctions may be made. *That* is most definite and limiting; *which* is least definite, and accordingly is used when the relative refers to an antecedent circumstance not expressed but implied in the previous clause. It is now seldom masculine or feminine, but is almost restricted to the neuter gender, and is commonly used instead of *what*, as if it were the neuter form of *who*.

Some compound relatives are, like the simple form *who*, indefinite, as—

    whoso,   *whoever,*   *whichever.*
                whosoever, *whichsoever.*

The former part of those compounded with *ever* is inflected as the simple form.

Some compounds of the old datives feminine, *there, where,* of the demonstrative and relative with prepositions are usually reckoned as adverbs, but may be used as equivalent to pronouns, *thereof, whereof, thereto, whereby,* &c.

He took up that *whereon* he lay, = *on which*.

5. Indefinite:—

(1) who;   (2) an, a;   (3) any;   (4) they;   (5) some;
(6) *Nom.* one.
    Obj. one.
    Poss. one's.

These are rather pronouns used with an indefinite sense: thus *who* is the relative, used indefinitely, in the phrase 'as *who* should say,' which is seldom used now.

An, a, are forms of the first numeral *an,* or *one*; *any* is a derivative of it.

They is the demonstrative pronoun used without reference to any particular persons, as '*They* say.'

One is the French word *on*, from Latin *homo*, a man (*homo, hominem*, French *homme, hom, om, on*), used in the sense of *they*, indefinite: it is not the same word as the English numeral *one*, though in some phrases it appears to have been confounded with it.

6. Distributive:—

Each, every, either, neither.

Distributive pronouns are singular, and always imply the previous mention or knowledge of a noun of the plural number: thus *either* and *neither* (*ne*, not, *either*) imply the mention or knowledge of a noun referring to two persons or things.

Each (*ech, ælc*) distributes two or more.

Every (*ever-each, æuer-ælc*) distributes more than two, and has also a sense of collection or plurality; and if we say 'Every one of them was there,' our meaning is almost the same as if we had said 'They were all there.' While in the expression '*all* and *every*,' *every* implies the separate individuality of the persons, in '*each* and *every*,' *each* implies the separate individuality of the persons, and *every* implies the inclusion of the whole number. Hence Shakespeare sometimes uses *every* with a plural verb; as—

        Smooth *every* passion
That in the nature of their lord rebel.

And *every* one to rest themselves betake.

Articles.

§ 39. The demonstrative pronoun *the*, and the indefinite *an*, *a*, are called **the Definite Article**, and **the Indefinite Article.**

The was at one time the masculine demonstrative, *that* being neuter, but now the definite article *the* is of all genders and numbers alike.

The indefinite article *an*, *a*, is a weakened use of the numeral *an*, the older form of *one*. *A* is used before a consonant or aspirate; *an* before all vowels except *u*, and before mute *h*. Some persons use *an* before words beginning with *u*.

The Definite Article—

(1) Individualises or specifies; that is, marks off the noun to which it is joined as the name of something which both speaker and hearer can in their minds separate from others of the same class.

> *The* boy is not here; i.e. the boy whom we know, who has been mentioned, of whom you inquire, &c.
>
> Thou art *the* man; i.e. of whom we have been speaking.
>
> *The* O'Donoghue; i.e. the chief who alone can be specified of the whole clan of that name.

In like manner it marks the subject of a sentence; for both speaker and hearer are supposed to know enough of the subject to individualise it in their minds.

> *The* beggar became king.

(2) Sometimes it generalises; that is, uses the individual for the whole class.

> *The* lion is carnivorous.

(3) In some ordinary phrases the definite article is omitted, as it would be too emphatic, or would wrongly imply the existence of a class of objects when there is no such class.

Is the Prime Minister *in town?*
The boy is off *to sea.*
The fox has run *to earth.*

The Indefinite Article—

(1) Specifies an individual of a class, but not any one in particular, as—

A man called on me to day.

(2) It sometimes generalises, as—

A man should bear himself bravely in misfortune; i.e. *any* man you like to mention, therefore *all* men.

In some sentences it would appear as if an indefinite article is used to distribute, as—

Three times *an* hour.

Fifteen shillings *a* week;

But *an, a,* in such phrases, are not really the indefinite article but a corruption of the preposition *on* (see § 59, i.) used with a dative case without any article;

Ic fæste tuwa *on wucan.* I fast twice *in the* week.

Comparative Table of Inflexions.

§ 40.   The First Personal Pronoun.

		10TH AND 11TH CENT.[1]	13TH AND 14TH CENT.[2]	MODERN.
SING.	Nom.	Ic	Ic, Ich	I
	Obj.	me	me	me
	Poss.	min	min, mi	mine, my
	Dat.	me	me	
DUAL.	Nom.	wit	wit	
	Obj.	unc	unc	
	Poss.	uncer	unker	
	Dat.	unc	unc	
PLUR.	Nom.	we	we	we
	Obj.	us	ous, us	us
	Poss.	ure	ure	our, ours
	Dat.	us	ous, us	

The Second Personal Pronoun.

		10TH AND 11TH CENT.	13TH AND 14TH CENT.	MODERN.
SING.	Nom.	thu	thu, thou	thou
	Obj.	the	the	thee
	Poss.	thin	thin, thi	thine, thy
	Dat.	the	the	
DUAL.	Nom.	git	git, get	
	Obj.	inc	gunk	
	Poss.	incer	gunker	
	Dat.	inc	gunk	
PLUR.	Nom.	ge	ge, yhe, ye	ye, you
	Obj.	eow	eow, yow, ou	you
	Poss.	eower	eower, gure, yure	your, yours
	Dat.	eow	eow, yow, ou	

---

[1] Vernon, Anglo-Saxon Guide, pp. 27, 28, 31.
[2] Morris and Skeat, Specimens of Early English, Part II. p. xxvii.

VERBS.

COMPARATIVE TABLE OF INFLEXIONS (*continued*).

The Third Personal Pronoun.

	10TH AND 11TH CENT.			13TH AND 14TH CENT.			MODERN.		
	M.	*F.*	*N.*	*M.*	*F.*	*N.*	*M.*	*F.*	*N.*
Nom.	he,	heo,	hit	he (ha),	heo,	hit (it)	he,	she,	it
Obj.	hine,	hi,	hit	hine (ine),	hi (hire),	hit (it)	him,	her,	it
Poss.	his,	hire,	his	his,	hire,	his	his,	hers,	its
Dat.	him,	hire,	him	him,	hire,	him			
Nom.		hi			hi (thai, thei)			they	
Obj.		hi			hi (his, hise)			them	
Poss.		hira			hire (here, heore)			their, theirs	
Dat.		him			hem (heom)				

The Interrogative Pronoun.

Nom.	hwá,	hwá,	hwæt	hua (huo),		huet (wat)	who,	what	
Obj.	hwone,	hwone,	hwæt	huam (hwan, wan)		huet (wat)	whom,	what	
Poss.	hwæs,	hwæs,	hwæs	huas (huos, wos)			whose,	whose	
Dat.	hwam,	hwæm,	hwam	huam(hwom,wom)					
Abl.	hwy,	hwy,	hwy						

VERB.

§ 41. **The Verb** has inflexion to mark distinctions of **Voice, Mood, Tense, Number, Person.**

Verbs are divided into **Transitive** and **Intransitive**.

A verb is **Transitive** when the action which it expresses may be exerted on an object (i. e. a noun in the objective case), without which the idea of the verb is incomplete; as *I strike him*.

A verb is **Intransitive** when it expresses state, or condition, or an action complete in itself and not communicated to any object; as *I live, I walk, I breathe.*

The object of a transitive verb is not always expressed; for in some cases an object of a general character is understood, which the mind easily supplies from the notion contained in the verb, and thus the verb approaches to the nature of an intransitive verb; as *men build, and time pulls down*—i.e. build buildings of all kinds, churches, houses, stations, &c.

Some intransitives may be changed into transitives by composition with prepositions, as—

He came,   *He overcame him;*

and often when the preposition is not compounded with the verb it becomes in sense absorbed in the verb, as—

He *speaks-of* thee.   You were *spoken-of.*

Some intransitives are used in a causative sense, and thus admit an object, as—

He ran *a horse* in the St. Leger.

He raced *his yacht* at Cowes.

Some verbs are used as both transitive and intransitive, as—

He *split* the nut; the nut *split* in two.

He *rent* his clothes.

The veil of the temple was *rent* in twain from the top to the bottom; and the earth did quake, and the rocks *rent*.

A different form is often given to the verb in its transitive and intransitive senses, the transitive form being derived from the intransitive by a modification of the stem-vowel; as—

He *falls*.   He *fells* the tree.
He *sits*.   He *sets* the lessons.
He *drinks*.   He *drenches* himself.

Some intransitive verbs are called **Impersonal Verbs**, because they are used in a construction called impersonal, which allows the verb to be used in the third person only, and without a subject expressed, or with a clause in place of a subject; as *meseems, methinks, methought* = it seems to me, it seemed to me. Or such verbs have the pronoun *it*, with an indefinite sense, in the place of a real subject; as *it snows, it rains.*

VOICES.

§ 42. The Verb has Two Voices:—

The Active Voice, in which the subject, or that of which the verb speaks, is the agent, a person or thing which does, or is, something; as *I kill, I live, I am.*

The Passive Voice, in which the subject is the patient, a person or thing to which something is done, which suffers something; as *I am killed.*

English verbs have one tense-form only belonging to the passive voice, the past participle; but they supply others by combining auxiliary verbs with this participle.

Intransitive verbs have no passive voice.

§ 43. Verb-forms are divided into two parts—i. **Finite**, ii. **Infinite**.

i. **The Verb Finite**, which is limited by mood and person as well as tense, has three **moods**, or manners (modes) of expressing its action or being:—

Indicative, for a direct statement, or a direct question; as—

> I *seek* him.
> What *do* mine eyes with grief behold?

Subjunctive, for an indirect statement, or an indirect question, expressing uncertainty, depending upon some statement or question expressed by another verb; as—

> Advise if this *be* worth attempting.
> He asked if that *were* worth attempting.

An indirect statement, or an indirect question, speaking of a thing not as a fact, but as a purpose or consequence, as possible, desirable, supposable, &c., in principal construction and not dependent on another verb, which is sometimes called the Conjunctive mood, is not expressed in English by a mood-form formed by inflexion, but by the help of auxiliary verbs; as—

  I *would* go.   I *may* go.   *May* I go.   *Could* I go.

Imperative, for a command or entreaty; as—

  Go home.

  Give us this day our daily bread.

The verb finite is also called personal, because its forms define the person of the subject of which it speaks.

 ii. **The Verb Infinite** has no limitation of mood or of person. It has two divisions—

Infinitive, a verbal substantive which, as a verb, may require a noun for an object; and, as a substantive, may stand for the subject, or complement, or object, in a sentence; as—

  Men are accustomed *to kill* animals.

  To kill is *to take* away life.

Participles, verbal adjectives, which as verbs may require an object, and as adjectives may qualify substantives; as—

  Trees *darkening* the water on each side.

  Man is a *cooking* animal.

  A *burnt* child dreads the fire.

Each of these forms has, in some constructions, the force of a gerund, having assimilated to itself what was a distinct gerund form in older English:—the infinitive from when it expresses a purpose; as—

  What went ye out into the wilderness *for to see*?
  Is this good *to eat*?
  The house is *to let*.

the form which has grown to resemble the participial form when it has the force of a substantive with a preposition; as—

  Apples are good for *eating*.
  And oft in *dying* called upon your name.

(Compare § 48, 2.)

TENSES.

§ 44. Tenses are forms expressing the time of the state, or action, of the verb.

Time is **Present, Past, Future.**

Action in time is conceived as—

(1) **Finished,**   **Perfect.**
(2) **Unfinished,**   **Imperfect.**
(3) **Undefined,** not finished, not unfinished, } **Aorist.**

In order therefore to express perfectly each kind of action in every time, a verb would require $3 \times 3 = 9$ tense-forms[1]. English has two only of these nine forms, the present aorist and the past aorist, as inflected tenses, but supplies the others by the use of auxiliary verbs combined with forms of the verb infinite.

i. Time Present.

Finished	*I have waited*	Present perfect
Unfinished	*I am waiting*	Present imperfect
Undefined	*I wait*	Present aorist.

ii. Time Past.

Finished	*I had waited*	Past perfect
Unfinished	*I was waiting*	Past imperfect
Undefined	*I waited*	Past aorist.

iii. Time Future.

Finished	*I shall have waited*	Future perfect
Unfinished	*I shall be waiting*	Future imperfect
Undefined	*I shall wait*	Future aorist.

Eight verbs are used as auxiliaries for supplying tense-forms—*be, have, shall, will, may, can, must, do;* and to these may be added some forms of the verbs *go* (I am going), *owe* (I ought), *let*.

---

[1] Compare Harper, Powers of the Greek Tenses, p. 7.

Numbers.

§ 45. Tenses have two **Numbers—Singular** and **Plural**; and each number has three Persons. These correspond to the numbers and persons of the subject of which the verb speaks, according as the subject stands for one or more than one, speaking, or spoken to, or spoken of. Usually, but not always, the personal pronouns are expressed with verb-forms; as—

>| I wait | We wait |
>| Thou waitest | Ye wait |
>| He waits | They wait. |

Conjugations.

§ 46. Verbs are divided into **Two Conjugations** or Classes, according to their mode of forming the inflexions which mark the past tense of the indicative mood and the past participle.

i. **The Strong Conjugation** (called also **Old** and **Irregular**), which forms the past tense by a change in the force of the vowel of the stem, as shown in the present tense; and forms the past participle by adding the syllable **-en**, with or without change of the vowel of the stem; as—

>| *fall,* | *fell,* | *fallen.* |
>| *drink,* | *drank,* | *drunken.* |

The pronunciation and spelling of English words have become so much changed that rules for the modification of the stem-vowels of strong verbs, which would explain the oldest forms, are useless for modern forms, in which almost any vowel appears able to be modified into any other.

The syllable -en in many verbs has coalesced with the termination, and ceased to be a distinct syllable, and from some verbs the inflexion has quite disappeared; as—

VERBS. 67

know, knew, known.
run, ran, run.
sing, sang, sung.

The verbs of the Strong Conjugation fall into three divisions:—

(1) Verbs in which the vowel of the participle is the same as the stem-vowel; as—
fall, fell, fallen.

(2) Verbs in which the vowel of the participle is the modified vowel of the past tense indicative.; as—
hang, hung, hung.

(3) Verbs in which the vowel of the participle differs from both the other forms; as—
drink, drank, drunken.

ii. **The Weak Conjugation** (called also **New**, and **Regular**), which forms the past tense of the indicative mood, and the past participle alike by adding the syllable -ed to the stem; as—

wait, waited, waited.

In many verbs the syllable -ed coalesces with the termination, ceasing to be a distinct syllable, and appears as d or t; or changes d into t; or is merged in a final t: and in some verbs it modifies the consonants or vowels of the final syllable; as—

breathe,	*breathed.*
learn (learned),	*learnt.*
lend,	*lent.*
quit (quitted),	*quit.*
feel,	*felt.*
pay (payed),	*paid.*
leave,	*left.*
lose,	*lost.*
have,	*had.*
make,	*made.*

sell,	*sold.*
clothe (clothed),	*clad.*

A few verbs whose stem has, or had in earlier English, a final guttural, form the past tense irregularly, both modifying the stem-vowel into **au** or **ou**, and taking the inflexion -t of the Weak conjugation; as—

catch,	*caught.*
reach,	*raught.*
teach,	*taught.*
bring,	*brought.*
buy,	*bought.*
may,	*might* [*moughte*].
owe,	*ought.*
seek (beseech),	*sought.*
think,	*thought.*
work,	*wrought.*

Some verbs ending in **d** or **t** appear to have no inflexion for the past tense or past participle, and therefore not to fall under either conjugation. They may be regarded as belonging to the Weak conjugation, the syllable -ed having coalesced with their final **d** or **t**; as—

shred,	*shred,*	*shred.*
hit,	*hit,*	*hit.*

Of these verbs the stem-vowel, if long in the present, is shortened; as—

lead,	*led,*	*led.*
read,	*read,*	*read.*

and of some both the uncontracted and the contracted forms are found; as—

The floods have *lifted* up their voice.
(Authorised Version.)

and—

The floods have *lift* up their voice.
(Prayer-book Version, Psalm xciii.)

VERBS.   69

There is in English a general tendency to discard Strong forms and to adopt Weak forms for verbs, as may be seen thus:—

(1) Many verbs have tense-forms of both conjugations; in some instances having originally belonged to the Strong conjugation alone, but having been adapted to the (seemingly) more regular formations of the Weak; as—

cleave,	clove and *cleft*,		cloven and *cleft*.	
help,	holp	„ *helped*,	holpen	„ *helped*.
hang,	hung	„ *hanged*,	hung	„ *hanged*.

(2) Many, which were once of the Strong conjugation, having formed new tenses according to the Weak, have in part or entirely lost their Strong forms[1]; as—

grave,	graved,		graven and *graved*.	
melt,	melted,		molten	„ *melted*.
crow,	crew and *crowed*,		crowed.	
heave,	hove	„ *heaved*,	heaved.	
leap,	[lep]	„ *leaped*,	leaped.	
snow,	[snew]	„ *snowed*,	snowed.	

(3) Derived verbs of English origin are usually of the Weak conjugation, thus from *fall, drink, rise,* are derived—

fell,   felled.
drench,   drenched.
raise,   raised.

(4) All foreign words adopted into English as verbs take the same mode of inflexion[2], 'the only verbal inflexion which can be properly said to be in a living and active state'; as—

index,	indexed.	telegraph,	telegraphed.
cash,	cashed.	taboo,	tabooed.

---

[1] It is very seldom that a verb which was Weak in older English has become Strong in later English. Chaucer used *wered* (weared):—'Of fustyan he *wered* a gepoun'; 'a blewe hood *wered* he'; 'but hood, for jolitee, ne *wered* he noon' (Prologue, 75, 564, 675): but modern English always uses *wore,* perhaps from analogy with *bear, swear,* &c.

[2] *Prove* (Fr. *prouver;* Lat. *probare*) has the Strong participle *proven,* retained in the legal phrase 'not *proven*'; and in poetry—

'Who hath *proven* him
King Uther's son?'

SCHEME OF VERB, WITH INFLECTED TENSE-FORMS.

§ 47. i. Strong Conjugation.

	Indicative.	Subjunctive.	Imperative.	Infinitive.
	Present.			
Sing.	I fall	I fall		
	Thou fallest	Thou fall	fall	[to] fall
	He falleth, falls	He fall		
				Participles.
Plur.	We fall	We fall		
	Ye fall	Ye fall	fall	*Present.* *Past.*
	They fall	They fall		falling fallen
	Past.			
Sing.	I fell	I fell		
	Thou fellest	Thou fell		[Gerund Forms.
	He fell	He fell		to fall
				falling]
Plur.	We fell	We fell		
	Ye fell	Ye fell		
	They fell	They fell		

ii. Weak Conjugation.

	Indicative.	Subjunctive.	Imperative.	Infinitive.
	Present.			
Sing.	I wait	I wait		
	Thou waitest	Thou wait	wait	[to] wait
	He waiteth, waits	He wait		
				Participles.
Plur.	We wait	We wait		
	Ye wait	Ye wait	wait	*Present.* *Past.*
	They wait	They wait		waiting waited
	Past.			
Sing.	I waited	I waited		
	Thou waitedst	Thou waited		[Gerund Forms.
	He waited	He waited		to wait
				waiting]
Plur.	We waited	We waited		
	Ye waited	Ye waited		
	They waited	They waited		

COMPARATIVE TABLE OF INFLEXIONS.

§ 48. The Weak Conjugation.

	10TH AND 11TH CENT.[1]		13TH AND 14TH CENT.[2]		MODERN ENGLISH.	
	Indic.	Subj.	Indic.	Subj.	Indic.	Subj.
	Present.		*Present.*		*Present.*	
Sing.	lufige	lufige	lovie, love	lovie, love	love	love
	lufast	lufige	lovest	lovie, love	lovest	love
	lufath	lufige	loveth	lovie, love	loveth, loves	love
Plur.	lufiath	lufion	lovieth, loveth	lovien, loven	love	love
	lufiath	lufion	lovieth, loveth	lovien, loven	love	love
	lufiath	lufion	lovieth, loveth	lovien, loven	love	love
	Past.		*Past.*		*Past.*	
Sing.	lufode	lufode	lovede	lovede	loved	loved
	lufodest	lufode	lovedest	lovede	lovedst	loved
	lufode	lufode	lovede	lovede	loved	loved
Plur.	lufodon	lufodon	loveden	loveden	loved	loved
	lufodon	lufodon	loveden	loveden	loved	loved
	lufodon	lufodon	loveden	loveden	loved	loved

Imperative.	Imperative.	Imperative.
Sing. lufa	love	love
Plur. lufiath, lufige	lovieth, loveth	love

Infinitive.	Infinitive.	Infinitive.
lufian	lovien, loven	[to] love

Gerund.	Gerund.	[Gerund.
to lufigenne	to lovienne, lovene	to love
		loving]

Participles.	Participles.	Participles.
lufigende	lovinde	loving
ge-lufod	y-loved, i-loved	loved

---

[1] Vernon, Anglo-Saxon Guide, p. 39.
[2] See Morris and Skeat, Specimens of Early English, Part II, p. xxxi. for the various forms in the different dialects.

In verbs, as in other parts of speech, the inflexions which remain are not all which were in use in the earlier stages of the language. A very gradual loss of inflexions may be traced, the most important losses being,—

1. The inflexion marking the Plural number; for the present tense the termination -eth in Southern dialects, and -en in Midland dialects, for all persons—

>All tho that b*eth*.
>These b*en* the points.

and for the past tense the termination -en—They glowed*en*.

in both the indicative and subjunctive moods: and the Southern plural termination -eth in the imperative mood—

>Lordynges, quoth he, now herken*eth* for the beste.

2. The inflexion marking the infinitive -an, later -en, by which the verb infinite was distinguished from the verb finite; as, sing*en*, to sing.

The distinctive inflexions of the gerund, -anne, later -enne; and of the present participle, -ande, later -ende, -inde; by which losses confusion has been introduced into the uses of these forms of the verb, as, infinitive and gerund—

>It is good *to hold* (*healdan, holden*) one's tongue.
>Bridles are good *to hold* (*to healdanne, to holdenne*) horses.

and participle and gerund—

>He was *holding* (*healdande, holdinde*) the handle.
>The handle was good for *holding* (*to healdanne, to holdenne*).

A verbal substantive in -ung, as halg-*ung*, hallow-*ing*, has also been assimilated to the same termination -ing, adding to the confusion between various constructions, since the same word may be a substantive, or a participle, or the gerund form of the verb infinite; as—

>The *passing* of Arthur.
>And Arthur *passing* thence to battle.
>It is only fit for *passing* the time.

The verbal substantive and the gerund cannot always be distinguished, for in some constructions the form so far is a substantive as to be qualified by an article, and so far has become a verb as to take a direct object; as—

>Nothing in his life
>Became him like *the leaving* it.

3. The augment or prefix, which at one time might be used with any part of the verb, and afterwards was a mark of the past participle, at one time ge-, *ge*-lufod, then y- or i-, as *y*-clept, *i*-drad; of which *y*-clept is still used by poets, and many words in provincial dialects keep the prefix, as *a-vound*, for *found*, in Dorset—Have ye *a-vound* the book.

4. It may be further noted that in modern English some inflexions are gradually passing from use; thus, the form -th of the third person singular of the present tense is giving way to the form -s; the second person singular of the past tense in -edst is seldom used; the ending -en of the past participle of strong verbs, as drunk-*en*, is disappearing, and there is a tendency to use only one form for the past tense indicative and the past participle of strong verbs, as weak verbs have only one form.

AUXILIARY VERBS.

§ 49. Auxiliary Verbs are used with forms of the verb infinite to express those relations of voice, mood, tense, which are not expressed by inflexions. They are—*be, have, shall, will, may, can, must, do,* and *ought, go, let*[1]. They are sometimes classed according to these relations of voice, mood, tense; thus *be* is an auxiliary of voice; *may, can, must* are auxiliaries of mood; *have, shall, will,* of tense. Their uses, however, are so various that this classification cannot be strictly maintained.

1. **Be** is irregular, having tenses from three distinct verbs, which are, however, in their origin very closely connected, *be* (from a verb *beon, ben*), *am*, and *was* (from a verb *wesan*). For the present tense indicative two forms exist, *am* and *be*; as—

'We *are* true men, we *are* no spies, we *be* twelve brethren.'

Be, however, has almost passed out of use as indicative, and is now commonly treated as a subjunctive form only. With the past participle of transitive verbs the auxiliary *be* supplies tense-forms for a passive voice. It is not always auxiliary, but sometimes an independent verb expressing existence; as—

O Adam, one Almighty *is*, from whom
All things proceed.
All things that *are*
Are with more spirit chased than enjoy'd.

In early English *be* was the auxiliary of future time, and supplied the place of a future tense, as *shall* and *will* do now. Instances of this use may be found as late as the sixteenth century; as—

That terribyll Trumpat, I heir tell,
Beis (= shall be) hard in Hevin, in erth, and Hell. (Lyndesay.)

The second person singular of the past tense in Early English was 'thou *were*' of both indicative and subjunctive moods, but during the sixteenth century the forms *wast* and *wert* came into literary use, formed according to the analogy of *hast, dost,* and of *art, shalt*. *Wast* was used of the indicative mood only, *wert* at first more usually of the subjunctive, but now of either mood.

---

[1] The verbs *may, can, shall, will,* and the old forms *dare, mote, owe,* are really past tenses *in form*, and present tenses *in meaning*, as *wot* (from *witan*, to know) is a past tense with present tense meaning; and their 3rd persons sing. have the form of the past, not of the present, as, he *may, can, shall, will;* and the old forms he *dare, mote, owe,* as 'God *wot;*' not he *mays, cans,* &c. The later-formed secondary past tenses of these verbs are naturally of the Weak conjugation, (see p. 69 (3),) *might, could, must, durst, wist.* See Grammar in Skeat's Mœso-Gothic Glossary.

2. **Have** is the auxiliary of perfect tenses, and expresses finished action; it is sometimes an independent verb expressing possession.

3. **Shall**, meaning *to owe, to be obliged*, is defective, no parts of the verb infinite being in use: it is always auxiliary.

4. **Will** is also a transitive verb, meaning 'to wish'; and in that sense is conjugated regularly in all its parts as a weak verb, *I will, he wills, willeth, willing*, &c., *willed* being the transitive form of the past tense, and *would* the auxiliary form.

Shall and *will* are both called signs of the future tense, because they supply a tense-form expressing future time. Shakespeare sometimes uses *shall* where modern usage prefers *will*—

> If much you note him,
> You *shall* offend him and extend his passion.

Should and *would* are used indifferently in the verses—

> And they brought young children to him, that he *should* touch them. (Mark x. 13.)

> And they brought unto him also infants, that he *would* touch them. (Luke xviii. 15.)

Modern English distinguishes thus between these two auxiliaries. *Shall* implies some constraint or the force of external circumstances affecting an action; while *will* implies wish or willingness, and freedom from external constraint, as if the action was entirely dependent on the actor's wishes. *Shall* is the usual auxiliary to express simple futurity, or the fact that a thing is coming to pass at a later time. But since there is an idea of constraint in the word *shall*, it is often more polite in speaking to others, or of others, to avoid it and to use *will*. Hence the simple future is expressed (1) in direct statement by *shall* for the first person, and *will* for the second and third persons; (2) in direct question by *shall* for the first and second persons, and by *will* for the third person; (3) in indirect statement and indirect question by *shall* for the first person, by either *shall* or *will* for the second person when the principal clause is in the second person, but *will* when the principal clause is in the first or the third person; by either *shall* or *will* for the third person when the principal clause is in the third person, but *will* when the principal clause is in the first or the third person. If the auxiliaries are changed the tense will express a promise; hence a distinction has been drawn between a predictive future and a promissive future.

Should and *would*, when used as the past tenses of *shall* and *will*, follow the same laws; but *should* is used also with all persons to express obligation; as—He feels he *should* do so.

A form *nill* (*ne* not, *will*), is used in the expression *willy nilly*, = will-I, nill-I, and sometimes also will-he, nill-he[1].

5, 6. **May** and **can** are auxiliaries of mood, and are both defective, no parts of the verb infinite being in use.

May once signified *power* or *might*, but now properly expresses right, permission, probability, or possibility, while *can*, which once signified *to know, to ken*, now expresses power. The older uses may be seen in the examples—

> For many a man so hard is of his herte
> He *may* not wepe though him sore smerte.
>
> I've seen myself, and served against the French,
> And they *can* well on horseback.

The use of *can* as an independent and transitive verb is obsolete. The past tense *could* was spelt *couthe, couth, coud*, but has been assimilated by false analogy to the spelling of *should* and *would*.

7. **Must** is the past tense of an obsolete present *mote*, he is able; it is now a present tense, and expresses necessity.

8. **Do** is conjugated in all its parts as a transitive verb, but is not auxiliary in the parts of the verb infinite. Tense-forms compounded with *do* as an auxiliary are sometimes called emphatic forms, but they were commonly used to express repeated or continued action; as—

> John *did* baptize in the wilderness.

The most ordinary use of this auxiliary is in interrogative and negative sentences; as—

> *Do* all men kill the things they *do* not love?
> *Do* not give it to him.

9. **Ought** is the past tense of the verb *owe* (*ágan*), which is conjugated as a transitive verb in all its parts, and has a more regular form *owed* of the past tense with a transitive force. *Ought* is employed with the force of a present tense as well as of a past tense. No other tense-form is used as an auxiliary.

10. **Let** is not really an auxiliary, but is a tense of a transitive verb commonly used to supply the place of tense-forms for the first and third persons of the imperative mood; as—

> *Let* him go.   *Let* us go.

One, two, or three auxiliaries may be used to make a tense-form; as—

I *am* loving.   I *have been* loving.   I *might have been* loving.

---

[1] Compare *will he, nill he*, Hamlet v. i; *will you, nill you*, Taming of the Shrew, ii. i. 'They, *will they, nill they*, shall fulfil the good pleasure of God.' (Cromwell's Letters and Speeches, Letter lxvii.—Carlyle.)

Table of Auxiliary Verbs.

Be.

Indicative.		Subjunctive.		Imperative.	Infinitive.
Present.	*Past.*	*Present.*	*Past.*		[to] be
SINGULAR.		SINGULAR.			
I am	I was	I be	I were		Participles.
Thou art	Thou wast (wert)	Thou be	Thou were (wert)	be	*Present.*
He is	He was	He be	He were		being
PLURAL.		PLURAL.			*Past.*
We are	We were	We be	We were		been
Ye are	Ye were	Ye be	Ye were	be	
They are	They were	They be	They were		

Old Form.

Indicative.

Present.

SINGULAR.

I am, be
Thou art, beest
He is, beeth, be,

PLURAL.

We are, beth, ben, be
Ye are, beth, ben, be
They are, beth, ben, be

Past.

SINGULAR.

I was
Thou were
He was

PLURAL.

We were
Ye were
They were

Have.

Indicative.		Imperative.	Infinitive.
Present.			[to] have
SINGULAR.	PLURAL.		Participles.
I have	We have		*Present.*
Thou hast	Ye have	have	having
He hath, has	They have		*Past.*
Past.			had
I had	We had		
Thou hadst	Ye had		
He had	They had		

VERBS.

SHALL.

Indicative.

Present.		Past.	
SING.	PLUR.	SING.	PLUR.
I shall	We shall	I should	We should
Thou shalt	Ye shall	Thou should(e)st	Ye should
He shall	They shall	He should	They should

WILL.

I will	We will	I would	We would
Thou wilt	Ye will	Thou would(e)st	Ye would
He will	They will	He would	They would

MAY.

I may	We may	I might	We might
Thou mayest	Ye may	Thou might(e)st	Ye might
He may	They may	He might	They might

CAN.

I can	We can	I could	We could
Thou canst	Ye can	Thou could(e)st	Ye could
He can	They can	He could	They could

MUST has no inflexions.

DO.

I do	We do	I did	We did
Thou doest, dost	Ye do	Thou diddest, didst	Ye did
He doeth, doth, does	They do	He did	They did

OUGHT.

		I ought	We ought
		Thou oughtest	Ye ought
		He ought	They ought

The phrase *going to* may be considered an auxiliary of the future tense. 'I am *going to* do it,' is equivalent to 'I *shall* do it,' or 'I *will* do it.'

§ 50. SCHEME OF A VERB (WEAK CONJUGATION) WITH ALL TENSE-FORMS, BY INFLEXION AND AUXILIARIES; according to Tense-Scheme, § 44.

Indicative Mood.

Present Tense-Forms.

	PRESENT-PERFECT.	PRESENT-IMPERFECT.	PRESENT-AORIST.
Sing.	I have waited	I am waiting	I wait
	Thou hast waited	Thou art waiting	Thou waitest
	He has waited	He is waiting	He waiteth, waits
Plur.	We have waited	We are waiting	We wait
	Ye have waited	Ye are waiting	Ye wait
	They have waited	They are waiting	They wait

Past Tense-Forms.

	PAST-PERFECT.	PAST-IMPERFECT.	PAST-AORIST.
Sing.	I had waited	I was waiting	I waited
	Thou hadst waited	Thou wast waiting	Thou waitedst
	He had waited	He was waiting	He waited
Plur.	We had waited	We were waiting	We waited
	Ye had waited	Ye were waiting	Ye waited
	They had waited	They were waiting	They waited

Future Tense-Forms.

	FUTURE-PERFECT.	FUTURE-IMPERFECT.	FUTURE-AORIST.
Sing.			
	I shall, will, have waited	I shall, will, be waiting	I shall, will, wait
	Thou shalt, wilt, have waited	Thou {shalt, wilt,} be waiting	Thou {shalt, wilt,} wait
	He shall, will, have waited	He shall, will, be waiting	He shall, will, wait
Plur.			
	We shall, will, have waited	We shall, will, be waiting	We shall, will, wait
	Ye shall, will, have waited	Ye shall, will, be waiting	Ye shall, will, wait
	They shall, will, have waited	They {shall, will,} be waiting	They {shall, will,} wait

VERBS.

[handwritten: Ext. 10 e / Place in Prize.]

...HEME OF. A VERB (WEAK CONJUGATION) WITH ALL TENSE-FORMS BY INFLEXION AND AUXILIARIES; according to Tense-Scheme, § 44.

Subjunctive Mood.

Present Tense-Forms.

PRESENT-PERFECT.	PRESENT-IMPERFECT.	PRESENT-AORIST.
I have waited	I be waiting	I wait
Thou have waited	Thou be waiting	Thou wait
He have waited	He be waiting	He wait
We have waited	We be waiting	We wait
Ye have waited	Ye be waiting	Ye wait
They have waited	They be waiting	They wait

Past Tense-Forms.

PAST-PERFECT.	PAST-IMPERFECT.	PAST-AORIST.
I had waited	I were waiting	I waited
Thou had waited	Thou wert waiting	Thou waited
He had waited	He were waiting	He waited
We had waited	We were waiting	We waited
Ye had waited	Ye were waiting	Ye waited
They had waited	They were waiting	They waited

Future Tense-Forms.

FUTURE-PERFECT.	FUTURE-IMPERFECT.	FUTURE-AORIST.

Sing.

shall, will, have waited | I shall, will, be waiting | I shall, will, wait
Thou shall, will, have waited | Thou shall, will, be waiting | Thou shall, will, wait
He shall, will, have waited | He shall, will, be waiting | He shall, will, wait

Plur.

We shall, will, have waited | We shall, will, be waiting | We shall, will, wait
Ye shall, will, have waited | Ye shall, will, be waiting | Ye shall, will, wait
They shall, will, have waited | They shall, will, be waiting | They shall, will, wait

§ 51. i. **Frequentative Verbs**, or verbs expressing repeated action, are formed from other verbs, usually by modifying the stem-vowel and adding—

(1) The termination -**er**, as—

beat,	batter.
climb,	clamber.
fret,	fritter.
gleam,	glimmer.
spit,	sputter.
wind, wend,	wander.

(2) The termination -**el** or -**le**, often with a modification of the final consonant of the stem; as—

drip,	dribble.
game,	gamble.
grab,	grapple.
nip,	nibble.
scrape,	scrabble.

ii. **Causative Verbs**, or verbs expressing that a thing is caused to have the quality implied by the root of the word, are formed from adjectives by adding the termination -**en**; as—

black,	blacken.
flat,	flatten.
long,	lengthen.
sweet,	sweeten.
white,	whiten.

Verbs in English have no distinctive final letter or syllable marking them off from other parts of speech, and so almost any word may be used as a verb; as—

To *foot* it.
To *tide* it over.
They *furthered* my plans.
The letter was *forwarded*.
To *weather* a storm.
The weather will *fair*.
Bosom up my counsel.
Weapons more violent, when next we meet
May serve to *better* us, and *worse* our foes
Or *equal* what between us made the odds.

PARTICLES.

§ 52. **Particles** are divided into four classes, **Adverbs, Prepositions, Conjunctions, Interjections**[1], because of differences in the ways of using them, and not because of differences in their nature. For it may be said that 'the preposition is an adverb of place, the conjunction is an adverb of manner, the interjection is an exclamatory adverb.' Or a preposition is sometimes called 'a transitive adverb, and a conjunction a relative adverb.' Thus we find that the same word may be an adverb and a preposition, as *after*—

> He came a long time *after*.
> He came *after* a long time.

Or an adverb and a conjunction, as *while*—

> And *while* the people clamoured for a king,
> Had Arthur crowned.

> Going to France ... all is prosperous to me; *while*, in returning to England, heavy misfortunes and adverse winds happen to me.

Or a conjunction and a preposition, as *for*—

> He will do this *for* he promised.
> He will do this *for* his promise' sake.

Or an adverb, and a preposition, and a conjunction, as *since*—

> That was done long *since*.
> That was done *since* yesterday.
> He will come, *since* he always keeps his promises.

---

[1] Compare Farrar, Greek Syntax, p. 32; Donaldson, Greek Grammar, p. 148.

Adverbs.

§ 53. **Adverbs** are so called because they usually qualify verbs; they may also qualify adjectives or adverbs, as—

He went *early*.

Ring out a *slowly* dying cause.

He is a *disgracefully* bad man.

He did that *very* badly.

Sometimes, but rarely, an adverb is used as an adjective qualifying a substantive, as—

Thine *often* infirmities.

Our *then* dictator,
Whom with all praise I point at, saw him fight.

Adverbs may be divided into five classes:—

i. **Adverbs of Place.**

Here, there, where, hence, hither, forth, above, off, backwards, away, asunder.

ii. **Adverbs of Time.**

Then, now, soon, often, seldom, while, whilom, anew, anon, betimes, formerly, still, ago.

Some, like *hence*, are adverbs of time as well as of place.

iii. **Adverbs of Number.**

Once, twice, thrice.

Many of these adverbs are old case-forms of pronouns or nouns, thus, *hence* (*hennes*), *thence* (*thennes*), *once* (*ones*), *needs*, are genitive cases, and to this adverbial form in *-es* some other words, *besides* (*biside* for *bisidan*), *amidst* (*amiddes* for *onmiddan*) have been assimilated; *here, there,* are datives singular; *seldom, whilom,* are datives plural.

iv. **Adverbs of Description**, expressing **quantity, quality, manner.**

Much, enough, almost, thus, so, quite, well, ill, badly, wisely, foolishly.

Adverbs of manner are usually formed by adding the syllable -ly to adjectives.

v. **Adverbs of Affirmation and Negation.**
Ay, yea, yes, nay, no, not.

PREPOSITIONS.

§ 54. **Prepositions** express originally relations of place and time, and are then used in wider senses to express various figurative relations arising out of these. The real prepositions are simple or compound forms from a few original roots; as—

About, above, after, against, among, at, but, by, before, behind, below, beneath, between, beyond, down, for, from, in, into, of, off, on, to, towards, unto, till, until, over, since, through, under, up, upon, with, within, without.

Ward or *wards* is used in composition only; as, to*wards*; or as a suffix to a substantive; as, to God-*ward*; they looked heaven-*wards*.

Many other words are used as prepositions, especially the participial form in **-ing**; as—

During the inquiry.

Prepositions are used with the objective case only, that is, the objective case alone admits a preposition to define its meaning more accurately in relation to other words in a sentence. The name itself, meaning 'a placing before,' expresses what is merely an accident in the use of the words, for prepositions may be placed after the nouns, although they usually come before; as—

He was there *before me*.
And *them* long time *before*, great Nimrod was.
I spoke *of him*.
He is the man *whom* I spoke *of*.

Several prepositions may define one noun; as—

He went forth *from out of* the city.

Pronouns are often compounded with prepositions following, and may then be classed as adverbs; as—

Wherein = in what.   *Thereupon* = upon that.

Conjunctions.

§ 55. **Conjunctions** join words, clauses, and sentences. Unlike adverbs, they must always stand at the beginning of the clauses or sentences which they introduce. They are—

i. **Coordinative,** or those which join words, or clauses and sentences which are independent one of another.

(1) Conjunctive, *and, also.*

(2) Disjunctive, *but, either, or, neither, nor.*

ii. **Subordinative,** or those which join clauses and sentences of which one is in a relation of dependence upon the other; as—

Although, because, if, since, that, unless.

Interjections.

§ 56. **Interjections** are words or cries expressing feelings of the mind; as—

Alas! Oh! Hurrah! Woe! Capital!

COMPOSITION AND DERIVATION.

§ 57. **Compound words** are formed in two ways—

i. **By joining words, both, or all, of which are also used as distinct and separate words;** as *mealtub*, of which the parts *meal* and *tub* are separate words, each having a distinct meaning, and when joined make a new word expressing a new idea: so *milkmaid, newspaper, railroad, quarterdeck, overlook, governor-general.*

ii. **By adding to a word an inseparable affix,** that is, one or more letters which cannot now be used as a distinct word; as, *be*stir, *un*tidy, bak*er*, king*dom*, man*hood*. This process may be distinguished from the former by the name 'Derivation.'

§ 58. Compound words of the first class are in reality phrases passing into words. The most important pass into substantives, adjectives, verbs.

Compound substantives are formed from—

(1) Substantives qualified or limited by preceding attributes, that is, adjectives, or substantives standing for adjectives, or particles standing for adjectives; as *grandfather, freeman, mankind, tarbarrel, wheelbarrow, bystander, forethought, aftergrowth, overthrow*. A few substantives are qualified by an adjective following; as *handful, pailful*.

(2) Substantives depending, as objects, on preceding verbs or prepositions; as *cutthroat, makeshift, marplot, pickpocket, scarecrow, spendthrift, afternoon, aftertime, outlaw*.

Compound adjectives are formed from—

(1) Adjectives, or participles, qualified by preceding attributes, that is, adjectives, or substantives standing as adjectives, or particles standing as adjectives; as *barebacked, cream-faced, meek-eyed, sad-coloured, best-nosed* and *loudest-toned, red-hot, sky-blue, snow-white, eagle-eyed, far-seeing, inborn, over-righteous*.

(2) Adjectives, or participles, qualified by preceding substantives in the objective case, either as direct objects, or as indirect objects or cases of extension; as *tale-bearing, time-serving, God-fearing, match-making, childlike, footsore, heartbroken, heartsick, sea-borne, weatherwise*.

Compound verbs are formed from—

(1) Verbs qualified by preceding particles; as *outrun, overset, undersell, upturn*.

(2) Verbs, qualified by preceding substantives, as direct or indirect objects, or cases of extension; as *backbite, browbeat, hamstring, shipwreck, waylay*.

Of compound words the latter word is generally principal, and the former is limiting or explanatory, making its meaning more distinct and precise.

§ 59. **Compound words of the second class,** or derived words, are in reality phrases which have already passed into words. The **inseparable affixes,** or portions which cannot be used as distinct words, are either **prefixes,** that is, additions to the beginning of words; or **suffixes,** that is, additions to the end of words.

i. **Prefixes** are usually particles, adverbs or prepositions, which have to some slight extent changed their old form or meaning; hence words formed by the aid of inseparable prefixes differ very little from the words already mentioned as compounded of verbs qualified by separable particles.

The most important prefixes are of English origin:—

A, a corruption of the prepositions *on, in*; as, *a*-bed, *on* bed, *a*-shore, *a*-board : *at*; as, *a*do, *a*-fore (aetforan) : *of*; as, *a*-down, *of* or *off* the dune, the hill. In some words it represents a syllable *and-*; as *a*long, *and*-lang; in others *er-* as *a*rise; or *ge-*; as, *a*-ware, *i*war.[1]

Be, a preposition meaning *about*, and *from about*; as, *be*-girt, girt *about*; *be*-reave, to strip *from about*; *be*-tray.

For (*fore*), meaning *forth, away, utterly*; as, *for*-give, to give *forth*; *for*-bid, to bid away, or prohibit; *for*-lorn, utterly lorn, or, lost; *for*-done, utterly wearied; *for*-go; *fore*-fend.

Fore, meaning *before*; as, *fore*-see, to see before, *fore*-tell; *fore*-stall, *fore*-mast.

Gain, meaning *against* (on-*gean*), *contrary to*; as, *gain*-say, to say *against*, oppose; *gain*-stand.

Mis, meaning *amiss, wrongly*; as, *mis*-deed, a wrong deed; *mis*-hap, an ill chance; *mis*-govern, to govern badly.

To, a preposition meaning *to* or *at*; as *to*-day, *to*-morrow, *to*-gether.

Un (answering to the Latin *in*), meaning *not*, having the effect of negativing the force of the word to which it is joined, and used mostly with substantives and adjectives; as, *un*-tired, not tired; *un*-able, not able; *un*-blushing, not blushing; and *un-* (answering to the German *ent-*) having the effect of reversing an action, used with verbs only, as *un*-bar, to free from bars; *un*-tie, to loosen.

With, meaning *against*; as, to *with*-stand, to stand *against*; *with*-hold, to hold against, and so to keep from a person.

---

[1] See Morris and Skeat, Specimens of Early English, Part II. p. xxxv.

COMPOSITION AND DERIVATION. 87

Some prefixes common in older English have now dropped out of use: as *ge-*, meaning together, as *ge*-fera, a companion: or giving verbs a transitive sense, as *ge*-thencan, to think of (this prefix has in many words been turned into *be-*, as *ge*leafe, *be*lief); *to-*, meaning in twain, apart, as *to*-torne, torn in pieces, ragged, *to*-brake, broken to pieces; *to-*, the preposition, used with verbs, as *to-nehen*, to draw nigh; *ymb-* or *umb-* or *um-*, meaning around, as *ymb-utan*, round about; *umb-iwette*, watered all round; *um*-lap, to surround, *um*-set, beset; *wan-*, meaning lack, want, as *wan*-hope, despair, *wan*-ton, lacking education, unrestrained.

Besides these English prefixes, since so many French, Latin, and Greek words have been introduced into English, a very large number of French, Latin, and Greek prefixes are in use with words of their own languages. A few have become naturalised, and are used in composition with words of English origin also.

Dis, meaning *apart, away*, having also a negative sense; as, *dis*arm, to take away arms: with English words, *dis*trust, want of trust; *dis*ease, want of ease, uneasiness, illness; *dis*believe, not to believe.

Em, en (the French form of the Latin preposition *in*), meaning *in*; as, *em*brace, to take in the arms; *en*sue, to follow: with English words, *em*bolden, *em*body, *en*dear, *dis*embodied.

Re, meaning *back again*; as, *re*cover, to take back; *re*creant, one who retracts his belief: with English words, *re*call, to call back; *re*build, to build again.

ii. The most important **suffixes** in like manner are those of English origin; and besides these several from French and Latin and Greek have been adopted, of which some have become naturalised, and are used in composition with words of English origin. The suffixes are used to form substantives, or adjectives, or verbs.

Substantive suffixes.

(1) **Personal**—

Eng.[1]	*-ar, -er, -yer,*	li*ar*, build*er*, murder*er*, bow*yer*.
	-ster,	spin*ster*, game*ster*, young*ster*.
Fr.	*-eer, -ier, -or (-eur),*	pion*eer*, bombard*ier*, tail*or*.
	-ee,	legat*ee*, feoff*ee*.
Fr.	*-ess,*	empr*ess*, murder*ess*.

(2) **Instrumental**—

Eng.	*-el, -le,*	shov*el*.

---

[1] Eng. = English; Fr. = French; Ital. = Italian; Lat. = Latin.

(3) Diminutive—

Eng.	-el, -le,	satch*el*, cocker*el*, padd*le*.
	-en,	maid*en*, kitt*en*.
	-ing, -ling,	farth*ing*, dar*ling*, gos*ling*.
	-kin,	lamb*kin*, pip*kin*.
	-ock, -ow,	hill*ock*, bull*ock*, shad*ow*, pill*ow*.
Fr.	-let, -et,	brace*let*, king*let*, flower*et*, latch*et*.
Lat. Fr.	-icle, -el, -le,	part*icle*, dams*el*, cast*le*, fem*ale*.

(4) Augmentative—

Eng.	-ard, -art,	drunk*ard*, bragg*art*.
Ital.	-oon, -on,	bass*oon*, ball*oon*, milli*on*.

(5) Expressive of an abstract idea of **condition, state, being**, &c.—

Eng.	-had, -head, -hood,	God*head*, man*hood*, priest*hood*.
	-dom,	king*dom*, free*dom*, martyr*dom*.
	-lock, -ledge,	wed*lock*, know*ledge*.
	-ness,	kind*ness*, white*ness*, rounded*ness*.
	-red,	kind*red*, hat*red*.
	-ship, -scape,	wor*ship*, king*ship*, land*scape*.
	-ter,	laugh*ter*, slaugh*ter*.
	-th,	streng*th*, bread*th*, weal*th*.
Fr. (Lat.)	-age,	marri*age*, steer*age*.
	-ance, -ence, -ency,	endur*ance*, persist*ence*, clem*ency*, dalli*ance*, ridd*ance*, hindr*ance*.
Fr.	-ment,	improve*ment*, nourish*ment*, defile*ment*.
Fr. (Lat.)	-ion, -ation,	act*ion*, starv*ation*.

(6) Collective—

Fr.	-ry, -ery (-erie),	jewel*ry*, poet*ry*, fai*ry*, rook*ery*.

Adjective suffixes.

(1) Expressive of **quality, material, nature**, &c.—

Eng.	-ish,	Engl*ish*, brown*ish*, fair*ish*.
	-ly,	man*ly*, god*ly*, earth*ly*.
	-y (-ig),	drear*y*, dream*y*.
Eng.	-en, -ern,	wood*en*, gold*en*, east*ern*.
Lat.	-ive, -tive,	sport*ive*, talk*ative*.
	-ian,	Grec*ian*, Austral*ian*, Shakespear*ian*.

COMPOSITION AND DERIVATION.

(2) Expressive of **fullness**—

Eng. *-ful,*   health*ful*, care*ful*, cheer*ful*, doubt*ful*.
      -some,   win*some*, glad*some*, whole*some*.
Fr.
(Lat.) } *-ous, -ose,*   glori*ous*, verb*ose*, oti*ose*.

(3) Expressive of **want**—

Eng. *-less,*   care*less*, fear*less*, fruit*less*.

(4) Expressive of **fitness**—

Lat. *-able, -ible, -ble, -ile,*   habit*able*, eat*able*, ed*ible*, frag*ile*.

(5) Expressive of **number**—

Eng. *-fold,*   mani*fold*, hundred*fold*.

Verb suffixes.

(1) **Frequentative**—

Eng. *-er,*   batt*er*, patt*er*, glimm*er*.
      -el, -le,   grov*el*, draw*l*, crack*le*.

(2) **Causative**—

Eng. *-en,*   length*en*, whit*en*, wid*en*.
Fr. *-fy,*   lique*fy*, grati*fy*, simpli*fy*.
Fr. *-ise,* }
Gr. *-ize,* }   equal*ise*, natural*ise*, mesmer*ise*.
      anathemat*ize*.

Besides these there are certain **Adverb suffixes**: as, *-ther*, expressing **movement towards**, as hi*ther*; *-ce* (*es*) expressing **movement from**, as hen*ce*; *-ward, -wards,* expressing **direction**, as home*ward*, heaven*wards*; *-wise·* and *-ly* (lic, like), expressing **manner**, as like*wise*, other*wise*, faithful*ly*, even*ly*.

The power of deriving new words by means of suffixes varies in the different stages of a language; one becomes very common, while another passes out of use. When a suffix is little used to form new words its force is gradually forgotten, and words compounded of it often lose their proper shape, or even become so changed as to seem compounds of some other more usual ending. Thus the suffix *-lock*, having become strange, has been changed, as in the form 'out of know*lych* of here syght,' till it is now scarcely to be recognised in know*ledge*. So too neighbour-*red* has been altered into the more common form neighbour*hood*; lif*lode* (life-leading), through lif*hood*, into liveli*hood*; right*wise* into right*eous*; fem*el* (femelle) into fe*male*, so as to appear the correlative of *male*.

SYNTAX.

§ 60. Syntax teaches the relations and right use of the different parts of speech and of their inflexions; or, in other words, teaches the laws of the arrangement and connection of words in a sentence.

§ 61. A sentence is a word, or a combination of words, expressing a thought or judgment.

A simple sentence is—

(1) A statement or assertion—
   Fire burns.

(2) A question—
   Dare he?
   Does fire burn?

(3) A command or wish—
   Fire, burn; and cauldron, bubble.

Every sentence contains two **members** or **parts**—

i. The person, or thing, about which something is said—**Subject**.

ii. What is said about that person, or thing—**Predicate**.

The Subject is, strictly speaking, a substantive in the nominative case.

The Predicate is, strictly speaking, a finite verb.

SUBJECT.	PREDICATE.
Fire	burns.
Men	die.
I	walk.

1. The subject and the predicate together can be expressed by one word—a finite verb, which, by its termination or by the manner of its use, implies the subject—
   Hearest?   Go.   Remember.

2. Any word, or combination of words (a phrase), which can express the force and sense of a substantive, may stand as the subject of a sentence—

 Pronoun, *He* fights.
 Adjective, *The just* shall live.
 Participle, *The beaten* run.
 Verb infinitive, *To lie* is disgraceful.
 Phrase, *England expects every man to do his duty*, was Nelson's signal.

3. The predicate may consist of a tense-form of an auxiliary verb (be, shall, &c.) called the copula or link, and a word completing the sentence, called the complement, or predicative-complement—

  Snow *is* *falling*.
  Men *are* *mortal*.

Some other verbs cannot express predication completely, and require a complement; as—

  He *became Cæsar*.

§ 62. Sentences thus consisting of subject and predicate only would express thoughts so vaguely and inaccurately as to be almost useless; therefore both **the subject and the predicate are often expanded** by the addition of words and phrases, which define and render more precise the sense in which they are used.

i. **The subject is expanded by the addition of attributes,** that is, of words assigning quality, and thus limiting or qualifying the subject and making its meaning more clear. These are **adjectives, or substantives, or phrases** which may stand in a sentence for them.

Thus the sentence 'Commander ruled' conveys very little information, but may be qualified and expanded—

(1) By an **adjective** (or pronoun or participle)—

  The commander ruled.
  The famous commander ruled.
  The conquering commander ruled.

(2) By a **substantive**, in agreement or apposition—

    The famous commander, *Cromwell*, ruled.

(3) By a **possessive case** of a substantive—

    England's famous commander ruled.

(4) By a **prepositional phrase**—

    The famous commander *of the Parliamentarians* ruled.

(5) By a **sentence**—

    The commander, *who gained the battle of Naseby*, ruled.

Many or all of the expansions may be used in the same sentence; as—

    England's famous conquering commander of the Parliamentarians, who gained the battle of Naseby, ruled.

ii. **The predicate is expanded by the addition of words (or clauses) to complete, or to define, the meaning of the verb**—

(1) By a **direct** (or nearer, or immediate) **object**, that is, a substantive in the objective case, or phrase, completing the meaning of a transitive verb; as—

    He gave *a book*.
    He loved *to hear the tale*.

(2) By an **indirect** (or remoter) **object**, that is, a substantive also in the objective case, or a preposition and substantive, to define more accurately the meaning of a verb transitive which already has a direct object, or of a verb intransitive without a direct object; as—

    He gave *me* a book.
    He gave a book *to me*.
    They spoke *to him*.

(3) **By objective cases of substantives, or absolute participial phrases, or adverbs, or adverbial phrases, or prepositional phrases,** expressing any circumstances limiting or qualifying an action or state, as place, time, cause, manner, measure, extent, &c.; as—

>He gave me a book *last week*.
>*They being present* he gave me a book.
>He *kindly* gave me a book.
>He behaved *more foolishly than before*.
>*In the kindest manner* he gave me a book.

(4) **A noun or verb infinite or phrase, is added to an expansion of the predicate,** especially to the direct object, asserting or predicating something additional concerning it; and this is called **the oblique predicate**; as—

>The king nominated him *general*.
>We have you *alone*.
>They declared him *to be an impostor*.

(5) The predicate, like the subject, may be expanded by a sentence—

>He gave me a book, *that I might keep it in remembrance of him*.

All words or phrases expanding either the subject or predicate of a sentence may themselves be expanded by qualifying words or phrases: thus, in the following examples, *flashing*, an expansion of the subject *she*, is itself expanded by an adverb and a direct object; *stiller*, an expansion of the object *lady*, is itself expanded by a phrase:—

>She *flashing* forth a haughty smile, began.
>At length I saw a lady within call
>*Stiller* than chiselled marble, standing there.

§ 63. **A Compound Sentence,** that is, a sentence that contains more than one finite verb, consists of two or more simple sentences, which are then termed its clauses.

These clauses are—

i. **Coordinate,** that is, clauses whose construction is independent of each other, and which are connected by coordinative conjunctions; as—

> They abandoned their native speech, and adopted the French tongue.
>
> She was subjugated by the Roman arms; but she received only a faint tincture of Roman arts and letters.

ii. **Subordinate,** that is, clauses whose construction is dependent on that of the main sentence, being connected with it by subordinative conjunctions, or relative or interrogative pronouns, or adverbs; as—

> He will come *if he be able.*
>
> He spoke loudly *that he might be heard.*
>
> I find not yet one lonely thought,
> *That cries against my wish for thee.*

Such subordinate clauses are usually expansions of the subject, or predicate, or object of the main sentence, and are equivalent to a substantive, or an adjective, or an adverb. They are therefore divided into—

> (1) **Substantival clauses,** standing in place of a substantive as subject or object, or in apposition to subject or object; usually introduced by 'that,' or an interrogative or relative word; as—
>
>> *That he could do no more* is clear.
>>
>> He said *that he could do no more.*
>>
>> *What was the matter* could not be found out.
>>
>> She knows not *what his greatness is.*
>
> (2) **Adjectival clauses,** standing in place of an attribute qualifying subject or object; usually introduced by some form of the relative pronoun or relative adverb; as—
>
>> There that man, *who fought so bravely,* was slain.
>>
>> I read of that glad year *which once had been.*
>>
>> This is the day *when he must die.*

(3) **Adverbial clauses,** standing in place of adverbs, qualifying and defining subject or predicate. These are usually introduced by an adverb or conjunction, and are equivalent to adverbs expressing place, time, cause, manner, condition, consequence, &c.; as—

>He lives *wherever he can find a resting-place.*
>The pagan English ate horses *until they exchanged their religion for Christianity.*
>They sat all night and day,
>*For every hour some horseman came
>With tidings of dismay.*
>He behaved *as an honourable man should.*
>I could not have done it *unless you had helped.*
>He smote him *that he died.*

Whatever the length of a compound sentence, it can always be reduced to its separate simple clauses, and the links which unite them one to another[1]; and whatever the length of a simple sentence or a simple clause, it can always be reduced to these two parts, subject and predicate, all other words being expansions either of the subject or of the predicate.

RULES OF SYNTAX.

RULES OF AGREEMENT. CONCORDS.

§ 64. **A verb finite in a sentence is in the same number and person as its subject;** as—

>*I wait,*
>*He waits,*
>*They wait.*

A collective noun as a subject, or two or more singular nouns forming a composite subject, will require the verb to be singular

---

[1] Compare Farrar, Greek Syntax, p. 51, iii, iv.

or plural according to the sense in which the subject is used; as—

> The multitude *was* divided.
> The multitude *pursue* pleasure.

In the former the idea of unity is predominant, and we think of the multitude as one body; while in the latter the idea of plurality is predominant, and we think of the many persons who compose the multitude. So—

> King and queen *were* there.
> Flesh and blood *hath* not revealed it unto thee.

The two constructions are sometimes combined; as—

> *This people*, who *knoweth* not the law, *are* cursed.
>
> Nodding *their* heads before her *goes*
> The merry *minstrelsy*.

This and many seeming irregularities may be explained by the law that 'the sense often overrides the grammar,' so that the predicate agrees with the meaning rather than the form of the subject; as—

> *A great company* of the priests *were* obedient to the faith.
> *The mayor* now, *with the city*, *are* to be flattered, not threatened.
> And *every mountain and island were* moved out of their places.
> As *every alien pen hath* got my use.
> And under thee their poesy *disperse*.

Sometimes the copula may agree with the complement instead of with the subject; as—

> The wages of sin *is death*.
> An high look, and a proud heart, and the plowing of the wicked *is sin*.

In Shakespeare and other writers of his time, and in some later authors, there are to be found frequent instances of a further irregularity or loose construction; a plural subject used with a singular predicate, or a singular subject with a plural predicate, where no 'agreement of sense' accounts for the want of 'agreement of form.' Such instances may be explained by a law that 'the

CASES OF SUBSTANTIVES.

ear often overrides the sense,' so as to make the predicate agree in form with the noun next preceding it, although such a construction may be quite ungrammatical[1]; as, in Shakespeare,

> *What cares* these roarers?
>
> The venom clamours of a jealous *woman*
> *Poisons* more deadly than a mad dog's tooth.
>
> Where lo! two lamps burnt out in *darkness lies*.

And in Chatterton,

> The wrinkled grass its silver *joys unfold*.
>
> The greatest of Creation's *blessings cloy*.

If, of two or more subjects of one predicate, one is of the first person, the predicate will be in the first person plural; and if one of the subjects is of the second person, and none of the first, the predicate will be in the second person plural.

§ 65. **A substantive qualifying a substantive, or noun-term, is in the same case**; as—

> *The river Thames* flows through London.
>
> *This* is *the river Thames*.

§ 66. **A relative agrees with its antecedent in gender, number, and person; but in case follows the rules of its own clause**; as—

> *Thou who* revellest now in triumph.
>
> *This* is *what* he did.
>
> There is *a reaper whose* name is Death.
>
> *He who* created us, *whose* we are, to *whom* all things are obedient, *whom* we see not with our eyes, upon *whom* we depend, is the eternal God.

The relative is sometimes made to agree with the sense rather than the form of the antecedent; as—

> The *multitude who* had come together.
>
> Each *legion*, to *whom* it was allotted.

---

[1] See Bacon's Advancement of Learning, ed. W. A. Wright, p. 293, Chatterton's works, ed. Skeat, i. 367.

Either relative or antecedent is commonly omitted; as—
How shall I curse whom God hath not cursed?
The petty cobwebs we have spun.
The man I trusted has deceived me.

Demonstrative pronouns agree in number with the noun to which they are attached.

CASES OF SUBSTANTIVES.

The Nominative Case.

§ 67. **The Nominative is the case of the subject—**

He waits.

They became kings.

It is I.

The Objective, or Accusative, Case.

§ 68. **The Objective expresses primarily the space over which motion is made, and the end or object towards which motion is directed.**

Hence it has two divisions—

i. **The case of extension;** expressing (1) the space over which, (2) the time during which, (3) the measure or amount to which, the action or state extends.

(1) The space over which; as—

He rode *twenty miles*.

The town is *fifty miles* away.

(2) The time during which; as—

She slept *nine hours*.

He is *eight years* old.

(3) The measure or amount to which; as—
> They were injured *a great deal.*
> They went *their way.*
> He ran *a race.*
> ... whatever creeps *the ground*,
> Insect or worm.

<small>Thus to this belong the cases called the cognate accusative, which expresses the same idea as the verb itself; and the accusative of limitation, which expresses a limited operation of the verb.</small>

ii. **The case of the end or object;** expressing (1) the place towards which motion is directed, (2) the object affected by the action of the subject.

(1) The place towards which; as—
> He is going *home.*
>
> Take some *home.*
>
> What time mine own might also flee,
> And ... arrive at last *the blessed goal.*

(2) The direct object, with a transitive verb; as—
> Why wilt thou kill *me*?
>
> Love *me*, love *my dog.*
>
> He longs *to die.*

(3) The indirect object, expressing that which is interested in an action or state, and completes the construction of many verbs transitive or intransitive; as—
> He gave *him* a book.
> Saddle *me* the ass.
> Give *sorrow* words.
> Oh! then return, the pledge redeem,
> Thou gav'st *the senate.*

The indirect object, in the early stages of the language, was expressed by the dative case, with or without a preposition: but as the dative case has become merged in the objective, the indirect object, when placed next after the verb, is expressed as the direct object; when placed in another position, by an objective case and preposition.

The relation of the indirect object, and all the other relations, which have been mentioned under the objective case, except the direct object of a transitive verb, may be expressed more precisely by the addition of a preposition, as—

    Saddle the ass *for me.*
    Whatever creeps *upon the ground.*
    He is going *towards home.*

The dative was the absolute case in early English: as the dative passed from use the objective was employed most commonly in an absolute clause; as—

    And, *them gathered together,* he said to them in parables.

But in English of the present day the nominative is mostly used; as—

    There on a day, *he sitting high in hall,*
    Before him came a forester of Dean.

The relation of the time at which an action takes place is also expressed now by the objective case; as—

    It was done *yesterday.*
    I will be with you *to-morrow.*

The Possessive, or Genitive, Case.

§ 69. The Possessive qualifies or defines a noun to which it is joined, and nearly resembles an adjective.

It usually expresses possession; as—

    Cæsar's gardens.
    I am sure to crush *somebody's* toes.

EXAMPLES OF ANALYSIS.

Sometimes the idea of possession is not very apparent, and the case may be called a genitive of relation; as—

> The *seven years'* war,
>
> The *king's* enemies,

in which last sentence the case is almost equivalent to a genitive expressing an object, 'those who oppose the king.'

When two or more nouns in the possessive case are in apposition, they are treated as a compound noun, the last only being inflected; as—

> The prophet *Merlin's* doom.
>
> Merlin, the *prophet's* doom.

This sentence in Early English would have been written, *Merlines* dom the prophet[1].

The possessive case always precedes the word which it qualifies, unless it stands as a complement; as—

> The earth is the *Lord's*.

The noun which the possessive case qualifies is sometimes omitted; as—

> The service was at *St. Paul's* [Cathedral].

The possessive relation may be expressed by the preposition *of* and an objective case; as—

> The gardens *of Cæsar*.
>
> The enemies *of the king*.

---

[1] See Piers Plowman (Clar. Press), ed. Skeat, p. xxi. note.

EXAMPLES OF ANALYSIS.

§ 70.   1. Nothing is new.

Subject   nothing
Predicate (copula and complement)   is new.

2. Thou knowest my ways.

Subject   thou
Predicate   knowest
  Expansion.
    Direct object.   my ways.

3. Still onward winds the dreary way.

Subject   way
  Expansions.
    Attributes   the, dreary
Predicate   winds
  Expansions.
    Adverbs of time and place   still, onward.

4. I vex my heart with fancies dim.

Subject   I
Predicate   vex
  Expansions.
    Direct object   my heart
    Prepositional-phrase of manner   with fancies dim.

5. I hear thee where the waters run.

Subject   I
Predicate   hear
  Expansions.
    Direct object   thee
    Subordinate adverbial clause of place   where the waters run.
      Subject   the waters
      Predicate   run.

6.   Unwillingly this rest
Their superstition yields me.

Subject	**superstition**
Expansion.	
Attribute	their
Predicate	**yields**
Expansions.	
Direct object	this rest
Indirect object	me
Adverb of manner	unwillingly.

7. She is, and is not; hence the pain to me.

Subject	**she**
Predicate, compound	**is,-and-is-not;**
Link, coupling clauses	hence
Subject	the pain
[*Predicate* understood]	[is]
Expansion.	
Indirect object	to me.

8. Thou layest down a law the rich would like.

Subject	**thou**
Predicate	**layest**
Expansions.	
Direct object	a law
Adverb of place	down
[*Link*, understood, coupling subordinate clause]	[that]
Subject	the rich
Predicate	would like.

9. This day a solemn feast the people hold
To Dagon their sea-idol, and forbid
Laborious works.

Subject	**people**
Expansion.	
Attribute	the

Predicate   hold
   Expansions.
      Direct object (with attributes)   a solemn feast
      Indirect object (with attributes) to Dagon, their sea-idol,
      Objective case of time   this day
Link, coupling coordinate clause   and
Predicate   forbid
   Expansion.
      Direct object (with attribute)   laborious works.

EXAMPLE OF A FORM OF PARSING.

§ 71.   O, there, perchance, when all our wars are done,
       The brand Excalibur will be cast away.

O	interjection.
there	adverb of place, qualifying *cast*.
perchance	adverb of manner.
when	adverb introducing a subordinate clause.
all	adjective, attribute of *wars*.
our	possessive pronoun, attribute of *wars*.
wars	substantive common, neuter gender, plural number. nominative case, subject of *are*. Sing. *war*.
are	auxiliary verb, from *be*; active voice, indicative mood, present tense, plural number, third person, agreeing with the subject *wars*. Parts—*am, was, being, been*; tense—*am, art, is, are, are, are*.
done	transitive verb, from *do*; passive voice, past participle; complement agreeing with *wars*. . Parts—*do, did, doing, done*.
the	definite article, attribute of *brand*.

brand	substantive common, neuter gender, singular number, nominative case, subject of *will*. Plur. *brands*.
Excalibur	substantive proper, neuter gender, singular number, nominative case, attribute of *brand*.
will	auxiliary verb, from *will*; active voice, indicative mood, present tense, singular number, third person, agreeing with the subject *brand*. Parts—*will, would*, —, —; tense—*will, wilt, will, will, will, will*: forming with *be* and *cast* a compound tense-form of the passive future-imperfect tense.
be	auxiliary verb from *be*; active voice, infinitive mood, present tense, depending on *will*. Parts—*am, was, being, been*; forming, with *will* and *cast*, a passive future-imperfect tense-form.
cast	transitive verb, from *cast*; weak conjugation, passive voice, past participle; complement agreeing with *brand*. Parts—*cast, cast, casting, cast*: forming, with (the auxiliaries of time and voice) *will* and *be*, a passive future-imperfect tense-form.
away	abverb of place, qualifying *cast*.

EXTRACTS.

1.

I walk.
Thou livest.
He is.
Water flows.
Light flashes.
He liveth.
Snow falls.
You slept.
We declare.
She cries.
She carried.
Birds sing.
Who comes?
Rememberest thou?
All laughed.
We fought.

He loved the commons.
The king asked counsel.
He vows revenge.
We repaired the boat.
The wolf left them.

They died.
He said.
Winds blew.
Kneel.
He hath.
The men ran.
A bird flew.
The bell rang.
It happened.
Remember.
The children swam.
An owl hooted.
Both escaped.
Which fell?
The boys played.
He spoke.

She saw the children.
Mars beheld the virgin.
He drank the wine.
They forgave us.
The winds prevented you.

They saved themselves.   You called me.
A man entered the house.   He bore the wrong.
The people seized him.   The boys failed.
All welcomed me.   He bought them.

2.

All good men praised him.

Duke William, the Norman, conquered England.

His personal strength was immense.

The story of these troubles is well known.

This Tarquinius was a great and mighty king.

What men are you?

Myself, well-mounted, hardly have escaped.

Here with Columbus were beings of a new world.

This monument is a colossal figure.

The characters of the two commanders were entirely dissimilar.

Sharp things were said.

He was weary of his crown.

He would return to his native country.

A single Englishwoman it was necessary to trust.

None of these things moved him.

One great error he committed.

The character of this man is a curious study.

His position was now most perilous.

And he drank of the cup and died.

This is William's story.

Many of these smaller enterprises were eminently unsuccessful.

In brief, acquit thee bravely.

Four hundred were already lost.

And King Offa reigned thirty-nine winters.

Good fortune come to thee.

They went and found the mariner to be right.

Here they endeavoured to make an entrance into the country.

We'll lay before this town our bones.

Of him we must now speak a little.

So weary bees in little cells repose.

The first of April died your noble mother.

Their fortunes grew old and feeble with themselves.

The House divided several times.

He himself put the crown on his head.

Ho! gunners, fire a loud salute; ho! gallants, draw your blades.

He hoped that the queen would be more successful.

If they do see thee they will murder thee.

Thou shalt not stir one foot to seek a foe.

If love be blind, love cannot hit the mark.

Thou shouldst have it, man, wert thou a born Turk.

He were no lion were not Romans hinds.

The swallow follows not summer more willingly than we your lordship.

Wherefore then didst not thou give mine enemy into mine hands when he was in thy power? Now art thou no true soldier, for that thou servest not thy lord the king faithfully.

If thou do ill, the joy fades, not the pains,
If well, the pain doth fade, the joy remains.

I'll catch it ere it come to ground.

And creep time ne'er so slow,
Yet it shall come for me to do thee good.

O, sir, when he shall hear of your approach,
If that young Arthur be not gone already,
Even at that news he dies.

What he hath won, that hath he fortified.

What shall he have that killed the deer?

The man that hath done this thing shall surely die.

Will ye not tremble at My presence, which have placed the sand for the bound of the sea by a perpetual decree that it cannot pass it?

I pray, can you read anything you see?

It was not he that achieved it; it was those that went before him, who had gradually got it.

Amber, science declares, is a kind of petrified resin, distilled by pines, that were dead before the days of Adam; which is now thrown up, in stormy weather, on that remote coast.

The love of variety or curiosity of seeing new things, which is the same, or at least a sister passion to it, seems woven into the frame of every son and daughter of Adam.

All animals that bite the grass or browse the shrub, whether wild or tame, wandered in this extensive circuit, secured from beasts of prey by the mountains which confined them.

> The adverse winds,
> Whose leisure I have stayed, have given him time
> To land his legions all as soon as I.

The notions of the earth, which were held at that period, were so wild, so vague, so tempting.

He was a courtly person, of good birth, a good speaker, a good musician.

He, as the richer personage, had the larger fleet and more men.

That he hoped for a reward was perfectly true.

Publius is a lover of the people, and seeks their good.

Flee, English! flee, English! dead is Edmund.

The end of government is the good of mankind.

Never did men more joyfully obey.

A tight house, warm apparel, and wholesome food, are sufficient motives to labour.

Having finished the fort, he commenced his attacks upon the Indians.

Home, sirrah, and take to some work.

Will you obey the heavenly voice, or will you not?

That he had resolved to take the command of his army in Ireland was soon rumoured all over London.

They refused Truth when she came; and now Truth knows nothing of them.

The houses, the furniture, the clothing of the rich, in a little time become useful to the inferior and middling ranks of people.

The two men shall give judgment on the shedder of blood.

If he shall appeal from their judgment, let the appeal be tried.

If their judgment be confirmed, cover his head.

Hang him with a halter on the accursed tree;

Scourge him either within the sacred limit of the city or without.

Hail, king! to-morrow thou shalt pass away.
Farewell! there is an isle of rest for thee.

Arise, go forth, and conquer as of old.

And whiter than the mist that all day long
Had held the field of battle was the king.

Then spake the king: My house hath been my doom.
But call not thou this traitor of my house,
Who hath but dwelt beneath one roof with me.
My house are rather they who sware my vows,
Yea, even while they brake them, own'd me king.

I heard the ripple washing in the reeds,
And the wild water lapping on the crag.

Doubt not, go forward; if thou doubt, the beasts
Will tear thee piecemeal.

A doubtful throne is ice on summer seas.

3.

And this our life, exempt from public haunt,
Finds tongues in trees, books in the running brooks,
Sermons in stones and good in everything.

And He that doth the ravens feed,
Yea, providently caters for the sparrow,
Be comfort to my age!

Blow, blow, thou winter wind,
Thou art not so unkind
   As man's ingratitude.

When shall we three meet again,
In thunder, lightning, or in rain?

What thou wouldst highly,
That wouldst thou holily; wouldst not play false,
And yet wouldst wrongly win.

Why, let the stricken deer go weep,
   The hart ungalled play;
For some must watch, while some must sleep:
   Thus runs the world away.

Who overcomes
By force, hath overcome but half his foe.

Was I deceived, or did a sable cloud
Turn forth her silver lining on the night?

They also serve who only stand and wait.

I am as free as nature first made man,
Ere the base laws of servitude began,
When wild in woods the noble savage ran.

Yon sun that sets upon the sea
    We follow in his flight;
Farewell awhile to him and thee,
    My native land, good night!

Britannia needs no bulwarks,
    No towers along the steep;
Her march is o'er the mountain-waves,
    Her home is on the deep.

She walks the waters like a thing of life,
And seems to dare the elements to strife.
Who would not brave the battle fire, the wreck,
To move the monarch of her peopled deck?

4. *Milton.*

Three poets, in three distant ages born,
Greece, Italy, and England did adorn.
The first in loftiness of thought surpassed,
The next in majesty, in both the last.
The force of nature could no farther go;
To make a third she joined the other two.

DRYDEN.

5. *The Destruction of Sennacherib.*

The Assyrian came down like the wolf on the fold,
And his cohorts were gleaming with purple and gold,
And the sheen of their spears was like stars on the sea,
When the blue wave rolls nightly on deep Galilee.

Like the leaves of the forest when summer is green,
That host with their banners at sunset were seen;
Like the leaves of the forest when autumn hath blown,
That host on the morrow lay withered and strown.

BYRON.

6. The Wolf and the Lion.

One day a wolf had taken a sheep from a fold, and was carrying it home to his own den, when he met a lion, who straightway laid hold of the sheep and bore it away. The wolf cried out that it was a great shame, and that the lion had robbed him. The lion laughed, and said, 'I suppose, then, that it was your good friend the shepherd who gave it to you.'

7. Sir John Moore.

Slowly and sadly we laid him down,
From the field of his fame fresh and gory;
We carved not a line, and we raised not a stone,
But we left him alone with his glory.

C. WOLFE.

8. The Snail.

To grass, or leaf, or fruit, or wall,
The snail sticks close, nor fears to fall,
As if he grew there house and all
                Together.

Within that house secure he hides,
When danger imminent betides
Of storm, or other harm besides
                Of weather.

V. BOURNE.

9.

When it was winter, and the snow lay all around, white and sparkling, a hare would often come jumping along and spring right over the little fir-tree. Oh! this made him so angry. But two winters went by, and when the third came the little tree had grown so tall that the hare was obliged to run round it.

10.

He went like one that hath been stunned,
    And is of sense forlorn;
A sadder and a wiser man
    He rose the morrow morn.

S. T. COLERIDGE.

11.

Oh! ever thus from childhood's hour
    I've seen my fondest hopes decay;
I never loved a tree or flower,
    But 'twas the first to fade away.
I never nursed a dear gazelle,
    To glad me with its soft black eye,
But when it came to know me well
    And love me, it was sure to die.

MOORE.

12.

The merry merry lark was up and singing,
    And the hare was out and feeding on the lea;
And the merry merry bells below were ringing,
    When my child's laugh rang through me.

KINGSLEY.

13.

The merry brown hares came leaping
    Over the crest of the hill,
Where the clover and corn lay sleeping
    Under the moonlight still.

KINGSLEY.

14.

A lion and some other beasts went out hunting together. When they had caught a fine stag, the lion divided the spoil into three parts, and said: 'The first I shall take as king; the second I shall take because I am the strongest; and as for the third part, let him take it who dares.'

15. *The Three Fishers.*

Three wives sat up in the lighthouse tower,
  And they trimm'd the lamps as the sun went down;
They look'd at the squall, and they look'd at the shower,
  And the night-rack came rolling up ragged and brown.
    But men must work, and women must weep,
    Though storms be sudden, and waters deep,
    And the harbour bar be moaning.
                    KINGSLEY.

16. *The Ancient Mariner.*

Farewell, farewell! but this I tell
  To thee, thou Wedding-Guest!
He prayeth well, who loveth well
  Both man and bird and beast.

He prayeth best who loveth best
  All things both great and small;
For the dear God who loveth us,
  He made and loveth all.
                  S. T. COLERIDGE.

17.

A fir-tree was one day boasting itself to a bramble. 'You are of no use at all; but how could barns and houses be built without me?' 'Good sir,' said the bramble, 'when the woodmen come here with their axes and saws, what would you give to be a bramble and not a fir?'

18. *The Inchcape Rock.*

No stir in the air, no stir in the sea,
The ship was as still as she could be,
Her sails from heaven received no motion,
Her keel was steady in the ocean.

Without either sign or sound of their shock
The waves flowed over the Inchcape Rock;
So little they rose, so little they fell,
They did not move the Inchcape Bell.

SOUTHEY.

19.

A wolf, seeing a goat feeding on the brow of a high rock, where he could not come at her, besought her to come down lower, for fear she should miss her footing at that height; 'and moreover,' said he, 'the grass is far sweeter and more abundant here below.' But the goat replied, 'Excuse me; it is not for my dinner that you invite me, but your own.'

20. *The Mouse.*

'When I went out into the wide world,' said the first mouse, 'I thought, as many think at my age, that I had already learned everything; but that was not the case. Years must pass before one gets so far. I went to sea once. I went in a ship that steered towards the north. They told me that the ship's cook must know how to manage things at sea; but it is easy enough to manage things when one has plenty of sides of bacon, and whole tubs of salt pork, and mouldy flour. One has delicate living on board. When at last we reached the port to which we were bound, I left the ship, and it was high up in the far north. I saw great pathless forests of pine and birch that smelt so strong that I sneezed, and thought of sausages.'

'I was born in the palace library,' said the second mouse. 'I and several members of our family never knew the happiness of getting into the dining-room, much less into the store-room; on my journey, and here to-day, are the only times I have seen a kitchen. We have indeed often been compelled to suffer hunger in the library, but we get a good deal of knowledge.'—ANDERSEN.

21.

The floor, moreover, of the place was laid
With coloured stones, wrought like a flowery mead;
And ready to the hand for every need,
Midmost the hall, two fair streams trickled down
O'er wondrous gem-like pebbles, green and brown,
Betwixt smooth banks of marble, and therein
Bright-coloured fish shone through the water thin.

But now be ready, for I long full sore
To hear the merry dashing of the oar,
And feel the freshness of the following breeze
That sets me free, and sniff the rough salt seas.

Therefore they gat them ready now for war,
With joyful hearts, for sharp they sniffed the sea,
And saw the great waves tumbling green and free
Outside the bar upon the way to Greece,
The rough green way to glory and sweet peace.
                                    MORRIS, *Jason.*

22. *The Oracle's Answer to Crœsus.*

I can count the sands, and I can measure the ocean;
I have ears for the silent, and know what the dumb man meaneth;
Lo! on my sense there striketh the smell of a shell-covered tortoise,
Boiling now on a fire with the flesh of a lamb in a cauldron,
Brass is the vessel below, and brass the cover above it.

23. *After Blenheim.*

My father lived at Blenheim then,
    Yon little stream hard by;
They burnt his dwelling to the ground,
    And he was forced to fly:
So with his wife and child he fled,
Nor had he where to rest his head.

With fire and sword the country round
    Was wasted far and wide,
And many a childing mother then
    And new-born baby died:
But things like that, you know, must be
At every famous victory.

They say it was a shocking sight
    After the field was won;
For many thousand bodies here
    Lay rotting in the sun;
But things like that, you know, must be
After a famous victory.

And everybody praised the Duke
    Who this great fight did win.
But what good came of it at last?
    Quoth little Peterkin.
Why that I cannot tell, said he,
But 't was a famous victory.

SOUTHEY.

24.

Farewell, then, and be joyful, for I go
Unto the people, many a thing to show,
And set them longing for forgotten things,
Whose rash hands toss about the crowns of kings.

But when he stood within that busy stead,
Taller he showed than any by a head,
Great limbed, broad shouldered, mightier far than all,
But soft of speech, though unto him did fall
Full many a scorn upon that day to get.

O Jove, by thy hand may all these be led
To name and wealth! and yet, indeed, for me,
What happy ending shall I ask from thee?
What helpful friends? what length of quiet years?
What freedom from ill care and deadly fears?
Do what thou wilt, but none the less believe
That all these things and more thou shouldst receive,
If thou wert Jason, I were Jove to-day.
MORRIS, *Jason.*

25.

From our old books I know
That Joseph came of old to Glastonbury,
And there the heathen Prince, Arviragus,
Gave him an isle of marsh whereon to build;
And there he built with wattles from the marsh
A little lonely church in days of yore,
For so they say, these books of ours, but seem
Mute of this miracle, far as I have read.
TENNYSON, *The Holy Grail.*

26. *Moses.*

We see the great Lawgiver looking round from his lonely elevation on an infinite expanse; behind him a wilderness of dreary sands and bitter waters, in which successive generations have sojourned, always moving, yet never advancing, reaping no harvest and building no abiding city; before him a goodly land, a land of promise, a land flowing with milk and honey. While the multitude below saw only the flat sterile desert in which they had so long wandered, bounded on every side by a near horizon, or diversified only by some deceitful mirage, he was gazing from a far higher stand, on a far lovelier country, following with his eye the long course of fertilizing rivers, through ample pastures, and under the bridges of great capitals, measuring the distances of marts and harbours, and portioning out all those wealthy regions from Dan to Beersheba.—MACAULAY, *Bacon*.

27. *Milanion's Prayer.*

O fairest, hear me now who do thy will,
Plead for thy rebel that he be not slain,
But live and love and be thy servant still;
Ah, give her joy and take away my pain,
And thus two long enduring servants gain
An easy thing this is to do for me,
What need of my vain words to weary thee!

But none the less, this place will I not leave
Until I needs must go my death to meet,
Or at my hands some happy sign receive
That in great joy we twain may one day greet
Thy presence here and kiss thy silver feet,
Such as we deem thee, fair beyond all words,
Victorious o'er our servants and our lords.

MORRIS, *Atalanta's Race*.

28. *The Passover.*

Night falls; the stars come out; the bright moon is in the sky. The household gathers round, and then takes place the hasty meal, of which every part is marked by the almost frantic haste of the first celebration, when Pharaoh's messengers were expected every instant to break in with the command, 'Get you forth from among my people! Go! Begone!' The guests of each household at the moment of the meal rose from their sitting and recumbent posture, and stood round the table on their feet. Their feet, usually bare within the house, were shod as if for a journey. Each member of the household, even the women, had staffs in their hands, as if for an immediate departure; the long Eastern garments of the men were girt up, for the same reason, round their loins. The roasted lamb was torn to pieces, each snatching and grasping in his eager fingers the morsel which he might not else have time to eat. Not a fragment is left for the morning, which will find them gone and far away. The cakes of bread which they broke and ate were tasteless from the want of leaven, which there had been no leisure to prepare.—STANLEY, *Jewish Church.*

29.

My eyes are dim with childish tears,
   My heart is idly stirred;
For the same sound is in my ears
   Which in those days I heard.
Thus fares it still in our decay;
   And yet the wiser mind
Mourns less for what age takes away
   Than what it leaves behind.

30.

You ask me, why, tho' ill at ease,
   Within this region I subsist,
   Whose spirits falter in the mist,
And languish for the purple seas?
It is the land that freemen till,
   That sober-suited Freedom chose,
   The land, where girt with friends or foes
A man may speak the thing he will.
TENNYSON.

31. *Toleration.*

When Abraham sat at his tent-door, according to his custom, waiting to entertain strangers; he espied an old man stooping and leaning on his staff, weary with age and travel, coming towards him, who was a hundred years of age. He received him kindly, washed his feet, provided supper, caused him to sit down; but observing that the old man eat and prayed not, nor begged for a blessing on his meat, he asked him why he did not worship the God of heaven; the old man told him that he worshipped the fire only, and acknowledged no other god; at which answer Abraham grew so zealously angry that he thrust the old man out of his tent, and exposed him to all the evils of the night and an unguarded condition. When the old man was gone, God called to Abraham, and asked him where the stranger was; he replied, 'I thrust him away because he did not worship Thee.' God answered him, 'I have suffered him these hundred years, although he dishonoured Me, and couldst not thou endure him one night when he gave thee no trouble?' Upon this, saith the story, Abraham fetched him back again and gave him hospitable entertainment and wise instruction. Go thou and do likewise, and thy charity will be rewarded by the God of Abraham.—JEREMY TAYLOR.

32.

Then rode Geraint into the castle court,
His charger trampling many a prickly star
Of sprouted thistle on the broken stones.
He look'd and saw that all was ruinous.
Here stood a shatter'd archway plumed with fern;
And here had fall'n a great part of a tower,
Whole, like a crag that tumbles from the cliff,
And like a crag was gay with wilding flowers:
And high above a piece of turret stair,
Worn by the feet that now were silent, wound
Bare to the sun, and monstrous ivy-stems
Claspt the gray walls with hairy-fibred arms,
And suck'd the joining of the stones, and look'd
A knot, beneath, of snakes, aloft, a grove.

TENNYSON, *Enid.*

33. *Toby.*

With all this inbred vulgar air, he was a dog of great moral excellence—affectionate, faithful, honest up to his light, with an odd humour as peculiar and as strong as his tail. My father, in his reserved way, was very fond of him, and there must have been very funny scenes with them, for we heard bursts of laughter issuing from his study when they two were by themselves; there was something in him that took that grave, beautiful, melancholy face. One can fancy him in the midst of his books, and sacred work and thoughts, pausing and looking at the secular Toby, who was looking out for a smile to begin his rough fun, and about to end by coursing and *gurrin'* round the room, upsetting my father's books, laid out on the floor for consultation, and himself nearly at times, as he stood watching him—and off his guard and shaking with laughter. Toby had always a great desire to accompany my father up to town; this my father's good taste and sense of dignity, besides his fear of losing his friend (a vain fear!), forbade, and as the decision of character of each was great and nearly equal, it was often a drawn game. Toby, ultimately, by making it his entire object, triumphed. He usually was nowhere to be seen on my father leaving; he however saw him, and lay in wait at the head of the street, and up Leith Walk he kept him in view from the opposite side like a detective, and then, when he knew it was hopeless to hound him home, he crossed unblushingly over, and joined company, excessively rejoiced of course.—*Horæ Subsecivæ*.

34. *Wasp.*

Once when she had three pups, one of them died. For two days and nights she gave herself up to trying to bring it to life—licking it, and turning it over and over, growling over it, and all but worrying it to awake it. She paid no attention to the living two, gave them no milk, flung them away with her teeth, and would have killed them, had they been allowed to remain with her. She was as one possessed, and neither ate, nor drank, nor slept, was heavy and miserable with her milk, and in such a state of excitement that no one could remove the dead pup. Early on the third day she was seen to take the pup in her mouth, and start across the fields towards the Tweed, striding like a race-horse—she plunged in, holding up her burden, and at the middle of the stream dropped it, and swam swiftly ashore; then she stood and watched the little dark lump floating away, bobbing up and down with the current, and losing it at last far down, she made her way home, sought out the living two, devoured them with her love, carried them one by one to her lair, and gave herself up wholly to nurse them: you can fancy her mental and bodily happiness and relief when they were pulling away—and theirs.—*Horæ Subsecivæ.*

35. *The City of the Phæacians.*

When we the city reach—a castled crown
Of wall encircles it from end to end,
And a fair haven, on each side the town,
Framed with fine entrance, doth our barks defend,
Which, where the terrace by the shore doth wend,
Line the long coast; to all and each large space,
Docks, and deep shelter, doth that haven lend;
There, paved with marble, our great market-place
Doth with its arms Poseidon's beauteous fane embrace.

WORSLEY, Odyssey.

36.

My worthy friend, Sir Roger, when we are talking of the malice of parties, very frequently tells us an accident that happened to him when he was a school-boy, which was at a time when the feuds ran high between the Roundheads and Cavaliers. This worthy knight, being then but a stripling, had occasion to enquire which was the way to St. Anne's Lane, upon which the person whom he spoke to, instead of answering his question, called him a young popish cur, and asked him who had made Anne a Saint? The boy, being in some confusion, enquired of the next he met, which was the way to Anne's Lane; but was called a prick-eared cur for his pains, and instead of being shewn the way, was told that she had been a Saint before he was born, and would be one after he was hanged. Upon this, says Sir Roger, I did not think fit to repeat the former questions, but going into every lane of the neighbourhood, asked what they called the name of that lane.—*Spectator.*

37. Genoa.

Some of you, I doubt not, remember Genoa; you have seen that queenly city with its streets of palaces, rising tier above tier from the water, girdling with the long lines of its bright white houses the vast sweep of its harbour, the mouth of which is marked by a huge natural mole of rock, crowned by its magnificent light-house tower. You remember how its white houses rose out of a mass of fig and olive and orange trees, the glory of its old patrician luxury; you may have observed the mountains behind the town spotted at intervals by small circular low towers, one of which is distinctly conspicuous where the ridge of the hills rises to its summit, and hides from view all the country behind it. Those towers are the forts of the famous lines, which, curiously resembling in shape the later Syracusan walls enclosing Epipolæ, converge inland from the eastern and western extremities of the city, looking down, the western line on the valley of the Polcevera, the eastern on that of the Bisagno, till they meet, as I have said, on the summit of the mountains, where the hills cease to rise from the sea, and become more or less of a table-land running off towards the interior, at the distance, as well as I remember, of between two and three miles from the outside of the city. Thus a very large open space is enclosed within the lines, and Genoa is capable, therefore, of becoming a vast entrenched camp, holding not so much a garrison as an army.— DR. ARNOLD, *Lectures on Modern History*.

38. Calypso's Cave.

Thither the long-winged birds retired to sleep,
Falcon and owl and sea-crow loud of tongue,
Who plies her business in the watery deep;

And round the hollow cave her tendrils flung
A healthy vine, with purpling clusters hung;
And fountains four, in even order set,
Near one another, from the stone out-sprung,
Streaming four ways their crystal-showery jet
Through meads of parsley soft and breathing violet.
WORSLEY, Odyssey.

39. *The Hand.*

Have you noticed that when you want to take hold of anything (a bit of bread, we will say), have you noticed that it is always the thumb who puts himself forward, and that he is always on one side by himself, whilst the rest of the fingers are on the other? If the thumb is not helping, nothing stops in your hand, and you don't know what to do with it. Try, by way of experiment, to carry your spoon to your mouth without putting your thumb to it, and you will see what a long time it will take you to get through a poor little plateful of broth. The thumb is placed in such a manner on your hand that it can face each of the other fingers, one after another, or all together, as you please; and by this we are enabled to grasp, as if with a pair of pincers, all objects, whether large or small. Our hands owe their perfection of usefulness to this happy arrangement, which has been bestowed on no other animal, except the monkey, our nearest neighbour. I may even add, while we are about it, that it is this which distinguishes the hand from a paw or a foot. My foot, which has other things to do than to pick up apples or lay hold of a fork, has also five fingers, but the largest cannot face the others; it is not a thumb, therefore, and it is because of this that my foot is not a hand.—JEAN MACÉ.

40. *The Brook.*

I slip, I slide, I gloom, I glance,
   Among my skimming swallows;
I make the netted sunbeam dance
   Against my sandy shallows.

I murmur under moon and stars
   In brambly wildernesses;
I linger by my shingly bars;
   I loiter round my cresses;

And out again I curve and flow
   To join the brimming river,
For men may come, and men may go,
   But I go on for ever.
                      TENNYSON.

41. *Calypso to Odysseus.*

Weep no more, luckless hero, weep no more,
Nor always thus consume thy life with pain.
Now will I send thee from this island-shore
Back to thy country o'er the watery plain.
Come thou and fall unto thy task amain.
Fell trees; with iron a broad craft prepare,
Made strongly to withstand the billows' strain,
And fix thwart timbers for the deck with care,
Which o'er the cloud-dark billows may thee safely bear.
                      WORSLEY, *Odyssey.*

42. *The Bee-eater.*

We had in this village, more than twenty years ago, an idiot boy, whom I well remember, who from a child showed a strong propensity to bees; they were his food, his amusement, his sole object. And as people of this cast have seldom more than one point in view, so this lad exerted all his few faculties on this one pursuit. In the winter he dozed away his time, within his father's house, by the fireside, in a kind of torpid state, seldom departing from the chimney corner; but in the summer he was all alert, and in quest of his game in the fields and on sunny banks. Honey-bees, humble-bees, and wasps were his prey wherever he found them: he had no apprehensions from their stings, but would seize them with naked hands, and at once disarm them of their weapons, and suck their bodies for the sake of their honey-bags. Sometimes he would fill his bosom, between his shirt and his skin, with a number of these captives; and sometimes would confine them in bottles. He was a very *merops apiaster*, or bee-bird, and very injurious to men that kept bees; for he would slide into their bee-gardens, and sitting down before the stools, would rap with his finger on the hives, and so take the bees as they came out. He has been known to overturn hives for the sake of honey, of which he was passionately fond. Where metheglin was making, he would linger round the tubs and vessels, begging a draught of what he called bee-wine. As he ran about, he used to make a humming noise with his lips, resembling the buzzing of bees.—WHITE's *Selborne.*

43. *Jotham's Parable.*

The trees went forth on a time to anoint a king over them; and they said unto the olive tree, Reign thou over us. But the olive tree said unto them, Should I leave my fatness, wherewith by me they honour God and man, and go to be promoted over the other trees? And the trees said to the fig tree, Come thou, and reign over us. But the fig

tree said unto them, Should I forsake my sweetness, and my good fruit, and go to be promoted over the trees? Then said the trees unto the vine, Come thou, and reign over us. And the vine said unto them, Should I leave my wine, which cheereth God and man, and go to be promoted over the trees? Then said all the trees unto the bramble, Come thou, and reign over us. And the bramble said unto the trees, If in truth ye anoint me king over you, then come and put your trust in my shadow; and if not, let fire come out of the bramble, and devour the cedars of Lebanon.—
JUDGES ix. 8–15.

44. *The Choice.*

When gentle winds but ruffle the calm sea,
My breast courageous grows, and earth to me
Dear as enticing ocean cannot be;
But when the great main roars, and white with foam
Huge waves tower up from it, and bellowing come
To burst on land, I wistful seek a home
In groves retired, where, when the storm descends,
It brings but music to the pine it bends.
Unblest whose house the wandering billows bear
With them, who strives with sea for fishy fare.
But I beneath the broad-leaved plane will lie,
Where some bright fountain, breaking forth hard by,
Delights, but not disturbs, with bubbling melody.

MOSCHUS, Garnett.

45.

This Indian lived here alone above three years; and although he was several times sought after by the Spaniards, who knew he was left on the island, yet they could never find him. He was in the woods hunting for goats, when Captain Watlin drew off his men, and the ship was under sail before he came back to shore. He had with him his gun, and a knife, with a small horn of powder, and a few shot; which being spent, he contrived a way, by notching his knife, to saw the barrel of his gun into small pieces, wherewith he made harpoons, lances, hooks, and a long knife; heating the pieces first in the fire, which he struck with his gun flint, and a piece of the barrel of his gun, which he hardened, having learnt to do that among the English. The hot pieces of iron he would hammer out and bend as he pleased with stones, and saw them with his jagged knife, or grind them to an edge by long labour, and harden them to a good temper as there was occasion. With such instruments as he made in that manner, he got such provisions as the island afforded, either goats or fish. He told us that at first he was forced to eat seal, which is very ordinary meat, before he had made hooks; but afterwards he never killed any seals but to make lines, cutting their skins into thongs. He had a little house, or hut, half a mile from the sea, which was lined with goatskin; his couch, or barbecu of sticks, lying along about two feet distance from the ground, was spread with the same, and was all his bedding. He had no clothes left, having worn out those he brought from Watlin's ship, but only a skin about his waist. He saw our ship the day before we came to an anchor, and did believe we were English; and therefore killed three goats in the morning, before we came to an anchor, and dressed them with cabbage, to treat us when we came ashore.—CAPTAIN DAMPIER, in Knight's *Knowledge is Power*.

46.

Then another of the King's Thanes arose and said, 'Truly the life of a man in this world, compared with that life whereof we wot not, is on this wise. It is as when thou, O King, art sitting at supper with thine Aldermen and thy Thanes in the time of winter, when the hearth is lighted in the midst and the hall is warm, but without the rains and the snow are falling, and the winds are howling; then cometh a sparrow and flieth through the house; she cometh in by one door and goeth out by another. Whiles she is in the house she feeleth not the storm of winter, but yet, when a little moment of rest is passed, she flieth again into the storm, and passeth away from our eyes. So is it with the life of man; it is but for a moment; what goeth afore it and what cometh after it, wot we not at all. Wherefore if these strangers can tell us aught, that we may know whence man cometh and whither he goeth, let us hearken to them and follow their law.'—FREEMAN, *Old English History for Children.*

47.

Alas! the meanest herb that scents the gale,
The lowliest flower that blossoms in the vale
Even where it dies, at spring's sweet call renews
To second life its odours and its hues.
But we, but man, the great, the brave, the wise,
When once in death he seals his failing eyes,
In the mute earth imprisoned, dark and deep,
Sleeps the long, endless, unawakening sleep.

MOSCHUS, Dean Milman.

48.

I began to consider about putting the few rags I had, which I called clothes, into some order. I had worn out all the waistcoats I had, and my business was now to try if I could not make jackets out of the great watch-coats which I had by me, and with such other materials as I had;

so I set to work a tailoring, or rather a botching, for I made most piteous work of it. However, I made shift to make two or three new waistcoats, which I hoped would serve me a great while; as for breeches or drawers, I made but a very sorry shift indeed, till afterward. I have mentioned that I saved the skins of all the creatures that I killed, I mean fourfooted ones, and I had hung them up stretched out with sticks in the sun, by which means some of them were so dry and hard that they were fit for little, but others it seems were very useful. The first thing I made of these was a great cap for my head, with the hair on the outside to shoot off the rain; and this I performed so well, that after this I made me a suit of clothes wholly of these skins, that is to say, a waistcoat, and breeches open at the knees, and both loose, for they were rather wanting to keep me cool than to keep me warm. I must not omit to acknowledge that they were wretchedly made; for if I was a bad carpenter, I was a worse tailor. After this I spent a great deal of time and pains to make me an umbrella; I was indeed in great want of one, and had a great mind to make one. I had seen them made in the Brazils, where they are very useful in the great heats which are there. And I felt the heats every jot as great here, and greater too, being nearer the Equinox; besides, as I was obliged to be much abroad, it was a most useful thing to me, as well for the rains as the heats. I took a world of pains at it, and was a great while before I could make anything likely to hold; nay, after I thought I had hit the way, I spoiled two or three before I made one to my mind; but at last I made one that answered indifferently well. The main difficulty I found was to make it let down. I could make it to spread, but if it did not let down too, and draw in, it was not portable for me any way but just over my head, which would not do. However, at last, as I said,

I made one to answer, and covered it with skins, the hair upwards, so that it cast off the rains like a penthouse, and kept off the sun so effectually that I could walk out in the hottest of the weather with greater advantage than I could before in the coolest, and when I had no need of it, could close it and carry it under my arm.—DEFOE, *Robinson Crusoe.*

49. *Sandanis' Counsel to Crœsus.*

Thou art about, oh, king, to make war against men who wear leathern trousers, and have all their other garments of leather; who feed not on what they like, but on what they can get from a soil that is sterile and unkindly; who do not indulge in wine, but drink water; who possess no figs nor anything else that is good to eat. If, then, thou conquerest them, what canst thou get from them, seeing that they have nothing at all? But if they conquer thee, consider how much that is precious thou wilt lose; if they once get a taste of our pleasant things, they will keep such hold of them that we shall never be able to make them loose their grasp.—RAWLINSON, *Herodotus.*

50. *Cleobis and Bito.*

There was a great festival in honour of the goddess Hêrê at Argos, to which their mother must needs be taken in a car. Now the oxen did not come home from the field in time; so the youths, fearful of being too late, put the yoke on their own necks, and themselves drew the car in which their mother rode. Five and forty furlongs did they draw her, and stopped before the temple. This deed of theirs was witnessed by the whole assembly of worshippers, and then their life closed in the best possible way. Herein, too, God showed forth most evidently how much better a thing

for man death is than life. For the Argive men stood thick around the car and extolled the vast strength of the youths; and the Argive women extolled the mother who was blessed with such a pair of sons; and the mother herself, overjoyed at the deed and at the praises it had won, standing straight before the image, besought the goddess to bestow upon Cleobis and Bito, the sons who had so mightily honoured her, the highest blessing to which mortals can attain. Her prayer ended, they offered sacrifice, and partook of the holy banquet, after which the two youths fell asleep in the temple. They never woke more, but so passed from the earth.—
RAWLINSON, *Herodotus*.

51. *Life*.

Time fleets, youth fades, life is an empty dream.
It is the echo of time; and he whose heart
Beat first beneath a human heart, whose speech
Was copied from a human tongue, can never
Recall when he was living yet knew not this.
Nevertheless long seasons pass o'er him
Till some one hour's experience shows what nothing,
It seemed, could clearer show; and ever after,
An altered brow and eye and gait and speech
Attest that now he knows the adage true
Time fleets, youth fades, life is an empty dream.
BROWNING, *Paracelsus*.

52.

It is related that a man of the pilgrims slept a long sleep, and then awoke, and saw no trace of the other pilgrims. So he arose and walked on; but he wandered from the way, and he proceeded until he saw a tent, and an old woman at its door, and he found by her a dog asleep. He approached the tent, saluted the old woman, and begged of her some food; whereupon she said to him, 'Go to yon valley, and catch as many serpents as will suffice thee, that I may broil some of them for thee.' The man replied, 'I dare not catch serpents, and I never ate them.' The old woman therefore said, 'I will go with thee, and catch some of them, and fear thou not.' Then she went with him, and the dog followed her, and she caught as many of the serpents as would suffice, and proceeded to broil some of them. The pilgrim could not refrain from eating, for he feared hunger and emaciation; so he ate of those serpents. And after this, being thirsty, he demanded of the old woman some water to drink; and she said to him, 'Go to the spring, and drink of it.' Accordingly he went to the spring; but he found its water bitter; yet he could not refrain from drinking of it, notwithstanding its exceeding bitterness, on account of the violence of his thirst. He therefore drank, and then returned to the old woman, and said to her, 'I wonder at thee, O thou old woman, and at thy residing in this place, and thy feeding thyself with this food, and thy drinking of this water.' 'How then,' said the old woman, 'is your country?' He answered her, 'Verily, in our country are spacious and ample houses, and ripe and delicious fruits, and abundant sweet waters, and excellent viands, and fat meats, and numerous sheep, and everything good, and blessings of which the like exist not save in the Paradise that God (whose name be exalted!) hath described to his just servants.' 'All this,' replied the old woman, 'I have heard; but tell me, have you any Sultan who ruleth over you, and oppresseth in his rule while ye are under his authority; and who, if any one of you committeth an offence, taketh his wealth, and destroyeth him, and who, if he desire, turneth you out from your houses?' The man answered her, 'That doth sometimes happen.' And the old woman rejoined, 'If so, by Allah, that dainty food and elegant life, and those delightful comforts, with oppression and tyranny, are penetrating poison; and our food, with safety, is a salutary antidote.—LANE's *Arabian Nights.*

53. *Cyrus.*

When the boy was in his tenth year, an accident, which I will now relate, caused it to be discovered who he was. He was at play one day in the village where the folds of the cattle were, along with the boys of his own age, in the street. The other boys who were playing with him chose the cowherd's son, as he was called, to be their king. He then proceeded to order them about; some he set to build him houses, others he made his guards, one of them was to be the king's eye, another had the office of carrying his messages, all had some task or other. Among the boys there was one, the son of Artembares, a Mede of distinction, who refused to do what Cyrus had set him. Cyrus told the other boys to take him into custody, and when his orders were obeyed, he chastised him most severely with the whip. The son of Artembares, as soon as he was let go, full of rage at treatment so little befitting his rank, hastened to the city and complained bitterly to his father of what had been done to him by the son of the king's cowherd. Artembares, in the heat of his passion, went to the king, accompanied by his son, and made complaint of the gross injury which had been done him. Pointing to the boy's shoulders, he exclaimed, 'Thus, oh! king, has thy slave, the son of a cowherd, heaped insult upon us.' At this sight and these words the king, wishing to avenge the son of Artembares for his father's sake, sent for the cowherd and his boy. When they came together into his presence, fixing his eyes on Cyrus, the king said, 'Hast thou then, the son of so mean a fellow as that, dared to behave thus rudely to the son of yonder noble, one of the first in my court?' 'My lord,' replied the boy, 'I only treated him as he deserved. I was chosen king in play by the boys of our village, because they thought me the best for it. He himself was one of the boys who chose me. All the others did according to my orders; but he refused, and made light of them, until at last he got his due reward. If for this I deserve to suffer punishment, here I am ready to submit to it.'—RAWLINSON, *Herodotus.*

54. *Jephthah's Daughter.*

Single I grew, like some green plant, whose root
    Creeps to the garden water-pipes beneath,
Feeding the flower; but ere my flower to fruit
    Changed, I was ripe for death.

My God, my land, my father—these did move
    Me from my bliss of life, that nature gave,
Lower'd softly with a threefold cord of love
    Down to a silent grave.

And I went mourning, 'No fair Hebrew boy
    Shall smile away my maiden blame among
The Hebrew mothers'—emptied of all joy,
    Leaving the dance and song,

Leaving the olive-gardens far below,
    Leaving the promise of my bridal bower,
The valleys of grape-loaded vines that glow
    Beneath the battled tower.

The light white cloud swam over us. Anon
    We heard the lion roaring from his den;
We saw the large white stars rise one by one,
    Or, from the darken'd glen,

Saw God divide the night with flying flame,
  And thunder on the everlasting hills.
I heard Him, for He spake, and grief became
  A solemn scorn of ills.

When the next moon was roll'd into the sky,
  Strength came to me that equall'd my desire.
How beautiful a thing it was to die
  For God and for my sire!

It comforts me in this one thought to dwell,
  That I subdued me to my father's will;
Because the kiss he gave me, ere I fell,
  Sweetens the spirit still.

Moreover it is written that my race
  Hew'd Ammon, hip and thigh, from Aroer
On Arnon unto Minneth. . . .
  . . . .

TENNYSON, *A dream of Fair Women.*

55.

Round great part of our coast we find terraces, from twenty to fifty feet above the level of the sea, and in some places the terrace runs with great persistence for a number of miles. Round the Firth of Forth, for example, on both shores, there is an old sea-cliff of solid rock, overlooking a raised beach or terrace, now often cultivated in cornfields and meadows, and then you come to the present sea beach. This terrace usually consists of gravel and sea-shells in great quantities, of the same species with those that lie upon the present beach, where the tide rises and falls every day. The some kind of terrace is found on the shores of the Firth of Clyde, and in almost all the other estuaries of Scotland, and in places round the west highlands on the coast of Scotland.

Similar or analogous raised beaches occur on the borders of Wales and in the south of England. In Devon and Cornwall there are the remains of old consolidated beaches clinging to the cliffs from twenty to thirty feet above the level of the sea. It is clear, therefore, that an elevation of the land has occurred in places to the extent of about forty feet, at a very recent period, long after all the living species of shell-fish inhabited our shores. Further, in the alluvial plains that border the Forth, and on the Clyde in the neighbourhood of Glasgow, at various times, in cutting trenches, canals, and other works, the bones of whales, seals, and porpoises have been found at a height of from twenty to thirty feet above the level of high-water mark. Now it is evident that whales did not crawl twenty or thirty feet above high-water mark to die, and therefore they must have either died upon the spot where their skeletons were found or been floated there after death. That part of the country therefore must have been covered with salt water, which is now occupied simply by common alluvial detritus. But the story does not stop there; for in the very same beds in which the remains of these marine mammalia have been discovered on the Clyde, canoes have been found in a state of preservation so perfect, that all their form and structure could be well made out. Some of them were simply scooped in the trunks of large trees, but others were built of planks nailed together, square-sterned boats indeed, built of well-dressed planks; and the inference has been drawn, that this last elevation took place at a time that is historical, and even since the Roman occupation of our island. — RAMSAY, *Physical Geology and Geography of Great Britain.*

56.

Of all the land far famed for goodly steeds,
Thou com'st, O stranger, to the noblest spot,
   Colonos, glistening bright,
Where evermore, in thickets freshly green,
   The clear-voiced nightingale
   Still haunts and pours her song,
   By purpling ivy hid,
And the thick leafage sacred to the God,
   With all its myriad fruits,
   By mortal's foot untouched,
   By sun's hot ray unscathed,
   Sheltered from every blast;
There wanders Dionysos evermore,
   In full, wild revelry,
And waits upon the nymphs who nursed his youth.

And yet another praise is mine to sing,
   Gift of the mighty God
To this our city, mother of us all,
   Her greatest, noblest boast,
   Famed for her goodly steeds,
   Famed for her bounding colts,
   Famed for her sparkling sea.
Poseidon, son of Kronos, Lord and King,
   To Thee this boast we owe,
   For first in these our streets
   Thou to the untamed horse
   Didst use the conquering bit;
   And here the well-shaped oar,
   By skilled hands deftly plied,

Still leapeth through the sea,
Following in wondrous guise,
The fair Nereids with their hundred feet.

PLUMPTRE, *Œdipus at Colonos.*

57. *The Porteous Riot at Edinburgh.*

The passive resistance of the Tolbooth gate promised to do more to baffle the purpose of the mob than the active interference of the magistrates. The heavy sledge-hammers continued to din against it without intermission, and with a noise which, echoed from the lofty buildings around the spot, seemed enough to have alarmed the garrison in the Castle. It was circulated among the rioters, that the troops would march down to disperse them, unless they could execute their purpose without loss of time; or that, even without quitting the fortress, the garrison might obtain the same end by throwing a bomb or two upon the street. Urged by such motives for apprehension, they eagerly relieved each other at the labour of assailing the Tolbooth door; yet such was its strength that it still defied their efforts. At length, a voice was heard to pronounce the words, 'Try it with fire.' The rioters, with an unanimous shout, called for combustibles, and as all their wishes seemed to be instantly supplied, they were soon in possession of two or three empty tar-barrels. A huge red glaring bonfire speedily arose close to the door of the prison, sending up a tall column of smoke and flame against its antique turrets and strongly-grated windows, and illuminating the ferocious and wild gestures of the rioters who surrounded the place, as well as the pale and anxious groups of those who, from windows in the vicinage, watched the progress of this alarming scene. The mob fed the fire with whatever they could find fit for the purpose. The flames roared and crackled among the heaps of nourishment piled on the fire, and a terrible shout soon announced that the door had kindled, and was in the act of being destroyed. The fire was suffered to decay, but, long ere it was quite extinguished, the most forward of the rioters rushed, in their impatience, one after another, over its yet smouldering remains. Thick showers of sparkles rose high in the air, as man after man bounded over the glowing embers, and disturbed them in their passage.—SCOTT, *Heart of Mid Lothian.*

58.

The ancestor of Gyges the Lydian was a shepherd, so the story runs, in the service of the reigning sovereign of Lydia, when one day a violent storm of rain fell, the ground was rent asunder by an earthquake, and a yawning gulf appeared on the spot where he was feeding his flocks. Seeing what had happened, and wondering at it, he went down into the gulf, and among other marvellous objects he saw, as the legend relates, a hollow brazen horse, with windows in its sides, through which he looked, and beheld in the interior a corpse, apparently of superhuman size; from which he took nothing but a golden ring off the hand, and therewith made his way out. Now when the usual meeting of the shepherds occurred, for the purpose of sending to the king their monthly report of the state of his flocks, this shepherd came with the rest, wearing the ring. And, as he was seated with the company, he happened to turn the hoop of the ring round towards himself, till it came to the inside of his hand. Whereupon he became invisible to his neighbours, who fell to talking about him as if he were gone away. While he was marvelling at this, he again began playing with the ring, and turned the hoop to the outside, upon which he became once more visible. Having noticed this effect, he made experiments with the ring, to see whether it possessed this virtue; and so it was, that when he turned the hoop inwards he became invisible, and when he turned it outwards he was again visible. After this discovery, he immediately contrived to be appointed one of the messengers to carry the report to the king; and upon his arrival he slew the king, and took possession of the throne.—PLATO, *Republic*, (Davies and Vaughan).

59.

Now these men,
Though brown indeed through dint of that hot sun,
Were comely and well-knit, as any one
I saw in Greece, and fit for deeds of war,
Though as I said of all men gentlest far;
Their arms were axe and spear, and shield and bow,
But nought of iron did they seem to know,
For all their cutting tools were edged with flint,
Or with soft copper, that soon turned and bent;
With cloths of cotton were their bodies clad,
But other raiment for delight they had
Most fairly woven of some unknown thing;
And all of them from little child to king
Had many ornaments of beaten gold:
Certes, we might have gathered wealth untold
Amongst them, had that then been in our thought,
But none the glittering evil valued aught.

MORRIS, *Earthly Paradise*.

60. The Old Margate Hoy.

All this time sat upon the edge of the deck quite a different character. It was a lad, apparently very poor, very infirm, and very patient. His eye was ever on the sea, with a smile; and, if he caught now and then some snatches of these wild legends, it was by accident, and they seemed not to concern him. The waves to him whispered more pleasant stories. He was as one, being with us, but not of us. He heard the bell of dinner ring without stirring; and when some of us pulled out our private stores, our cold meat and our salads, he produced none, and seemed to want none. Only a solitary biscuit he had laid in; provision for the one or two days and nights, to which these vessels were oftentimes obliged to prolong their voyage. Upon a nearer acquaintance with him, which he seemed neither to court nor decline, we learned that he was going to Margate, with the hope of being admitted into the Infirmary there for seabathing. His disease was a scrofula, which appeared to have eaten all over him. He expressed great hopes of a cure; and when we asked him, whether he had any friends where he was going, he replied 'he *had* no friends.'—CHARLES LAMB.

61.

Come, Antony, and young Octavius, come,
Revenge yourselves alone on Cassius,
For Cassius is a-weary of the world;
Hated by one he loves; braved by his brother;
Checked like a bondman; all his faults observed,
Set in a note-book, learned and conned by rote,
To cast into my teeth. O, I could weep
My spirit from mine eyes! There is my dagger,

And here my naked breast; within, a heart
Dearer than Plutus' mine, richer than gold;
If that thou be'st a Roman, take it forth;
I, that denied thee gold, will give my heart:
Strike, as thou didst at Caesar; for I know,
When thou didst hate him worst, thou lovedst him better
Than ever thou lovedst Cassius.
SHAKESPEARE, Julius Cæsar.

62.

As I am one, who, by my profession, am obliged to look into all kinds of men, there are none whom I consider with so much pleasure, as those who have anything new or extraordinary in their characters, or ways of living. For this reason I have often amused myself with speculations on the race of people called Jews, many of whom I have met with in most of the considerable towns which I have passed through in the course of my travels. They are, indeed, so disseminated through all the trading parts of the world, that they are become the instruments by which the most distant nations converse with one another, and by which mankind are knit together in a general correspondence. They are like the pegs and nails in a great building, which, though they are but little valued in themselves, are absolutely necessary to keep the whole frame together.—*Spectator*.

63.

The mountain wooded to the peak, the lawns
And winding glades high up like ways to Heaven,
The slender coco's drooping crown of plumes,
The lightning flash of insect and of bird,
The lustre of the long convolvuluses
That coil'd around the stately stems, and ran

Ev'n to the limit of the land, the glows
And glories of the broad belt of the world,
All these he saw; but what he fain had seen
He could not see, the kindly human face,
Nor ever hear a kindly voice, but heard
The myriad shriek of wheeling ocean-fowl,
The league-long roller thundering on the reef,
The moving whisper of huge trees that branch'd
And blossom'd in the zenith, or the sweep
Of some precipitous rivulet to the wave,
As down the shore he ranged, or all day long
Sat often in the seaward-gazing gorge,
A shipwreck'd sailor, waiting for a sail;
No sail from day to day, but every day
The sunrise broken into scarlet shafts
Among the palms and ferns and precipices;
The blaze upon the waters to the east;
The blaze upon his island overhead;
The blaze upon the waters to the west;
Then the great stars that globed themselves in Heaven,
The hollower-bellowing ocean, and again
The scarlet shafts of sunrise—but no sail.

TENNYSON, *Enoch Arden.*

64. *Of Gardens.*

And because the breath of flowers is far sweeter in the air (where it comes and goes like the warbling of music) than in the hand, therefore nothing is more fit for that delight than to know, what be the flowers and plants that do best perfume the air. Roses damask and red are fast flowers of their smells, so that you may walk by a whole row of them, and find nothing of their sweetness, yea, though it be in a morning's dew. Bays likewise yield no smell, as they grow; rosemary little, nor sweet-marjoram. That which, above all others, yields the sweetest smell in the air, is the violet; specially the white double violet which comes twice a-year, about the middle of April and about Bartholomew-tide. Next to that is the musk-rose. . . . . Then sweet-briar. Then wall-flowers, which are very delightful to be set under a parlour, or lower chamber window. Then pinks and gilly-flowers, specially the matted pink and the clove gilly-flower. Then the flowers of the lime tree. Then the honeysuckles, so they be somewhat afar off. Of bean-flowers I speak not, because they are field flowers. But those which perfume the air most delightfully, not passed by as the rest, but being trodden upon and crushed, are three; that is burnet, wild thyme, and water-mints. Therefore you are to set whole alleys of them, to have the pleasure, when you walk or tread.—BACON.

65.

Never stoops the soaring vulture
On his quarry in the desert,
On the sick and wounded bison,
But another vulture, watching
From his high aerial look-out,
Sees the downward plunge, and follows;
And a third pursues the second,
Coming from the invisible ether,
First a speck, and then a vulture,
Till the air is dark with pinions.
So disasters come not singly;
But as if they watched and waited,
Scanning one another's motions,

When the first descends, the others
Follow, follow, gathering flock-wise
Round their victim, sick and wounded,
First a shadow, then a sorrow,
Till the air is dark with anguish.
              LONGFELLOW, *Hiawatha*.

66. *Alexander*.

Alexander was bred and taught under Aristotle, the great philosopher, who dedicated divers of his books of philosophy unto him : he was attended with Callisthenes and divers other learned persons, that followed him in camp, throughout his journeys and conquests. What price and estimation he had learning in doth notably appear in these three particulars: first, in the envy he used to express that he bare towards Achilles, in this, that he had so good a trumpet of his praises as Homer's verses; secondly, in the judgement or solution he gave touching that precious cabinet of Darius, which was found among his jewels; whereof question was made what thing was worthy to be put into it; and he gave his opinion for Homer's works; thirdly, in his letter to Aristotle, after he had set forth his books of nature, wherein he expostulateth with him for publishing the secrets or mysteries of philosophy; and gave him to understand that himself esteemed it more to excel other men in learning and knowledge than in power and empire. And what use he had of learning doth appear, or rather shine, in all his speeches and answers, being full of science and use of science, and that in all variety.—BACON, *Advancement of Learning*.

67.

Therefore, O friends, if ye are of my mind,
When we are passed the French and English strait
Let us seek news of that desired gate
To immortality and blessed rest
Within the landless waters of the west,
But still a little to the southward steer.
Certes no Greenland winter waits us there,
No year-long night, but rather we shall find
Spice-trees set waving by the western wind,
And gentle folk who know no guile at least,
And many a bright-winged bird and soft-skinned beast,
For gently must the year upon them fall.

Morris, *Earthly Paradise.*

68. *A Thunderstorm.*

The thunder muttered far off, but there was neither rain nor visible lightning. But on the opposite horizon appeared a mass of dark blue cloud, which rose rapidly, and advanced in the direct line of the tower. Before it rolled a lighter but still lurid volume of vapour, which curled and wreathed like eddying smoke before the denser blackness of the unbroken cloud. Then followed the flashing of lightning, the rolling of thunder, and a deluge of rain like the bursting of a waterspout. They sate some time in silence, watching the storm as it swept along, with wind, and driving rain, and whirling hail, bringing for a time almost the darkness of night, through which the forked lightning poured a scarcely interrupted blaze. Suddenly came a long dazzling flash, that seemed to irradiate the entire circumference of the sky, followed instantaneously by one of those crashing peals of thunder, which always indicate that something very near has been struck by the lightning. . . . . One of two horses in a gentleman's carriage had been struck dead, and a young lady in the carriage had been stunned by the passing flash, though how far she was injured by it could not be immediately known. The other horse, it appeared, had been prancing in terror, and had nearly overthrown the carriage; but he had been restrained by the vigorous arm of a young farmer, who had subsequently carried the young lady into the house.—*Gryll Grange.*

69.

My children ! on this day ye cease to have
A father. All my days are spent and gone;
And ye no more shall lead your wretched life,
Caring for me. Hard was it, that I know,
My children ! yet one word is strong to loose,
Although alone, the burden of these toils,
For love in larger store ye could not have
From any than from him who standeth here,
Of whom bereaved ye now shall live your life.
     PLUMPTRE, *Œdipus at Colonos.*

70.

That the British infantry soldier is more robust than the soldier of any other nation, can scarcely be doubted by those who, in 1855, observed his powerful frame distinguished amidst the united armies of Europe; and notwithstanding his habitual excess in drinking, he sustains fatigue and wet, and the extremes of cold and heat, with incredible vigour; when completely disciplined, and three years are required to accomplish this, his port is lofty and his movements free, the whole world cannot produce a nobler specimen of military bearing, nor is the mind unworthy of the outward man. He does not indeed possess that presumptuous vivacity which would lead him to dictate to his commanders, or even to censure real errors although he may perceive them; but he is observant and quick to comprehend his orders, full of resources under difficulties, calm and resolute in danger, and more than usually obedient and careful of his officers in moments of imminent peril.—SIR W. NAPIER.

71.

The time when we first begin really to know anything about Britain is between fifty and sixty years before the birth of our Lord Jesus Christ. You know, I suppose, that this is the way in which Christian nations reckon time; such a thing happened so many years before, or so many years after, the birth of Christ. At that time the greatest people in the world were the Romans. These were originally the people of the city of Rome in Italy. They were not so bold at sea as the Phœnicians, nor were they so clever and learned a people as the Greeks. They could not build such fine temples, or carve such beautiful statues, or make such eloquent speeches and poems as the Greeks could; but they were the best soldiers and the wisest law-makers that the world ever saw. At Rome, in the best days of Rome, every man knew both how to command and how to obey. The Romans chose their own rulers; but when they had chosen them, they submitted to all their lawful commands. They made their own laws; but they did not think that, because they made the laws, they might therefore break them. Thus they were able gradually to conquer, first all Italy, and then nearly all the world that they knew of, that is, all the countries round about the Mediterranean Sea. The people of Italy itself they gradually admitted to the same rights as themselves, so that at the time of which I am speaking, every Italian was reckoned as a Roman; but the lands out of Italy they made into Provinces, and the people of those lands were their subjects. There was no King at Rome, but the people of the Provinces had to obey the laws made by the Senate and People of Rome, and to be governed by the magistrates whom the Romans sent to rule over them. The Romans were very proud of their freedom in having no King or master of any kind, and for a long time they were worthy of their freedom, and used it well.—FREEMAN, *Old English History for Children.*

72.

'Friends,' said the captain, 'the state of the weather advises each one of us to commend himself to God, and to prepare for death.' He was asked by some who knew a little about seamanship, for how many hours he thought he could keep the ship together. He said he could promise nothing, but certainly not more than three hours. What were the folks on board doing meanwhile? Not a few of them fell flat on the deck, and began to worship the sea, pouring all the oil they could get hold of upon the waves, soothing it, just as we are wont to do to an irritated prince. O most merciful sea, most noble sea, most wealthy sea! O most beautiful sea! grow calm and save us. Many prayers of this kind they kept chanting to the deaf sea. Some were only seasick, most of them kept making vows. One Englishman was there, who kept promising mountains of gold to our Lady of Walsingham, if ever he set foot on land alive. Some made many promises to the wood of the Cross in one place, and others to it in another. A few promised to turn Carthusians. One there was who bound himself to go to St. James of Compostella, with bare feet and head, his body covered only with a shirt of iron mail, and begging his bread along the road. I could not but laugh, as I heard one vowing as loud as he could bellow, lest he should not be attended to, a wax figure as big as the saint to the St. Christopher who stands on the top of the church in Paris, more like a mountain than a statue. While he was thus vociferating at his best, an acquaintance that happened to be standing next to him, gave him a nudge, and added a hint. 'Mind what you promise,' he says, 'even if you sell by auction everything you possess, you could not pay this.' The other replied in a more subdued tone, so that Christopher should not hear forsooth, 'Hold your tongue, you idiot. Do you think I am speaking my real mind? If only once I set my foot ashore, I shall not give him as much as a tallow candle.'—ERASMUS, *Colloquia* (Lowe).

73. *The Ugly Duck.*

Towards evening the Duck came to a miserable peasant's hut. Here lived a woman with her Tom Cat and her Hen. And the Tom Cat could arch his back and purr, he could even give out sparks; but for that one had to stroke his fur the wrong way. In the morning the strange Duckling was at once noticed, and the Tom Cat began to purr, and the Hen to cluck. What is this? said the woman, and looked all round: but she could not see well, and therefore she thought the Duckling was a fat duck that had strayed. 'This is a rare prize,' she said. 'Now I shall have duck's eggs. I hope it is not a drake.' And so the Duckling was admitted on trial for three weeks; but no eggs came. And the Tom Cat was master of the house, and the Hen was the lady, and always said 'We and the world,' for she thought they were half the world, and by far the better half. 'Can you lay eggs?' she asked. 'No.' 'Then you will have the

goodness to hold your tongue.' And the Tom Cat said, 'Can you curve your back, and purr, and give out sparks?' 'No.' 'Then you cannot have any opinion of your own when sensible people are speaking.' And the Duckling sat in a corner and was melancholy; then the fresh air and the sunshine streamed in; and it was seized with such a strange longing to swim on the water, that it could not help telling the Hen of it. 'What are you thinking of?' said the Hen. 'You have nothing to do, that is why you have these fancies. Purr or lay eggs, and they will pass over.' 'But it is so charming to swim on the water,' said the Duckling, 'so refreshing to let it close over one's head, and to dive down to the bottom.' 'Yes, that must be a mighty pleasure, truly,' quoth the Hen, 'ask the Cat about it, he is the cleverest animal I know, ask him if he likes to swim on the water, or to dive down. Ask our mistress, the old woman; no one in the world is cleverer than she. Do you think she has any desire to swim or to let the water close over her head?' 'You don't understand me,' said the Duckling. 'We don't understand you! Then pray who is to understand you? You surely don't pretend to be cleverer than the Tom Cat and the woman, I won't say anything of myself. Don't be conceited, child. You may believe me, I speak for your good. I tell you disagreeable things, and by that one may always know one's true friends. Only take care that you learn to lay eggs, or to purr and give out sparks.'—
ANDERSEN.

74. *The Centaur.*

But louder still the noise he hearkened grew,
Until at last in sight the Centaur drew,
A mighty grey horse, trotting down the glade,
Over whose back the long grey locks were laid,

That from his reverend head abroad did flow:
For to the waist was man, but all below
A mighty horse, once roan, now well-nigh white
With lapse of years; with oak-wreaths was he dight
Where man joined unto horse, and on his head
He wore a gold crown, set with rubies red,
And in his hand he bare a mighty bow,
No man could bend of those that battle now.

MORRIS, *Jason*.

75.

But slow as moves a lion from the fold,
Which dogs and youths with ceaseless toil hath worn,
Who all night long have kept their watch, to guard
From his assault the choicest of the herd;
He, hunger-pinched, hath oft the attempt renewed,
But nought prevailed; by spears on every side,
And javelins met, wielded by stalwart hands,
And blazing torches, which his courage daunt;
Till with the morn he sullenly withdraws.

LORD DERBY, *Homer*.

76. *The Sedge-warbler.*

It mattered not to the Sedge-warbler whether it were night or day! She built her nest down among the willows and reeds and long thick herbage that bordered the great river's side, and in her sheltered covert she sang songs of mirth and rejoicing both by day and night. 'Where does the great river go to?' asked the little ones, as they peered out of their nest one lovely summer night and saw the moonbeams dancing on the waters, as they hurried along. Now the Sedge-warbler could not tell her children where the great river went to; so she laughed, and said they must ask the

Sparrow who chattered so fast, or the Swallow who travelled so far, next time one or other came to perch on the willow-tree to rest. . . . The mother-bird would sometimes leave the little ones below, and go up into the willow branches to sing alone; and as the season advanced she did this oftener and oftener; and her song was plaintive and tender then, for she used to sing to the tide of the river as it swept along, she knew not whither, and think that some day she and her husband and children should all be hurrying to the Unknown Land whence she had come. . . . At first she used to sing these ditties only when alone, but by degrees she began to let her little ones hear them now and then, for were not they going to accompany her? . . . Then the little ones asked her where the Unknown Land was. But she smiled, and said she could not tell them, for she did not know. . . . 'Why should we leave the reed-beds and the willow-trees? Cannot we all build nests here, and live here always? Mother, do not let us go away anywhere else. I want no other land, and no other home but this. There are all the other aits in the great river to choose from, where we shall each settle; there can be nothing in the Unknown Land more pleasant than the reed-beds and willow-trees here. . . . Think of the red glow in the morning sky, mother, and the soft haze, and the beautiful rays of warm light across the waters! Think of the grand noonday glare, when the broad flags and reeds are all burnished over with heat. Think of these evenings, mother, when we can sit about in the branches, here, there, anywhere, and watch the great sun go down behind the sky; or fly to the aits of the great river, and sing in the long green herbage there, and then come home by moonlight, and sing till we fall asleep; and wake singing again, if any noise disturb us, if a boat chance to paddle by, or some of those strange bright lights shoot up with a noise into the sky from distant gardens. . . . Sing those dreadful songs about another land no more?' And the Sedge-warbler changed her note, and sang . . . of her own young days, . . . and how a voice seemed to rise within her that said, 'This is not your rest.' And how at last they had left their home together, and came and settled down among the reed-beds of the great river. 'And where is the place you came from, mother?' . . . 'My child, it is the Unknown Land. Far, far away, I know, but where, I do not know. Only the voice that called me thence is beginning to call again.'. . . Long before the sunbeams could pierce the heavy haze one autumn morning, the young Sedge-warblers rose for the last time over their much loved reed-beds, and took flight, they knew not whither.—*Parables from Nature.*

77. *The Canadian Boat Song.*

Faintly as tolls the evening chime,
Our voices keep tune and our oars keep time.
Soon as the woods on the shore look dim,
We'll sing at St. Anne's our parting hymn.
Row, brothers, row, the stream runs fast,
The Rapids are near and the daylight is past.

Why should we yet our sail unfurl?
There is not a breath the blue wave to curl;
But when the wind blows off the shore,
Oh! sweetly we'll rest our weary oar.
Blow, breezes, blow, the stream runs fast,
The Rapids are near and the daylight is past.

MOORE.

78. *The Rooks' Parliament.*

The origin of these creatures, these men, whom we equally fear and dislike, is decidedly the most useful of all subjects of study. How can it be otherwise? Their treatment of us, and our feelings to them, can never be placed on a proper footing, until we know something of the nature of the people themselves. . . . *How* came this creature in the land, and *whence?* *Why* is he here at all? . . . He comes near us and we fly: he pursues us again, and again we retire before him. Old solitudes and woodland homes are invaded, and made public; and we seek fresh retreats, only to be driven out afresh. . . . Now the *why* of our yielding our place to man is fear. We can none of us deny it. . . . But the *why* of this fear? What is that? Well! I am told on all sides that it is our sense of man's superiority to ourselves. . . . So it was said, at least; but of this, what proofs? was my next demand; and no one could give me an answer. . . . I shouted for proofs till I was hoarse, but every one turned away silent. Who can wonder, then, that my next enquiry was a doubt. Is man superior to ourselves after all? . . . Now all common observation is against the superiority of man. While we fly swiftly through the sky, behold him creeping slowly along the ground. While we soar to the very clouds, a brief jump and come down again is all his utmost efforts can accomplish, though I have seen him practising to get higher and higher, in his leaps, as if at a game. And at all times, if one of his legs is up, the other is obliged to be down, or the superior creature would be apt to tumble on his nose. . . . Again, while we are clothed in a natural glossy plumage, available equally for summer or winter, behold man, not possessing in himself the means of protection against any sort of weather whatever! Neither

M

the warmth of summer nor the cold of winter suits his uncomfortable skin. In all seasons he must wear clothes. Clumsy incumbrances, with which he is driven by a sad necessity to supply the place of the feathers or fur with which every other creature on earth but himself is blessed. What sort of superiority is this? One more instance out of many, and I shall have said enough for the present. . . . While we are satisfied with ourselves and all around us, man is ever discontented and uneasy, seeking rest in everlasting change, but neither finding it himself, nor allowing it to others, as we know to our bitter cost. Ah, my friends, if restless dissatisfaction be a proof of superiority, who would not be glad to be an inferior animal? . . . One objection remains to be answered. . . . While standing under our roosting-trees, these creatures, men, will occasionally level at us sticks, of the most contemptible size, but which, owing to some contrivance which I have not at present had the time to investigate, make suddenly an abominable banging noise and a very unpleasant smoke. And no sooner do our youngsters see and hear all this, than some of them are pretty sure to fall down upon the ground, as if crouching at the very feet of our foe. . . . The prostrate young ones are carried away unresisting, and are never heard of more. Now this has actually been brought forward as a proof of the superiority of man; though in what way wanton cruelty proves superiority, I confess I am unable to see. My friends, man is not our superior, was never so, for he is neither more nor less than a degenerated brother of our own race.—*Parables from Nature*, Third Series.

79.

But swifter the next day the river ran
With higher banks, and now the woods began
To be of trees that in their land they knew,
And into clumps of close-set beeches grew,·
And oak-trees thinly spread, and there-between
Fair upland hillocks well beset with green;
And 'neath the trees great herds of deer and neat,
And sheep and swine, fed on the herbage sweet,
Seeming all wild as though they knew not man,
For quite untented here and there they ran,
And while two great bucks raised the armed brow
Each against each (since time of fight was now)
About them would the swine squeal, and the sheep
In close-drawn flock the faint republic keep,
With none to watch; nor saw they fence or fold
Nor any husbandry did they behold.
MORRIS, Jason.

80.

The resistance offered by the native chiefs of Ireland was feeble compared with that which was offered by the Saxons to the Norman conquerors of England. The most stubborn stand was made by the inhabitants of the Danish towns. There was no protracted and wavering battle like that of Hastings. The loose Irish armies more than once flung their naked bodies, their feeble targets, and their clumsy swords on the mailed and disciplined Norman ranks; but the issue of the struggle was scarcely more doubtful than that of the struggle between the Spaniards and the Mexicans. Superiority in war, produced by better weapons and tactics, and by a greater aptitude both for obedience and of

command, is in early times a high test of comparative civilization: and thus, in early times, conquest in some degree justifies itself as the ascendancy of a civilizing power.—
GOLDWIN SMITH, *Irish History and Irish Character*.

81.

But through the town few eyes were sealed with sleep
When the sun rose; yea, and the upland sheep
Must guard themselves for that one morn at least,
Against the wolf; and wary doves may feast
Unscared that morning on the ripening corn.
Nor did the whetstone touch the scythe that morn;
And all unheeded did the mackerel shoal
Make green the blue waves, or the porpoise roll
Through changing hills and valleys of the sea.
   For 'twixt the thronging people solemnly
The heroes went afoot along the way
That led unto the haven of the bay,
And as they went the roses rained on them
From windows glorious with the well-wrought hem
Of many a purple cloth; and all their spears
Were twined with flowers that the fair earth bears;
And round their ladies' tokens were there set
About their helmets, flowery wreaths, still wet
With beaded dew of the scarce vanished night.
                            MORRIS, *Jason*.

82.

Supposing half a dozen or a dozen men were cast ashore from a wreck on an uninhabited island, and left to their own resources, one, of course, according to his capacity, would be set to one business and one to another, the strongest to dig and to cut wood, and to build huts for the rest; the most dexterous to make shoes out of bark and coats out of skins; the best educated to look for iron or lead in the rocks, and to plan the channels for the irrigation of the fields. But though their labours were thus naturally severed, that small group of shipwrecked men would understand well enough that the speediest progress was to be made by helping each other, not by opposing each other: and they would know that this help could only be properly given so long as they were frank and open in their relations, and the difficulties which each lay under properly explained to the rest. So that any appearance of secresy or separateness in the actions of any of them would instantly, and justly, be looked upon with suspicion by the rest, as the sign of some selfish or foolish proceeding on the part of the individual. If, for instance, the scientific man were found to have gone out at night, unknown to the rest, to alter the sluices, the others would think, and in all probability rightly think, that he wanted to get the best supply of water to his own field; and if the shoemaker refused to show them where the bark grew which he made the sandals of, they would naturally think, and in all probability rightly think, that he didn't want them to see how much there was of it, and that he meant to ask from them more corn and potatoes in exchange for his sandals than the trouble of making them deserved.—RUSKIN, *Political Economy of Art.*

83.

O child, I pray the Gods to spare thine head
The burden of a crown; were it not good
That thou shouldst live and die within this wood
That clothes the feet of Pelion, knowing nought
Of all the things by foolish men so sought;

For there, no doubt, is everything man needs,—
The quiver, with the iron-pointed reeds,
The cornel bow, the wood-knife at the side,
The garments of the spotted leopard's hide,
The bed of bear-skin in the hollow hill,
The bath within the pool of some green rill;
There shall the quick-eyed centaurs be thy friends,
Unto whose hearts such wisdom great Jove sends
They know the past and future, and fear nought
That by the fates upon them may be brought.
And when the spring brings love, then mayst thou find,
In some fair grassy place, the wood-nymphs kind,
And choose thy mate, and with her, hand in hand,
Go wandering through the blossoming sweet land;
And nought of evil there shall come to thee,
But like the golden age shall all things be;
And when upon thee falls the fated day,
Fearless and painless shalt thou pass away.

MORRIS, *Jason*.

84.

It happened at Athens, during a public representation of some play exhibited in honor of the Commonwealth, that an old gentleman came too late for a place suitable to his age and quality. Many of the young gentlemen who observed the difficulty and confusion he was in, made signs to him that they would accommodate him if he came where they sate. The good man bustled through the crowd accordingly; but when he came to the seats to which he was invited, the jest was to sit close, and expose him, as he stood out of countenance, to the whole audience. The frolic went round all the Athenian benches. But on those occasions there were also particular places assigned for foreigners.

When the good man skulked towards the boxes appointed for the Lacedemonians, that honest people, more virtuous than polite, rose up all to a man, and with the greatest respect received him among them. The Athenians being suddenly touched with a sense of the Spartan virtue, and their own degeneracy, gave a thunder of applause; and the old man cried out, 'The Athenians understand what is good, but the Lacedemonians practise it.'—*Spectator.*

85. *Arion and the Dolphin.*

In Periander's days there lived a minstrel of Lesbos, Arion by name, who was second to none as a player on the lute. This Arion, who spent most of his time with Periander, sailed to Italy and Sicily, and having earned by his minstrelsy great store of treasure, hired a Corinthian ship to go back to Corinth, for whom should he trust rather than the Corinthians, whom he knew so well? When the crew were out at sea, they took counsel together to throw Arion overboard, and keep his treasure. But he divined their intent, and besought them to take his money, but spare his life. But the ship-men refused, and bade him either straightway kill himself on board, so that he might be buried on shore, or leap into the sea of his own freewill. Then Arion, being in a sore strait, begged, since it must be so, that he might don his vestments, and sing one strain standing on the quarter-deck; and when he had ended his song he promised to despatch himself. The seamen consented, well pleased once more to hear the master of all singers, and made space to hear him, withdrawing into the midship; and he chanted a lively air, and then plunged overboard, all as he was. So they sailed away to Corinth, and thought no more of Arion. But, lo! a dolphin took the minstrel up on his back, and landed him safely at the promontory Tænarus in Laconia, whence he made his way to Corinth, all in his sacred robes, and told there all that had befallen him. But Periander did not believe him, and kept him under guard. At last the ship-men came, and when Periander asked them what had become of Arion, they said they had left him safe and sound at Tarentum, in Italy. Then Periander produced Arion in his vestments, just as he was when he leapt overboard, and they were struck dumb, and could deny their guilt no more. And Arion set up, as a thank-offering to the god, an effigy of a man riding on a dolphin.—HERODOTUS, *Ancient Classics for English Readers.*

86.

So, with the wind behind them, and the oars
Still hard at work, they went betwixt the shores
Against the ebb, and now full oft espied
Trim homesteads here and there on either side,
And fair kine grazing, and much woolly sheep,
And skin-clad shepherds, roused from mid-day sleep,
Gazing upon them with scared wondering eyes.
So now they deemed they might be near their prize;
And at the least knew that some town was nigh,
And thought to hear new tidings presently;
Which happed indeed, for on the turn of tide,
At ending of a long reach, they espied
A city wondrous fair, which seemed indeed
To bar the river's course; but, taking heed
And drawing nigher, soon found out the case,
That on an island builded was the place
The more part of it; but four bridges fair
Set thick with goodly houses everywhere,
Crossed two and two on each side to the land,

Whereon was built, with walls on either hand,
A towered outwork, lest that war should fall
Upon the land, and midmost of each wall
A noble gate; moreover did they note
About the wharves full many a ship and boat.
And they beheld the sunlight glistering
On arms of men and many a warlike thing,
As nigher to the city they were borne,
And heard at last some huge deep booming horn
Sound from a tower o'er the watery way,
Whose last loud note was taken up straightway
By other watchers further and more near.
MORRIS, Jason.

87. *Of Studies.*

Read not to contradict, and confute; nor to believe and take for granted; nor to find talk and discourse; but to weigh and consider. Some books are to be tasted, others to be swallowed, and some few to be chewed and digested. That is, some books are to be read only in parts; others to be read, but not curiously; and some few to be read wholly, and with diligence and attention. Some books also may be read by deputy, and extracts made of them by others. But that would be only in the less important arguments, and the meaner sort of books; else distilled books are, like common distilled waters, flashy things. Reading maketh a full man; conference, a ready man; and writing an exact man. And therefore, if a man write little, he had need have a great memory; if he confer little, he had need have a present wit; and if he reads little, he had need have much cunning, to seem to know that he doth not. Histories make men wise; poets witty; the mathematics subtle; natural philosophy deep; moral grave; logic and rhetoric able to contend.

Nay, there is no stond or impediment in the wit, but may be wrought out by fit studies; like as diseases of the body may have appropriate exercises. . . . So if a man's wit be wandering, let him study the mathematics; for in demonstrations, if his wit be called away never so little, he must begin again.—BACON, *Essays.*

88. *Samson.*

At length for intermission sake they led him
Between the pillars; he his guide requested,
(For so from such as nearer stood we heard,)
As overtired, to let him lean awhile
With both his arms on those two massy pillars
That to the arched roof gave main support.
He unsuspicious led him; which when Samson
Felt in his arms, with head awhile inclined,
And eyes fast fix't he stood, as one who pray'd,
Or some great matter in his mind resolv'd.
At last with head erect thus cri'd aloud.
  Hitherto, lords, what your commands impos'd
I have performed, as reason was, obeying,
Not without wonder or delight beheld.
Now of my own accord such other trial
I mean to show you of my strength, yet greater;
As with amaze shall strike all who behold.
This uttered, straining all his nerves he bowed;
As with the force of winds and waters pent,
When mountains tremble, those two massy pillars,
With horrible convulsion to and fro
He tugged, he shook, till down they came and drew
The whole roof after them, with burst of thunder
Upon the heads of all who sat beneath,

Lords, ladies, captains, counsellors, or priests,
Their choice nobility and flower, not only
Of this, but each Philistian city round,
Met from all parts to solemnize this feast.
Samson with these immixt inevitably
Pulled down the same destruction on himself;
The vulgar only scaped who stood without.
                    MILTON, *Samson Agonistes.*

89. *How they brought the good news from Ghent
unto Aix.*

I sprang to the stirrup, and Joris, and he;
I galloped, Dirck galloped, we galloped all three;
'Good speed!' cried the watch, as the gate-bolts undrew:
'Speed!' echoed the wall to us galloping through;
Behind shut the postern, the lights sank to rest,
And into the midnight we galloped abreast.

Not a word to each other; we kept the great pace
Neck by neck, stride by stride, never changing our place;
I turned in my saddle, and made its girths tight,
Then shortened each stirrup, and set the pique right,
Rebuckled the cheek-strap, chained slacker the bit,
Nor galloped less steadily Roland a whit.

'Twas moonset at starting; but, while we drew near
Lokeren, the cocks crew and twilight dawned clear;
At Boom, a great yellow star came out to see;
At Düffeld, 'twas morning as plain as could be;
And from Mecheln church-steeple we heard the half-chime,
So Joris broke silence with, 'Yet there is time.'

At Aerschot, up leaped of a sudden the sun,
And against him the cattle stood black every one,
To stare through the mist at us galloping past,
And I saw my stout galloper, Roland, at last,
With resolute shoulders each butting away
The haze, as some bluff river headland its spray;

And his low head and crest, just one sharp ear bent back
For my voice, and the other pricked out on his track;
And one eye's black intelligence,—ever that glance
O'er its white edge at me, his own master, askance!
And the thick heavy spume-flakes which aye and anon
His fierce lips shook upwards in galloping on.

By Hasselt, Dirck groaned; and cried Joris, 'Stay spur!
Your Roos galloped bravely, the fault's not in her,
We'll remember at Aix'—for one heard the quick wheeze
Of her chest, saw the stretched neck, and staggering knees,
And sunk tail, and horrible heave of the flank,
As down on her haunches she shuddered and sank.

So we were left galloping, Joris and I,
Past Loos and past Tongres, no cloud in the sky;
The broad sun above laughed a pitiless laugh,
'Neath our feet broke the brittle bright stubble like chaff;
Till over by Dalhem a dome-tower sprang white,
And 'Gallop,' cried Joris, 'for Aix is in sight!'

'How they'll greet us!' and all in a moment his roan
Rolled neck and croup over, lay dead as a stone;
And there was my Roland to bear the whole weight
Of the news which alone could save Aix from her fate,
With his nostrils like pits full of blood to the brim,
And with circles of red for his eye-sockets' rim.

Then I cast my loose buff-coat, each holster let fall,
Shook off both my jack-boots, let go belt and all,
Stood up in the stirrup, leaned, patted his ear,
Called my Roland his pet name, my horse without peer;
Clapped my hands, laughed and sang, any noise, bad or good,
Till at length into Aix Roland galloped and stood.

And all I remember is friends flocking round
As I sate with his head 'twixt my knees on the ground,
And no voice but was praising this Roland of mine,
As I poured down his throat our last measure of wine,
Which (the burgesses voted by common consent)
Was no more than his due who brought good news from
   Ghent.   BROWNING.

90. *Strongbow.*

Giraldus has given us a minute account of the personal appearance and the character of Strongbow. The countenance of the renowned adventurer was feminine, and his voice was thin; 'he was gentle and courteous in his manners; what he could not gain by force he gained by address; in peace he was more ready to obey than command; when not in battle was more a soldier than a general, in battle more a general than a soldier; always took his companions into counsel and undertook no enterprise without their advice; in action was the sure rallying-point of his troops; and of unshaken constancy in either fortune of war, neither to be disturbed by adversity nor to be thrown off his balance by success.' Strongbow's Irish ally, Dermot, is described by the same writer as 'tall and huge; warlike and daring, with a voice hoarse from shouting in battle; desiring to be feared rather than loved; an oppressor of the noble, a raiser up of the low; tyrannical to his own people and detested by strangers; one who had his hand against every man and every man's hand against him.' His followers, after a victory, having thrown a heap of heads at his feet, the savage clapped his hands with delight, yelled forth his thanks to God, and seizing by the hair and ears a head which he recognised as that of a hated enemy, he tore off part of the nose and lips with his teeth. Without insisting on the details of the two portraits, we have no difficulty in recognising the first as typical of a conquering race, the second as typical of a race destined to be conquered.—GOLDWIN SMITH, *Irish History and Irish Character.*

91. *Œnone.*

O mother Ida, many-fountained Ida,
Dear mother Ida, harken ere I die.
I waited underneath the dawning hills,
Aloft the mountain lawn was dewy-dark,
And dewy-dark aloft the mountain pine;
Beautiful Paris, evil-hearted Paris,
Leading a jet-black goat white-horned, white-hooved,
Came up from reedy Simois all alone.

O mother Ida, harken ere I die.
Far off the torrent called me from the cleft:
Far up the solitary morning smote
The streaks of virgin snow. With down-dropt eyes
I sat alone; white-breasted like a star
Fronting the dawn he moved; a leopard skin
Drooped from his shoulder, but his sunny hair
Clustered about his temples like a God's;
And his cheek brightened as the foam-bow brightens
When the wind blows the foam, and all my heart
Went forth to embrace him coming ere he came.

EXTRACTS. 175

O mother, hear me yet before I die.
They came, they cut away my tallest pines,
My dark tall pines, that plumed the craggy ledge
High over the blue gorge, and all between
The snowy peak and snow-white cataract
Fostered the callow eaglet—from beneath
Whose thick mysterious boughs in the dark morn
The panther's roar came muffled, while I sat
Low in the valley. Never, never more
Shall low Œnone see the morning mist
Sweep thro' them; never see them overlaid
With narrow moonlit slips of silver cloud,
Between the loud stream and the trembling stars.

TENNYSON.

92.

The Mediterranean Sea with its various branches, penetrating far into the great Continent, forms the largest gulf of the ocean, and, alternately narrowed by islands or projections of the land, and expanding to a considerable breadth, at once separates and connects the three divisions of the Old World. The shores of this inland sea were in ancient times peopled by various nations, belonging in an ethnographical and philological point of view to different races, but constituting in their historical aspect one whole. This historic whole has been usually, but not very appropriately, entitled the history of the ancient world. It is in reality the history of civilization among the Mediterranean nations; and as it passes before us in its successive stages, it presents four great phases of development, the history of the Coptic or Egyptian stock dwelling on the southern shore, the history of the Aramæan or Syrian nation, which occupied the east coast and extended into the interior of Asia as far as the Euphrates and Tigris, and the histories of the twin peoples, the Hellenes and Italians, who received as their heritage the countries bordering on its European shores. Each of these histories was in its earlier stages connected with other regions and with other cycles of historical evolution, but each soon entered on its own peculiar career. The surrounding nations of alien or even of kindred extraction, the Berbers, and Negroes of Africa, the Arabs, Persians, and Indians of Asia, the Celts and Germans of Europe, came into manifold contact with the peoples inhabiting the borders of the Mediterranean, but they neither imparted unto them nor received from them any influences of really decisive effect upon their respective destinies.—MOMMSEN, *History of Rome.*

93. *Mercy.*

The quality of mercy is not strained,
It droppeth as the gentle rain from heaven
Upon the place beneath; it is twice blest;
It blesseth him that gives, and him that takes:
'Tis mightiest in the mightiest; it becomes
The throned monarch better than his crown;
His sceptre shows the force of temporal power,
The attribute to awe and majesty,
Wherein doth sit the dread and fear of kings;
But mercy is above the sceptred sway;
It is enthroned in the hearts of kings,
It is an attribute to God himself;
And earthly power doth then show likest God's
When mercy seasons justice. Therefore, Jew,
Though justice be thy plea, consider this,
That, in the course of justice, none of us
Should see salvation; we do pray for mercy;

And that same prayer doth teach us all to render
The deeds of mercy. I have spoke thus much
To mitigate the justice of thy plea;
Which if thou follow, this strict court of Venice
Must needs give sentence 'gainst the merchant here.
                    SHAKESPEARE, *Merchant of Venice.*

94. *Friedrich Wilhelm I, King of Prussia.*

He was not tall of stature, this arbitrary King: a florid-complexioned stout-built man; of serious, sincere, authoritative face. Man of short firm stature; stands at his ease, and yet like a tower. Most solid; eyes steadfastly awake; cheeks slightly compressed, too, which fling the mouth rather forward. . . . Face, figure and bearing, all in him is expressive of robust insight, and direct determination; of healthy energy and authority, a certain air of royalty reduced to its simplest form. The face, in pictures, is not beautiful or agreeable; yet it may have been originally handsome. High enough arched brow, rather copious cheeks and jaws; nose smallish, inclining to be stumpy: large gray eyes, bright with steady fire and life; often enough gloomy and severe, but capable of jolly laughter too. Eyes naturally with a kind of laugh in them, which laugh can blaze out into fearful thunderous rage, if you give him provocation. Especially if you lie to him; for that he hates above all things. . . . For the rest, a handsome man of his inches; conspicuously well-built in limbs and body, and delicately finished off to the very extremities. His feet and legs were very fine. The hands, if he would have taken care of them, were beautifully white; fingers long and thin: a hand at once nimble to grasp, delicate to feel, and strong to clutch and hold; what may be called a beautiful hand, because it is the usefullest.—
CARLYLE, *History of Frederick the Great.*

95.

As when a falcon bird of swiftest flight,
From some high mountain-top, on tim'rous dove
Swoops fiercely down; she, from beneath, in fear,
Evades the stroke: he, dashing through the brake,
Shrill-shrieking, pounces on his destin'd prey;
So, wing'd with desp'rate hate, Achilles flew,
So Hector, flying from his keen pursuit,
Beneath the walls his active sinews plied.
They by the watch-tow'r, and beneath the wall
Where stood the wind-beat fig-tree, rac'd amain
Along the public road, until they reach'd
The fairly-flowing fount whence issued forth,
From double source, Scamander's eddying streams.

LORD DERBY, *Homer*.

96. *Queen Mary.*

Queen Mary, the daughter of Henry VIII and of his queen Catharine, daughter of Ferdinand the Catholic, king of Aragon, is a princess of great worth. In her youth she was rendered unhappy by the events of her mother's divorce; by the ignominy and threats to which she was exposed after the change of religion in England, she being unwilling to bend to the new one'; and by the dangers to which she was exposed by the Duke of Northumberland, and the riots among the people when she ascended the throne. She is of short stature, well made, thin and delicate, and moderately pretty; her eyes are so lively that she inspires reverence and respect, and even fear, wherever she turns them; nevertheless, she is very short-sighted. Her voice is deep, almost like that of a man. She understands five languages, English, Latin, French, Spanish, and Italian, in which last, however, she does not venture to discourse. She is also much skilled in ladies' work, such as producing all sorts of embroidery with the needle. She has a knowledge of music, chiefly on the lute, on which she plays exceedingly well. As to the qualities of her mind, it may be said of her that she is rash, disdainful, and parsimonious rather than liberal. She is endowed with great humility and patience, but withal high-spirited, courageous, and resolute, having during the whole course of her adversity been guiltless of any the least approach to meanness of comportment; she is, moreover, devout and staunch in the defence of her religion. . . . The cabals she has been exposed to, the evil disposition of the people towards her, the present poverty and the debt of the crown, and her passion for King Philip, from whom she is doomed to live separate, are so many other causes of the grief by which she is overwhelmed. She is, moreover, a prey to the hatred which she bears to my Lady Elizabeth, and which has its source in the recollection of the wrongs she experienced on account of her mother, and in the fact that all eyes and hearts are turned towards my Lady Elizabeth as successor to the throne.—MICHELE.

97.

There rac'd they, one in flight, and one pursuing;
Good he who fled, but better who pursu'd,
With fiery speed; for on that race was stak'd
No common victim, no ignoble ox:
The prize at stake was mighty Hector's life.

Meanwhile on Hector, with untiring hate,
The swift Achilles press'd; as when a hound,
Through glen and tangled brake, pursues a fawn,
Roused from its lair upon the mountain side;

And if awhile it should evade pursuit,
Low crouching in the copse, yet quests he back,
Searching unwearied, till he find the trace;
So Hector sought to baffle, but in vain,
The keen pursuit of Peleus' active son.
Oft as he sought the shelter of the gates
Beneath the well-built tow'rs, if haply thence
His comrades' weapons might some aid afford;
So oft his foeman, with superior speed,
Would cut him off, and turn him to the plain.
He tow'rd the city still essay'd his flight;
And as in dreams, when one pursues in vain,
One seeks in vain to fly, the other seeks
As vainly to pursue; so could not now
Achilles reach, nor Hector quit, his foe.

LORD DERBY, *Homer*.

98. *Edward I.*

His head spherical, his eyes round, and gentle and dove-like when he was pleased, but fierce as a lion's and sparkling with fire when he was disturbed; his hair black and crisp; his nose prominent and rather raised in the middle. His chest was broad; his arms were agile; his thighs long; his feet arched; his body was firm and fleshy, but not fat. He was so strong and active that with his hand he could leap into his saddle. Passionately fond of hunting, whenever he was not engaged in war, he amused his leisure with his dogs and falcons. He was rarely unwell, and did not lose either his teeth or sight by age. Temperate by habit, he never devoted himself to the luxuries of his palace. He never wore his crown after the day of his coronation, thinking it rather a burden than an honor. He declined the royal garments of purple and went about in the plain and common dress of a plebeian. Being once asked why he did not wear richer apparel, he answered with the consciousness of true greatness, that it was absurd to suppose that he could be more estimable in fine than in simple clothing. No man was more acute in counsel, more fervid in eloquence, more self-possessed in danger, more cautious in prosperity, more firm in adversity. Those whom he once loved he scarcely ever forsook; but he rarely admitted into his favour any that had excited his dislike. His liberalities were magnificent. He was considerably above the average height, and very majestic in his bearing.—JOHN OF LONDON, *Commemoratio*.

99.

For Arthur when none knew from whence he came,
Long ere the people chose him for their king,
Roving the trackless realms of Lyonnesse,
Had found a glen, gray boulder and black tarn.
A horror lived about the tarn, and clave
Like its own mists to all the mountain side:
For here two brothers, one a king, had met
And fought together; but their names were lost.
And each had slain his brother at a blow,
And down they fell and made the glen abhorr'd:
And there they lay till all their bones were bleach'd,
And lichen'd into colour with the crags:
And he, that once was king, had on a crown
Of diamonds, one in front, and four aside.
And Arthur came, and labouring up the pass
All in a misty moonshine, unawares
Had trodden that crown'd skeleton, and the skull
Brake from the nape, and from the skull the crown
Roll'd into light, and turning on its rims
Fled like a glittering rivulet to the tarn:

And down the shingly scaur he plunged and caught,
And set it on his head, and in his heart
Heard murmurs 'lo, thou likewise shalt be king.'
TENNYSON, *Elaine*.

100. *On Plantations.*

Planting of countries is like planting of woods; for you must make account to lose almost twenty years profit, and expect your recompence in the end. For the principal thing, that hath been the destruction of most plantations, hath been the base and hasty drawing of profit in the first years. It is true, speedy profit is not to be neglected as far as may stand, with the good of the plantation, but no further. It is a shameful and unblessed thing to take the scum of people, and wicked condemned men, to be the people with whom you plant; and not only so, but it spoileth the plantation. For they will ever live like rogues, and not fall to work, but be lazy and do mischief and spend victuals and be quickly weary, and then certify over to their country to the discredit of the plantation. The people wherewith you plant ought to be gardeners, ploughmen, labourers, smiths, carpenters, joiners, fishermen, fowlers, with some few apothecaries, surgeons, cooks, and bakers. In a country of plantation first look about what kind of victual the country yields of itself to hand; as chestnuts, walnuts, pineapples, olives, dates, plums, cherries, wild honey, and the like; and make use of them. Then consider what victual or esculent things there are which grow speedily and within the year; as parsnips, carrots, turnips, onions, radish, artichokes of Jerusalem, maize, and the like. For wheat, barley, and oats, they ask too much labour; but with pease and beans you may begin, both because they ask less labour, and because they serve for meat, as well as for bread. And of rice likewise cometh a great increase, and it is a kind of meat. Above all, there ought to be brought store of biscuit, oatmeal, flour, meal, and the like, in the beginning till bread may be had. For beasts or birds take chiefly such as are least subject to diseases, and multiply fastest; as swine, goats, cocks, hens, turkeys, geese, house-doves, and the like. The victual in plantations ought to be expended almost as in a besieged town, that is, with certain allowance.... Consider likewise what commodities the soil where the plantation is doth naturally yield, that they may some way help to defray the charge of the plantation; so it be not, as was said, to the untimely prejudice of the main business, as it hath fared with tobacco in Virginia. Wood commonly aboundeth but too much; and therefore timber is fit to be one. If there be iron ore, and streams whereupon to set the mills, iron is a brave commodity where wood aboundeth. Making of bay salt, if the climate be proper for it, would be put in experience. Growing silk likewise, if any be, is a likely commodity. Pitch and tar, where store of firs and pines are, will not fail. So drugs and sweet woods, where they are, cannot but yield great profit. But moil not too much under ground; for the hope of mines is very uncertain, and useth to make the planters lazy in other things.—BACON, *Essays*.

101.

A. The virtues of sovereigns are such as tend to the maintenance of peace at home, and to the resistance of foreign enemies. Fortitude is a royal virtue; and though it be necessary in such private men as shall be soldiers, yet, for other men, the less they dare, the better it is both for the commonwealth and for themselves. Frugality (though perhaps you will think it strange) is also a royal virtue; for it increases the public stock, which cannot be too great for the public use, nor any man too sparing of what he has in trust for the good of others. Liberality also is a royal virtue; for the commonwealth cannot be well served without extraordinary diligence and service of ministers, and great fidelity to their Sovereign; who ought therefore to be encouraged, and especially those that do him service in the wars. In sum, all actions and habits are to be esteemed good or evil by their causes and usefulness in reference to the commonwealth, and not by their mediocrity, nor by their being commended. For several men praise several customs, and that which is virtue with one, is blamed by others; and, contrarily, what one calls vice, another calls virtue, as their present affections lead them.

B. Methinks you should have placed among the virtues that, which, in my opinion, is the greatest of all virtues, religion.

A. So I have, though, it seems, you did not observe it.—HOBBES.

102.

O kind hosts and dear,
Hearken a little unto such a tale
As folk with us will tell in every vale
About the yule-tide fire, when the snow
Deep in the passes, letteth men to go
From place to place: now there few great folk be,
Although we upland men have memory
Of ills kings did us; yet as now indeed
Few have much wealth, few are in utter need.
Like the wise ants a kingless, happy folk
We long have been, not galled by any yoke,

But the white leaguer of the winter tide
Whereby all men at home are bound to bide.
Alas, my folly! how I talk of it,
As though from this place where to-day we sit
The way thereto was short—Ah, would to God
Upon the snow-freed herbage now I trod!
     Morris, *Earthly Paradise*.

103.

The sources of the noblest rivers which spread fertility over continents, and bear richly laden fleets to the sea, are to be sought in wild and barren mountain tracts, incorrectly laid down in maps, and rarely explored by travellers. To such a tract the history of our country during the thirteenth century may not unaptly be compared. Sterile and obscure as is that portion of our annals, it is there that we must seek for the origin of our freedom, our prosperity, and our glory. Then it was that the great English people was formed, that the national character began to exhibit those peculiarities which it has ever since retained, and that our fathers became emphatically islanders, islanders not merely in geographical position, but in their politics, their feelings, and their manners. Then first appeared with distinctness that constitution which has ever since, through all changes, preserved its identity; that constitution of which all the other free constitutions in the world are copies, and which, in spite of some defects, deserves to be regarded as the best under which any great society has ever yet existed during many ages. . . . Then it was that the courage of those sailors who manned the rude barks of the Cinque Ports first made the flag of England terrible on the seas. Then it was that the most ancient colleges which still exist at both the great national seats of learning were founded. Then was formed that language, less musical indeed than the languages of the south, but in force, in richness, in aptitude for all the highest purposes of the poet, the philosopher, and the orator, inferior to the tongue of Greece alone. Then too appeared the first faint dawn of that noble literature, the most splendid and the most durable of the many glories of England.— MACAULAY, *History of England.*

104. *Queen Elizabeth.*

But for a tablet or picture of smaller volume (not presuming to speak of your majesty that liveth), in my judgement the most excellent is that of Queen Elizabeth, your immediate predecessor in this part of Britain; a prince that, if Plutarch were now alive to write lives by parallels, would trouble him I think to find for her a parallel amongst women. This lady was endued with learning in her sex singular, and rare even amongst masculine princes; whether we speak of learning, of language, or of science, modern or ancient, divinity or humanity; and unto the very last year of her life she accustomed to appoint set hours for reading, scarcely any young student in an university more daily or more duly. As for her government, I assure myself, I shall not exceed, if I do affirm that this part of the island never had forty-five years of better times; and yet not through the calmness of the season, but through the wisdom of her regiment. For if there be considered of the one side, the truth of religion established, the constant peace and security, the good administration of justice, the temperate use of the prerogative, not slackened, nor much strained, the flourishing state of learning, sortable to so excellent a patroness, the convenient state of wealth and means, both of crown and subject, the habit of obedience, and the moderation of discontents; and there be considered on the other side the differences of religion, the troubles of neighbour countries, the ambition of Spain, and opposition of Rome; and then that she was solitary and of herself: these things, I say, considered, as I could not have chosen an instance so recent and so proper, so I suppose I could not have chosen one more remarkable or eminent to the purpose now in hand, which is concerning the conjunction of learning in the prince with felicity in the people.—BACON, *Advancement of Learning.*

105. *Pride.*

But pride begets the mood
Of wanton, tyrant power;
Pride filled with many thoughts, yet filled in vain,
Untimely, ill-advised,
Scaling the topmost height,
Falls to the abyss of woe,
Where step that profiteth
It seeks in vain to take.
I ask our God to stay
The labours never more
That work our country's good;
I will not cease to call on God for aid.
PLUMPTRE, *Œdipus the King.*

106.

If we consider our own country in its natural prospect, without any of the benefits and advantages of commerce, what a barren uncomfortable spot of earth falls to our share! Natural historians tell us, that no fruit grows originally among us, besides hips and haws, acorns and pignuts, with other delicates of the like nature; that our climate of itself, and without the assistances of art, can make no further advances towards a plum than to a sloe, and carries an apple to no greater perfection than a crab: that our melons, our peaches, our figs, our apricots, and cherries, are strangers among us, imported in different ages, and naturalized in our English gardens; and that they would all degenerate and fall away into the trash of our own country, if they were wholly neglected by the planter, and left to the mercy of our sun and soil. Nor has traffick more enriched our vegetable world, than it has improved the whole face of nature among us. Our ships are laden with the harvest of every climate; our tables are stored with spices and oils and wines; our rooms are filled with pyramids of China, and adorned with the workmanship of Japan; our morning's draught comes to us from the remotest corners of the earth. We repair our bodies by the drugs of America, and repose ourselves under Indian canopies. . . . Nature indeed furnishes us with the bare necessaries of life, but traffick gives us greater variety of what is useful, and at the same time supplies us with everything that is convenient and ornamental. Nor is it the least part of this our happiness, that whilst we enjoy the remotest products of the north and south, we are free from those extremities of weather which give them birth; that our eyes are refreshed with the green fields of Britain, at the same time that our palates are feasted with fruits that rise between the tropics.—*Spectator*.

107. *Wolsey.*

So farewell to the little good you bear me.
Farewell! a long farewell, to all my greatness!
This is the state of man; to-day he puts forth
The tender leaves of hopes; to-morrow blossoms,

And bears his blushing honours thick upon him;
The third day comes a frost, a killing frost,
And, when he thinks, good easy man, full surely
His greatness is a-ripening, nips his root,
And then he falls, as I do. I have ventured,
Like little wanton boys that swim on bladders,
This many summers in a sea of glory,
But far beyond my depth; my high-blown pride
At length broke under me and now has left me,
Weary and old with service, to the mercy
Of a rude stream, that must for ever hide me.
Vain pomp and glory of this world, I hate ye;
I feel my heart new open'd. O, how wretched
Is that poor man that hangs on princes' favours!
There is, betwixt that smile we would aspire to,
That sweet aspect of princes, and their ruin,
More pangs and fears than wars or women have;
And when he falls, he falls like Lucifer,
Never to hope again.
                    SHAKESPEARE, *Henry VIII*.

108.

She then an axe of huge dimensions gave,
  On both sides bladed, steel of temper fine,
Into the strong clasp of Odysseus brave,
  Beautiful, helved with olive, work divine,
  And well-curved hatchet, whose metallic shine
Lightened afar. Anon the way she led
  To the isle's margin, where the soaring pine,
    Alder, and poplar black, were thickly spread,
Fitted to float with ease,—sapless long since and dead.

So having shown him where the wood grew tall
Calypso, nymph divine, returning went
Homeward. But he the forest-trees made fall,
Eager to reap his work's accomplishment.
Nor did his vigour from the task relent
Till twenty he had felled, and each with care
Meted and planed. Then nymph Calypso lent
Augers, and he the pierced planks fitted fair
And with firm bolts and joints the good ship did prepare.

As is the wide-walled compass which a man
Makes for a merchant-craft which he doth build,
Such for his broad bark did Odysseus plan,
And set the upright ribs, and sockets drilled
For thwart deck-timbers, and the space unfilled
With horizontal planks did overlay,
And planted the tall mast with art well skilled,
And to its place the sail-yard did convey,
And shaped the rudder well to rule her onward way.

Also an osier bulwark woven deep
To breast the dashings of the angry tide,
That he securely through the waves might sweep,
He wrought; and ballast for the ship supplied.
Divine Calypso linen did provide
For sails, which he contriving not in vain
Well fashioned, and each rope and cable tied,
Bound down the strong sheets, fit for every strain,
And launched the ship with levers on the noble main.

'Twas the fourth day, and all his task was o'er.
Him on the fifth Calypso, nymph divine,
Robed in sweet raiment, culled from her own store,
And bathed, and to his good bark did consign.

Two skins, one filled with water, one with wine,
She gave him, and a wallet stored with meat,
And in his wake along the rippling brine
Breathed a warm wind, exceeding soft and sweet,
Which with spread sails Odysseus did right gladly greet.
                                WORSLEY, *Odyssey*.

109. *Frozen Words.*

We were separated by a storm in the latitude of 73, insomuch that only the ship which I was in, with a Dutch and a French vessel, got safe into a creek of Nova Zembla. We landed in order to refit our vessels, and store ourselves with provisions. The crew of each vessel made themselves a cabin of turf and wood, at some distance from each other, to fence themselves against the inclemencies of the weather, which was severe beyond imagination. We soon observed, that in talking to one another we lost several of our words, and could not hear one another at above two yards distance, and that too when we sat very near the fire. After much perplexity, I found that our words froze in the air before they could reach the ears of the person to whom they were spoken. I was soon confirmed in this conjecture, when, upon the increase of the cold, the whole company grew dumb, or rather deaf; for every man was sensible, as we afterwards found, that he spoke as well as ever; but the sounds no sooner took air, than they were condensed and lost. It was now a miserable spectacle to see us nodding and gaping at one another, every man talking, and no man heard. One might observe a seaman, that could hail a ship at a league distance, beckoning with his hands, straining with his lungs, and tearing his throat, but all in vain. We continued here three weeks in this dismal plight. At length, upon a turn of wind, the air about us began to thaw. Our cabin was immediately filled with a dry clattering sound, which I afterwards found to be the crackling of consonants that broke above our heads, and were often mixed with a gentle hissing which I imputed to the letter S, that occurs so frequently in the English tongue. I soon after felt a breeze of whispers rushing by my ear; for those being of a soft and gentle substance, immediately liquefied in the warm wind that blew across our cabin. These were soon followed by syllables and short words, and at length by entire sentences, that melted sooner or later, as they were more or less congealed; so that we now heard everything that had been spoken during the whole three weeks that we had been silent, if I may use that expression. . . . When this confusion of voices was pretty well over, though I was afraid to offer at speaking, as fearing I should not be heard, I proposed a visit to the Dutch cabin which lay about a mile farther up into the country. At about half a mile's distance from our cabin, we heard the groanings of a bear, which at first startled us: but upon enquiry we were informed by some of our company that he was dead, and now lay in salt, having been killed upon that very spot about a fortnight before, in the time of the frost. Not far from the same place we were likewise entertained with some posthumous snarls and barkings of a fox. We at length arrived at the little Dutch settlement, and upon entering the room, found it filled with sighs that smelt of brandy, and several other unsavoury sounds that were altogether inarticulate. My valet, who was an Irishman, fell into so great a rage at what he heard, that he drew his sword; but not knowing where to lay the blame, he put it up again. We were stunned with these confused noises, but did not hear a single word till about half an hour after; which I ascribed to the harsh and obdurate sounds of that language, which wanted more time than ours to melt and become audible. After having here met with a very hearty welcome, we went to the French cabin, who, to make amends for their three weeks' silence, were talking and disputing with greater rapidity and confusion than ever I heard in an assembly even of that nation. Their language, as I found, upon the first giving of the weather, fell asunder and dissolved.—ADDISON.

110. *The Battle of Senlac.*

All this was bravely and cleverly done; but it could not recover the battle, now that King Harold's wise orders had once been disobeyed. The English line was now broken; the hill was defenceless at many points; so the Normans could now ride up, and the battle was now fought on the hill. The fight was by no means over yet; the English had lost their great advantage of the ground; but King Harold and all his mighty men were still there; so they still formed their shield-wall and fought with their great axes. . . . The English seem to have gradually lost their close array, so that the battle changed into a series of single combats; here one or two Frenchmen cutting down an Englishman, here one or two Englishmen cutting down a Frenchman. Very valiant deeds of this sort were done by many men in both armies. They had now been fighting ever since nine in the morning, and twilight was now coming on. Luck had no doubt now turned against the English; still they were by no means beaten yet, and it is by no means clear that they would have been beaten after all, if King Harold had only lived till night-fall. Here, as always in these times, everything depended on one man. Harold still lived and fought by his Standard, and it was against that point that all the efforts and all the devices of the Normans were now aimed. The Norman archers had begun the fight and the Norman archers were now to end it. Duke William now bade them shoot up in the air that the arrows might fall like bolts from heaven. This device proved the most successful of all; some men were pierced right through their helmets; others had their eyes put out; others lifted up their shields to guard their heads, and so could not wield their axes so well as before. King Harold still stood close by the Golden Dragon, with his axe in his hand, and his shield pierced with several arrows. But now the hour of our great King was come. Every foe who had come near him had felt the might of that terrible axe, but his axe could not guard him against this awful shower of arrows. One shaft, falling, as I said, from heaven, pierced his right eye; he clutched at it and broke off the shaft; his axe dropped from his hand, and he fell, all disabled by pain, in his own place as King between the two royal ensigns. Twenty Norman knights now swore to take the Standard, now that the King no longer defended it; they rushed on; most of them were killed by the English who still fought around their wounded King; but those who escaped succeeded in beating down the Standard of the Fighting Man and in bearing off the Golden Dragon. That ancient ensign, which had shone over so many battle-fields, was never again carried before a true English King. Then four knights, one of whom was Count Eustace, rushed upon King Harold as he lay dying; they killed him with several wounds, and mangled his body. Such was the end of the last native King of the English, Harold the son of Godwine. He fell by the most glorious of deaths, fighting for the land and the people which he had loved so well.—FREEMAN, *Old English History for Children.*

111. *The Coming of Guinevere.*

Yea, but I know: the land was full of signs
And wonders ere the coming of the Queen.
So said my father, and himself was knight
Of the great Table—at the founding of it;
And rode thereto from Lyonnesse, and he said
That as he rode, an hour or maybe twain
After the sunset, down the coast, he heard
Strange music, and he paused and turning—there
All down the lonely coast of Lyonnesse,
Each with a beacon-star upon his head,
And with a wild sea-light about his feet,
He saw them—headland after headland flame
Far on into the rich heart of the west:
And in the light the white mermaiden swam,
And strong man-breasted things stood from the sea,
And sent a deep sea-voice thro' all the land,
To which the little elves of chasm and cleft
Made answer, sounding like a distant horn.
So said my father—yea, and furthermore,
Next morning, while he past the dim-lit woods,
Himself beheld three spirits mad with joy
Come dashing down on a tall wayside flower,
That shook beneath them, as the thistle shakes
When three gray linnets wrangle for the seed:
And still at evenings on before his horse
The flickering fairy-circle wheel'd and broke
Flying, and link'd again, and wheel'd and broke
Flying, for all the land was full of life.
And when at last he came to Camelot,
A wreath of airy dancers hand-in-hand
Swung round the lighted lantern of the hall;

And in the hall itself was such a feast
As never man had dream'd; for every knight
Had whatsoever meat he long'd for served
By hands unseen; and even as he said
Down in the cellars merry bloated things
Shoulder'd the spigot, straddling on the butts
While the wine ran; so glad were spirits and men
Before the coming of the sinful Queen.
TENNYSON.

112. *Achilles.*

The character of Achilles differs from that of all other heroes of poetry and romance in these respects: it is more intense; it is more colossal in scale; it ranges over a wider compass, from the borders of savagery to the most tender emotions and the most delicate refinements. Yet all its parts are so accurately graduated, and so nicely interwoven, that the whole tissue is perfectly consistent with itself. The self-government of such a character is indeed very partial. But any degree of self-government is a wonder, when we consider over what volcanic forces it is exercised. It is a constantly recurring effort at rule over a constantly recurring rebellion; and there is a noble contrast between the strain put upon his strength, in order to suppress his own passion, and the masterful ease with which he prostrates all his enemies in the field. The command, always in danger, is never wholly lost. It is commonly re-established by a supreme and desperate struggle; and sometimes, as in the first Assembly after the intervention of Athenê, we see the tide of passion flowing to a point at which it resembles a horse that has gained its utmost speed, yet remains under the full control of its rider. Ferocity is an element in his character, but is not its base. It is always grounded in, and springing from some deeper sentiment, of which it is the manifestation. His ferocity towards the Greeks grows out of the intensity of his indignation at the foul wrong done, with every heightening circumstance of outward insult, not merely to him, but in his person to every principle of honour, right, and justice, in the manner of Briseis; as well as to the real attachment he felt for her. His ferocity towards Hector is the counterpart and recoil of the intensity of his passionate love for the dead Patroclos. Magnitude, grandeur, majesty, form the framework on which Homer has projected the character of Achilles. And these are in their truest forms; those forms which contract to touch the smaller, as they expand to grasp the greater things. The scope of this character is like the sweep of an organ over the whole gamut, from the lowest bass to the highest treble, with all its diversities of tone and force as well as pitch. From the fury of the first Assembly, he calms down to receive with courtesy the pursuivants who demand Briseis. From the gentle pleasure of the lyre, he kindles into the stern excitement of the magnificent Debate of the Ninth Book. From his terrible vengeance against the torn limbs of Hector he melts into tears, at the view and the discourse of Priam. The sea, that home of marvels, presents no wider, no grander contrasts, nor offers us an image more perfect according to its kind in each of its varying moods. Foils, too, are employed with skill to exalt the hero. The half-animated bulk and strength of Ajax (who was also greatly beautiful) exhibit to us the mere clay of Achilles, without the vivifying fire. The beauty of Nireus, wedded to effeminacy, sets off the transcendant, and yet manful and heroic, beauty of Achilles; and the very ornaments of gold, which in Nastes the Carian only suggest Asiatic luxury and relaxation, when they are borne on the person of the great

Achaian hero, seem but a new form of tribute to his glorious manhood.—GLADSTONE, *Juventus Mundi*.

113. *Hannibal.*

Then Hannibal called his soldiers together, and told them openly that he was going to lead them into Italy. 'The Romans,' said he, 'have demanded that I and my principal officers should be delivered up to them as malefactors. Soldiers, will you suffer such an indignity? The Gauls are holding out their arms to us, inviting us to come to them, and to assist them in revenging their manifold injuries. And the country which we shall invade, so rich in corn and wine and oil, so full of flocks and herds, so covered with flourishing cities, will be the richest prize that could be offered by the gods to reward your valour.' One common shout from the soldiers assured him of their readiness to follow him. He thanked them, fixed the day on which they were to be ready to march, and then dismissed them.—DR. ARNOLD, *History of Rome*.

114.

And here the fulness of his mind, and his strong sense of being the devoted instrument of his country's gods to destroy their enemies, haunted him by night as they possessed him by day. In his sleep, so he told Silenus, he fancied that the supreme god of his fathers had called him into the presence of all the gods of Carthage, who were sitting on their thrones in council. There he received a solemn charge to invade Italy; and one of the heavenly council went with him and with his army, to guide him on his way. He went on, and his divine guide commanded him, 'See that thou look not behind thee.' But after a while, impatient of the restraint, he turned to look back; and there he beheld a huge and monstrous form, thick set all over with serpents; wherever it moved, orchards and woods and houses fell crashing before it. He asked his guide in wonder, what that monster form was? The god answered, 'Thou seest the desolation of Italy; go on thy way, straight forwards, and cast no look behind.' Thus, with no divided heart, and with an entire resignation of all personal and domestic enjoyments for ever, Hannibal went forth, at the age of twenty-seven, to do the work of his country's gods, and to redeem his early vow.—DR. ARNOLD, *History of Rome.*

115.

    They, lifting in their arms the corpse,
Upraised it high in air; then from behind
Loud yelled the Trojans, as they saw the Greeks
Retiring with their dead; and on they rushed,
As dogs that in advance of hunter youths
Pursue a wounded boar: awhile they run,
Eager for blood; but when, in pride of strength,
He turns upon them, backward they recoil,
This way and that in fear of death dispersed:
So onward pressed awhile the Trojan crowd,
With thrust of swords, and double-pointed spears.
But ever as the Ajaces turned to bay,
Their colour changed to pale, not one so bold
As, dashing on, to battle for the corpse.
Thus, they with anxious care, from off the field
Bore towards the ships their dead; but on their track
Came sweeping on the storm of battle, fierce,
As, on a sudden breaking forth, the fire
Seizes some populous city, and devours

House after house amid the glare and blaze,
While roar the flames before the gusty wind;
So fiercely pressed upon the Greeks' retreat
The clattering tramp of steeds and armèd men.
But as the mules, with stubborn strength endued,
That down the mountain through the trackless waste
Drag some huge log, or timber for the ships,
And spent with toil and sweat, still labour on
Unflinching; so the Greeks with patient toil
Bore on their dead; the Ajaces in their rear
Stemming the war, as stems the torrent's force
Some wooded cliff, far stretching o'er the plain;
Checking the mighty river's rushing stream,
And flinging it aside upon the plain,
Itself unbroken by the strength of flood:
So firmly, in the rear, the Ajaces stemmed
The Trojan force; yet these still onward pressed,
And 'mid their comrades proudly eminent,
Two chiefs, Æneas, old Anchises' son,
And glorious Hector, in the van were seen.
Then, as a cloud of starlings or of daws
Fly screaming, as they see the hawk approach,
To lesser birds the messenger of death;
So before Hector and Æneas fled,
Screaming, forgetful of their warlike fame,
The sons of Greece; and scattered here and there
Around the ditch lay store of goodly arms,
By Greeks abandoned in their hasty flight.

Lord Derby, *Homer*.

116.

He that goeth about to persuade a multitude, that they are not so well governed as they ought to be, shall never want attentive and favourable hearers; because they know the manifold defects whereunto every kind of regiment is subject; but the secret lets and difficulties, which in public proceedings are innumerable and inevitable, they have not ordinarily the judgment to consider. And because such as openly reprove supposed disorders of state are taken for principal friends to the common benefit of all, and for men that carry singular freedom of mind; under this fair and plausible colour whatsoever they utter passeth for good and current. That which wanteth in the weight of their speech, is supplied by the aptness of men's minds to accept and believe it. Whereas on the other side, if we maintain things that are established, we have not only to strive with a number of heavy prejudices deeply rooted in the hearts of men, who think that herein we serve the time, and speak in favour of the present state, because thereby we either hold or seek preferment; but also to bear such exceptions as minds so averted beforehand usually take against that which they are loth should be poured into them.—HOOKER, *Ecclesiastical Polity*.

117. *Hannibal's Passage of the Rhone.*

Here Hannibal obtained from the natives on the right bank, by paying a fixed price, all their boats and vessels of every description with which they were accustomed to traffic down the river; they allowed him also to cut timber for the construction of others; and thus in two days he was provided with the means of transporting his army. But finding that the Gauls were assembled on the eastern bank to oppose his passage, he sent off a detachment of his army by night with native guides, to ascend the right bank, for about two and twenty miles, and there to cross as they could, where there was no enemy to stop them. The woods which then lined the river, supplied this detachment with the means of constructing barks and rafts enough for the passage; they took advantage of one of the many islands in this part of the Rhone, to cross where the stream was divided; and thus they all reached the left bank in safety. There they took up a strong position, probably one of those strange masses of rock which rise here and there with steep cliffy sides like islands out of the vast plain, and rested for four and twenty hours after their exertions in the march and the passage of the river. Hannibal allowed eight and forty hours to pass from the time when the detachment left his camp; and then, on the morning of the fifth day after his arrival on the Rhone, he made his preparations for the passage of his main army. The mighty stream of the river, fed by the snows of the high Alps, is swelled rather than diminished by the heats of summer; so that, although the season was that when the southern rivers are generally at their lowest, it was rolling the vast mass of its waters along with a startling fulness and rapidity. The heaviest vessels were therefore placed on the left, highest up the stream, to form something of a breakwater for the smaller craft crossing below; the small boats held the flower of the light armed foot, while the cavalry were in the larger vessels; most of the horses being towed astern swimming, and a single soldier holding three or four together by their bridles. Everything was ready, and the Gauls on the opposite side had poured out of their camp, and lined the bank in scattered groups at the most accessible points, thinking that their task of stopping the enemy's landing would be easily

accomplished. At length Hannibal's eye observed a column of smoke rising on the farther shore, above or on the right of the barbarians. This was the concerted signal which assured him of the arrival of his detachment; and he instantly ordered his men to embark, and to push across with all possible speed. They pulled vigorously against the rapid stream, cheering each other to the work; while behind them were their friends, cheering them also from the bank: and before them were the Gauls singing their war songs, and calling them to come on with tones and gestures of defiance. But on a sudden a mass of fire was seen on the rear of the barbarians; the Gauls on the bank looked behind, and began to turn away from the river; and presently the bright arms and white linen coats of the African and Spanish soldiers appeared above the bank, breaking in upon the disorderly line of the Gauls. Hannibal himself, who was with the party crossing the river, leaped on shore amongst the first, and forming his men as fast as they landed, led them instantly to the charge. But the Gauls, confused and bewildered, made little resistance; they fled in utter rout; whilst Hannibal, not losing a moment, sent back his vessels and boats for a fresh detachment of his army; and before night his whole force, with the exception of his elephants, was safely established on the eastern side of the Rhone.—
DR. ARNOLD, *History of Rome.*

118. *Moses.*

The end was at last come. It might still have seemed that a triumphant close was in store for the aged Prophet. His eye was not dim nor his natural force abated. He had led his people to victory against the Amorite kings; he might still be expected to lead them over into the land of

Canaan. But so it was not to be. From the desert plains of Moab he went up to the same lofty range whence Balaam had looked over the same prospect. The same, but seen with eyes how different! The view of Balaam has been long forgotten; but the view of Moses has become the proverbial view of all time. It was the peak dedicated to Nebo on which he stood, He lifted up his eyes westward, and northward, and southward, and eastward. Beneath him lay the tents of Israel ready for the march; and over against them, distinctly visible in its grove of palm trees, the stately Jericho, key of the Land of Promise. Beyond was spread out the whole range of the mountains of Palestine, in its fourfold masses; all Gilead, with Hermon and Lebanon in the east and north; the hills of Galilee, overhanging the Lake of Gennesareth; the wide opening where lay the plain of Esdraelon, the future battle-field of the nations; the rounded summits of Ebal and Gerizim; immediately in front of him the hills of Judæa, and, amidst them, seen distinctly through the rents in their rocky walls, Bethlehem on its narrow ridge, and the invincible fortress of Jebus. To him, so far as we know, the charm of that view lay in the assurance that this was the land promised to Abraham, to Isaac, and to Jacob, and to their seed, the inheritance—with all its varied features of rock and pasture, and forest and desert—for the sake of which he had borne so many years of toil and danger, in the midst of which the fortunes of his people would be unfolded worthily of that great beginning. To us, as we place ourselves by his side, the view swells into colossal proportions, as we think how the proud city of palm-trees is to fall before the hosts of Israel; how the spear of Joshua is to be planted on height after height of those hostile mountains. . . . All this he saw. He saw it with his eyes, but he was not to go over thither. It was his

last view. From that height he came down no more. . . .
No man knoweth of his sepulchre unto this day.—STANLEY,
Jewish Church.

119.

But toward the south a little now they bent,
And for awhile o'er landless sea, they went,
But on the third day made another land
At dawn of day, and thitherward did stand;
And since the wind blew lightly from the shore,
Somewhat abeam, they feared not with the oar
To push across the shallowing sea and green,
That washed a land the fairest they had seen,
Whose shell-strewn beach at highest of the tide
'Twixt sea and flowery shore was nowise wide,
And drawn a little backward from the sea
There stood a marble wall wrought cunningly,
Rosy and white, set thick with images,
And overtopped with heavy-fruited trees,
Which by the shore ran, as the bay did bend,
And to their eyes had neither gap nor end;
Nor any gate; and looking over this,
They saw a place not made for earthly bliss,
Or eyes of dying men, for growing there
The yellow apple and the painted pear,
And well-filled golden cups of oranges
Hung amid groves of pointed cyprus trees;
On grassy slopes the twining vine-bough grew,
And hoary olives 'twixt far mountains blue,
And many-coloured flowers, like as a cloud
The rugged southern cliffs did softly shroud;
And many a green-necked bird sung to his mate
Within the slim-leaved, thorny pomegranate,

That flung its unstrung rubies on the grass,
And slowly o'er the place the wind did pass
Heavy with many odours that it bore
From thymy hills down to the sea-beat shore,
Because no flower there is, that all the year,
From spring to autumn, beareth otherwhere,
But there it flourished; nor the fruit alone
From 'twixt the green leaves and the boughs outshone,
For there each tree was ever flowering.
Nor was there lacking many a living thing
Changed of its nature, for the roe-deer there
Walked fearless with the tiger, and the bear
Rolled sleepily upon the fruit-strawn grass,
Letting the coneys o'er his rough hide pass,
With blinking eyes, that meant no treachery.
Careless the partridge passed the red fox by;
Untouched the serpent left the thrushes brown,
And as a picture was the lion's frown.
But in the midst there was a grassy space
Raised somewhat over all the flowery place,
On marble terrace-walls wrought like a dream;
And round about it ran a clear blue stream,
Bridged o'er with marble steps, and midmost there
Grew a green tree, whose smooth grey boughs did bear
Such fruit as never man elsewhere had seen,
For 'twixt the sunlight and the shadow green
Shone out fair apples of red gleaming gold.
Moreover round the tree, in many a fold,
Lay coiled a dragon, glittering little less
Than that which his eternal watchfulness
Was set to guard.

MORRIS, *Jason*.

123. *Vesuvius.* A. D. 79.

My uncle was at that time with the fleet under his command at Misenum. On the 24th of August, about one in the afternoon, my mother desired him to observe a cloud which appeared of a very unusual size and shape. . . . He immediately arose, and went out upon an eminence, from whence he might more distinctly view this very uncommon appearance. It was not at that distance discernible from what mountain this cloud issued, but it was found afterwards to ascend from Mount Vesuvius. I cannot give a more exact description of its figure than by likening it to that of a pine-tree, for it shot up to a great height in the form of a trunk, which extended itself at the top into a sort of branches: it appeared sometimes bright, and sometimes dark and spotted, as it was more or less impregnated with earth and cinders. . . . My uncle ordered the galleys to put to sea, and went himself on board with an intention of assisting not only Retina but many other places, for the population is thick on that beautiful coast. When hastening to the place from whence others fled with the utmost terror, he steered his direct course to the point of danger, and with so much calmness and presence of mind, as to be able to make and dictate his observations upon the motion and figure of that dreadful scene. He was now so nigh the mountain, that the cinders, which grew thicker and hotter the nearer he approached, fell into the ships, together with pumice stones, and black pieces of burning rock; they were likewise in danger, not only of being aground by the sudden retreat of the sea, but also from the vast fragments which rolled down from the mountain, and obstructed all the shore. . . . [After he had landed,] the eruption from Mount Vesuvius flamed out in several places with much violence, which the darkness of the night contributed to render still more visible and dreadful. But my uncle, in order to soothe the apprehensions of his friend, assured him it was only the burning of the villages, which the country people had abandoned to the flames; after this he retired to rest, and it is most certain he was so little discomposed as to fall into a deep sleep; for being pretty fat, and breathing hard, those who attended without actually heard him snore. The court which led to his apartment being now almost filled with stones and ashes, if he had continued there any time longer, it would have been impossible for him to have made his way out; it was thought proper, therefore, to awaken him. He got up and went to Pomponianus and the rest of his company, who were not unconcerned enough to think of going to bed. They consulted together whether it would be most prudent to trust to the houses, which now shook from side to side with frequent and violent concussions; or to fly to the open fields, where the calcined stones and cinders, though light indeed, yet fell in large showers and threatened destruction. In this distress they resolved for the fields as the less dangerous situation of the two. . . . They went out, then, having pillows tied upon their heads with napkins; and this was their whole defence against the storm of stones that fell around them. It was now day everywhere else, but there a deeper darkness prevailed than in the most obscure night; which, however, was in some degree dissipated by torches and other lights of various kinds. They thought proper to go down further upon the shore, to observe if they might safely put out to sea; but they found the waves still run extremely high and boisterous. There my uncle, having drunk a draught or two of cold water, threw himself down upon a cloth which was spread for him, when immediately the flames, and a strong smell of sulphur which was the forerunner of them, dispersed the rest of the company, and obliged him to rise. He raised himself up with the assistance of two of his servants, and instantly fell down dead, suffocated, as I conjecture, by some gross and noxious vapour, having always had weak lungs, and being frequently subject to a difficulty of breathing. As soon as it was light again, which was not till the third day after this melancholy accident, his body was found entire, and without any marks of violence upon it, exactly in the same posture that he fell, and looking more like a man asleep than dead.—PLINY, *Letters*.

121. *Vesuvius*, A.D. 79.

There had been, for many days before, some shocks of an earthquake, which the less surprised us as they are extremely frequent in Campania; but they were so particularly violent that night, that they not only shook everything about us, but seemed indeed to threaten total destruction. My mother flew to my chamber, where she found me rising in order to awaken her. We went out into a small court belonging to the house, which separated the sea from the buildings. . . . Though it was now morning, the light was exceedingly faint and languid; the buildings all around us tottered; and though we stood upon open ground, yet, as the place was narrow and confined, there was no remaining there without certain and great danger; we therefore resolved to quit the town. The people followed us in the utmost consternation; and as to a mind distracted with terror every suggestion seems more prudent than its own, pressed in great crowds about us in our way out. At a convenient distance from the houses, we stood still, in the midst of a most dangerous and dreadful scene. The chariots which we had ordered to be drawn out were so agitated backwards and forwards, though upon the most level ground, that we could not keep them steady, even by supporting them with large stones. The sea seemed to roll back upon itself, and to be driven from its banks by the convulsive motion of the earth; it is certain at least the shore was considerably enlarged, and many sea animals were left upon it. On the other side a black and dreadful cloud, bursting with an igneous serpentine vapour, darted out a long train of fire, resembling flashes of lightning, but much larger. . . . Soon afterward, the cloud seemed to descend, and cover the whole ocean, as it certainly did the island of Capreæ and the promontory of Misenum. . . . The ashes now began to fall upon us, though in no great quantity. I turned my head, and observed behind us a thick smoke, which came rolling after us like a torrent. I proposed, while we yet had any light, to turn out of the high road, lest she should be pressed to death in the dark by the crowd that followed us. We had scarce stepped out of the path, when darkness overspread us; not like that of a cloudy night, or when there is no moon, but of a room when it is shut up and all the lights extinguished. Nothing then was to be heard but the shrieks of women, the screams of children, and the cries of men; some calling for their children, others for their parents, others for their husbands, and only distinguishing each other by their voices; one lamenting his own fate, another that of his family; some wishing to die from the very fear of dying; some lifting their hands to the gods;. but the greater part imagining that the last and eternal night was come, which was to destroy the gods and the world together. At length a glimmering light appeared, which we imagined to be rather the forerunner of an approaching burst of flames, as in truth it was, than the return of day. However, the fire fell at a distance from us; then again we were immersed in thick darkness, and a heavy shower of ashes rained upon us, which we were obliged every now and then to shake off, otherwise we should have been crushed and buried in the heap. . . . At last this dreadful darkness was dissipated by degrees, like a cloud of smoke; the real day returned, and soon the sun appeared, though very faintly, and as when an eclipse is coming on. Every object that presented itself to our eyes (which were extremely weakened) seemed changed, being covered over with white ashes, as with a deep snow. We returned to Misenum, where we refreshed ourselves as well as we could, and passed an anxious night between hope and fear, though indeed with a much larger share of the latter; for the earthquake still continued.—PLINY, *Letters*.

122.

The eastward rocks of Almería's bay
Answer long farewells of the travelling sun
With softest glow as from an inward pulse
Changing and flushing; all the Moorish ships
Seem conscious too, and shoot out sudden shadows;
Their black hulls snatch a glory, and their sails
Show variegated radiance, gently stirred
Like broad wings poised. Two galleys moored apart
Show decks as busy as a home of ants
Storing new forage; from their sides the boats,
Slowly pushed off, anon with flashing oar
Make transit to the quay's smooth-quarried edge,
Where thronging Gypsies are in haste to lade
Each as it comes with grandames, babes, and wives,
Or with dust-tinted goods, the company
Of wandering years. Nought seems to lie unmoved,
For 'mid the throng the lights and shadows play,

And make all surface eager, while the boats
Sway restless as a horse that heard the shouts
And surging hum incessant. Naked limbs
With beauteous ease bend, lift, and throw, or raise
High signalling hands. The black-haired mother steps
Athwart the boat's edge, and with opened arms,
A wandering Isis outcast from the gods,
Leans towards her lifted little one. The boat
Full-laden cuts the waves, and dirge-like cries
Rise and then fall within it as it moves
From high to lower and from bright to dark.
Hither and thither, grave white-turbaned Moors
Move helpfully, and some bring welcome gifts,
Bright stuffs and cutlery, and bags of seed
To make new waving crops in Africa.

. . . . . .

The younger heads were busy with the tale
Of that great Chief whose exploits helped the Moor.
And, talking still, they shouldered past their friends,
Following some lure which held their distant gaze
To eastward of the quay, where yet remained
A low black tent close guarded all around
By armed Zincali. Fronting it above,
Raised by stone steps that sought a jutting strand,
Fedalma stood and marked with anxious watch
Each laden boat the remnant lessening
Of cargo on the shore, or traced the course
Of Nadar to and fro in hard command
Of noisy tumult; imaging oft anew
How much of labour still deferred the hour
When they must lift the boat and bear away
Her father's coffin, and her feet must quit
This shore for ever. Motionless she stood,

Black-crowned with wreaths of many-shadowed hair;
Black-robed, but wearing wide upon her breast
Her father's golden necklace and his badge.
Her limbs were motionless, but in her eyes
And in her breathing lip's soft tremulous curve
Was intense motion as of prisoned fire
Escaping subtly in outleaping thought.
GEORGE ELIOT, *The Spanish Gypsy*.

123. *The Teeth.*

I told you before that it was their business to dress and prepare what was presented to them. And in order to do their work in the best way possible, they divide their labour; some cut up, others tear, and others pound. First, there are those flat teeth in front of the two jaws, just below the nose. Touch yours with the tip of your finger; you will find that they terminate in sharp-edged plates, like knives. These are called *incisors*, from the Latin word *incidere*, which means to cut, and it is with them that we bite bread and apples, where the first business is to cut. The next sort are those little pointed teeth, which come after the *incisors*, on each side of both jaws. You will easily find them; and if you press against them a little, you will feel their points. If we call the first set the knives of the mouth, we may call these its forks. They serve to pierce whatever requires to be torn, and they are called *canine* teeth, from the Latin word *canis*, a dog, because dogs make great use of them in tearing their food. They place their paws upon it, and plunging the canine teeth into it, pull off pieces by a jerk of the head. The last set, which are placed at the back of the jaw, are called *molars*, from the Latin word *mola*, which means a mill-stone. They perform the same office as a miller's mill-stone; that is to say, they grind everything that comes in their way. This set have flat square tops, with little inequalities on the surface, which you can feel the moment you lay your finger on them. These are the largest and strongest of the three sets, and with them we even crack nuts, when we prefer the risk of breaking our teeth to the trouble of fetching the nut-crackers. Now, I will answer for it that you cannot explain to me why we always place what is hard to break between the *molars*, and never employ the *incisors* in the work? I will tell you the reason, however, if you will first tell me why, when you are going to snip off the tip of your thread (which offers very little resistance), you do it with the point of your scissors; whereas you put any tough thing which is likely to resist strongly, a match, for instance, close up to their hinge. Now take your scissors in your left hand; hold the lower ring of the handle firmly between your thumb and closed hand, so that its blade shall remain straight and immoveable; then with your other hand cause the upper ring to go up and down, and watch its blade as it moves. Now, you have before you the pattern of the two jaws on one side of your face, from the ear to the nose; the upper one, which never moves, and the lower one, which goes up and down. The *incisors* are at the points, they gallop up and down, and are worthless for doing hard work; the *molars* are at the hinges, and move slowly; and if anything tough has to be dealt with, it comes to them as a matter of course; hence they are the nut-crackers. But, besides this power of moving up and down, the lower jaw possesses another less obvious one, by means of which it goes from right to left. It is chiefly by this second action of the jaw that the food is pounded. Try to chew a bit of bread by only moving your jaw up and down, and you will soon tire of the attempt. One word more to complete my description of the teeth; that portion of them which is in the jaw is called the *root;* and the *incisors,* which cannot work hard because they have but little resisting power, possess only small and short roots; whereas the *canines,* whose duty it is to tear the food sideways, would run the risk of being dragged out and left sticking in the substances they are at work upon, if they were not well secured; these, therefore, have roots which go much deeper into the jaw, and in consequence of this they give us more pain than the others when we have to go to the dentist; those famous *eye-teeth,* which so terrify people on such occasions, are the *canines* of the upper jaw, and lie, in fact, just below the eye. The *molars* meanwhile would be in danger of being shaken in the sideway movement, while chewing; so they do as you would do if you were pushed aside. Now you would throw out your feet right and left in order to steady yourself, and thus the molars, which have always two roots, throw them out right and left for the same purpose; and some have three, some four, and they require no less for the business they have to do.— JEAN MACÉ.

124.

Indoors, warm by the wide-mouthed fire-place, idly the farmer
Sat in his elbow-chair, and watched how the flames and the smoke-wreaths
Struggled together like foes in a burning city. Behind him,
Nodding and mocking along the wall, with gestures fantastic,
Darted his own huge shadow, and vanished away into darkness.
Faces, clumsily carved in oak, on the back of his armchair

Laughed in the flickering light, and the pewter plates on the
    dresser
Caught and reflected the flame, as shields of armies the
    sunshine.
Fragments of song the old man sang, and carols of Christ-
    mas,
Such as at home, in the olden time, his fathers before him
Sang in their Norman orchards and bright Burgundian vine-
    yards.
Close at her father's side was the gentle Evangeline seated,
Spinning flax for the loom, that stood in the corner behind
    her.
Silent awhile were its treadles, at rest was its diligent shuttle,
While the monotonous drone of the wheel, like the drone of
    a bagpipe,
Followed the old man's song, and united the fragments
    together.
As in a church, when the chant of the choir at intervals
    ceases,
Footfalls are heard in the aisles, or words of the priest at
    the altar,
So, in each pause of the song, with measured motion the
    clock clicked.   LONGFELLOW, *Evangeline.*

125.

Once in an ancient city, whose name I no longer remember,
Raised aloft on a column, a brazen statue of Justice
Stood in the public square, upholding the scales in its left
    hand,
And in its right a sword, as an emblem that justice presided
Over the laws of the land, and the hearts and homes of the
    people.

Even the birds had built their nests in the scales of the
  balance,
Having no fear of the sword that flashed in the sunshine
  above them.
But in the course of time the laws of the land were cor-
  rupted;
Might took the place of right, and the weak were oppressed,
  and the mighty
Ruled with an iron rod. Then it chanced in a nobleman's
  palace
That a necklace of pearls was lost, and ere long a suspicion
Fell on an orphan girl who lived as maid in the household.
She, after form of trial condemned to die on the scaffold,
Patiently met her doom at the foot of the statue of Justice.
As to her Father in heaven her innocent spirit ascended,
Lo! o'er the city a tempest rose; and the bolts of the
  thunder
Smote the statue of bronze, and hurled in wrath from its
  left hand
Down on the pavement below the clattering scales of the
  balance,
And in the hollow thereof was found the nest of a magpie,
Into whose clay-built walls the necklace of pearls was in-
  woven.   LONGFELLOW, *Evangeline*.

126. *The Siege of Genoa.*

It is not at once that the inhabitants of a great city, accustomed to the daily sight of well-stored shops and an abundant market, begin to realize the idea of scarcity; or that the wealthy classes of society, who have never known any other state than one of abundance and luxury, begin seriously to conceive of famine. But the shops were emptied, and the store-houses began to be drawn upon; and no fresh supply or hope of supply appeared. Winter passed away, and spring returned, so early and so beautiful on that garden-like coast, sheltered as it is from the north winds by its belt of mountains, and open to the full rays of the southern sun. Spring returned and clothed the hill sides within the lines with its fresh verdure. But that verdure was no longer the mere delight of the careless eye of luxury, refreshing the citizens by its liveliness and softness when they rode or walked up thither from the city to enjoy the surpassing beauty of the prospect. The green hill sides were now visited for a very different object; ladies of the highest rank might be seen cutting up every plant which it was possible to turn to food, and bearing home the common weeds of our roadsides as a most precious treasure. The French general pitied the distress of the people, but the lives and strength of his garrison seemed to him more important than the lives of the Genoese, and such provisions as remained were reserved in the first place for the French army. Scarcity became utter want, and want became famine. In the most gorgeous palaces of that gorgeous city, no less than in the humblest tenements of its humblest poor, death was busy; not the momentary death of battle or massacre, nor the speedy death of pestilence, but the lingering and most miserable death of famine. Infants died before their parents' eyes, husbands and wives lay down to expire together. A man whom I saw at Genoa in 1825, told me that his father and two of his brothers had been starved to death in this fatal siege. So it went on, till, in the month of June, when Napoleon had already descended from the Alps into the plain of Lombardy, the misery became unendurable, and Massena surrendered. But before he did so, twenty thousand innocent persons, old and young, women and children, had died by the most horrible of deaths which humanity can endure. . . . Now is it right that such a tragedy as this should take place, and that the laws of war should be supposed to justify the authors of it? . . . For the thing was done deliberately; the helplessness of the Genoese was known; their distress was known; it was known that they could not force Massena to surrender; it was known that they were dying daily by hundreds. . . . Now on which side the law of nations should throw the guilt of most atrocious murder, is of little comparative consequence, or whether it should attach it to both sides equally: but that the deliberate starving to death of twenty thousand helpless persons should be regarded as a crime in one or both of the parties concerned in it, seems to me self-evident.—ARNOLD, *Lectures on Modern History.*

127. *The Trial of the Seven Bishops.*

At ten the Court again met. The crowd was greater than ever. The jury appeared in their box; and there was a breathless stillness. Sir Samuel Astry spoke. 'Do you find the defendants, or any of them, guilty of the misdemeanour whereof they are impeached, or not guilty?' Sir Roger Langley answered, 'Not Guilty.' As the words were uttered, Halifax sprang up and waved his hat. At that signal, benches and galleries raised a shout. In a moment ten thousand persons, who crowded the great hall, replied with a still louder shout, which made the old oaken roof crack; and in another moment the innumerable throng without set up a third huzza, which was heard at Temple Bar. The boats which covered the Thames gave an answering cheer. A peal of gunpowder was heard on the water, and another, and another; and so, in a few moments, the glad tidings went flying past the Savoy and the Friars to London Bridge, and to the forest of masts below. As the news spread, streets and squares, marketplaces and coffeehouses, broke forth into acclamations. Yet were the acclamations less strange than the weeping. For the feelings of men had been wound up to such a point that at length the stern English nature, so little used to outward signs of emotion, gave way, and thousands sobbed aloud for very joy. Meanwhile, from the outskirts of the multitude, horsemen were spurring off to bear along all the great roads intelligence of the victory of our Church and nation. . . . The acquitted prelates took refuge in the nearest chapel from the crowd which implored their blessing. Many churches were open on that morning throughout the capital; and many pious persons repaired thither. The bells of all the parishes of the City and liberties were ringing. The jury meanwhile could scarcely make their way out of the hall. They were forced to shake hands with hundreds. 'God bless you!' cried the people; 'God prosper your families! you have done like honest good-natured gentlemen; you have saved us all to-day.' As the noblemen who had attended to support the good cause drove off, they flung from their carriage windows handfuls of money, and bade the crowd drink to the health of the King, the Bishops, and the jury. . . . The King had that morning visited the camp on Hounslow Heath, . . . and was in Lord Feversham's tent when the express arrived. He was greatly disturbed, and exclaimed in French, 'So much the worse for them.' He soon set out for London. While he was present, respect prevented the soldiers from giving a loose to their feelings; but he had scarcely quitted the camp when he heard a great shouting behind him. He was surprised, and asked what that uproar meant. 'Nothing,' was the answer; 'the soldiers are glad that the Bishops are acquitted.' 'Do you call that nothing?' said James. And then he repeated, 'So much the worse for them.' . . . That joyful day was followed by a not less joyful evening. . . . Never within the memory of the oldest, not even on that night on which it was known through London that the army of Scotland had declared for a free Parliament, had the streets been in such a glare with bonfires. Round every bonfire crowds were drinking good health to the Bishops and confusion to the Papists. The windows were lighted with rows of candles. Each row consisted of seven; and the taper in the centre, which was taller than the rest, represented the Primate. The noise of rockets, squibs, and firearms, was incessant. One huge pile of faggots blazed right in front of the great gate of Whitehall.—MACAULAY, *History of England.*

128. *The Shield of Achilles.*

And first a shield he fashioned, vast and strong,
With rich adornment; circled with a rim,
Threefold, bright-gleaming, whence a silver belt
Depended; of five folds the shield was formed;
And on its surface many a rare design
Of curious art his practised skill had wrought.
    Thereon were figured earth, and sky, and sea,
The ever-circling sun, and full-orbed moon,
And all the signs that crown the vault of Heaven;
Pleiads and Hyads, and Orion's might,
And Arctos, called the Wain, who wheels on high
His circling course, and on Orion waits;
Sole star that never bathes in the ocean wave.
    And two fair populous towns were sculptured there:
In one were marriage pomp and revelry,

And brides, in gay procession, through the streets
With blazing torches from their chambers borne,
While frequent rose the hymeneal song.
Youths whirled around in joyous dance, with sound
Of flute and harp; and, standing at their doors,
Admiring women on the pageant gazed.
  Meanwhile a busy throng the forum filled:
There between two a fierce contention rose,
About a death-fine; to the public one
Appealed, asserting to have paid the whole;
While one denied that he had aught received.
Both were desirous that before the Judge
The issue should be tried; with noisy shouts
Their several partisans encouraged each.
The heralds stilled the tumult of the crowd:
On polished chairs, in solemn circle, sat
The reverend Elders; in their hands they held
The loud-voiced heralds' sceptres; waving these,
They heard the alternate pleadings; in the midst
Two talents lay of gold, which he should take
Who should before them prove his righteous cause.
  Before the second town two armies lay,
In arms refulgent; to destroy the town
The assailants threatened, or among themselves
Of all the wealth within the city stored
An equal half, as ransom, to divide.
The terms rejecting, the defenders manned
A secret ambush; on the walls they placed
Women and children mustered for defence,
And men by age enfeebled; forth they went,
By Mars and Pallas led; these, wrought in gold,
In golden arms arrayed, above the crowd
For beauty and stature, as befitting Gods,

Conspicuous shone; of lesser height the rest.
But when the destined ambuscade was reached,
Beside the river, where the shepherds drove
Their flocks and herds to water, down they lay,
In glittering arms accoutred; and apart
They placed two spies, to notify betimes
The approach of flocks of sheep and lowing herds.
These, in two shepherds' charge, ere long appeared,
Who, unsuspecting as they moved along,
Enjoyed the music of their pastoral pipes.
They on the booty, from afar discerned,
Sprang from their ambuscade; and cutting off
The herds, and fleecy flocks, their guardians slew.
Their comrades heard the tumult where they sat
Before their sacred altars, and forthwith
Sprang on their cars, and with fast-stepping steeds
Pursued the plunderers, and o'ertook them soon.
There on the river's bank they met in arms,
And each at other hurled their brazen spears.
And there were figured Strife, and Tumult wild,
And deadly Fate, who in her iron grasp
One newly wounded, one unwounded bore,
While by the feet from out the press she dragged
Another slain: about her shoulders hung
A garment crimsoned with the blood of men.
Like living men they seemed to move, to fight,
To drag away the bodies of the slain.

And there was graven a wide-extended plain
Of fallow land, rich, fertile, mellow soil,
Thrice ploughed; where many ploughmen up and down
Their teams were driving; and as each attained
The limit of the field, would one advance,
And tender him a cup of generous wine:

Then would he turn, and to the end again
Along the furrow cheerly drive his plough.
And still behind them darker showed the soil,
The true presentment of a new-ploughed field,
Though wrought in gold; a miracle of art.
   There too was graven a corn-field, rich in grain,
Where with sharp sickles reapers plied their task,
And thick, in even swathe, the trusses fell;
The binders, following close, the bundles tied:
Three were the binders; and behind them boys
In close attendance waiting, in their arms
Gathered the bundles, and in order piled.
Amid them, staff in hand, in silence stood
The King, rejoicing in the plenteous swathe.
A little way removed, the heralds slew
A sturdy ox, and now beneath an oak
Prepared the feast; while women mixed, hard by,
White barley porridge for the labourers' meal.
   And, with rich clusters laden, there was graven
A vineyard fair, all gold; of glossy black
The bunches were, on silver poles sustained;
Around, a darksome trench; beyond, a fence
Was wrought, of shining tin; and through it led
One only path, by which the bearers passed,
Who gathered in the vineyard's bounteous store.
There maids and youths, in joyous spirits bright,
In woven baskets bore the luscious fruit.
A boy, amid them, from a clear-toned harp
Drew lovely music; well his liquid voice
The strings accompanied; they all with dance
And song harmonious joined, and joyous shouts,
As the gay bevy lightly tripped along.
   Of straight-horned cattle too a herd was graven;

Of gold and tin the heifers all were wrought:
They to the pasture, from the cattle-yard,
With gentle lowings, by a babbling stream,
Where quivering reed-beds rustled, slowly moved.
Four golden shepherds walked beside the herd,
By nine swift dogs attended; then amid
The foremost heifers sprang two lions fierce
Upon the lordly bull: he, bellowing loud,
Was dragged along, by dogs and youths pursued.
The tough bull's-hide they tore, and gorging lapped
The intestines and dark blood; with vain attempt
The herdsmen following closely, to the attack
Cheered their swift dogs; these shunned the lions' jaws,
And close around them baying, held aloof.

 And there the skilful artist's hand had traced
A pasture broad, with fleecy flocks o'erspread,
In a fair glade, with fold, and tents, and pens.

 There, too, the skilful artist's hand had wrought,
With curious workmanship, a mazy dance,
Like that which Dædalus in Cnossus erst
At fair-haired Ariadne's bidding framed.
There, laying each on other's wrists their hand,
Bright youths and many-suitored maidens danced:
In fair white linen these ; in tunics those,
Well woven, shining soft with fragrant oils;
These with fair coronets were crowned, while those
With golden swords from silver belts were girt.
Now whirled they round with nimble practised feet,
Easy, as when a potter, seated, turns
A wheel, new fashioned by his skilful hand,
And spins it round, to prove if true it run :
Now featly moved in well-beseeming ranks.
A numerous crowd, around, the lovely dance

Surveyed, delighted; while an honoured Bard
Sang, as he struck the lyre, and to the strain
Two tumblers, in the midst, were whirling round.
About the margin of the massive shield
Was wrought the mighty strength of the ocean stream.
LORD DERBY, *Homer*.

GLOSSARY.

ABBREVIATIONS.

D. = Danish.
Du. = Dutch.
E. = English.
Fr. = French.
G. = German.
Gael. = Gaelic.
Gr. = Greek.
Hebr. = Hebrew.
It. = Italian.
L. = Latin.
L. L. = Late Latin.
O. Fr. = Old French.
Port. = Portuguese.
Scand. = Scandinavian.
Sp. = Spanish.
Sw. = Swedish.
Teut. = Teutonic.
W. = Welsh.

Adj. = adjective, adv. = adverb, conj. = conjunction, contr. = contracted or contraction, dim. = diminutive, freq. = frequentative, interj. = interjection, pp. = past participle, prep. = preposition, pron. = pronoun, s. or subs. = substantive, v. = verb.

Abandon, v. [Fr. *abandonner*, to place at a person's command; *bandon*, L. L. *bandum*, D. *band*, It. *bando*, proclamation, command] to give up, forsake.

Abate, v. [Fr. *abattre*, L. L. *ab*, from, *battere*] to beat down, lessen. *Abated.*

Abeam, adv. [E. *on*, *beam*, a tree] the part of the vessel where the breadth is greatest, because the chief supports, beams, are there.

Abhor, v. [L. *ab*, *horrere*, dread, shrink from] to dread, loathe, detest, hate. *Abhorred.*

Abide, v. [E. *at*, *bidan*, to wait] to wait for, endure; wait, live, dwell. *Abode.*

Able, adj. [Fr. *habile*, L. *habilis*, *habere*, to have] having power, powerful, skilful.

Abominable, adj. [L. *ab*, from, *ominalis*, *omen*] from which one would turn away as from a bad omen; hateful, horrible.

Abound, v. [L. *abundare*, to overflow; *ab*, *unda*, a wave] to overflow, to be plentiful. *Abounded.*

About, adv. prep. [E. *on*, *be*, *utan*] near by the outside, round, near, concerning, nearly.

Above, adv. prep. [E. *on*, *be*, *ufan*] near by the up side, higher, more than, superior to.

Abraham, s., a patriarch of the Hebrew race, who migrated from the land of Chaldæa into Canaan.

Abreast, adv. [E. *on*, *breost*, breast] with breasts in a line, side by side.

Abroad, adv. [E. *on*, *brád*, broad] in

Q 2

a broad, open, space; at large, out of the country.

Absolutely, adv. [L. *absolutus; ab, solutus*, loosed from] like one loosed from control; freely, in an unlimited manner.

Absurd, adj. [L. *absurdus; ab*, from, *surdus*, a deaf man] like an answer from a deaf man; not to the point, unreasonable, foolish.

Abundance, s. [L. *abundantia*, overflow] abounding, plenty.

Abundant, adj. [L. *abundantem*, overflowing] abounding plentiful.

Abyss, s. [Gr. *abyssos; a*, not, *byssos*, depth, bottom] a bottomless depth, a depth which cannot be measured.

Accept, v. [L. *acceptum, accipere; ad*, to, *capere*, to take] to take to oneself, to receive. *Accepted*.

Accessible, adj. [L. *accessibilis, accessus, accedere; ad, cedere*, to approach] able to be approached or come at.

Accident, s. [L. *accidentem, accidens, accidere; ad, cadere*, to fall to] that which falls to one, a thing unexpected, chance.

Acclamation, s. [L. *acclamationem, acclamare; ad, clamare*, to cry to] a shout, applause.

Accommodate, v. [L. *accommodatus; ad, commodare, com, modus*, to suit with measure] to suit, fit, adapt, supply. *Accommodated*.

Accompany, v. [Fr. *accompagner, compagne*, L. *companio; con, cum, panis*, bread] to go with, associate with. *Accompanied*.

Accomplish, v. [Fr. *accomplir*, L. *complere*, to fill] to complete, fulfil, finish. *Accomplished*.

Accomplishment, s. [E. *accomplish*] fulfilment, completion, end.

Accord, v. [Fr. *accorder*, L. *ad*, to, L. L. *cordare, cor*, the heart] to agree, harmonize. *Accorded*.

Accord, s., agreement, harmony.

Account, s. [Fr. *acconter, compter*, L. *ad, computare*] reckoning, value, statement, relation.

Accoutre, v. [Fr. *accoûtrer*, O. Fr. *accoustrer, cousteur*, L. *ad, custodire*, to keep the sacred vestments] to dress, put on arms, equip. *Accoutred*.

Accurate, adj. [L. *accuratus; ad*, to, *curare, cura*, care] cared for, done with care, correct, exact. Adv. *accurately*.

Accursed, adj. [E. *accurse; at, cursian*, to curse] under a curse, cursed, doomed.

Accustom, v. [O. Fr. *accoustumer*, L. *ad*, to, *consuetudinem*, habit] to make a habit, to practise, to become used. *Accustomed*.

Achieve, v. [Fr. *achever, chef*, L. *ad*, to, *caput*, head] to bring to a head, finish, accomplish, attain to, gain.

Acknowledge, v. [E. *a, knowledge*] to own a knowledge of, to admit, confess. *Acknowledged*.

Acorn, s. [E. *æc, oc*, an oak, *æcern*, adj., of the oak, oaken, corrupted as if from *oak-corn*] the fruit of the oak.

Acquaintance, s. [E. *acquaint*, Fr. *accointer*, L. *ad -cognitare, cognitus*] knowledge, a person known.

Acquit, v. [Fr. *acquitter*, L. *ad-quietare, ad*, to, *quietem, quies*, rest] to give rest, to set free. *Acquitted*. Cf. **Quit, Quiet, Quite**.

Across, adv. prep. [E. *at, cross*] from one side to another, on the other side, over.

Act, s. [L. *actum, agere*, to do] a thing done, deed.

Action, s. [L. *actionem, agere*] a doing, a thing done.

Active, adj. [Fr. *active*, L. *activus, agere*] doing, working, busy, quick.

GLOSSARY. 229

Actually, adv. [L. *actualis*] really.
Acute, adj. [L. *acutus, acuere,* to sharpen] sharp, discerning, sensible, clever.
Adage, s. [L. *adagium*] a saying, proverb, maxim.
Add, v. [L. *addere, dare*] to put to, increase, sum up. *Added.*
Address, s. [Fr. *adresser,* L. *dirictiare, directus, regere*] speech, manner.
Administration, s. [L. *administrationem ; ad, minister*) the managing, conducting, doing; the body of persons managing.
Admit, v. [Fr. *admettre,* L. *ad, mittere,* send to] to let in, allow, confess. *Admitted.*
Adorn, v. [L. *ad, ornare*] to deck, decorate. *Adorned.*
Advance, v. [Fr. *avancer, avant,* L. *ab, ante,* from before] to go forward, bring forward, promote. *Advanced.*
Advance, s. a movement forward.
Advantage, s. [Fr. *avantage, avant,* L. *ab, ante*] a state of advance, benefit, gain.
Adventurer, s. [E. *adventure,* Fr. *aventure,* L. *ad venturus, venire,* come to] one who seeks adventures, tries what is to come, one who goes about seeking his fortune.
Adverse, adj. [L. *ad, versus,* opposite] turned against, opposite, hostile.
Adversity, s. [Fr. *adversité,* L. *adversitatem, ad, versus*] opposing fortune, misfortune, distress.
Advice, s. [Fr. *avis,* L. *ad,* L. *visum,* an opinion] notice, instruction, warning, counsel.
Advise, v. [Fr. *aviser,* L. *ad, visere,* to see to] to counsel. *Advised.*
Aerial, adj. [L. *aerialis, aerius, aer*] of, or, in the air; lofty.
Afar, adv. [E. *at, far*] away, at a distance.

Affection, s. [Fr. *affection,* L. *affectionem, affectus; ad, facere*] a state of feeling towards, kindly feeling, love. Adj. *affectionate.*
Affirm, v. [Fr. *affirmer,* L. *affirmare; ad, firmare*] to say strongly, assert, declare, maintain. *Affirmed.*
Afford, v. [E. *forthian,* to help, assist] to be able to buy or sell, to grant, to yield. *Afforded.*
Afoot, adv. [E. *on foot*] walking.
Afore, adv. [E. *on fore*] before.
Afraid, adj. *affrayed,* pp. of verb *affray* [Fr. *effrayer,* L. *ex -frigidare,* to freeze with fright, *frigidus,* cold] scared, terrified, frightened.
Afresh, adv. [Fr. *frais, fraiche,* It. *fresco,* G. *fresc*] again, anew.
Africa, s., a name given to the continent which lies south of the Mediterranean Sea. Adj. *African.*
After, adv. prep. [E. *æft,* behind, comp. *æfter*] comparative of *aft;* more behind, later.
Afternoon, s., the time after the noon or midday.
Afterwards, adv., at a later time.
Again, adv. [E. *on, gen,* opposite] another time.
Against, prep. [corruption of E. *againes, again*] opposite to, close to, until.
Age, s. [Fr. *âge, aage, edage,* L. *ætaticum, ætas,* time] time of life, latter part of life, a period. Adj. *aged,* old.
Agile, adj. [Fr. *agile,* L. *agilis*] nimble, active.
Agitate, v. [L. *agitatus, agitare, agere*] to move often, disturb, shake. *Agitated.*
Ago (agone), adv. [E. pp. of *of-gán,* to go off] past, since.
Agreeable, adj. [F. *agréable,* L. *ad, gratabilis, gratus*] pleasing.
Aground, adv. [E. *on, ground*] on the ground, stranded.

Ah, interj., exclamation of surprise, &c.

Aid, v. [Fr. *aider,* L. L. *aiutare,* L. *adjutare;* frequentative of *juvare*] to help, assist. *Aided.*

Aid, s. [Fr. *aide*] help, assistance.

Aim, v. [O. Fr. *esmer,* L. *æstimare*] to estimate, seek after, level at, point at. *Aimed.*

Air, s. [Fr. *air,* L. *aer*] that which blows, atmosphere, a melody, manner.

Airy, adj. [*air*] of the air, open to the air, light.

Aisle, s. [L. *axilla,* a wing] the wing or side of a church, a side-passage of a church.

Ait, s. [E. *eyot,* dim. of *ey,* island] a small island.

Alarm, v. [Fr. *alarmer,* It. *all' arme,* L. *ad illa arma,* to arms] to call to arms, to warn of danger, to frighten. *Alarmed.*

Alas, interj. [Fr. *hélas,* O. Fr. *hé! las!* L. *ah, lassus,* wearied] an exclamation of sorrow.

Alder, s. [E. *alr*] the water-tree.

Alderman, s. [E. *ealdor, eald, man*] an elder man; formerly the title of the chief magistrate of a shire, now of the officer next below the mayor in a city or borough.

Alert, adj. [Fr. *alerte,* O. Fr. *à l'erte,* It. *all' erta,* L. *erectus, erigere,* to set up] on one's guard, brisk, active.

Alien, adj. [L. *alienus,* of another] of another country, foreign, apart from.

Alive, adj. [E. *on, lif*] having life, lively.

All, adj., the whole.

Allah, s. [Arabic] God.

Alley, s. [Fr. *allée, aller,* to walk] a narrow passage, a walk in a garden. Pl. *alleys.*

Allow, v. [Fr. *allouer,* L. *allaudare; ad, laudare,* to praise] to approve, permit, grant. *Allowed.*

Allowance, s. [E. *allow*] permission, that which is allowed, a grant.

Alluvial, adj. [L. *alluvialis, alluvium; ad, luere,* to wash to] washed from higher land upon lower.

Ally, s. [Fr. *allié,* L. *alligare; ad, ligare,* to bind to] one bound by treaty or by friendship; a confederate, friend. Pl. *allies.*

Almighty, adj. [E. *ealmihtig, all, might*] having all power.

Almost, adv. [E. *all, most*] mostly all, nearly.

Aloft, adv. [E. *on, loft, lyft,* the air] in the air, on high.

Alone, adv. [E. *all one*] by one's self, singly.

Along, adv. [E. *andlang*] by the length, lengthwise, onward.

Aloof, adv. [E. *on, luff, lyft,* the air] to windward, out of reach, away.

Aloud, adv. [E. *on, loud, hlud,* a sound] with a sound.

Alp, s. [Gael.] a mountain; *Alps,* the mountains of Switzerland.

Already, adv. [E. *all, ræd, rathe,* early] prepared, now, so soon.

Also, adv. [E. *all so*] in such manner, likewise, too.

Altar, s. [L. *altare*] a high place for sacrifices, a table.

Alter, v. [L. *alterare; alter,* another] to make otherwise, change. *Altered.*

Alternate, adj. [L. *alternatus, alter*] by turns, one after another. Adv. *alternately.*

Although, adv. [F. *all, though*] granting all that, notwithstanding.

Altogether, adv. [E. *all, to, gathered*] all collected into one place, united, wholly.

Always, adv. [E. *all ways*] through all ways, at all times.

Amain, adv. [E. *on, maegen,* may] with main, with strength, strongly, mightily.

Amaze, v. [E. *on, maze*] to make confused, to astonish. *Amazed.*

GLOSSARY.

Amber, s. [Fr. *ambre,* Arab. *anbar*] yellow fossil resin.

Ambition, s. [L. *ambitionem* (canvassing for votes), *ambitus, ambire,* to go round] desire of place, power, honour, fame.

Ambuscade, s. [Fr. *embuscade,* It. *imboscata, bosco,* a wood] a hiding in a wood, lying in wait.

Ambush, s. [Fr. *embuscher,* It. *imboscare, bosco*] a lying in wait, shelter.

Amends, s. pl. [Fr. *amender,* L. *a,* from, *menda,* a fault] atonement, recompense.

Amid, Amidst, prep. [E. *on, middan, middes,* middle] in the middle, among.

Among, Amongst, prep. [E. *on, mang, mængan,* to mingle] mingled with.

Ample, adv. [Fr. *ample,* L. *amplus*] large, large enough, abundant.

Amuse, v. [Fr. *amuser,* O. Fr. *muser*] to delight, entertain. *Amused.*

Amusement, s. [Fr. *amusement*] pastime, pleasure.

Analogous, adj. [Gr. *analogia; ana, logos,* relation to] bearing analogy to, having proportion to.

Ancestor, s. [Fr. *ancestre,* L. *antecessor; ante,* before, *cessor, cedere,* to go] those who have gone before, forefathers.

Anchor, s. [L. *ancora,* Gr. *agkura, agkos,* a bend] a bent instrument for holding a vessel.

Anchor, v., to hold a vessel by an anchor. *Anchored.*

Ancient, adj. [Fr. *ancien,* L. *antianus, ante,* before] that which has been before, remote in time, old.

And, conj., also.

Anew, adv. [E. *on, new*] in a new time, way, form; over again.

Angry, adj. [E. *anger,* L. *angor,* vexation] with anger, subject to anger, vexed.

Anguish, s. [Fr. *angoisse,* L. *angustiæ,* a strait, *angere,* to strangle] difficulty, pain, misery.

Animal, s. [L. *animal, anima,* life, breath] a thing that breathes, a living creature.

Animate, v. [L. *animatus, animare, anima*] to give breath or life to, to encourage. *Animated,* made full of life, spirited.

Annals, s. pl. [L. *annales, annus,* a year] history with events arranged under their several years, chronicles.

Announce, v. [Fr. *annoncer,* L. *annuntiare; ad, nuntiare,* to report to] to report, publish, tell. *Announced.*

Anoint, v. [Fr. *oindre,* L. *in,* upon, *ungere*] to smear with oil, to pour oil upon. *Anointed.*

Anon, adv. [E. *on, in, an,* one] in one minute, at once, after a short time.

Another, adj. [E. *an, other*] one more.

Answer, v. [E, *and,* again, *swerian,* to swear] to swear in turn, reply, succeed. *Answered.*

Answer, s., a reply, response.

Ant, s. [E. contr. of *æmet*] an insect, emmet.

Antidote, s. [Gr. *anti,* against, *doton,* given] a thing given against, i. e. as a remedy for, or preventive of, another; a remedy for poison.

Antique, adj. [Fr. *antique,* L. *antiquum, ante,* before] of time before, ancient, old.

Anxious, adj. [L. *anxius, angere,* to strangle] in difficulty, troubled, disturbed about the future.

Any, indef. pr. adj. [E. *ænig, ane*] an, one, used indefinitely.

Apart, adj. [Fr. *à, part,* L. *ad, partem, pars,*] aside, not with all, separate.

Apartment, s. [*apart*] a place divided from the rest of the house, a room.

Apothecary, s. [L. *apothecarius*, Gr. *apo*, away, *theke*, a storehouse] one who keeps drugs, a dispenser of drugs. Pl. *apothecaries*.

Apparel, s. [Fr. *appareil*, L. *ad*, L. L. *pariculus*, *par*] putting like to like, a suit of clothing, clothes, dress.

Apparent, adj. [L. *apparentem*, *apparere*; *ad*, *parere*] appearing, present, evident, plain. Adv. *apparently*.

Appeal, v. [Fr. *appeler*, L. *appellare*, to call to] to call to, to refer to. *Appealed*.

Appear, v. [Fr. *apparoir*, L. *apparere*; *ad*, *parere*, to come forth to] to become visible to, to seem. *Appeared*.

Appearance, s. [*appear*] a becoming visible, seeming, show, form.

Applause, s. [L. *applausus*; *ad*, *plaudere*, to clap the hands for] clapping of the hands, praise.

Apple, s. [E. *æpl*] a fruit; the pupil or centre of the eye.

Appoint, v. [Fr. *appointer*, *point*, L. *ad*, to, *punctum*, a point] to bring to a point, to settle, fix. *Appointed*.

Apprehension, s. [L. *apprehensionem*; *ad*, *prehendere*, to draw to] taking, taking in the mind, understanding, arrest, fear.

Approach, v. [Fr. *approcher*, L. *appropiare* (*appropinquare*), *prope*, near] to draw near to, to come towards. *Approached*.

Approach, s., a coming near, a means of coming near, a path.

Appropriate, v. [L. *appropriatus*; *ad*, *proprius*, to one's own] to add to one's own, to make one's own, to take for one's self. *Appropriated*.

Apricot, s. [Fr. *abricot*, Port. *albericoque*; through Arabian from L. *præcocia*, as if from *præ*, early, *coquere*, to ripen] a wall-fruit introduced into Italy from Armenia.

April, s. [L. *Aprilis*; *aperire*, to open] the fourth month of the year, when buds are opening.

Apt, adj. [Fr. *apte*, L. *aptus*, fitted] fit, suitable, inclined. Subs. *aptness*.

Aptitude, s. [Fr. *aptitude*, L. *aptitudinem*, *aptus*] a state of fitness, suitability.

Arab, s. [Fr. *Arabe*, L. *Arabem*] a man of Arabia; a wanderer.

Arabian, adj. [*Arabia*] of Arabia.

Aramæan, adj. [*Aramæa*, *Aram*, son of Shem, Gen. x. 22] a name given to one of the branches of the Semitic family of peoples and languages; it includes Syrian and Chaldean.

Arbitrary, adj. [L. *arbitrarius*; *arbiter*, a judge] decisive, absolute, despotic.

Arch, s. [Fr. *arche*, L. *arcus*, a bow] a curve, a segment of a circle. Adj. *arched*.

Archer, s. [Fr. *archer*, *arche*, L. *arcus*] a bowman.

Archway, s. [E. *arch*, *way*] a covered way, a way under an arch.

Arctos, s. [Gr. *arktos*] the Bear, the name by which the Greeks knew the constellation which we call the Great Bear, or Charles' wain or waggon.

Argument, s. [L. *argumentum*, *arguere*, to show] a proof; reasoning intended to prove.

Ariadne, s., daughter of Minos, king of Crete, for whom Daedalus made the labyrinth in which the Minotaur was confined.

Arise, v. [E. *er*, *risan*, to rise up] to get up, move upwards, proceed from. *Arise*, *arose*, *arisen*.

Arm, **Arms**, s. the shoulder-joint. Pl. *arms*, weapons.

Arm, v. [Fr. *armer*, L. *armare*] to get arms, to put on armour. *Armed*.

Armchair, s. [E. *arm*, *chair*] a chair with arms.

GLOSSARY. 233

Army, s. [Fr. *armée*, L. *armata, armare*] an armed body of men.

Around, adv. prep. [E. *on, round*] about, on all sides of.

Arrangement, s. [Fr. *arrangement, arranger, range*, Teut. *hring*, a ring] a placing in ranks, putting in order, contrivance.

Array, s. [O. Fr. *arroy*, E. *ræd*, ready] arrangement, order, dress, equipment.

Arrive, v. [Fr. *arriver*, L. *adripare; ad, ripa*, to the bank] to draw near, come. *Arrived.*

Arrival, s., a drawing near, coming.

Arrow, s., a weapon to be shot from a bow.

Art, s. [Fr. *art*, L. *artem, ars*] knowledge in working, skill, cunning; a profession.

Artichoke, s. [Fr. *artichaut*, It. *articiocco*] a plant; Jerusalem artichoke, the *girasole* (L. *gyrus*, a circle, *sol*, sun) turning to the sun, sunflower.

As, adv. conj. [E. *eall-swa*] all so, corruption of *also*; like, for example.

Ascend, v. [L. *ascendere; ad, scandere*, to climb] to climb up, to mount, to go up. *Ascended.*

Ascendancy, s. [*ascendant*] superiority.

Ascribe, v. [L. *ascribere; ad scribere*, to write in addition] to impute, assign to. *Ascribed.*

Ash, s. [E. *æsc*] a kind of tree.

Ash, s. [E. *asca*] remains after burning, calcined dust. Most commonly used in plural, *ashes.*

Ashore, adv. [E. *on, shore*] on the shore, on land.

Asia, s., the name of the Eastern quarter of the globe. Adj. *Asiatic.*

Aside, adv. [E. *on, side*] at the side, out of the way.

Ask, v. [E. *ascian, acsian*] to seek an answer, to enquire. *Asked.*

Askance, adv. [It. *a, scancio*] athwart, across, slanting.

Asleep, adv. [E. *on, sleep*] sleeping.

Aspect, s. [L. *aspectus, aspicere*, to look at] look, appearance, view.

Aspire, v. [Fr. *aspirer*, L. *aspirare; ad spirare*, to breathe upon] to seek after, to aim at. *Aspired.*

Assail, v. [Fr. *assailir*, L. *assilire; ad, salire*, to leap on] to attack, assault. *Assailed.*

Assault, s. [Fr. *assaut*, O. Fr. *assalt*, L. *assultum, assilire; ad, salire*] a sudden attack, onset.

Assemble, v. [Fr. *assembler*, L. *ad, simulare, simul*, together] to gather into one place. *Assembled.*

Assembly, s. [Fr. *assemblée, assembler*] a gathering, meeting. Pl. *assemblies.*

Assert, v. [L. *assertus, asserere; ad, serere*, to join] to maintain, say positively. *Asserted.*

Assign, v. [Fr. *assigner*, L. *assignare; ad, signum*, a mark] to mark out for, to allot. *Assigned.*

Assist, v. [Fr. *assister*, L. *assistere; ad, sistere, stare*, to stand] to be present at, to help, aid. *Assisted.*

Assistance, s. [Fr. *assistance*] help, aid.

Assurance, s. [Fr. *assurance, assurer*] certainty, confidence, courage.

Assure, v. [Fr. *assurer*, L. *ad, securare, securus*, without anxiety] to make sure, to give certainty, confirm, assert. *Assured.*

Astern, adv. [E. *on, stern*] at the steering part of a vessel, at the hinder part, behind.

Asunder, adv. [E. *af*, off, *sundrian*, to cut] separate, separately, apart.

At, prep., close by.

Athens, s. [Gr. *Athenai*] the ancient capital of Attica, and modern capital of Greece. Adj. *Athenian.*

GLOSSARY.

Athwart, adv. prep. [E. *on*, *thwart*] across.

Atrocious, adj. [Fr. *atroce*, L. *atrocem*, cruel] full of cruelty, wickedness.

Attach, v. [Fr. *attacher*, *tâche*, O. Fr. *tasche*, L. L. *tacsa*, *taxare*] to draw to, to fasten. *Attached.*

Attachment, s. [Fr. *attachement*, *attacher*] a fastening, affection.

Attack, v. [Fr. *attaquer*, variation of *attacher*] to fasten upon so as to hurt, to assault, injure. *Attacked.*

Attain, v. [Fr. *atteindre*, L. *attingere*; *ad*, *tangere*] to reach, touch, gain, obtain. *Attained.*

Attempt, s. [L. *ad*, *temptare*, *tentare*, to try] a trial, effort.

Attend, v. [Fr. *attendre*, L. *attendere*; *ad*, *tendere*, to stretch to] to stretch the mind towards, to give the mind to, to listen. *Attended.*

Attention, s. [Fr. *attention*, L. *attentionem*, *tendere*] the act of attending, giving the mind, listening.

Attentive, adj. [Fr. *attentif*, *attendre*] full of attention.

Attest, v. [Fr. *attester*, L. *attestari*; *ad*, *testari*, to witness] to give witness to, to witness, prove, certify. *Attested.*

Attribute, s. [Fr. *attribut*, L. *attributum*; *ad*, *tribuere*, to assign] a thing assigned, a belonging, a quality, an adjective.

Auction, s. [L. *auctionem*, *auctus*, *augere*, to increase] a public sale at which the price is increased by each offer.

Audible, adj. [Fr. *audible*, L. *audibilis*, *audire*, to hear] that can be heard.

Audience, s. [Fr. *audience*, L. *audientiam*, *audiens*, *audire*] the act of hearing, the people hearing, the hearers, the power of hearing.

Auger, s. [E. *nafgar*, *nafu*, navel, *gar*, gore] a centre-bit, a tool for boring.

Aught, s. [E. *a*, ever, *wiht* (whit), a thing] anything.

August, s. [L. *augustus*] the name of the eighth month, from the Roman Emperor Octavius Augustus.

Author, s. [Fr. *auteur*, L. *auctorem*, *augere*, to increase] a worker, beginner, maker, maker of books, writer.

Authoritative, adj. [Fr. *autoritatif*, *autorité*] full of authority.

Authority, s. [Fr. *autorité*, L. *auctoritatem*, *auctor*] lawful power, rule, permission.

Autumn, s. [Fr. *automne*, L. *auctumnus*, *auctus*, *augere*] the season of increase, the months of August, September, October.

Available, adj. [E. *avail*, Fr. *valoir*, L. *valere*] able to be used, profitable.

Avenge, v. [Fr. *venger*, L. *vindicare*, to claim] to inflict retribution, to punish. *Avenged.*

Average, s. [Fr. *avarie*, L. L. *havaria*, damage, Teut. *haferei*, damage at sea; Scand. *haf*, the sea] (originally) contribution by the various owners of a cargo to pay the losses of those whose goods had been damaged in transit; even distribution of inequalities; mean proportion.

Average, v., to fix an average, bear mean proportion. *Averaged.*

Avert, v. [L. *avertere*; *a*, *vertere*, to turn from] to keep off, to turn away. *Averted.*

Awake, v. [E. *on*, *wacan*] to rouse from sleep, to watch. *Awoke*, *awaken* or *awaked*.

Awake, adj., roused, watching.

Away, adv. [E. *on weg*, way] on the road, absent, far off.

Awe, s. [E. *ege*, fear] dread, solemn fear. Adj. *awful*.

GLOSSARY. 235

Awhile, adv. [E. *a=an*, one, *while*] at a time, for some time.
Axe, s., a tool for chopping or hewing.
Aye, adv. [E. *aa, æ*] ever, always, for all time.

Babe, Baby, s. [*ba*, the sound an infant makes] an infant, a very young child.
Back, s. [E. *bæc*] the hinder part of the body, the rear.
Back, adv., behind, again, to a former place, or time, or state.
Backward,-s, adv. [E. *back*] towards the back, in a back direction.
Bacon, s. [O. Fr. *bacon*, a pig] the salted flesh of the pig.
Bad, adj., not good, evil, ill, vicious. Comp. *worse*, sup. *worst*.
Badge, s., a mark, a distinction.
Baffle, v. [O. Fr. *beffler*, to mock] to mock, elude, frustrate, to render unavailing. *Baffled*.
Bag, s., a thing which bulges, a small sack, poke, pouch.
Bagpipe, s. [E. *bag, pipe*] a musical instrument made of pipes and bags for bellows.
Baker, s. [E. *bake*] one who bakes.
Balance, s. [Fr. *balance*, L. *bilancem; bis*, twice, *lanx*, a dish, scale] a pair of scales, an instrument for weighing, equality, a sum which makes an account equal.
Ballast, s., a load to steady a boat or vessel.
Bang, v. [from the sound] to beat so as to make a loud sound, to strike violently. *Banged*.
Bank, s. [E. *banc*: cf. **Bench**] a back, mound of earth, ridge, a place where money is deposited, so called from money-lenders sitting at benches in streets at their business.
Banner, s. [Fr. *bannière*, It. *bandiera, banda*, G. *band*, a strip] a flag, ensign, standard, a signal for troops.

Banquet, s. [Fr. *banquet, banque*, It. *banca*, G. *banc*] a feast at benches or tables, a feast.
Bar, s., a branch, rod, pole, a pole so placed as to stop a passage, a bank stopping the passage into a river or harbour.
Bar, v., to fasten with a bar, shut in, shut out, hinder. *Barred*.
Barbarian, s. [L. *barbarus*, Gr. *barbaros*, one who did not speak sense] a foreigner, an uncivilised person, a rough.
Bard, s. [W. *bardd*] a minstrel, singer, poet.
Bare, adj., open, stripped, naked, uncovered.
Bare, v., to strip, uncover, make naked. *Bared*.
Bark, s. [E. *beorgan*, to cover] the covering or rind of a tree.
Bark, v., to cry like a dog, make a loud snappish noise. *Barked*.
Bark, s. [It. *barca*] a vessel, a three-masted vessel with no yards on the mizen mast.
Barley, s. [E. *berlic, bere*] a plant of the family of grasses, producing a large grain used for bread and for malting.
Barn, s. [E. *berern; bere*, barley, *ern*, a place] the place for storing barley, a farm storehouse.
Barrel, s. [E. *bar*] a cask made of bars or staves.
Barren, adj., unbearing, unfruitful.
Bartholomew-tide, s., the time at which St. Bartholomew's day comes, August 24.
Base, s. [Fr. *base*, L. *basis*, Gr. *basis*, going, *bainein*, to go] a stepping (cf. **Stepping-stones**), that on which one steps, foundation, bottom.
Base, adj. [Fr. *bas*, L. *bassus, basis*] what is at the bottom, low (with a moral sense), mean, vicious, vile.
Basket, s. [W. *basgod, basg*, network] a vessel made of plaited twigs.

GLOSSARY.

Bass, s. [Fr. *basse,* It. *basso,* L. *bassus,* low] the lowest, deepest-toned part in music.

Bath, s., a bathing-place, a place to wash in, a wash.

Bathe, v. [E. *bath*] to lie in water, to wash, dip in water. *Bathed.*

Battle, s. [Fr. *bataille,* L. *batalia*] a beating, fight, engagement.

Battle, v., to fight, struggle. *Battled.*

Bay, adj. [Fr. *bai,* L. *badius*] reddish-brown, used mostly of horses.

Bay, s. [Fr. *baie,* L. *bacca,* a berry] a shrub, the laurus or laurel of the Romans, called *bay* from its number of berries.

Bay, s. [Fr. *baie,* L. *baia*] a bend or hollow of the sea coast, a bend, bow.

Bay, v. [Fr. *aboyer*] to bark as a dog, to bark frequently. *Bayed.*

Be-, or **Bi-,** a prefix, (1) about, or all round; (2) transitive sign.

Beach, s. [from root of E. *bank*] the shore, bank by the sea.

Beacon, s. [E. *beacen*] a sign, watch-fire on a height, the height on which the fire was placed. See **Beckon.**

Bead, s. [E. *bid,* to pray] a perforated ball. These small balls were strung, and were used to count off the number of prayers said — hence called beads, or prayers. Cf. **Bedesman, Beadsman,** one who prays for another. Adj. *beaded.*

Bean, s., a plant producing a kind of pulse, the fruit of the plant.

Bear, v. [E. *beran*] (1) to carry, endure. *Bore* and *bare, borne.* (2) To bring forth, to have young. *Bore* and *bare, born.*

Bear, s. [E. *bera,* a wild animal] a wild beast with rough, shaggy hair.

Bearing, s., behaviour.

Beast, s. [Fr. *beste,* L. *bestia*] an animal, a brute.

Beat, v. [root E. *bat*] to strike, overcome, surpass. *Beat, beaten.*

Beauty, s. [Fr. *beauté,* O. Fr. *belté,* L. *bellitatem, bellus, bonus*] goodness, fairness, elegance, good looks. Adj. *beauteous, beautiful.* Adv. *beautifully.*

Because, conj. [E. *be, cause*] for the reason that.

Beckon, v. [E. *beacen,* a sign] to sign, point, call by a signal. *Beckoned.*

Become, v. [E. *be, cuman,* to come] to come about, to come into, to change into. *Became, become.*

Bed, s., a place to lie on, a layer, lair, couch, sleeping-place.

Bedding, s. [E. *bed*] things belonging to a bed, bed-clothes.

Bee, s., an insect that makes honey.

Bee-bird, s. [E. *bee*] a bird that eats bees, *Merops Apiaster.*

Beech, s. [E. *bece, boc*] a forest tree producing nuts.

Beersheba, s., a town in Canaan in the extreme south of Judah, often spoken of as the southern limit of the land.

Befall, v. [E. *be, fall*] to fall to, happen, come to pass. *Befell, befallen.*

Befit, v. [E. *be, fit*] to fit, to suit. *Befitted.*

Before, adv. [E. *be, fore*] by the front part, in front of, earlier.

Beforehand, adv., earlier, sooner.

Beg, v. [E. *beggian (bedegian, bedecian), biddan,* to pray, ask] to ask, to go about asking. *Begged.*

Beget, v. [E. *be, get*] to cause to be produced, produce. *Begot (begat), begotten.*

Begin, v. [E. *beginnan, be,* root *gen*] to come into being, commence. *Began, begun.*

GLOSSARY. 237

Begone, interj. [E. imperat. *be*, pp. *gone*] go away! be off!

Behave, v. [E. *be, have*] to bear (oneself), carry, conduct. *Behaved.*

Behind, adv. prep. [E. *be, hind*] about the hind part, at the back, in the rear, after.

Behold, v. [E. *be, hold*] to look upon, see. *Beheld, (beholden) beheld.*

Being, s. [E. *be*] existence, a living creature.

Believe, v. [E. *be, lyfan*, to give leave] to give assent, trust, credit. *Believed.*

Bell, s. [E. *bellan*, to sound] a metal vessel giving a sound.

Bellow, v. [E. *bell*] to sound loudly, to low, to roar. *Bellowed.*

Belong, v. [E. *be, long*, reaching] to reach about, to relate to, to be the property of one. *Belonged.*

Below, adv. prep. [E. *be, low*] in a low place, beneath, under.

Belt, s. [L. *balteus*, a girdle] a band, girdle.

Bench, s. [softened form of E. *baenc*] a bank, seat, form.

Bend, v. [E. *bendan*] to curve, make crooked, to incline, induce. *Bended* or *bent.*

Beneath, adv. prep. [E. *be, neath, benyðan*] about the under part, under, below, lower than.

Benefit, s. [O. Fr. *benefait* (*bienfait*), L. *bene*, well, *factum*, done] a good deed, a kindness, advantage.

Berber, s., an inhabitant of Northern Africa.

Bereave, v. [E. *be, reáfian*, to rob, reave] to deprive utterly, to make destitute. *Bereaved* or *bereft.*

Beseech, v. [E. *be, seek*, softened form] to seek earnestly, implore, entreat. *Besought.*

Beset, v. [E. *be, set*] to set about, surround, besiege. *Beset.*

Besides, adv. prep. [E. *be, side*] by the side, moreover, in addition to.

Besiege, v. [E. *be*, Fr. *siége*, L. *sedere*, to sit] to sit down about, to blockade, invest. *Besieged.*

Best, adj. [E. contr. of *betest*] most good, most excellent. Good, (*bet*) *better, best.*

Bestow, v. [E. *be, stow*, a station] to stow away, to put by, give. *Bestowed.*

Betide, v. [E. *be, tidan*, to happen] to happen, to befall. *Betided*, or *betid.*

Betimes, adv. [E. *be, time*] by the right time, in good time, early.

Better, adj. [E. *bet*] more good, superior. Good, (*bet*) *better*, *best.*

Between, prep. [E. *be, twain, twa*, two] by two, in the middle of two.

Betwixt, prep. [E. *be, tweox, twa*, two] by two, between two.

Bevy, s. [Fr. *bevée*] a brood, a group of girls.

Bewilder, v. [E. *be, wild*] to make wild, to perplex. *Bewildered.*

Beyond, adv. prep. [E. *be, yon*] by that side, at a distance, further than, remote from.

Bid, v. [E. *biddan*, to pray] to ask, pray, command. *Bid* or *bade, bidden.*

Bide, v. [E. *bidan*, to wait on] to stay, wait. (*Bode*), *bided.*

Big, adj., swollen, large, great.

Billow, s. [form of E. *bulge*] a great swollen wave.

Bind, v. [E. *bindan*] to band together, to unite, to tie, to oblige. *Bound, (bounden) bound.* Subs. *binder.*

Birch, s., a forest tree with a smooth white bark.

Bird, s. [E. *brid*] one of a brood, a feathered animal. (Orig. any young creature.)

Birth, s. [E. *bear*] a bearing, bringing forth, origin, the thing born.

Biscuit, s. [Fr. L. *bis*, twice, Fr. *cuit*, L. *coctus, coquere*, cooked] twice baked, bread baked hard.

Bishop, s. [softened form of E. *biscop*, L. *episcopus*, Gr. *episkopos*, an overseer] an officer of the Church in charge of a diocese.

Bison, s. [Gr. *bison*] a large wild species of bull, having humped shoulders and a shaggy mane.

Bit, s. [E. *bite*] a piece bitten off, a small piece, a tool which bites, a part of the bridle bitten by the horse.

Bite, v. [E. *bitan*] to tear with the teeth, to wound. *Bit, bitten.*

Bitter, adj. [E. *bite*] biting to the taste, sharp, acid, painful, harsh. Adv. *bitterly.*

Bitterness, s. [E. *bitter*] quality of being bitter, malice, sorrow, pain.

Black, adj. [E. *blæc*] colourless, dark, dismal. Subs. *blackness.*

Bladder, s. [E. *blæddre, blæsan*, to blow] that which is blown out, a thin bag of skin.

Blade, s. [E. *blǽd*, a leaf] a leaf, anything leaf-shaped, a sword, the flat part of an oar. Adj. *bladed*, fitted with a blade.

Blame, v. [Fr. *blâmer*, O. Fr. *blasmer*, L. *blasphemare*, Gr. *blasphemein*, to find fault with] to censure, find fault with. *Blamed.*

Blame, s., fault-finding, censure.

Blast, s. [E. *blǽst, blǽsan*, to blow] air blown, a rush or gust of air.

Blaze, s. [E. *blǽsan*, to blow] a rush of light, a bright light, a flame.

Blaze, v., to flame, shine brightly. *Blazed.*

Bleach, v. [softened form of *bleak*, E. *blæc*] to make colourless, to whiten, to become white, to pale. *Bleached.*

Blenheim, s., a village near the bank of the Danube, near which the English and their allies under the Duke of Marlborough gained a great victory over the French and Bavarians under Marshal Tallard, A.D. 1704.

Bless, v. [E. *blessian*, to consecrate] to make happy, to wish happy, to praise. *Blessed* or *blest.*

Blessing, s. [E. *bless*] a prayer for happiness, benediction.

Blind, adj., sightless, dark.

Blink, v. [E. *blican*] to wink, twinkle, to see dimly, open and shut the eyes. *Blinked.*

Bliss s., joy, happiness.

Bloat, v. [Sw. *blota*, to soak in water] to puff out, to swell. *Bloated.*

Blood, the red fluid in the arteries, kindred.

Blossom, v. [E. *blosm*, bloom] to blow, to put forth flowers, to flourish. *Blossomed.*

Blow, v. [E. *blowian*, to shine] to put forth flowers, to bloom. *Blew, blown.*

Blow, v. [E. *bláwan*, to breathe] to breathe hard, to drive by wind. *Blew, blown.*

Blow, s., a stroke, hit, sudden accident, great misfortune.

Blue, adj. [E. *bleu*] a colour, the colour of the sky.

Bluff, adj., abrupt, rough, blustering.

Blushing, adj. [E. *blush*, bloom, blow] reddening, colouring.

Boar, s., a male swine.

Board, s. [E. *brád*, broad, by metathesis] a broad piece of timber, a table for food, people sitting at a table.

Boast, s., talking big, magnifying oneself.

Boasting, s., the act of bragging, vaunting. self-exaltation.

Boat, s. [E. *bát*] a small open vessel.

Bob, v., to move quickly, to jerk up and down. *Bobbed.*

Bodily, adj. [E. *body*] belonging to body, real. Adv. in a body, really, completely.

Body, s. [E. *bodig*, root *bot*, a lump] the trunk, mass, framework, substance, a number of persons together.

Boil, v. [Fr. *bouillir*, L. *bullire*] to bubble with heat, to be heated. *Boiled*.

Boisterous, adj. [E. *boistous*, W. *bwyst*, wild] wild, noisy, disorderly.

Bold, adj., daring, courageous, steep.

Bolt, s., a round head, an arrow with a round head, a pin, bar, large nail.

Bomb, s. [Fr. *bomb*, from the sound] a booming, sounding ball; a hollow ball of iron filled with powder.

Bondman, s. [E. *bind*, *man*] one who is bound, a slave, serf.

Bone, s. [E. *bán*] the hard framework of an animal.

Bonfire, s. [W. *ban*, high, E. *fire*] a beacon-fire, a large fire upon open ground.

Book, s. [E. *boc*, a beech-tree] a collection of paper bound together, so called from the early books of the Teutonic nations having been written on beechen blocks.

Boom, v. [from the sound] to make a rumbling noise. *Boomed*.

Border, s. [Fr. *bordure*, Du. *bord*, an edge] an edge, fringe.

Border, v., to touch upon, to be close to, to fringe. *Bordered*.

Bosom, s. [E. *bosm*] the front part of the body, breast, heart.

Botch, v. [E. *boss*, a lump] to patch, to mend in a clumsy way. *Botched*.

Both, adj. [E. *ba*, *twa*] two together, two.

Bottle, s. [Fr. *bouteille*, L. *buticula*, *butica*, a flask] a vessel that bulges, a vessel for holding liquid, a glass vessel.

Bottom, s. [E. *botm*] the under part, the lowest part.

Bough, s. [E. *bugan*, to bend] the bent part of a tree, a branch.

Boulder, s. [Fr. *boule*, E. *bole*] a stone rounded by natural causes.

Bound, s., a limit, end.

Bound, v., to mark by a bound, limit, enclose. *Bounded*.

Bound, v. [Fr. *bondir*, L. *bombitare*] to spring, jump. *Bounded*.

Bounteous, adj. [E. *bounty*, Fr. *bonté*, L. *bonitatem*, *bonus*, good] abounding in goodness, abundant, plentiful.

Bow, v. [E. *bugan*, to bend] to bend, incline the body, make to bend. *Bowed*.

Bow, s. [E. *bugan*] a bending of the body, a salute, the curved forepart of a ship.

Bow, s. [E. *bugan*] a bent instrument for shooting arrows.

Bower, s. [E. *bur*, a room] a chamber, an enclosure in a garden, an arbour.

Box, s. [L. *buxus*] a tree, a chest made of the box-tree, a chest.

Boy, s., a male child.

Brake, s., fern, a place full of fern, a thicket.

Bramble, s. [E. *bremel*, thorn] the blackberry plant.

Branch, s., a shoot, arm of a tree.

Branch, v., to spread into arms, to divide into branches. *Branched*.

Brandy, s. [E. *brand wine*, *burnt wine*] spirit distilled from wine.

Brass, s. [E. *braes*, fire] metal bright as live coal, alloy of copper and zinc.

Brave, adj. [Fr. *brave*, It. *bravo*] showy, gaudy, fine, bold, noble. Adv. *bravely*.

Brave, v., to meet boldly, dare, defy. *Braved*.

Brazen, adj. [E. *brass*] made of brass.

Brazils, s. [Port. *brasil*, bright red; *braza*, live coals, O. G. *bras*, fire] a country on the west of South America, once called Santa Cruz, afterwards Brasil, from an excellent bright red (brasil) dye which was brought from it.

Bread, s. [E. *breówan*, to brew] meal baked, food.

Breadth, s. [E. *broad*] measure from side to side, width.

Break, v. [E. *brecan*] to part by force, to burst, to tear apart, to separate. *Broke (brake), broken.*

Breaker, s. [E. *break*] a wave bursting on the shore.

Breakwater, s. [E. *break, water*] a ledge or wall in a harbour to break the waves.

Breast, s. [E. *breost*] the upper part of the body, the bosom.

Breast, v., to meet in front, to face, to struggle against. *Breasted.*

Breath, s. [E. *braeð*] vapour, air, a stream of air. Adj. *breathless,* without breath.

Breathe, v. [E. *breath*] to take in and give forth air, to live. *Breathed.*

Breeches, s., pl. only [O. F. *bragues*, L. *bracca*, a Teutonic word] trousers.

Breed, v. [E. *breodan*] to generate, bring forth, nourish. *Bred* or *breeded.*

Breeze, s. [Fr. *brise*] a cool wind.

Bridal, s. [E. *bride, ale*] the bride's ale or feast, a wedding. Adj. belonging to a wedding.

Bridge, s. [E. *bricg*, softened form] a building uniting the banks of a river.

Bridge, v., to join the banks of a river by a building, unite. *Bridged.*

Bridle, s. [E. *bridel, bit*] the means of guiding a horse, a rein, a check.

Brief, adj. [Fr. *bref*, L. *breve*] short.

Brief, s., a short writing, summary, writ, the summary of instructions given to a barrister about his case.

Brier, s., bramble, a thorny shrub, species of rose.

Bright, adj. [E. *beorht*] clear, burning, shining, bright.

Brighten, v. [E. *bright*] to make bright, become bright. *Brightened.*

Brim, s., the lip, edge, margin.

Brim, v., to rise to the brim, to be full to the brim. *Brimmed.*

Brine, s., the sea, salt water, a salt pickle.

Bring, v., to fetch, carry to, carry with one. *Brought.*

Britain, s. [E. *Bryten*, L. *Britannia*, Fr. *Bretaine*] a name by which the Romans called England. The name appears to have belonged to the Bretones, a tribe of Belgic Celts on the Somme below Amiens, and to have been brought with them when they crossed the Channel and settled on the southern coast of this island, and from them to have been given to the whole island.

British, adj., belonging to Britain.

Brittle, adj. [E. *brytan*, to break] easily broken, fragile.

Broad, adj. [E. *brád*] extended, wide.

Broil, v. [Fr. *brûler*, L. *per -ustulare, ustus,* burnt] to cook over the coals. *Broiled.*

Bronze, s. [It. *bronzo*, glowing coals] an alloy of copper and tin, a cast of bronze.

Brook, s. [E. *brecan*, to break] a stream breaking forth, a bubbling stream.

Broth, s. [E. *brod, breówan*, to brew] liquor in which flesh has been boiled or brewed, soup.

Brother, s. [E. *broðor*] a son born of the same parents, a close friend.

Brow, s. [E. *bræw*] the ridge over the eyes, a ridge, the edge of a hill.

Brown, adj. [E. *brun, byrnan*, to burn] of a burnt colour, dusky, tawny.

Browse, v. [O. Fr. *brouster, broust,* a

sprig] to nibble off sprigs, feed upon shoots of trees. *Browsed.*
Bubbling, adj. [E. *bubble*] murmuring, rising in bubbles.
Buck, s., the male goat, the male deer, a male.
Buckle, v. [Fr. *boucle*, L. *bucula, bucca*, a cheek] to fasten with a buckle or knob, to link. *Buckled.*
Buff, adj. [*buffalo*] light yellow (the colour of leather of buffalo skin).
Build, v. [E. *byldan*] to make, construct, erect a house. *Builded* or *built.*
Building, s. [*build*] a structure, house.
Bulk, s. [hard form of E. *bulge*] large size.
Bulwark, s. [G. *boll, werk*] a work made of tree-boles or trunks, an outwork, fortification, defence.
Bundle, s. [E. *byndel, bind*] a thing bound, a collection of things bound together.
Burden, s. [E. *beran*, to bear] a thing borne, a load, weight.
Burgess, s. [L.L. *burgensis*, Teut. *burg*, a fort] one who lives in a borough.
Burn, v. [E. *byrnan*] to be on fire, to consume by fire, to be heated. *Burned* or *burnt.*
Burnet, s., Gilbert Burnet, bishop of Salisbury in the reign of William III and Mary, wrote a History of the Reformation.
Burst, v. [E. *berstan*] to break open, rush forth. *Burst.*
Burst, s., a sudden rush.
Bury, v. [E. *byrian, birgan*] to hide in the ground, to cover over, inter. *Buried.*
Business, s. [O. Fr. *besognes*, affairs; but treated as if from E. *busy*] duty, employment, trade.
Bustle, v., to hurry, stir quickly, to be active. *Bustled.*
Busy, s. [E. *bysig*] working, active, employed.

Busy, v., to set to work, employ, make active, occupy. *Busied.*
But, conj. [E. *be, utan*, out] except, leaving out.
Butt, s. [Fr. *botte*] a large cask.
Butt, v., to push, strike with the head. *Butted.*
Buy, v. [E. *bige, bycgan*] to get for money, purchase. *Bought.*
Buzzing, s., a humming sound, whirring.
By (bi, be), adv. prep., about, around, near, close, by means of (expressing an instrumental sense).

Cabal, s. [Fr. *cabale*, Hebr. *kabala*, secret tradition] a small party with a secret purpose, a plot, conspiracy.
Cabbage, s. [Fr. *caboche*, L. L. *cabo*, L. *caput*, a head] a plant whose head is eatable.
Cabin, s. [Fr. *cabane*, L.L. *capanna*] a hut, a room on board ship.
Cabinet, s. [Fr. *cabinet, cabane*] a small cabin, a closet.
Cable, s. [Fr. *cable*, L. *capulum, capere*, to hold] a rope, a rope for fastening a vessel.
Cæsar, s., Gaius Julius Cæsar, a Roman general and emperor; born of patrician family B.C. 100; invaded Britain B.C. 55 and 54; murdered at Rome B.C. 44.
Cake, s. [from same root as E. *cook*] a piece of cooked dough, a hard compressed mass.
Calcine, v. [Fr. *calciner*, L. *calcem, calx*, lime] to reduce to powder by burning. *Calcined.*
Call, v., to cry aloud for, name. *Called.*
Call, s., a cry, demand, summons.
Callow, adj. [E. *calu, calo*, bald] not covered with feathers, unfledged, young.
Calm, adj. [Fr. *calme*, It. *calma*, L. *cauma*, the noonday heat, Gr. *kauma, kaiein*, to burn] quiet, still, serene, resting. Subs. *calmness.*

Calm, v., to make quiet, soothe. *Calmed*.

Calypso, s., a nymph, daughter of Atlas, who detained Odysseus in the island of Ogygia, while on his way home from Troy.

Camelot, s., the name of the supposed place of King Arthur's court.

Camp, s. [Fr. *camp*, L. *campus*, a plain] the ground on which an army is posted, the tents of an army, an army in tents.

Campania, s. [L. *campus*, a plain] a level district on the west coast of Italy.

Can, v. See pp. 75, 77.

Canaan, s., a country situated on the eastern coast of the Mediterranean Sea; also called Palestine.

Canal, s. [L. *canalis*, *canna*, a reed] a passage for water, an artificial watercourse.

Candle, s. [L. *candela*, *candere*, to be bright] a light made of wax or tallow attached to a wick, a waxlight, taper.

Canine, adj. [Fr. *canine*, L. *caninus*, *canis*, a dog] belonging to a dog, like a dog.

Canoe, s. [Sp. *canoa*, a West Indian word] a small boat, a boat made of the hollowed trunk of a tree.

Canopy, s. [Fr. *canopé*, L. *conopeum*, Gr. *konopeion*, a mosquito-curtain, *konops*, a mosquito] a covering, a curtain.

Cap, s., a covering, a top, a cover for the head.

Capable, adj. [Fr. *capable*, L. *capabilis*, *capere*, to take] able to take hold of, competent, skilful.

Capacity, s. [Fr. *capacité*, L. *capacitatem*, *capax*] power of holding, ability, skill.

Capital, s. [Fr. *capital*, L. *capitalis*, *caput*, a head] the chief city, the head of a pillar or column, a 'arge letter, money.

Captain, s. [Fr. *capitaine*, It. *capitano*, L. *caput*] the head officer, the chief, the commander of a company of soldiers.

Captive, s. [Fr. *captif*, L. *captivus*, *capere*, to take] a person taken, a prisoner.

Car, s. [Fr. *car*, L. *carrus*] a waggon, a small carriage.

Care, s. [E. *caru*] attention, heed, anxiety, trouble. Adj. *careful*, *careless*.

Care, v., to take heed, to be anxious. *Cared*.

Career, s. [Fr. *carrière*, L. *carrus*] a road for a car, course, way, path in life.

Cargo, s. [Sp. *cargo*, *cargar*, L. *carricare*, to load, *carrus*, a car] what a ship carries, a shipload.

Carol, s. [Fr. *carole*, It. *carola*, L. *chorulus*, *chorus*, a dance] a dance, a dance with song, a song.

Carpenter, s. [Fr. *charpentier*, L. *carpentarius*, *carpentum*, a carriage] a wheelwright, a worker in wood.

Carriage, s. [Fr. *carriage*, It. *carriagio*, L. *carrus*] the act of carrying, that which carries, a car, vehicle, price paid for carrying.

Carrot, s. [Fr. *carotte*, L. *carota*] an edible root of a reddish colour.

Carry, v. [Fr. *carrier*, L. *carrus*] to bear on a car, to bear, transport. *Carried*.

Carthusian, s., a member of a religious order founded, 1084, by Bruno of Cologne, at Chartreuse in Dauphiné, whence the name.

Carve, v. [E. *ceorfan*] to cut, to engrave. *Carved*.

Case, s. [Fr. *caisse*, L. *capsa*, *capere*, to hold] a receptacle, covering, chest, box.

Case, s. [Fr. *cas*, L. *casus*, *cadere*, to fall] that which befalls, an event, state, condition.

Cast, v., to throw, throw into shape, turn over in the mind. *Cast*.

Cast, s., a throw, a throwing into shape, shape, form.

GLOSSARY. 243

Castle, s. [Fr. *castel*, L. *castellum, castrum*] a fortified building.
Cat, s. [L. *catus*, G. *katze*] a domestic animal of the same family as the tiger.
Cataract, s. [Fr. *cataracte*, L. *cataracta*, Gr. *katarraktes*, a waterfall] a waterfall, rush of water.
Catch, v. [Fr. *cacher*, L. *coactare*] to chase, lay hold of, seize. *Caught.*
Cater, v. [Fr. *acater*, L. *ad, captare*] to get, to provide food. *Catered.*
Catholic, adj. [L. *catholicus*, Gr. *katholikos*, universal] universal, general, embracing all.
Cattle, s. [Fr. *catel*, L. (*catallum*), *captale*, the principal sum in a loan, *capitale, caput*] valuable property, beasts of a farm, oxen.
Cauldron, s. [Fr. *chaudron*, L. *calidarium, calere*, to be hot] a vessel for heating liquid, a large kettle.
Cause, s. [L. *causa*] a reason, inducement.
Cause, v., to induce, bring about, effect. *Caused.*
Cautious, adj. [L. (*cautiosus*) *cautus, cavere*, to beware] wary, careful.
Cavalier, s. [It. *cavaliere, cavallo*, L. *caballus*, a horse] a horseman, a knight, gentleman, a royalist in the reign of Charles I.
Cavalry, s. [It. *cavalerie, cavallo*] a troop of horse, horse-soldiers.
Cave, s. [Fr. *cave*, L. *cavus*, hollow] a hollow place, a den.
Cease, v. [Fr. *cesser*, L. *cessare*] to stop. *Ceased.*
Ceaseless, adj. [E. *cease*] endless, without a stop.
Cedar, s. [Fr. *cèdre*, L. *cedrus*, Gr. *kedros*] a fragrant evergreen tree.
Celebration, s. [Fr. *célébration*, L. *celebrationem, celebrare*] the act of making famous, praising, a ceremony.
Cell, s. [L. *cella*] a hollow place, hut, small room.
Cellar, s. [L. *cellarium, cella*] an underground cell.
Celt, s., the name of a branch of the Indo-European family of nations, including the French as descendants of the Gauls, the Welsh, the Irish, the Gaelic people of Scotland, and the people of Brittany.
Censure, s. [Fr. *censure*, L. *censura*] blame, fault-finding.
Censure, v., to find fault with, to blame. *Censured.*
Centaur, s. [Fr. *centaure*, L. *centaurus*, Gr. *kentauros, kentein*, to pierce] a fabulous monster, man above and horse below, mentioned by Greek poets.
Centre, s. [Fr. *centre*, L. *centrum*, Gr. *kentron*, a point] the middle point, the middle.
Century, s. [Fr. *centurie*, L. *centuria, centum*] a hundred years.
Certain, adj. [Fr. *certain*, L. *certus*] fixed, appointed, sure. Adv. *certainly.*
Certify, v. [Fr. *certifier*, L. *certificare, certum facere*] to make certain, to declare, assert, *Certified.*
Chaff, s. [E. *ceaf*] the case covering grain, husk, refuse, worthless stuff.
Chain, v. [Fr. *chaîne*, L. *catena*] to fasten with a chain, fasten, bind. *Chained.*
Chair, s. [Fr. *chaire*, L. *cathedra*, Gr. *kathedra*] a seat.
Chamber, s. [Fr. *chambre*, L. *camera*] a covered room.
Chance, v. [Fr. *chance*, L. *cadentia, cadere*, to befall] to befall, happen, come to pass. *Chanced.*
Change, v. [Fr. *changer*, L. L. *cambiare*] to alter, vary, barter. *Changed.*
Change, s., alteration, variation, variety, movement.

R 2

Channel, s. [Fr. *channel*, L. *canalis, canna*, a reed] a watercourse, passage, narrow sea.

Chant, v. [Fr. *chanter*, L. *cantare*] to sing, intone. *Chanted.*

Chant, s., a song, sacred music.

Chapel, s. [Fr. *chapelle*, L. *capella*, a hood, the canopy over an altar] a place of worship, originally a recess forming part of a church.

Character, s. [Fr. *caractère*, L. *character*, Gr. *charakter*] a mark, a sign, quality, description.

Charge, v. [Fr. *charger*, L. *carricare, carrus*] to load, to lay upon, to impose commands upon, attack. *Charged.*

Charge, s., a load, command, duty, attack.

Charger, s. [E. *charge*] a horse used in a charge, a warhorse.

Chariot, s. [Fr. *chariot, char*, L. *carrus*] a carriage.

Charity, s. [Fr. *charité*, L. *caritatem, carus*, dear] love, affection, kindness, kindness in giving money.

Charm, s. [Fr. *charme*, L. *carmen*] an enchantment, a spell, fascination.

Charming, adj. [E.*charm*] pleasing, delightful.

Chasm, s. [Gr. *chasma*, a gap] a fissure, cleft, open place between rocks.

Chastise, v. [O. Fr. *chastier*, L. *castigare, castus*, pure] to correct, punish. *Chastised.*

Chatter, v. [E. freq. of *chat*] to talk much, to keep talking. *Chattered.*

Check, v. [Fr. *échec*, O. Fr, *eschac*, stop to the king, Pers. *schach*, king] a term in the game of chess, to stop, to hinder. *Checked.*

Cheek, s. [E. *ceaca*] the jaw, side of the face.

Cheer, s. [Fr. *chère*, L.L. *cara*, Gr. *kara*, the head] countenance, look, joyful look, joy, a joyful shout.

Cheer, v., to encourage, to raise a shout. *Cheered.*

Cherry, s. [E. *cirse*, L. *cerasus*, Gr. *Kerasos*, a place on the Euxine Sea whence the cherry came into Italy] a small stone-fruit.

Chest, s. [E. *cist*, L. *cista*] a box, case.

Chestnut, s. [E. *chesteyn*, O. Fr. *chastagne*, L. *castanea, Castana*, a city of Pontus, whence the nut came into Italy] a nut with a prickly husk or covering.

Chew, v. [E. *ceowan*] to bite, crush with the jaws. *Chewed.*

Chief, adj. [Fr. *chef*, L. *caput*] head, principal, a leading man. Adv. *chiefly.*

Child, s. [E. *cild*] offspring, a young person, boy or girl. Adj. *childish*, like a child.

Childhood, s. [E. *child*] state of a child, time of being a child.

Chime, s., bells ringing in harmony, agreement of sound, agreement.

Chimney, s. [Fr. *cheminée*, L. *caminata, caminus*] a fireplace, a passage for smoke from the fireplace.

China, s., a large populous country in the east of Asia.

Choice, s. [Fr. *chois, choisir*, O. F. *coisir*, E. *ceosan*] act of choosing, preference, thing chosen.

Choir, s. [Fr. *chœur*, L. *chorus*, G. *choros*] a band of singers, the part of a church in which the singers sit.

Choose, v. [E. *ceosan*] to prove, to select, to pick. *Chose, chosen.*

Christ, s. [L. *Christus*, Gr. *Christos, chriein*, to anoint] the Anointed, a title or name given to our Lord.

Christian, s. [L. *Christianus*, Gr. *Christos*] a disciple of Christ.

Christmas, s. [*Christ, mass*, L. *missa*] orig. a mass or service in remembrance of Christ, the birthday of Christ, December 25th.

Church, s. [E. *circe, cyrice*, Gr. *kuriakos (oikos)*, the Lord's house] a building set apart for worship of God, people who worship God.

Cinder, s. [Fr. *cendre*, L. *cinerem, cinis*] ash, burnt coal.

Cinque-ports, s. [Fr. *cinque*] five ports on the S. E. coast of England; viz. Dover, Hastings, Hythe, Romney, Sandwich, with jurisdiction vested in a Warden, instituted by William I in 1078. Two other ports, Winchelsea and Rye, were added to the number later.

Circle, s. [L. *circulus*] a plane figure bounded by a line everywhere equally distant from a point called the centre, a ring. Adj. *circling*.

Circuit, s. [Fr. *circuit*, L. *circuitus, circum, ire*, to go round] a going round, a round.

Circular, adj. [L. *circularis, circus*] round.

Circulate, v. [L. *circulatus, circulare*] to send round, go round. *Circulated*.

Circumference, s. [L. *circum, ferre*] a line drawn round a thing, the limit of a circle.

Circumstance, s. [L. *circum, stantia, stare*] that which accompanies, the surroundings.

Citizen, s. [O. Fr. *citeien (citoyen)* L. L. *civitadanus, civitas*] a dweller in a city.

City, s. [Fr. *cité*, L. *civitatem, civitas*, a state] a town, a town that is the seat of a bishop's see.

Civilise, v. [Fr. *civiliser, civil*, L. *civilis, civis*, a citizen] to make civil, to soften, refine. *Civilised*.

Civilisation, s. [Fr. *civilisation, civiliser*] the act of civilising, refinement, polished manners.

Clap, v., to slap, to make a noise by striking the hands. *Clapped* or *clapt*.

Clasp, s. [E. *claspe, clap*] a thing which fastens with a snap, a fastening.

Clasp, v., to fasten, embrace, hug. *Clasped*.

Class, s, [Fr. *classe*, L. *classem*] a rank, order, degree, division, kind.

Clattering, adj. [E. *clatter*] making a rattling sound.

Clay, s. [E. *claeg*] that which clogs, a soft sticky earth, earth.

Clear, adj. [Fr. *clair*, L. *clarus*] distinct, loud, open, bright, evident.

Cleave, v. [E. *clifan, claeg*] to stick, cling, adhere closely. *Clave* or *cleaved*, *cleaved*.

Cleave, v. [E. *clufan*, to cut] to cut, separate. *Clove*, or *cleft*, or *cleaved*; *cloven, cleft, cleaved*.

Cleft, s. [E. *cleave*, to cut] a place split open, a crack, rift, opening.

Clever, adj. skilful, wise, cunning, expert. Subs. *cleverness*.

Click, v., to make a sharp sound, to tick. *Clicked*.

Cliff, s. [E. *cleave*] a sharp cut rock, a precipice, crag.

Climate, s. [Fr. *climate*, L. *clima*, Gr. *klima*, a slope] the inclination of a land towards the pole, temperature and moisture of a land.

Cling, v. [E. *clingan*] to stick close, hang closely. *Clang* or *clung, clung*.

Clock, s. [Fr. *cloche*, a bell] a machine for measuring time, at first the hour of the day was struck by bells.

Close, v. [Fr. *clos*, L. *clausus, claudere*, to shut] to shut, end, finish. *Closed*.

Close, s., an end, a finish.

Close, adj., shut, narrow, confined. Adv., secretly, tightly, in a narrow manner.

Cloth, s. [E. *cláð*] covering, a garment, woven stuff. Pl. *cloths*, woven stuffs; *clothes*, garments.

Clothe, v. [E. *cloth*] to put on coverings, to dress. *Clad* or *clothed*.

Clothed, s. [E. *clothe*] garment, dress.

Cloud, s. [E. *clod*] a mass of vapour, a mass.

Cloudy, adj. [E. *cloud*] full of clouds, obscure, dark, gloomy.

Clove, s. [Sp. *clavo*, L. *clavus*, a nail] the flower-bud of a spice-tree of Molucca, so called from its shape.

Clover, s. [E. *clæfer*, *cleave*] a plant with a split leaf, trefoil.

Cluck, v, [from the sound] to call as a hen does, to make a sharp sound. *Clucked*.

Clump, s. [E. *lump*] a thick piece, mass, cluster of trees.

Clumsy, adj. [E. *clomsen*, to be benumbed] shapeless, awkward.

Cluster, s. [E. *clyster*] a group, a bunch.

Cluster, v., to collect in bunches, cling in groups. *Clustered*.

Clutch, v. [E. *clouch*, a claw] to grasp, catch at, seize. *Clutched*.

Cnossus, s., a town in the island of Crete.

Coast, s. [O. Fr. *coste*, L. *costa*, a rib, side] the edge, the edge of land touching on the sea, the sea-line.

Coat, s. [Fr. *cotte*, L. *cotta*, a rug] a covering, an outer garment, an animal's fur.

Cock, s. [a word formed from the sound] a male bird, the male domestic fowl.

Cocoa, s. [Port. *cacao*] a preparation of the seeds of the chocolate plant.

Coffeehouse, s. [Fr. *café*, Arab. *cahwa*] a house in which coffee is supplied.

Coffin, s. [L. *cophinus*, Gr. *kophinos*, a basket] a box to hold a dead body.

Cohort, s. [Fr. *cohorte*, L. *cohortem*, *cohors*] a division of the Roman army, about 600 men, a body of armed men.

Coil, v. [O. Fr. *coillir*, L. *colligere; con, legere*, to gather together] to wind round. *Coiled*.

Cold, adj. [E. *cool*] cooled, deprived of heat.

College, s. [Fr. *collége*, L. *collegium; con, legere*, to gather together] a society of persons, a building in which such a society lives, a society devoted to education.

Colossal, adj. [L. *colossus*, Gr. *kolossos*] like the colossus, very large, gigantic, immense.

Colour, s. [Fr. *couleur*, L. *colorem*, *color*] hue, tint, stain, appearance, false appearance, pretence.

Colour, v., to put colour upon, to tint, dye, stain. *Coloured*.

Colt, s., a young animal, a young horse.

Column, s. [L. *columna*] a pillar, a long mass of troops, a long row of lines.

Combat, s. [Fr. *combat, combattre*, L. L. *battuere*] a battle, fight.

Combustible, adj. [Fr. *combustible*, L. *combustus; cum, urere*, to burn] able to be burned, liable to burn.

Come, v. [E. *cuman*] to move to, to draw near, approach. *Came, come*.

Comely, adj. [E. *come*] becoming, suitable, pleasing, beautiful.

Comfort, v. [Fr. *conforter*, L. *con, fortis*, strong] to strengthen, help, encourage, console. *Comforted*.

Comfort, s., help, encouragement, consolation.

Command, v. [Fr. *commander*, L. *cum, mandare*] to give orders, order, summon. *Commanded*.

Command, s. an order.

Commander, s. [E. *command*] one who orders.

Commence, v. [Fr. *commencer*, It. *cominciare*, L. *con, cum, initiare*] to begin, to arise. *Commenced*.

Commend, v. [Fr. *commander*] to give into the charge of, entrust to, praise. *Commended*.

Commerce, s. [Fr. *commerce*, L. *con, mercem, merx*, goods] exchange of goods, trade, traffic.

Commit, v. [L. *committere*] to entrust, hand over, do. *Committed*.

Commodity, s. [Fr. *commodité*, L. *commoditatem; cum, modus*] suitable measure, advantage.

Common, adj. [Fr. *commun*, L. *communis*] shared by several, usual, general, of small value, poor. Adv. *commonly*.

Commonwealth, s. [E. *common, wealth*] the well-being of the state, the government, a republic.

Companion, s. [Fr. *compagnon*, L. *companionem, cum, panis*, bread] a sharer of food, a comrade, fellow-traveller, partner.

Company, s. [Fr. *compagnie*, L. *cum, panis*] association, a number of partners.

Comparative, adj. [L. *comparativus, comparare*] in relation to something else.

Compare, v. [Fr. *comparer*, L. *comparare*] to bring together, to match. *Compared*.

Compass, s. [Fr. *compas*, L. *cum, passus*, a step] a circuit, circle, range. Pl. *compasses*, an instrument for making a circle.

Compel, v. [L. *compellere*, to drive together] to drive, force, insist. *Compelled*.

Complain, v. [Fr. *complaindre*, L. *cum, plangere*, to beat the breast] to wail, lament, murmur. *Complained*.

Complaint, s. [Fr. *complainte*] an expression of pain or sorrow.

Complete, v. [L. *cum, pletus, plere*, to fill] to fulfil, to finish. *Completed*.

Complexion, s. [Fr. *complexion*, L. *complexionem, complecti*, to enfold] a combination, appearance, disposition, colour of the skin.

Comport, v. [Fr. *comporter*, L. *cum, portare*, to carry] to behave, conduct. *Comported*.

Comportment, s. [Fr. *comportment, comporter*] bearing, behaviour, carriage, conduct.

Compostella, s., a town in Galicia in Spain, where was a famous shrine of Santiago, or Saint James.

Comprehend, v. [L. *comprehendere*] to take hold of, understand. *Comprehended*.

Compress, v. [L. *compressus; cum, premere*] to press together. *Compressed*.

Comrade, s. [Fr. *camarade*, Sp. *camarada*, L. *camera*, a chamber] a chamber-companion, a companion in a journey, partner.

Con, v. [E. *cunnan*] to know, to study, pore over. *Conned*.

Conceited, adj. [*conceit*, It. *concetto*, a fancy, L. *conceptum, concipere*, to think] imagining self of great importance, vain.

Conceive, v. [Fr. *concevoir*, L. *concipere, capere*] to take in, to take into the mind, to think, imagine. *Conceived*.

Concern, v. [Fr. *concerner*, L. *cum, cernere*, to see] to have relation to, to affect. *Concerned*.

Concert, v. [Fr. *concerter*, L. *cum, certare*, to strive] to plan, contrive, arrange. *Concerted*.

Concussion, s. [Fr. *concussion*, L. *concussionem, concutere, cum, quatere*, to shake] a shaking, a shock.

Condemn, v. [Fr. *condemner*, L. *cum, damnare*] to declare guilty, to blame. *Condemned*.

Condense, v. [Fr. *condenser*, L. *cum, densare*] to thicken, compress. *Condensed*.

Condition, s. [Fr. *condition*, L. *conditionem; cum, datum, dare*] state, quality, manner.

Coney, s. [L. *cuniculus*] a rabbit.

Confer, v. [Fr. *conférer*, L. *cum, ferre*] to bring together, to hold a conversation, to give. *Conferred*.

Conference, s. [Fr. *conférence*, L. *cum, ferre*] a meeting, conversation.

Confess, v. [Fr. *confesser*, L. *confessari*, freq. of L. *fateri*] to avow, admit, acknowledge. *Confessed*.

Confine, v. [Fr. *confiner*, L. *cum, finire*] to limit, enclose, shut up, restrain. *Confined*.

Confirm, v. [Fr. *confirmer*, L. *cum, firmare*] to make firm, strengthen, establish, ratify. *Confirmed.*

Confuse, v. [Fr. *confus*, L. *confusus; fundere*] to mix, perplex, disorder, confound. *Confused.*

Confusion, s. [Fr. *confusion*, L. *confusionem; fundere*] mixture, disorder.

Confute, v. [L. *confutare*, to check] to disprove, to prove to be wrong. *Confuted.*

Congeal, v. [Fr. *congeler*, L. *congelare; gelu*, frost] to freeze hard, become stiff. *Congealed.*

Conjecture, s. [L. *conjectura, jactura, jacere*] a cast, guess, opinion.

Conjecture, v., to make a cast, to guess. *Conjectured.*

Conjunction, s. [L. *conjunctionem; junctio, jungere*, to join] a joining, union, a word which joins.

Connect, v. [L. *connectere; nectere*] to link together, join. *Connected.*

Conquer, v. [Fr. *conquerir*, L. *conquirere; quaerere*, to seek] to overcome, vanquish. *Conquered.*

Conqueror, s. [E. *conquer*] one who conquers.

Conquest, s. [O. Fr. *conqueste*, L. *conquisitus; quaerere*] victory.

Conscious, adj. [L. *conscius; scire*, to know] knowing, aware.

Consciousness, s. [E. *conscious*] knowledge.

Consent, v. [Fr. *consentir*, L. *consentire*, to think with] to agree. *Consented.*

Consent, s., agreement.

Consequence, s. [Fr. *conséquence*, L. *consequentia; sequi*, to follow] that which follows, result, effect, importance.

Consider, v. [Fr. *considérer*, L. *considerare*] to look closely into, to attend to, contemplate. *Considered.*

Considerable, adj. [Fr. *considérable, considérer*] worth regard, important, large.

Consign, v. [Fr. *consigner*, L. *con, signare, signum*, a seal] to give under seal, to intrust. *Consigned.*

Consist, v. [Fr. *consister*, L. *cum, sistere, stare*, to stand] to stand in agreement with, to be made of. *Consisted.*

Consistent, adj. [L. *consistentem, sistere*] agreeing.

Consolidate, v. [L. *consolidatus, solidus*] to make solid, strengthen. *Consolidated.*

Consonant, s. [L. *consonantem; sonare*, to sound] a letter that needs a vowel to be sounded with it.

Conspicuous, adj. [L. *conspicuus*] easily seen, prominent.

Constant, s. [Fr. *constant*, L. *constantem; stare*] standing firm, unchanging. Subs. *constancy.*

Consternation, s. [Fr. *consternation*, L. *consternationem; sternere*, to lay low] a throwing into confusion, fright, fear.

Constitute, v. [L. *constitutus; statuere, stare*] to appoint, fix, settle. *Constituted.*

Constitution, s. [L. *constitutionem; statuere*] settlement, usage by which a country is governed.

Construct, v. [L. *constructus; struere*, to build] to put together, build. *Constructed.*

Construction, s. [L. *constructionem; struere*] building, making, a thing built.

Consult, v. [L. *consultus; consulere*] to talk together, to ask for advice. *Consulted.*

Consultation, s. [L. *consultationem; consulere*] the act of consulting.

Consume, v. [Fr. *consumer*, L. *consumere; sumere*, to take] to destroy, waste, spend. *Consumed.*

Contact, s. [Fr. *contact*, L. *contactus, tangere*] touch, union, meeting.

Contemptible, adj. [Fr. *contemp-*

GLOSSARY. 249

tible, L. *contemptus, temnere*, to despise] fit to be despised, mean.

Contend, v. [L. *contendere*] to strive against, to fight. *Contended.*

Continent, s. [Fr. *continent*, L. *continentem*, touching, *tenere*] an expanse of land containing several countries which touch one another.

Continue, v. [Fr. *continuer*, L. *continuus, tenere*] to remain, persist, carry on, extend. *Continued.*

Contract, v. [L. *contractus, trahere*] to draw together, lessen, shorten. *Contracted.*

Contradict, v. [L. *contra, dictus, dicere*] to oppose in words, deny. *Contradicted.*

Contrary, adj. [L. *contrarius, contra*] opposite, opposed.

Contribute, v. [L. *contributus, tribuere*] to give with others, to give a share. *Contributed.*

Contrive, v. [Fr. *controuver*, It. *trovare*, L. *turbare*] to seek out, invent, devise, manage. *Contrived.*

Contrivance, s. [E.*contrive*] a plan, invention, scheme.

Control, s. [Fr. *contrôle, contrerôle*, L. *contra, rotula*, a roll] a check-roll, check, restraint, authority, power.

Convenient, adj. [L. *convenientem, veniens, venire*] becoming, fit, suitable.

Converge, v. [Fr. *converger*, L. *convergere*] to turn towards, incline together. *Converged.*

Converse, v. [Fr. *converser*, L. *conversari, vertere*, to turn] to discourse, to talk. *Conversed.*

Convey, v. [O.Fr. *convoier*, L.L. *conviare*,L.*via*] to take on the way, send on the way, carry. *Conveyed.*

Convolvulus, s. [L. *cum, volvere*, to roll] a creeping plant, which rolls its tendrils round other things for support.

Convulsion, s. [L. *convulsionem; vulsus, vellere*, to tear] agitation, disturbance, spasm.

Convulsive, adj. [Fr. *convulsif*, L. *cum, vulsus, vellere*] spasmodic, agitated.

Cook, s. [E. *cóc*, L. *coquus*] one who prepares food by means of fire.

Cool, adj., not warm, calm, impudent.

Copious, adj. [L. *copiosus, copia*, plenty] plentiful, abundant.

Copper, s. [Germ. *kupfer*, L. *cuprum, cyprium*, Gr. *kupros*, the island of Cyprus, from which copper came] a reddish metal.

Copse, s. [E. *coppice*, O. Fr. *copeiz, couper*, to cut] a small wood that may be cut for firewood.

Coptic, adj., belonging to *Copts*, Egyptian.

Copy, s. [Fr. *copie*, L. *copia*, plenty] an imitation. Pl. *copies.*

Copy, v., to make a transcript, imitate. *Copied.*

Cord, s. [Fr. *chorde*, L. *chorda*, Gr. *chorde*] string, a small rope.

Corinth, s., a city of Greece, on the isthmus which joins the Peloponnesus, or Morea, to the mainland.

Corinthian, adj. [L. *Corinthianus, Corinthus*] a dweller in Corinth, belonging to Corinth.

Corn, s., the seed of various species of grasses, grain.

Cornel,s.[Fr.*cornille*,L. *corniculus, cornus*] the cornel-tree, cherry.

Corner, s. [Fr. *corne*, L. *cornua, cornu*, a horn] the horn where two lines meet, an angle.

Coronation, s. [L. *coronationem, corona*, a crown] the act of crowning.

Coronet, s. [L. *corona*] a small crown.

Corpse, s. [Fr. *corps*, L. *corpus*, a body] a dead body.

Correspondence, s. [Fr. *correspondance*, L. *cum, respondere*, to answer] relation, fitness, intercourse by letters.

Corrupt, adj. [L. *corruptus, cum, rumpere*, to break] impure, defiled, erroneous.

Cost, s. [O. Fr. *coust, couster*, L. *con, stare*, to stand] the price in which a thing stands a person, value.

Cotton, s. [Fr. *coton*, Arab. *qoton*] a soft fibrous down obtained from the seed-pod of a plant growing in tropical countries.

Couch, s. [Fr. *couche, coucher*, L. *collocare, locus*] a place for rest, a bed, lounge, sofa.

Council, s. [Fr. *concile*, L. *concilium*] an assembly for consultation, a meeting.

Counsel, s. [Fr. *conseil*, L. *consilium*] advice, deliberation.

Counsellor, s. [E. *counsel*] an adviser, a barrister.

Count, v. [Fr. *compter*, L. *computare*] to sum, add together, reckon. *Counted*.

Count, s., reckoning, number.

Countenance, s. [Fr. *contenance, contenant*, L. *cum, tenere*, to hold together] protection, support, appearance, the face.

Counterpart, s. [Fr. *contrepart*, L. *contra, partem*] opposite part, likeness.

Country, s. [Fr. *contrée*, L. *contra*, against] that which is over against the town, rural district, native land.

Courage, s. [Fr. *courage*, L. *cor*, the heart] spirit, heartiness, bravery.

Courageous, adj. [Fr. *courageux, courage*] full of courage, brave.

Course, s. [Fr. *cours*, L. *cursus, currere*, to run] a running, way, career.

Course, v., to run, go quickly, pursue, run dogs after a hare. *Coursed*.

Court, s. [O. Fr. *court*, L. *cohortem*] an enclosed place, the dwelling of the sovereign.

Court, v., to pay attention to, to make love to. *Courted*.

Courteous, adj. [Fr. *courtois, court*] with the manners of the court, polished.

Courtesy, s. [Fr. *courtoisie, court*] courtly manners, politeness.

Courtly, adj. [E. *court*] well-mannered, polished, respectful.

Cover, s. [Fr. *couvert, couvrir*, L. *co-operire*] a screen, protection.

Cover, v., to clothe, screen, protect. *Covered*.

Covert, s. [Fr. *couvert*] a covered place, shelter, thicket.

Cow, s., the female of the bull; pl. *cows* and *kine*, which latter is properly a genitive formed thus: sing. *cu*, pl. *cy(kye)*, genitive *cuna (kine)*.

Cowherd, s. [E. *cow-herd*] a keeper of cows.

Crab, s., an animal of the order crustacea, usually called a shellfish, having ten legs, breathing through gills, living either in the sea or on land.

Crack, v. [from the sound] to split with a noise, to burst. *Cracked*.

Crackle, v. [freq. of E. *crack*] to crack often. *Crackled*.

Crackling, s., roasted skin of pork.

Craft, s. [E. *cræft*] strength, power, power of taking in, ability, art, cunning.

Crag, s. [W. *craeg*] a rock, a rough rock, a cliff.

Crash, v. [from the sound] to break with a noise. *Crashed*.

Crawl, v., to draw on by the claws, move slowly, creep. *Crawled*.

Creature, s. [Fr. *créature*, L. *creatura, creare*, to make] a thing created, an animal.

Creek, s. [E. *crecca*] a bend in the shore, an inlet.

Creep, v. [E. *creopan*] to move by bending the body, move slowly, crawl. *Creeped* or *crept*.

Cress, s. [E. *cerse*] a pungent plant eaten raw and used in salad.

Crest, s. [Fr. *creste*, L. *crista*] a tuft of hair or feathers, a plume.

Crew, s. [a form of E. *crowd*] a mass of people, a company, a ship's company.

Crime, s. [Fr. *crime*, L. *crimen*, a charge] a fault, offence against law.

Crimson, adj. [It. *cremesino*, Turkish *kermes*, a worm from which the dye was got] dark red.

Crisp, adj. [O. Fr. *crespe*, L. *crispus*] curled, wavy, frizzled.

Crop, s. [E. *crop*, top] produce, yield of land.

Cross, s. [Fr. *croix*, L. *crucem, crux*] two lines athwart.

Cross, v., to mark with a cross, thwart, pass over. *Crossed.*

Crouch, v. [softened from E. *crook*] to bend down, lie close to the ground, cringe. *Crouched.*

Croup, s. [from the sound] inflammation of the throat producing a cough.

Croup, s. [Fr. *croupe*, Norse *kroppr*] a horse's rump.

Crow, v. [from the sound] to croak, to make a noise like a cock, to boast. *Crew* or *crowed, crowed.*

Crowd, s. [E. *crud*, W. *crwd*, a lump] a lump, mass, collection of people.

Crown, s. [G. *krone*, L. *corona*] a ring, circle, diadem.

Cruelty, s. [O. Fr. *cruelté*, L. *crudelitatem, crudelis*] brutality, unkindness.

Crush, v. [from the sound] to break with a noise, bruise, ruin. *Crushed.*

Cry, v. [Fr. *crier*, It. *gridare*, L. *quiritare*] to make a loud sound, wail, lament, weep. *Cried.*

Cry, s., a shrill sound. Pl. *cries.*

Cull, v. [Fr. *cueillir*, L. *colligere, cum, legere*] to gather, collect pick. *Culled.*

Cultivate, v. [L. *cultivatus, cultus*,

colere] to till, to attend to. *Cultivated.*

Cunning, adj. [E. *cunnan*, to know] knowing, skilful, wise, crafty. Adv. *cunningly.*

Cup, s. [Fr. *coupe*, L. *cuppa*] a round hollow vessel.

Cupid, s. [L. *cupido, cupere*, to desire] the God of love among the Romans, son of Venus the goddess of love.

Cur, s., a poor·dog, a small dog, a surly fellow.

Cure, s. [Fr. *cure*, L. *cura*] care, healing, a remedy.

Curiosity, s. [Fr. *curiosité*, L. *curiositatem, curiosus, cura*] anxiety to know, inquisitiveness.

Curious, adj. [Fr. *curieux*, L. *curiosus, cura*] inquisitive, full of care, rare.

Curl, v. [E. *crull*, by metathesis] to coil, wreathe, twist. *Curled.*

Current, adj. [L. *currentem, currere*, to run] running, passing, flowing.

Current, s. a stream.

Curve, s. [L. *curvus*] a bend, an arch.

Curve, v., to bend round, to arch. *Curved.*

Custody, s. [L. *custodia, custos*, a guard] keeping, imprisonment.

Custom, s. [O. Fr. *coustume*, L. L. *costuma*, L. *consuetudinem*] habit, use.

Cut, v., to take off a piece, cleave, divide. *Cut, cut.*

Cutlery, s. [E. *cutler*, Fr. *coutelier*, L. *cultellus, culter*, a knife] the stock of a cutler, knives.

Cycle, s. [Fr. *cycle*, Gr. *kuklos*] a circle, a round of years, a series.

Cypress, s. [Fr. *cyprès*, L. *cupressus*, Gr. *kuparissos*] an evergreen tree.

Dædalus, s., a famous artist of Athens, who visited Crete and made a labyrinth for King Minos. The legend related that he made himself wings and flew from Crete to Sicily.

Dagger, s. [E. *dag, dig,* Fr. *dague*] a knife or sword for stabbing.

Daily, adj. [E. *day*] happening day by day, every day.

Dainty, adj. [W. *dantaidd, dant,* tooth] toothsome, delicate, nice.

Damask, s. [*Damascus*] cloth from Damascus, silk, variegated stuff.

Damson, s. [corruption of *Damascene, Damascus*] a plum from Damascus, a small black plum.

Dan, s., a son of the patriarch Jacob; the tribe called from him; a town, formerly Laish, in the northern part of Palestine, occupied by a colony of Danites, and afterwards counted as the limit of the land towards the north.

Dance, v. [Fr. *danser*] to stamp with the feet, to move in measure. *Danced.*

Dancer, s. [E. *dance*, Teut. *dansôn*] one who dances.

Danger, s. [Fr. *danger,* L. *dominiarium, dominus,* a lord] the power of a lord, penalty, peril, risk, hazard. Adj. *dangerous.*

Danish. adj. [*Dane*] belonging to the Danes, the people of Denmark.

Dare, v. to be bold, to endure, venture. *Dared* or *durst, dared.*

Daring, s. bravery, courage.

Darius, s., the King of Persia, whose power was overthrown by Alexander of Macedon in the battle of Arbela on the plains near the Tigris, B.C. 331. He was murdered in Bactria by Bessus, one of his satraps, B.C. 330.

Dark, adj. [E. *dearc*] without light, obscure. Subs. *darkness;* adj. *darksome.*

Dart, v., to throw violently, hurl rapidly, shoot, dash. *Darted.*

Dash, v. [from the sound] to throw with a rushing sound. *Dashed.*

Date, s. [L. *datum, dare,* to give] a given time, a fixed time, time.

Daughter, s. [E. *dohter*] a female child.

Daunt, v. [O. Fr. *danter (dompter),* L. *domitare, domare,* to tame] to frighten, dishearten. *Daunted.*

Daw, s. [from the cry] a chattering bird of the crow family, *Corvus Monedula.*

Dawn, v. [E. *dagian,* to become day; *dæg*] to become day, to brighten, to grow light. *Dawned.*

Dawn, s., early morning.

Day, s. [E. *dæg*] light, from morning till night, twelve hours, the time of one revolution of the earth, twenty-four hours.

Dazzle, s. [freq. of E. *daze*] to stupefy with excess of light, to astonish. *Dazzled.*

Dead, adj. [E. *die*] having died, dulled, overwhelmed, without life. Adj. *deadly,* like death, causing death.

Deaf, adj., dull, stopped, unable to hear.

Deal, v. [E. *dæl,* a part] to portion, divide, allot. *Dealed* or *dealt.*

Deal, s., the wood of the fir-tree, which is easily parted, or split into planks, or boards.

Dear, adj. [E. *deore*] of high price, valuable, beloved.

Death, s. [E. *dead*] condition, of being dead, end of life.

Debate, s. [Fr. *débattre*] a dispute, discussion.

Debt, s. [Fr. *débit,* L. *debitum, debere,* to owe] a thing owed, a payment due.

Decay, v. [O. Fr. *dechoir, decaier,* L. *decadere, cadere,* to fall] to fall away, to fall to pieces, waste away. *Decayed.*

Decay, s., wasting, ruin.

Deceitful, adj. [E. *deceit*] full of deceit, lying, false.

Deceive, v. [Fr. *decevoir,* L. *decipere, capere,* to take] to take in, mislead, cheat. *Deceived.*

Decidedly, adv. [E. *decide*] certainly, surely, in a determined way.

Decision, s. [Fr. *décision*, L. *decisionem, decidere, caedere*, to cut] settlement, determination.

Decisive, adj. [Fr. *décisif*, L. *decidere*] positive, determined.

Deck, s. [E. *decan*, to cover] a covering, the covering of a vessel.

Declare, v. [Fr. *déclarer*, L. *declarare, de, clarus*, clear] to make clear, to proclaim, show. *Declared.*

Decline, v. [Fr. *décliner*, L. *declinare*] to slope downwards, fail, decay, refuse. *Declined.*

Decree, s. [Fr. *décret*, L. *decretum, cernere*, to decide] a decision, law, command.

Dedicate, v. [L. *dedicatus, dicare*] to give as sacred, consecrate, assign. *Dedicated.*

Deed, s. [E. *do*] a thing done, act, fact.

Deem, v. [E. *deman*, to distinguish] to judge, decide, think. *Deemed.*

Deep, adj. [E. *deop, dip, dib*] stretching down, hidden, crafty. Adv. *deeply.*

Deer, s. [E. *deor*, a wild animal] an animal of the cervine family, a stag, hind, roe.

Defect, s. [L. *defectus, deficere, facere*] a fault, blemish.

Defence, s. [Fr. *defense*, L. *defensus, defendere*, to ward off] safeguard, protection. Adj. *defenceless.*

Defend, v. [Fr. *défendre*, L. *defendere*] to ward off, to protect, guard. *Defended.*

Defendant, s. [Fr. *défendant*, L. *defendere*] a defender, the person who defends a lawsuit.

Defer, v. [L. *deferre*] to put off, delay, give way to. *Deferred.*

Defiance, s. [Fr. *défiance, défier*, L. *dis, fides*] disowning of allegiance, a challenge.

Defray, v. [Fr. *défrayer*, L. L. *fredum*, a fine to buy peace, G. *friede*, peace] to pay a fine, pay expenses, pay. *Defrayed.*

Deftly, adv. [E. *deft, dæfe*, fit] fitly, cleverly, in a handy manner.

Defy, v. [Fr. *défier*, It. *disfidare*, L. *dis, fides*] to renounce allegiance, challenge, offer combat. *Defied.*

Degenerate, adj. [L. *degeneratus, de, genus*, a race] degraded, sunk into a low condition. Subs. *degeneracy.*

Degenerate, v., to fall into a degraded state, to become worse. *Degenerated.*

Degree, s. [Fr. *degré*, L. *de, gradus*, a step] grade, order, rank, a step, small portion.

Deliberate, adj. [L. *deliberatus, librare, libra*, a balance] weighing carefully in the mind, cautious, thoughtful.

Delicate, adj. [Fr. *délicat*, L. *delicatus, deliciae*] pleasing, tender, refined, gentle, in 'weak health. Pl. *delicates*, rarities, delicacies.

Delicious, adj. [L. *deliciosus, deliciae*] full of delight, charming, very pleasing.

Delight, v. [O. Fr. *delit*, L. *delectare*] to please, charm. *Delighted.*

Delight, s., pleasure, joy, rapture. Adj. *delightful.*

Deliver, v. [Fr. *délivrer*, L. *deliberare, liber*] to set free, to set free from oneself and give to another, hand over. *Delivered.*

Deluge, s. [Fr. *déluge*, L. *diluvium, luere*, to wash] an overflowing of water, a flood.

Demand, v. [Fr. *demander*, L. *de, mandare*, to order] to send for from, to require from, insist, claim. *Demanded.*

Demand, s., a claim, requisition.

Demonstration, s. [L. *demonstrationem, de, monstrare*, to show] showing, proof.

Den, s. [E. *dene*, a valley] a narrow valley, a beast's lair.

Dense, adj. [L. *densus*] close, thick.

Dentist, s. [Fr. *dentiste*, L. *dentem, dens*] one who repairs teeth.

Deny, v. [Fr. *dénier*, L. *denegare, negare*] to say no to, gainsay, contradict, disown. *Denied.*

Depart, v. [Fr. *départir*, L. *dis, partiri*, to sever] to go away, leave. *Departed.*

Departure, s. [E. *depart*] going away, leaving.

Depend, v. [L. *dependere*] to hang upon, to rely on. *Depended.*

Depth, s. [E. *deep*] deepness, a deep place.

Deputy, s. [Fr. *député, députer*, L. *deputare*, to send] a substitute, an officer in another's place.

Dermot, s., chieftain, or king, of Leinster, who when driven from his dominions offered to become the vassal of Henry II of England, and so led' to the earliest English conquest of Ireland. He was reinstated by Richard (Strongbow) of Chepstow, 1169, and died 1170.

Descend, v. [L. *descendere, scandere*, to climb] to go down. *Descended.*

Describe, v. [L. *describere, scribere*, to write] to write an account of, represent. *Described.*

Description, s. [Fr. *description*, L. *descriptionem, de, scriptus, scribere*] an account, representation.

Desert, s. [Fr. *désert*, L. *desertum, deserere*, to leave] desolate, forsaken, a wild, wilderness.

Deserve, v. [L. *deservire*] to earn, merit, to be worthy. *Deserved.*

Desire, s. [Fr. *désir*, L. *desiderium, desiderare*, to long for] aim, wish, anxiety, longing. Adj. *desirous.*

Desire, v., to long for, wish earnestly. *Desired.*

Desolation, s. [L. *desolationem, de solus*, alone] destruction, waste.

Despatch, v. [O. Fr. *despescher*, L. *dis, impactare, pangere*, to fasten] to send away quickly, to finish, to kill. *Despatched.*

Desperate, adj. [L. *desperatus, de, sperare*, to hope] hopeless, rash.

Destine, v. [Fr. *destiner*, L. *destinare*, to fix] intend, appoint. *Destined.*

Destiny, s. [Fr. *destinée*, L. *destinere*] end, appointment, fate.

Destroy, v. [Fr. *destruire*, L. *de, struere*, to build] to pull down, undo, demolish, overthrow. *Destroyed.*

Destruction, s. [L. *destructionem, struere*] pulling down, ruin, overthrow.

Detachment, s. [Fr. *détacher, de, attacher*] a body of troops separated from the main force.

Detail, v. [Fr. *détailler, tailler*, L.L. *taliare*, to cut] to set out in every part, to enumerate. *Detailed.*

Detective, s. [Fr. *détectif*, L. *detectus, detegere*, to uncover] one who detects.

Determination, s. [L. *de, terminationem, terminus*, a bound] fixing an end, end, resolution, purpose.

Detest, v. [Fr. *détester*, L. *de, testari*, to witness] to abhor, hate. *Detested.*

Detritus, s. [L. *detritus, de, terere*, to rub] stuff worn down from rocks.

Development, s. [Fr. *développement*] opening, unrolling, unfolding, growth.

Device, s. [Fr. *deviser*, L. *divisus, dividere*] a contrivance, scheme, plan, design, emblem.

Devon, s., the land of the Damnonii, a county in the west of England.

Devote, v. [L. *devotus, devovere*, to vow] to set apart by vow, dedicate, doom. *Devoted.*

Devour, v. [Fr. *dévorer*, L. *devorare*] to swallow, consume. *Devoured.*

Devout, adj. [Fr. *dévot*, L. *devotus, vovere*] religious, pious.
Dew, s. [E. *deaw*, moist] moisture on substances exposed in the open air when no rain or visible wet is falling. Adj. *dewy*.
Dexterous, adj. [L. *dexter*, the right hand] handy, clever, ready, expert.
Diamond, s. [Fr. *diamant*, It. *diamante*, Gr. *adamanta, adamas*] a very hard precious stone.
Dictate, v. [L. *dictatus, dictare, dicere*, to say] to tell with authority, to tell another what to write. *Dictated.*
Die, v., to lose life, perish, wither. *Died, died* or *dead*.
Differ, v. [L. *differre, dis, ferre*, to carry] to be unlike, disagree. *Differed*.
Difference, s. [Fr. *différence*, L. *differentia, ferre*] unlikeness, disagreement.
Different, adj. [Fr. *différent*, L. *differentem, ferre*] unlike.
Difficulty, adv. [E. *difficult*] with difficulty, hardly.
Difficulty, s. [Fr. *difficulté*, L. *difficultatem, dis, facilis*, easy] perplexity, embarrassment, obstacle.
Dig, v., to pierce, stab, turn up the earth. *Dug* or *digged.*
Digest, v. [L. *digestus, dis, gerere*, to bear] to get rid of (as food), dissolve, classify, think over. *Digested.*
Dight, v. [E. *dihtan*, L. *dictare*] to prepare, compose, arrange, dress. *Dight.*
Dignity, s. [Fr. *dignité*, L. *dignitatem, dignus*, worthy] worth, honour, grandeur, high position.
Diligence, s. [Fr. *diligence*, L. *diligentia, diligere*, to be careful] industry, carefulness, attention.
Diligent, adj. [Fr. *diligent*, L. *diligentem, diligere*] attentive, industrious, careful.
Dim, adj., dull, somewhat dark, obscure.

Dimension, s. [Fr. *dimension*, L. *dimensionem, mensus, metiri*, to measure] a measurement, extent.
Diminish, v. [Fr. *diminuer*, L. *di, minuere, minus*, less] to lessen, decrease. *Diminished.*
Din, s. [from the sound] noise, a continuous sound.
Dinner, s. [Fr. *dîner*, O. Fr. *disner*, L.L. *disnare*, L. *de,caenare, caena*] the midday meal, the chief meal.
Dint, s. [from the sound] a blow, marks of a blow, force.
Dionysos, s. [Gr. *Dionusos*] the god of wine among the Greeks.
Direct, adj. [L. *directus, dirigere*, to straighten] straight, open, plain.
Dirge, s. [L. *dirige*, the first word of an old Latin funeral anthem, Psalm v. 8] a funeral service, a mournful song.
Dis: di, a Latin prefix, in composition implies separation, and so obtains the force of negation, *not*, or of opposition as *dis*agreeable, not agreeable, or the reverse of agreeable; the derivation of such compounded words is to be found under the simple forms.
Disable, v. [*dis, able*] to make unable, to maim, weaken. *Disabled.*
Disarm, v. [*dis, arm*] to take arms from. *Disarmed.*
Disaster, s. [Fr. *desastre*, L. *astrum*, a star] ill-fortune, evil chance.
Discern, v. [Fr. *discerner*, L. *dis, cernere*, to see] to see clearly, to perceive. *Discerned.*
Discipline, v. [Fr. *discipline*, L. *disciplina, discere*, to learn] to train, correct, order. *Disciplined.*
Discompose, v. [*dis, compose*, L. L. *compausare*] to disorder. *Discomposed.*
Discontent, s. [*dis,content*] want of content, uneasiness.
Discontent, v., to dissatisfy. *Discontented.*
Discourse, s. [Fr. *discours*, L. *dis, cursus, currere*, to run] a speech

running over several subjects, conversation, a sermon.

Discourse, v., to talk, hold a conversation, make a speech. *Discoursed*.

Discover, v. [*dis, cover*] to uncover, show, find out, invent. *Discovered*.

Discovery, s. [E. *discover*] disclosure, finding, revelation, invention.

Discredit, s. [Fr. *discrédit, crédit*. L. *creditus, credere*] want of credit, ill-repute.

Discredit, v., to disbelieve, disgrace. *Discredited*.

Disdainful, adj. [E. *disdain*, O. Fr. *desdaigner*, L. *dis, dignari, dignus*, worthy] full of disdain, scornful, contemptuous.

Dislike, s. [*dis, like*] aversion, hate.

Dismal, adj. [E. *dizzy, daze*] dull, dark, uncheerful.

Dismiss, v. [L. *dimissus, dimittere*] to send away, allow to go. *Dismissed*.

Disperse, v. [Fr. *disperser*, L. *dispersus, spargere*, to scatter] to scatter, separate. *Dispersed*.

Disposition, s. [L. *dispositionem, positus, ponere*] arrangement, tendency, temperament.

Dispute, v. [Fr. *disputer*, L. *dis, putare*, to think] to disagree, controvert, quarrel. *Disputed*.

Dissatisfaction, s. [*dis, satisfaction, satisfy*] displeasure, dislike.

Disseminate, v. [L. *dis, seminatus, seminare, semen*, a seed] to spread, to sow. *Disseminated*.

Dissipate, v. [L. *dissipatus, dissipare*] to scatter, waste. *Dissipated*.

Dissolve, v. [Fr. *dissolver*, L. *dis, solvere*] to loosen, melt. *Dissolved*.

Distance, s. [Fr. *distance*, L. *distantia, dis, stare*, to stand] space, interval.

Distant, adj. [Fr. *distant*, L. *dis, stantem, stare*] remote, separate, indistinct.

Distil, v. [Fr. *distiller*, L. *dis, stillare*] to drop, flow in drops, extract spirit from. *Distilled*.

Distinct, adj. [L. *dis, tinctus, tingere*, to dye] clearly marked off, clear, plain. Adv. *distinctly*; subs. *distinctness*.

Distinction, s. [L. *distinctionem, dis, tingere*] a mark, difference.

Distinguish, v. [Fr. *distinguissant, distinguer* L. *dis, tingere*] to, mark as different, to make famous. *Distinguished*.

Distracted, adj. [E. *distract*, L. *dis, tractus, trahere*, to draw] torn by emotions, wild.

Distress, s. [O. Fr. *destresse*, L. *dis, stringere*] pain, grief.

Disturb, v. [L. *dis, turbare, turba*, a crowd] to confuse, confound. *Disturbed*.

Ditch, s. [soft form of E. *dyke, dig*] a trench.

Ditty, s. [O. Fr. *ditté, dicté*, L. *dictum, dicere* to tell] a story, poem, song.

Dive, v. [E. *deofan*] to plunge into water. *Dived*.

Divers, adj. [Fr. *divers*, L. *di, versus, vertere*, to turn] differing, various, many.

Diversify, v. [Fr. *diversifier*, L. *diversum, facere*] to make diverse, to vary. *Diversified*.

Diversity, s. [Fr. *diversité*, L. *diversitatem, vertere*] variety.

Divide, v. [L. *dividere*] to separate into two, separate. *Divided*.

Divine, adj. [L. *divinus, divus*, a God] belonging to the Gods, sacred.

Divine, v. [L. *divinus*, a soothsayer] to foretell, guess. *Divined*.

Divinity, s. [Fr. *divinité*, L. *divinitatem, divinus*] matters belonging to God, the deity.

Division, s. [Fr. *division*, L. *divisionem, divisus, dividere*] separating, parting, a part.

Divorce, s. [Fr. *divorce*, L. *divortium, vertere*] dissolution of marriage, separation.

GLOSSARY.

Do, see pages 75, 77.
Dock, s., a hollowed place for shipbuilding, an inclosed basin for vessels.
Dolphin, s. [L. *delphin*, Gr. *delphin*] a large fish.
Dome, s. [Fr. *dôme*, It. *duomo*, Gr. *doma*, a building] a vaulted roof, cupola.
Domestic, adj. [Fr. *domestique*, L. *domesticus*, *domus*, a house] belonging to the house, fond of home.
Don, v. [E. *do*, *on*] to put on, assume. *Donned*.
Doom, s. [E. *dom*, *deem*] judgment, sentence.
Doom, v., to sentence, condemn. *Doomed*.
Door, s. [E. *dor*, *duru*] an opening, the gate of a house, an entrance.
Double, adj. [Fr. *double*, L. *duplus*, *duplex*; *duo*, two, *plica*, -a fold] twofold.
Doubt, v. [O. Fr. *doubter*, L. *dubitare*, *dubius*, *duo*] to incline two ways, hesitate, distrust. *Doubted*.
Doubt, s., suspense, hesitation, distrust. Adj. *doubtful*.
Dove, s. [E. *duva*, *dufian*, to dive] the bird that dives swiftly through the air, a pigeon.
Down, adv. prep. [E. *adown*, *of*, *dune*, from the hill] to a lower place, on the ground.
Doze, v., to fall to sleep, to sleep lightly. *Dozed*.
Dozen, adj. [Fr. *douzaine*, *douze*, L. *duodecim*] twelve, a set of twelve.
Drag, v., to haul, pull, draw forcibly. *Dragged*.
Dragon, s. [Fr. *dragon*, L. *draconem*, Gr. *drakon*, *derkomai*, I see] a serpent, a fabulous creature (so called from its bright eyes).
Drake, s. [E. *ened*, duck, *rick*, rule] the male duck.
Draught, s. [E. *drag*] the act of drawing, that which is drawn, a current of air.

Draw, v. [softened form of E. *drag*] to pull, haul gently, entice. *Drew*, *drawn*. Subs. *drawer*.
Dread, s. [E. *drædan*] awe, fear, terror. Adj. *dreadful*.
Dream, s., an appearance in sleep, a vision.
Dream, v., to see in sleep, to think in sleep, to behave as a person asleep. *Dreamed* or *dreamt*.
Dreary, adj. [E. *drearig*, *dreosan*, to fall] troubled, dejected, gloomy.
Dress, v. [Fr. *dresser*, L. *directus*, *dirigere*] to arrange, prepare, clothe, trim. *Dressed* or *drest*.
Dress, s., clothing.
Dresser, s. [Fr. *dressoir*, *dresser*] a kitchen table for preparing meat.
Drill, v. [E. *thirlian*, by metathesis] to shake, pierce, exercise, exercise soldiers. *Drilled*.
Drink, v. [E. *drincan*] to take in liquid, suck in, imbibe. *Drank*, *drunken* or *drunk*.
Drive, v. [E. *drifan*] to urge, push violently, hurry on, guide. *Drave* or *drove*, *driven*.
Drone, s. [from the sound] the male non-working bee, an idler.
Dronish, adj. [E. *drone*] like a drone, idle, lazy.
Droop, v. [E. *drop*] to hang, to be sad. *Drooped*.
Drop, v., to fall in drops, to let fall. *Dropped* or *dropt*.
Drug, s. [Fr. *drogue*] aromatic herbs, medicines.
Dry, adj. [E. *drig*] free from moisture, thirsty, severe, uninteresting.
Duck, s. [E. *duck*, to dip] the bird that dips its head in the water.
Duckling, s. [dim. of E. *duck*] a young duck.
Due, adj. [Fr. *dû*, *devoir*, L. *debere*] owed, proper, fit, a debt. Adv. *duly*.
Duke, s. [Fr. *duc*, L. *ducem*, *dux*] a leader, nobleman of the highest rank in England.
Dumb, adj., dull, silent, unable to speak.

S

Durable, adj. [L. *durabilis, durare,* to last] able to endure, lasting, strong.

During, prep. [pres. part. E. *dure*] lasting through.

Dust, s., powder, fine particles of earth.

Dutch, adj. [G. *deutsch, deut,* the people] a name by which the Germans call themselves, but which the English have confined to the branch of the German race which lives in Holland; belonging to the Hollanders.

Duty, s. [O. Fr. *deuté, devoir,* L. *debere*] what is due, obligation.

Dwell, v., to delay, linger, stay, live. *Dwelt.*

Dwelling, s. [E. *dwell*] a house.

Each, distr. pr. [E. *ælc, æ,* ever; *lic,* like] one by one, every one separately.

Eager, adj. [Fr. *aigre,* L. *acrem, acer*] sharp, ardent, vehement.

Eaglet, s. [E. *eagle,* Fr. *aigle,* L. *aquila*] a young eagle.

Ear, s., the organ of hearing.

Early, adj. [E. *ær,* ere, *lic*] beforehand, in time, soon.

Earn, v. [E. *earnian, ear,* to plough] to gain by labour, to get, to deserve. *Earned.*

Earth, s. [E. *eorðe, ear,* to plough] ploughland, land, the world. Adj. *earthly.*

Earthquake, s. [E. *earth, quake*] a shaking of the earth, a convulsion of the earth.

Ease, s. [Fr. *aise*] quiet, rest. Adj. *easy;* Adv. *easily.*

East, s., the rising, the place of sunrise, the countries east of Europe. Adj. *eastern;* Adv. *eastward.*

Eat, v. [E. *etan*] to consume food, to devour, consume. *Ate* or *eat, eaten.*

Ebal, s., a mountain on the north side of the town of Shechem, or Samaria, in Palestine, from which part of the Law of Moses was proclaimed.

Ebb, v. [E. *ebba,* the going away of the tide] to fall, decline. *Ebbed.*

Echo, s. [L. and Gr. *echo*] a repeated sound, sound driven back. Pl. *echoes.*

Echo, v., to send back a sound, to repeat. *Echoed.*

Eclipse, s. [L. *eclipsis,* Gr. *ekleipsis, leipein,* to fail] a failing of light, hiding.

Eddy, s. [E. *ythian,* to boil, *yth,* a wave] a whirlpool, a whirling rush of water.

Edge, s. [E. *ecg,* a point] a border, sharp side. Adj. *edged,* having an edge.

Educate, v. [L. *educatus, educare*] to train, cultivate, teach. *Educated.*

Effect, s. [L. *effectum, e, facere*] result, consequence.

Effectually, adv. [E. *effectual,* L. *effectualis, effectum*] thoroughly, to some purpose.

Effeminacy, s. [E. *effeminate,* L. *effeminatus, femina,* a woman] womanishness, weakness of character.

Effigy, s. [Fr. *effigie,* L. *effigiem, e, fingere,* to form] a figure, likeness, representation of a person.

Effort, s. [Fr. *effort,* L. *e, fortis,* strong] a strong attempt, struggle.

Egyptian, adj. [*Egypt*] belonging to Egypt, a native of Egypt.

Eight, num. adj. [E. *eahta*] twice four, the cardinal next after seven.

Either, pr. [E. *ægther*] one of two, see page 57.

Elbow, s. [E. *ell,* arm, *boga,* a bow] the bend of the arm.

Elegant, adj. [Fr. *elegant,* L. *elegantem, elegans*] graceful, refined, tasteful.

Element, s. [Fr. *élément,* L. *elementum*] a first principle, ingredient.

Elephant, s. [Fr. *éléphant,* L.

elephantem, perhaps from Hebrew, *Aleph, hindi*, Indian bull] a large thick-skinned quadruped with trunk and two ivory tusks.

Elevation, s. [L. *elevationem, e, levare*, to lift] lifting up, height.

Elf, s. [E. *ælf*] a little spirit supposed to haunt woods, a fairy.

Elizabeth, s., Queen of England, daughter of Henry VIII and Anne Boleyn, born 1533, reigned 1558-1603.

Eloquence, s. [Fr. *éloquence*, L. *eloquentia, e, loqui*, to speak] fluent speech, oratory.

Eloquent, adj. [Fr. *éloquent*, L. *eloquentem, e, loqui*] speaking with ease and fluency.

Else, adj. [E. *elles*, otherwise; *el*, other] other, besides.

Elsewhere, adv. [E. *else*] in another place.

Em-. See **En-**.

Emaciation, s. [L. *emaciationem, e, macere*, to waste] wasting, thinness.

Embank, v. [E. *bank*] to enclose with a mound, bank up. *Embanked*.

Embark, v. [E. *bark*] to put on board a bark or ship, go on board, commence. *Embarked*.

Embers, s. [E. *æmyrian*] burning ashes.

Emblem, s. [Fr. *emblème*, Gr. *emblema, en*, in, *ballein*, to lay] an inlaid ornament, a picture, type, symbol.

Embrace, v. [O. Fr. *embracer, brace*, L. *brachium*] to fold in the arms. *Embraced*.

Embroidery, s. [E. *broider, bredan, bregdan*, to weave] woven work, ornamental needlework.

Eminence, s. [Fr. *éminence*, L. *eminentia, e, minere*, to threaten] elevation, height, greatness.

Eminent, adj. [Fr. *éminent*, L. *eminentem, e, minere*] high, standing out, illustrious.

Emotion, s. [L. *emotionem, e, motus, movere*, to move] movement of the feelings, agitation.

Emphatical, adj. [E. *emphatic*, Fr. *emphatique*, L. and Gr. *emphasis, emphainein*, to show] impressive, forcible.

Empire, s. [Fr. *empire*, L. *imperium*] dominion, the dominion of an absolute monarch.

Employ, v. [Fr. *employer*, L. *in, plicare*, to fold] to turn to one's purpose, to use. *Employed*.

Empty, adj.[E.*æmtig, æmta*, leisure] idle, having nothing in it, void.

Empty, v., to make void. *Emptied*.

En-, a prefix meaning *in*, the French form of the Latin preposition *in*; em- before the letters *b* and *p*.

Enable, v. [E. *able*] to strengthen, make able. *Enabled*.

Encircle, v. [E. *in, circle*] to enclose in a circle, surround. *Encircled*.

Enclose, v. [E. *in, close*] to shut in. *Enclosed*.

Encourage, v. [Fr. *encourager*, see **Courage**] to give heart to, embolden. *Encouraged*.

End, s., the last part, finish. Adj. *endless*.

End, v., to finish, put a stop to. *Ended*.

Endeavour, s. [Fr. *en, devoir*, L. *debere*, to owe] an attempt, exertion.

Endow, v. [Fr. *endouer*, L. *dotare, dotem, dos*] to give a dowry to, to enrich with, give in trust for. *Endowed*.

Endue, v. [L. *induere*] to put on, invest. *Endued*.

Endure, v. [Fr. *endurer*, L. *in, durare, durus*, hard] to harden, to be firm, to bear. *Endured*.

Enemy, s. [Fr. *ennemi*, L. *inimicus, in*, not, *amicus, amare*, to love] a foe, an opponent.

Energy, s. [Fr. *energie*, Gr. *ener-*

geia, ergon, a work] active power, force.

Engage, v. [Fr. *engager, gage,* It. *gaggio,* L. *vadium,* O. H. G. *weddi,* a pledge] to pledge, to promise, to hire. *Engaged.*

England, s. [E. *Engle, land*] the land of the Angles.

English, adj. [E. *Englisc, Engle*] belonging to England, the people of England.

Enjoy, v. [E. *in, joy*] to delight in. *Enjoyed.*

Enjoyment, s. [E. *enjoy*] pleasure, delight.

Enlarge, v. [E. *in, large*] to make larger. *Enlarged.*

Enough, adj. adv. [E. *genug*] plenty, sufficient.

Enquire. See Inquire.

Enrich, v. [E. *in, rich*] to make rich. *Enriched.*

Ensign, s. [Fr. *enseigne,* L. *insignia, insigne*] a mark, a banner.

Enter, v. [Fr. *entrer,* L. *intrare*] to go in, come in, engage in. *Entered.*

Enterprise, s. [Fr. *entreprise, entreprendre,* L. *inter, prendere,* to take] a thing taken in hand, an undertaking, adventure.

Enterprising, adj. [E. *enterprise*] adventurous, bold.

Entertain, v. [Fr. *entretenir,* L. *inter, tenere*] to hold in talk, receive, amuse. *Entertained.*

Entertainment, s. [E. *entertain*] reception, amusement.

Enthrone, v. [E. *in, throne*] to place on a throne. *Enthroned.*

Entice, v. [O. Fr. *entiser,* Fr. *tison,* a firebrand, L. *titionem, titio*] to excite, tempt, lead on, allure. *Enticed.*

Entire, adj. [Fr. *entier,* L. *integer*] whole, unbroken. Adv. *entirely.*

Entitle, v. [E. *in, title*] to give a title to, style, qualify. *Entitled.*

Entrance, s. [L. (*intrantia*), *intrans, intrare*] a going in, passage in.

Entrenched, adj. [E. *entrench, trench,* Fr. *trancher,* to cut] protected by trenches, fortified.

Envy, s. [Fr. *envie,* L. *invidia, in, videre,* to see] pain at seeing others' success, ill-will.

Envy, v. [Fr. *envier,* L. *invidere*] to feel pain at others' success. *Envied.*

Epipolæ, s., a long broad ridge on the north west of Syracuse, sloping down towards the city and commanding it, occupied by the Athenians during their siege of the city, B.C. 414.

Equal, adj. [L. *aequalis, aequus*] even, of like qualities, uniform. Adv. *equally.*

Ere, adv. [E. *ær*] before, sooner. Superl. *erst.*

Erect, adj. [L. *erectus, erigere,* to straighten] upright, straight.

Error, s. [L. *error, errare,* to wander] a mistake.

Erst. See **Ere.**

Eruption, s. [L. *eruptionem, e, rumpere,* to burst] an outburst.

Escape, v. [Picard Fr. *escaper,* L. L. *excappare,* to slip out of the cloak, *cappa,* a cape or cloak] to slip away, to get clear off. *Escaped.*

Esculent, adj. [L. *esculentus, esca, edere,* to eat] fit for food, eatable.

Esdraelon, s., a valley and plain in the northern part of Palestine, to the south-west of the sea of Galilee.

Especially, adv. [E. *especial,* Fr. *espèce,* L. *species*] chiefly, particularly.

Espy, v. [O. Fr. *espier,* E. *spy*] to catch sight of, discover. *Espied.*

Establish, v. [O. Fr. *establir,* L. *stabilire, stabilis, stare,* to stand] to set up firmly. *Established.*

Estate, s. [O. Fr. *estat,* L. *status, stare*] a fixed condition, property.

Esteem, v. [Fr. *estimer,* L. *aestimare*] to value, consider, think highly of. *Esteemed.*

GLOSSARY. 261

Estimable, adj. [Fr. *estimable*, L. *aestimare*] worthy, deserving.
Estimation, s. [L. *aestimationem*, *aestimare*] esteem, value, honour.
Estuary, s. [L. *aestuarium, aestuare, aestus*, tide] the part of a river into which the tide comes, a wide river-mouth.
Eternal, adj. [Fr. *éternal*, L. *aeternus, aeviternus, aevum*, Gr. *aion*, time] lasting through all time, everlasting.
Ether, s. [Fr. *éther*, L. *aether*, Gr. *aither*] bright air, clear air.
Ethnology, s. [Gr. *ethnos*, a nation, *logos*, science] the science which treats of the races of man.
Euphrates, s., a river which rises in the mountains of Taurus in Armenia, flows south-west, south, and then south-east into the Persian Gulf.
Europe, s., the north-western continent or division of the Eastern Hemisphere; the name means either [Gr. *eurus, ope*, broad face] the 'broad face' which the coast near Mount Athos would present to an Asiatic Greek; or 'the west,' the land of the setting sun, name given by the Phœnicians of the east. Adj. *European*.
Evade, v. [Fr. *évader*, L. *evadere*, to get off] to escape, elude. *Evaded.*
Even, adv. [E. *æfen*, level] just so, likewise, so much as.
Evening, s. [E. *æfen*, even, *æf* = off] the sinking of the day, going off of the light.
Event, s. [L. *eventus, venire*, to come] that which comes to pass, result.
Ever, adv. [E. *æfre*] for an age, for all time, always, at any time.
Everlasting, adj. [E. *ever, last*] remaining always, eternal.
Evermore, adj. [E. *ever, more*] always in time to come.
Every, pron. [E. *æfre, ælc, evereche*] the whole one by one; see page 57.

Evident, adj. [Fr. *évident*, L. *e, videntem, videre*, to see] visible, plain, clear, certain. Adv. *evidently*.
Evil, adj. [E. *yfel*] bad, wicked, base.
Evolution, s. [L. *evolutionem, e, volutus, volvere*, to roll] unrolling, working out.
Exact, adj. [Fr. *exact*, L. *exactus, ex, agere*, to work] worked out, correct, accurate. Adv. *exactly*.
Exalt, v. [Fr. *exalter*, L. *exaltare, ex, altus*, high] to raise to a height. *Exalted.*
Example, s. [Fr. *exemple*, L. *exemplum*] a pattern.
Exceed, v. [Fr. *excéder*, L. *ex, cedere*, to go] to go beyond, surpass. *Exceeded.*
Excel, v. [Fr. *exceller*, L. *ex, cellere*] to surpass, be eminent. *Excelled.*
Excellent, adj. [Fr. *excellent*, L. *excellentem, ex, cellere*] surpassing, meritorious, of great worth. Subs. *excellence*.
Except, prep. [L. *exceptus, ex, capere*, to take] taken out, omitted.
Exception, s. [L. *exceptionem, ex, capere*] taking out, a thing taken out, something not according to rule.
Excess, s. [Fr. *excès*, L. *excessus, ex, cedere*, to go] going beyond.
Exchange, v. [Fr. *exchanger*, see **Change**] to change away, barter. *Exchanged.*
Exchange, s., barter, change.
Excite, v. [Fr. *exciter*, L. *excitare, ex, ciere*] to rouse, stir. *Excited.*
Excitement, s. [Fr. *excitement*] an excited state, agitation.
Exclaim, v. [O. Fr. *exclamier*, L. *ex, clamare*, to cry] to cry aloud, shout. *Exclaimed.*
Excuse, v. [Fr. *excuser*, L. *excusare, causa*, an action at law] to free from blame, acquit, justify. *Excused.*
Execute, v. [Fr. *exécuter*, L. *exsecutus, ex, sequi*, to follow] to

follow out, finish, put to death. *Executed.*

Exempt, adj. [L. *exemptus, emere,* to buy] bought off, free from, not liable to.

Exercise, s. [Fr. *exercice,* L. *exercitium, exercere*] exertion, practice, use.

Exercise, v., to exert, practise, discipline, train. *Exercised.*

Exert, v. [L. *exsertus,* uncovered, ready for work, *ex, serere*] to work hard, strain. *Exerted.*

Exertion, s. [L. *exertionem, ex, serere*] hard work, labour.

Exhibit, v. [L. *exhibitus, ex, habere*] to put out, show. *Exhibited.*

Exist, v. [Fr. *exister,* L. *ex, sistere*] to be alive, live. *Existed.*

Expand, v. [L. *ex, pandere,* to spread] to spread open. *Expanded.*

Expanse, s. [L. *expansus, pandere*] a spreading, extent, space.

Expect, v. [L. *ex, spectare*] to look out for, wait for. *Expected.*

Expend, v. [L. *ex, pendere*] to lay out, spend. *Expended.*

Experience, s. [Fr. *expérience,* L. *experientia, experiri,* to try] proof, test, knowledge gained by trial.

Experiment, s. [L. *experimentum, experiri*] a trial.

Expire, v. [Fr. *expirer,* L. *ex, spirare*] to breathe out, die, end. *Expired.*

Explain, v. [L. *explanare, planus,* even] to make plain or easy, expound. *Explained.*

Exploit, s. [Fr. *exploit,* L. *explicitare, ex, plicare,* to unfold] a thing done openly, a noble deed.

Explore, v. [Fr. *explorer,* L. *explorare*] to search, examine. *Explored.*

Expose, v. [Fr. *exposer,* L. L. *expausare*] to put forth, to publish. *Exposed.*

Expostulate, v. [L. *expostulatus, postulare,* to demand] to reason earnestly, remonstrate. *Expostulated.*

Express, v. [L. *expressus, premere*] to press out, declare, speak. *Expressed.*

Express, s., a special messenger.

Expression, s. [L. *expressionem, pressus, premere*] manner of putting forth, look, speech.

Expressive, adj., full of expression.

Extend, v. [L. *extendere*] to stretch, spread. *Extended.*

Extensive, adj. [Fr. *extensif,* L. *ex, tensus, tendere*] stretching far.

Extent, s. [E. *extend*] space.

Extinguish, v. [Fr. *extinguir,* L. *ex, tinguescere, tinguere*] to quench, put out. *Extinguished.*

Extol, v. [L. *ex, tollere,* to raise] to exalt by praise, to praise. *Extolled.*

Extract, s. [L. *extractum, ex, trahere,* to draw] a portion taken out, a passage from a book.

Extraction, s. [L. *extractionem, trahere*] taking out, descent, lineage.

Extraordinary, adj. [L. *extraordinarius, ordinem, ordo,* a row] out of the common.

Extreme, adj. [L. *extremus, ex*] outermost, very far off, utmost. Adv. *extremely.*

Extremity, s. [Fr. *extrémité,* L. *extremitatem, extremus, ex*] the utmost part, very great distress.

Eye, s. [E. *eage*] the organ of sight.

Face, s. [Fr. *face,* L. *facies, facere*] the make or appearance, countenance, look.

Face, v., to turn the face to, oppose, meet. *Faced.*

Fact, s. [L. *factum, facere,* to do] a deed, act.

Faculty, s. [Fr. *faculté,* L. *facultatem, facilis,* easy] power, quality.

Fade, v. [Fr. *fade,* L. *vapidus,* without flavour] to become weak, wither, lose colour. *Faded.*

Fagot, s. [W. *ffagod, ffasgu*, to bind] a bundle of sticks.

Fail, v. [Fr. *faillir*, L. *fallere*, to err] to err, slip, miss, decay. *Failed*.

Fain, adj. [E. *fægen*] joyful, glad. Adv. gladly, willingly.

Faint, adj. [Fr. *feinte, feindre*, L. *fingere*, to feign] empty, without strength, feeble, not in earnest, feigned. Adv. *faintly*.

Fair, adj. [E. *faeger*] bright, beautiful.

Fairy, s. [Fr. *féerie*, L. *fataria, fata, fatum*] an imaginary being supposed to influence man's fate, an elf.

Faithful, adj. [E. *faith*] full of faith, trusty. Adv. *faithfully*.

Falcon, s. [It. *falcone*, L. *falconem, falx*] a bird with a hooked bill, a hawk.

Fall, v. [E. *feallan*] to drop, slip, go downwards. *Fell, fallen*.

Fallow, adj. [E. *fealo*, yellow, brown] land lying untilled.

False, adj. [L. *falsus, fallere*] deceiving, untrue, lying.

Falter, v. [freq. of E. *fail*] to fail often, totter, stammer, hesitate. *Faltered*.

Fame, s. [L. *fama*] rumour, report, good report, glory. Adj. *famed*.

Family, s. [L. *familia*] a household, offspring of one father, race.

Famine, s. [Fr. *famine*, L. *fames*, hunger] scarcity of food.

Famous, adj. [L. *famosus, fama*] of great fame, glorious.

Fancy, s. [Fr. *fantasie*, L. *phantasia*, Gr. *phainein*, to show] the faculty which makes past impressions appear to the mind, imagination.

Fancy, v., to imagine. *Fancied*.

Fane, s. [L. *fanum*] a temple, shrine.

Fantastic, adj. [Fr. *fantastique*, see **Fancy**] fanciful, odd.

Far, adv., at a distance. *Far, farther, farthest*.

Fare, v. [E. *faran*] to go, get on, do, prosper. *Fared*. **Farewell**, may you fare well, or may it go well with you.

Fare, s., passage, price of passage, entertainment, food.

Farmer, s. [E. *farm*] one who farms, one who cultivates land.

Fashion, s. [Fr. *façon*, L. *factionem, facere*, to make] the make of a thing, manner, custom, style.

Fast, adj. [E. *fæst*] firm, unbroken, quick.

Fat, adj. [E. *fett, fedan*, to feed] well-fed, stout, gross. Subs. *fatness*.

Fatal, adj. [Fr. *fatal*, L. *fatalis, fatum*] bringing fate, deadly.

Fate, s. [L. *fatum*] destiny, doom.

Father, s. [E. *fæder*] a male parent.

Fatigue, s. [Fr. *fatigue, fatiguer*, L. *fatigare*, to tire] weariness, toil, exhaustion.

Fault, s. [O. Fr. *faulte*, It. *faltare*, L. *fallere*] mistake, error, failing.

Favour, s. [Fr. *faveur*, L. *favorem*] kindness, patronage.

Favourable, adj. [E. *favour*] friendly, helpful, well-disposed.

Fawn, s. [Fr. *faon*, L. L. *foetonum, foetus*, a young animal] a young deer.

Fear, s. [E. *fær*, a coming suddenly on] alarm at danger, dread, anxiety. Adj. *fearful, fearless*.

Fear, v., to feel alarm, dread. *Feared*.

Feast, s., [Fr. *feste*, L. *festum*] a holiday, entertainment, banquet.

Feast, v., to keep holiday, to have a grand meal. *Feasted*.

Feather, s. [E. *feder*] one of the growths which make the covering of a bird.

Feature, s. [Fr. *faiture*, L. *factura, facere*] the make, appearance, countenance, distinct part of the countenance.

Feeble, adj. [Fr. *faible*, L. *flebilis*, lamentable, *flere*, to weep] weak, faint.

Feed, v. [E. *food*] to provide with food, nourish. *Fed*.

Feel, v. [E. *felan*] to touch, handle, know surely. *Felt*.

Felicity, s. [Fr. *félicité*, L. *felicitatem, felix*, happy] happiness.

Fell, v. [E. *fall*] to cause to fall, knock down. *Felled*.

Fellow, s. [E. *felaw, feoh*, money, *law*, society] a partner, mate, person.

Feminine, adj. [L. *femininus, femina*, a woman] of a woman, female, womanish, gentle.

Fence, s. [Fr. *defense*, L. *defensus, defendere*, to ward off] a defence, protection, hedge.

Fence, v. to enclose with a hedge, protect, keep off. *Fenced*.

Ferdinand, s., king of Arragon, 1474; married Isabella queen of Castile, uniting the two kingdoms, 1479, retired to Arragon, on her death, 1506.

Fern, s. [E. *fearn, faran*, to go, because the seed was thought to be used by witches to give the power of going invisibly] a plant with featherlike fronds.

Ferocious, adj. [Fr. *féroce*, L. *ferocem*] fierce, savage.

Ferocity, s. [Fr. *férocité*, L. *ferocitatem, ferox*] fierceness, savageness.

Fertilise, v. [Fr. *fertiliser*, L. *fertilis*] to make fruitful. *Fertilised*.

Fertility, s. [Fr. *fertilité*, L. *fertilitatem, fertilis, ferre*, to bear] fruitfulness, power of bearing much fruit.

Fervid, adj. [L. *fervidus, fervere*, to boil] burning, heated, excited.

Festival, s. [Fr. *festival*, L. *festivalis, festivus, festus*] a holiday.

Fetch, v. [softened form of E. *feccan*] to bring, go after. *Fetched*.

Feud, s. [O. Fr. *faide*, G. *fehde*] a quarrel, strife.

Feversham, s., Lewis Duras, earl of Feversham, was commander of the forces of King James II. at Sedgemoor, July 6, 1685, and till the king's abdication, 1688.

Few, adj. [E. *feawa*] a small number, not many.

Fibre, s. [Fr. *fibre*, L. *fibra*] a thread.

Fidelity, s. [Fr. *fidelité*, L. *fidelitatem, fidelis, fidus*] faithfulness.

Field, s. [E. *feld*] the open country, a meadow.

Fierce, adj. [Fr. *féroce*, L. *ferocem*] savage, rough. Adv. *fiercely*.

Fiery, adj. [E. *fire*] made of fire, blazing, hot, excited.

Fifth, adj. [E. *five*] ordinal next after fourth.

Fifty, adj. [E. *fif, tig*, ten] five times ten, five tens.

Fig, s. [E. *fic*, L. *ficus*] a fruit-tree producing a rich luscious fruit, a small unimportant thing.

Fight, v. [E. *feohtan*] to strike with the hands, to contend, strive. *Fought*, (*foughten*) *fought*.

Fight, s., a strife, battle, contention.

Figure, s. [Fr. *figure*, L. *figura, fingere*] shape, form.

Fill, v. [E. *fyllan*] to pour into a thing till it will hold no more, satisfy. *Filled*.

Find, v. [E. *findan*] to come upon, meet with. *Found*.

Fine, adj. [Fr. *fin*, L. *finitus, finis*, an end] perfect, beautiful, delicate, small.

Finger, s. [E. *fang*] that which takes hold, a digit, one of the extremities of the hand.

Finish, v. [Fr. *finissant, finir*, L. *finire*] to end, conclude. *Finished*.

Fir, s., a resinous tree, the pine.

Fire, s., heat and light of burning, flame.

Fire, v., to set on fire, kindle, inflame. *Fired*.

Firm, adj. [L. *firmus*] strong, not easily moved, resolute. Adv. *firmly*.

First, adj. [E. *fore*] most forward, foremost.

Firth, s. [E. *frith*] a narrow sea, an arm of the sea.

Fish, s. [E. *fisc*] an oviparous animal living in water. Pl. *fish*, and *fishes*. Adj. *fishy*.

Fisherman, s. [E. *fisher*] a man who catches fish.

Fit, adj. [Fr. *fait*, O. Fr. *faict*, L. *factus, facere*] made, suited, proper.

Fit, v., to be suitable, to suit, to be adapted to. *Fitted* or *fit*.

Five, adj., the cardinal number next after four.

Fix, v. [L. *fixus, figere*] to fasten, bind, steady. *Fixed*.

Flag, s. [E. *fleogan*, to fly] a cloth flying in the wind, an ensign.

Flake, s. [E. *fleogan*] a piece that flies, scale, slice.

Flame, s. [Fr. *flamme*, L. *flamma*] a blaze of fire.

Flame, v., to blaze, burn brightly. *Flamed*.

Flank, s. [Fr. *flanc*, L. *flaccus*, flabby] the side, the part of the side unprotected by bone.

Flash, s., a sudden rush of flame, bright light. Adj. *flashy*, showy, dazzling.

Flash, v., to burst into flame, to burst forth. *Flashed*.

Flat, adj., smooth, level, even.

Flax, s. [E. *fleax*] a plant whose fibres are made into thread and woven into linen cloth.

Flee, v. [E. *fleon*, from root of *fleogan*, to fly] to run away, escape. *Fled*.

Fleet, s. [E. *flota*, a ship, *flow*] a company of ships.

Fleet, v. [E. *fleotan*, *flow*] to pass quickly. *Fleeted*.

Flesh, s. [E. *flæsc*] the substance on the bone of animals, meat. Adj. *fleshy*.

Flicker, v. [E. *fliccerian*, freq. of *fleogan*, to fly] to flutter, waver. *Flickered*.

Flight, s. [E. *flyht, fleogan*] act of flying, fleeing, escape.

Fling, v., to throw, cast, heave. *Flung*.

Flint, s., a hard stone, stone used for arrow heads.

Float, v. [E. *flot, flow*] to flow, swim, to cause to swim. *Floated*.

Flock, s. [E. *floc, fleogan*, to fly] a flight of birds, assembly, crowd.

Flock, v., to assemble in a crowd, rush in a crowd. *Flocked*.

Flood, s. [E. *flód, flow*] an overflow, deluge.

Floor, s. [E. *flór*] a flat surface, bottom of a room.

Florid, adj. [L. *floridus, flos*, a flower] abounding in flowers, bright, reddish.

Flour, s. [Fr. *fleur*, L. *florem, flos*] the finest part of meal.

Flourish, v. [Fr. *florissant, florir*, L. *florescere, flos*] to flower, to prosper. *Flourished*.

Flow, v. [E. *fleowan*] to glide, like water. *Flowed*.

Flower, s. [Fr. *fleur*, L. *florem, flos*] blossom of a plant. Adj. *flowery*, adorned with flowers.

Flush, v. [E. *flow*] to redden with a flow of blood, blush. *Flushed*.

Flute, s. [O. Fr. *flaute*, L. *flatum, flare*, to blow] a musical instrument sounded by blowing into holes.

Fly, v. [E. *fleogan, fleon*] to move on wings, move quickly. *Flew, flown*.

Foam, s. [E. *fám*] air bubbles on the sea, froth, scum.

Foe, s. [E. *fáh, fian*, to hate] a hater, an enemy.

Foil, s. [L. *folia, folium*, a leaf] a leaf of gold, gold leaf used as ornament, anything used to adorn or set off another.

Fold, s. [E. *fald*] a bending, an enclosure for sheep.

Folk, s. [E. *folc*] a crowd, the people. Pl. *folk*, or *folks*.

Follow, v. [E. *folgian*] to go after, pursue, seek. *Followed*.

Follower, s., one who follows.

Folly, s. [Fr. *folie, fol*, L. *follis*, an air bag] the state of a fool, silliness, emptiness.

Fond, adj. [E. *fonne*, a fool] silly, simple, loving, affectionate.

Food, s. [E. *fóda*] what brings up the body, nourishment.

Foolish, adj. [E. *fool*] like a fool, silly.

Foot, s. [E. *fót*] the lower part of the leg, bottom.

For, prep. conj. (in front of), in place of, on account of, because.

Forage, s. [Fr. *fourrage*, O. Fr. *fourre*, L. L. *fodrum*, E. *foder, food*] food for cattle.

Forbid, v. [E. *for, bid*] to bid away, bid not to do a thing. . *Forbade* or *forbad, forbidden*.

Force, s. [Fr. *force*, L. *forcia, fortia, fortis*, strong] strength, power.

Force, v., to compel, coerce. *Forced*.

Foreign, adj. [O. Fr. *forain*, L. L. *foraneus, foras*, out of doors] from abroad, from another country. Subs. *foreigner*.

Forerun, v. [E. *fore, run*] to run before, precede, come before. *Foreran, forerun*.

Forest, s. [O. Fr. *forest*, L.L. *forestis, foris*] outlying unenclosed land, a district under special game laws, a large wood.

Forget, v. [E. *for*, away, *get*] to lose from the memory. *Forgot* or *forgat, forgotten*.

Forgetful, adj., apt to forget.

Forgive, v. [E. *for*, away, *give*] to give away, pardon. *Forgave, forgiven*.

Fork, s. [L. *furca*] an instrument divided into prongs.

Fork, v., to divide into prongs, separate into two parts, to pierce with a fork. *Forked*.

Forlorn, adj. [E. *for*, utterly, *loren, leosan*, to lose] deserted, lost.

Form, s. [Fr. *forme*, L. *forma*] shape, fashion.

Form, v.. to make, shape. *Formed*.

Former, see page 51.

Forsake, v. [E. *forsacan*, to declare opposition, *sacu*, strife] to renounce, leave. *Forsook, forsaken*.

Forsooth, adv. [E. *for, sooth*, truth] in truth, surely, indeed.

Fort, s. [Fr. *fort*, L. *fortis*] a strong place, stronghold.

Forth, adv. [E. *fore*] onward, forward, outside.

Forth, s., the name of a large frith, or arm of the sea, on the western coast of Scotland.

Fortify, v. [Fr. *fortifier*, L. *fortificare, fortem, facere*] to make strong, to make into a fort. *Fortified*.

Fortitude, s. [Fr. *fortitude*, L. *fortitudinem, fortis*] strength of mind, bravery, endurance.

Fortnight, s., [E. *fourteen, night*] two weeks.

Fortress, s. [Fr. *forteresse*, L. L. *fortalitia, fortis*] a fort, castle, stronghold.

Fortune, s. [Fr. *fortune*, L. *fortuna, fors*] lot, chance success.

Forty, adj. [E. *four, tig*, ten] four times ten, four tens.

Forum, s. [L. *Forum*, the market-place at Rome, near which were the law-courts, an open space, a law-court.

Forward, adv. [E. *fore*] onward. Adj., ready; Verb, to send on, help.

Foster, v. [E. *fostrian*, to feed, *food*] to nourish, take care of, cherish. *Fostered*.

Foul, adj. [E. *fúl*] dirty, impure, unfair.

Found, v. [Fr. *fonder*, L. *fundere*, to cast down] to lay a basis, establish, begin. *Founded*.

Fount, s. [Fr. *font*, L. *fontem, fons*] a spring of water.

Fourfold, adj. [E. *four, fold*] multiplied by four.

Fourth, see page 52.

GLOSSARY.

Fowl, s. [E. *fugol, fleogan,* to fly] a bird, a domestic bird.

Fowler, s. [E. *fowl*] a birdcatcher.

Fox, s. [E. *feax,* hair, the hairy animal] a small animal of the dog family, noted for its cunning, preserved in England to be hunted; fem. *vixen.*

Fragment, s. [Fr. *fragment,* L. *frangere,* to break] a broken piece, a part.

Frame, v., to form, shape, make, to enclose in a frame. *Framed.*

Frame, s., structure, union of parts, form, a case enclosing something.

Frank, adj. [Fr. *franc,* G. *frank*] the name of the German conquerors of Gaul, who were free while the former inhabitants were conquered and enslaved] free, open, candid.

Free, adj. [E. *freo*] not bound, at liberty.

Free, v., to set at liberty. *Freed.*

Freedom, s. [E. *free*] the condition of being free, liberty.

Freeze, v. [E. *freosan*] to harden into ice, to harden because of cold, to shiver. *Froze, frozen.*

French, adj. [E. *Francisc, Frank*] belonging to France.

Frequent, adj. [L. *frequentem, frequens*] happening often. Adv. *frequently.*

Fresh, adj. [O. Fr. *fraische,* G. *frisc*] lively, new. Subs. *freshness;* Adv. *freshly.*

Friar, s. [Fr. *frère,* L. *frater,* a brother] a brother of a religious order.

Friend, s. [E. *freond, freon,* to love] a lover, a beloved acquaintance.

Fro, adv., from.

Frolic, s. [G. *fröh,* joy; *lich,* condition] a game, sport, freak; originally an adjective meaning joyous.

Frolic, v., to play, gambol. *Frolicked.*

Front, s [Fr. *front,* L. *frontem, frons,* forehead] the fore part.

Front, v., to face, stand opposite to. *Fronted.*

Frost, s. [E. *froze, freeze*] frozen dew, temperature cold enough to make ice.

Frown, s. [Fr. *frogner*] a knitting of the brows, a scowl.

Frugality, s. [Fr. *frugalité,* L. *frugalitatem, frugalis, fruges,* fruit] thrift, carefulness.

Fruit, s. [Fr. *fruit,* L. *fructum, frui,* to use] produce of trees, or of the land; any produce.

Full, adj. [E. *fill*] filled, having all that can be contained. Subs. *fulness.*

Fun, s. [E. *fon,* a fool] sport, jest, amusement. Adj. *funny.*

Fur, s., the short hair of animals.

Furlong, s. [E. *fuhr,* furrow, *long*] 220 yards.

Furnish, v. [Fr. *fournir,* O. Fr. *fornir, fromir,* O. H. G. *frumjan,* to procure] to complete, store, provide. *Furnished.*

Furniture, s. [Fr. *fourniture, fournir*] goods of a house, decoration.

Further, adj. adv., see page 51.

Furthermore, adv., see page 49.

Fury, s. [L. *furia, furere*] rage, madness.

Future, adj. [L. *futurus*] coming, what will be in later time, referring to coming time.

Gain, v. [Fr. *gagner*] to earn, win, acquire. *Gained.*

Gait, s. [E. *gate,* a way] a way of walking, walk.

Gale, s. [Norw. *galen,* raging] a raging wind, storm.

Galilee, s., a Hebrew word meaning 'frontier,' given as a name to the northern part of Canaan, where the Israelites were much mingled with the Phœnicians, and afterwards used as the name of the entire northern third of the land.

Gall, v., to rub into a sore, vex, annoy. *Galled.*

Gallant, adj. [Fr. *galant, galer*, E. *gâl*] fine, spirited, brave, courteous.

Gallery, s. [It. *galleria*] a balcony, an upper stage in a building, a covered way in a fortress.

Galley, s. [Fr. *galée*, a ship's beak] a large beaked ship.

Gallop, v. [Fr. *galoper*, G. *gahlaupan*, to leap] to leap in running as a horse does. *Galloped.*

Game, s., play, sport; animals hunted or shot in sport.

Gamut, s. [*gamma*, the Greek G, last note of the musical scale of Guy of Arezzo, *ut*, the first note of the scale] the musical scale.

Gap, s. [E. *geap*, wide] an opening.

Gape, v. [E. *gap*] to open wide, yawn, stare. *Gaped.*

Garden, s. [E. *garth*] a small yard, an enclosure for flowers and fruit.

Gardener, s. [E. *garden*] one who works in a garden.

Garment, s. [Fr. *garnement, garnir*, to furnish] clothing.

Garrison, s. [Fr. *garnison, garnir*, E. *warnian*, to warn, beware] a guard of soldiers for a fortress.

Gate, s., a hole, passage, way, entrance.

Gather, v. [E. *gaderian*] to draw into a heap, collect. *Gathered.*

Gaul, s. [Fr. *Gaule*, L. *Gallia*] the land of the Galli; the name by which the Romans knew the country which we call France.

Gay, adj. [Fr. *gai*, G. *jähe*, O. H. G. *gâki*, quick] merry, lively.

Gaze, v. [E. *geseán, seon*, to see] to look earnestly, look steadily. *Gazed.*

Gaze, s., a steady look.

Gazelle, s. [Fr. *gazelle*, Ar. *gazal*] a wild goat.

Gem, s. [L. *gemma*] a precious stone, anything very precious.

General, adj. [L. *generalis, genus*, a race] common to a whole class, usual.

General, s., the chief commander of an army.

Generation, s. [L. *generationem, generare, genus*] origin; in time, a period of about thirty years.

Generous, adj. [L. *generosus*, nobly born, *genus*] free, liberal, open.

Gennesareth, s. [Hebr. *Gani*, gardens, *Sar*, prince] the Garden of Princes; a richly-watered and fertile plain, of about five miles in width and six or seven in length, between the mountains and the lake which has obtained the name Lake of Gennesareth, in the north of Palestine.

Genoa, s., a seaport on the most northern bend of the south coast of Italy. Adj. *Genoese.*

Gentle, adj. [Fr. *gentil*, L. *gentilis, gens*, a clan] well-born, mild, refined. Adv. *gently.*

Geographical, adj. [E. *geography*; Gr. *ge*, earth, *graphe*, a written account] concerning geography, the science describing the world.

Gerizim, s., a mountain on the south side of Shechem in Canaan, from which part of the Law of Moses was proclaimed, and on which the Samaritans had a temple.

German, adj. [L. *Germanus*, G. *wehr, man*, warman] belonging to Germany; of the German, Teutonic, race.

Gesture, s. [L. *gestura, gerere*, to bear] a movement of the body.

Get, v. [E. *gitan*] to seize, obtain, receive. *Got* or *gat, gotten* or *got.*

Ghent, s., a town at the junction of the river Lys with the Schelde, in the province of East Flanders, in Belgium.

Gift, s. [E. *give*] a thing given, present.

Gilead, s., a rough mountainous

GLOSSARY. 269

district on the eastern side of the river Jordan.

Gillyflower, s. [E. *girofloure*, Fr. *giroflée*, It. *garofalo*, Gr. *karyophyllus*, the clove-tree, so called from the smell] a stock.

Gipsy, s. [E. *Egyptian*] a wandering race from India, by mistake thought to be from Egypt; a dark-faced person, a vagabond.

Giraldus, s., a Welshman, hence called Giraldus Cambrensis, who went as companion and preceptor to Ireland with John, son of King Henry III; he wrote a Latin history of the Conquest of Ireland, 1154–1189.

Gird, v. [E. *gyrd*] to enclose, circle, clothe. *Girded* or *girt*.

Girl, s., a female child, a young woman.

Girth, s. [E. *gird*] a band, girdle.

Give, v. [E. *gifan*] to bestow, grant, hand over. *Gave, given*.

Glad, adj. [E. *glæd*] smooth, joyous, happy, bright. Adv. *gladly*.

Gladden, v. [E.*glad*] to make glad. *Gladdened*.

Glade, s., a passage letting light into a wood, an open space between trees.

Glance, s., a sudden ray of light, darting look.

Glance, v., to dart a look, glide obliquely. *Glanced*.

Glare, s., a dazzling light, stare.

Glasgow, s., the commercial capital of Scotland, on the river Clyde.

Gleam, v. [E. *glǽm*] to shine brightly *Gleamed*.

Glen, s. [W. *llyn*] a valley.

Glimmer, v. [freq. of E. *gleam*] to keep shining, to flicker. *Glimmered*.

Glisten, v. [E. *glistenan, glas,* shining] to sparkle with light. *Glistened*.

Glitter, v. [E. *glitian*] to sparkle. *Glittered*.

Globe, s. [Fr. *globe*, L. *globus*] a ball, sphere, the earth.

Gloom, s., darkness, sadness, sorrow. Adj. *gloomy*.

Glory, s. [L. *gloria*] fame, honour. Adj. *glorious*.

Glory, v., to triumph, boast, rejoice. *Gloried*.

Glossy, adj. [E. *gloss, glas*, shining] shining, smooth.

Glow, v., to shine as a fire, to be red-hot. *Glowed*.

Glow, s., brightness, redness, heat.

Go, v. [E. *gán*] to walk, move, depart. [*Went*], *gone*.

Goat, s. [E. *gát*] a horned animal closely allied to the sheep.

God, s., the supreme being. Fem. *goddess*.

Godwine, s., a famous Englishman, son of Wulfnoth, Earl of the West Saxons from 1020–1053, father of Harold II King of England.

Gold, s. [E. *gealw*, yellow, gold] a yellow metal. Adj. *golden*.

Good, adj. [E. *gód*] proper, virtuous, pious. Subs. *goodness*.

Goose, s. [E. *gós*] a large web-footed bird of gray colour, a silly person. Pl. *geese*.

Gorge, s. [Fr. *gorge*, L. *gurges*] a throat, narrow passage.

Gorge, v., to swallow greedily, overfeed. *Gorged*.

Gorgeous, adj. [O. Fr. *gorgias*, proud, *gorge*] stately, grandly adorned.

Gory, adj. [E. *gór, gore*, blood] blood-stained.

Govern, v. [Fr. *gouverner*, L. *gubernare*] to regulate, direct, rule. *Governed*.

Government, s. [Fr. *gouvernement, gouverner*] rule, system of governing, persons having power.

Gradual, adj. [Fr. *graduel*, L. *gradualis, gradus*, a step] step by step, by degrees. Adv. *gradually*.

Graduate, v. [L. *graduatus*,

Graduare, gradus] to get a degree, to mark by degrees, divide. *Graduated.*

Grand, adj. [Fr. *grand*, L. *grandem*] large, important, stately.

Grandame, s. [Fr. *grand, dame*] grandmother.

Grandeur, s. [Fr. *grandeur, grand*] greatness, importance.

Grant, v. [L. L. *graantum*, O. Fr. *craanter, creancer, creance*, L. *credentia, credere*, to trust] to allow, entrust, give. *Granted.*

Grape, s. [Fr. *grappe*, a bunch, G. *krappen*] the fruit of the vine, which grows in the form of a bunch of berries.

Grasp, v. [E. *grab*] to catch hold of, seize, hold in the hand. *Grasped.*

Grasp, s., a seizing.

Grass, s. [from same root as E. *grow*] growing herbs. Pl. *grass*, and *grasses*.

Grated, adj. [E. *grate, crate*, L. *crates*] enclosed by bars, rubbed upon a rough surface.

Grave, s. [E. *grafan*, to dig] a burying place, tomb, a hole.

Grave, adj. [Fr. *grave*, L. *gravem*, heavy] solemn, serious, important.

Gravel, s. [Fr. *gravelle*, O. Fr. *grave*, sand] small stones.

Gray, adj. [E. *græg*] speckled, black and white, dun and white.

Graze, v.[E. *grate*] to scrape, touch slightly. *Grazed.*

Great, adj., large, grand. Subs. *greatness.*

Greece, s. [L. *Graecia*] the name by which the Romans knew Hellas, the south-eastern peninsula of Europe. The Graeci were a small tribe settled on the Illyrian coast.

Greek, adj. [Fr. *grec*, L. *graecus*] belonging to Greece.

Green, adj. [from same root as E. *grow*] the colour of growing herbs.

Greenland, s., the north-eastern part of America; a Danish colony, discovered by sailors from Iceland about 980, who are said to have given it this name from its appearance as compared with their own land. It was colonised by a Danish mission under Hans Egede, 1720-3.

Greet, v. [E. *grétan*] to meet, salute, address. *Greeted.*

Grey, see **Gray**.

Grief, s. [Fr. *grief*, L. *gravem*, heavy] heaviness of mind, sorrow, sadness.

Grind, v. [from the sound] to grate, break small, crush. *Ground.*

Groan, v. [from the sound] to make a moaning sound. *Groaned.*

Gross, adj. [Fr. *gros*, L. *grossus*, coarse[thick, coarse, fat.

Ground, s. [E. *grund*] the surface of the land, land, foundation, a reason.

Ground, v., to place on the ground, found, begin. *Grounded.*

Group, s. [Fr. *groupe*, It. *groppo*] a bunch, collection, throng.

Grove, s. [E. *græf, grafan*, to dig] a place where trees have been planted, collection of trees, small wood.

Grow, v., to increase, develop. *Grew, grown.*

Growl, v. [from the sound] to make a snarling sound, snarl, murmur angrily. *Growled.*

Guard, v. [O. Fr. *guarder*, G. *warten*, to keep] to keep, take care of, protect. *Guarded.*

Guard, s., a keeper, protector.

Guardian, s. [L. L. *guardianus*, E. *warden, ward*] a keeper, protector.

Guest, s. [E. *gæst*] a stranger, visitor.

Guide, v. [Fr. *guide*, It. *guida*, Goth. *witan*] to show, to direct, lead. *Guided.*

Guide, s., a leader.

Guile, s. [Fr. *guile*, E. *wile*] fraud, deceit, trick.

Guilt, s. [E. *gylt, gildan*, to pay] a debt, crime, wickedness. Adj.

guilty, wicked; *guiltless*, free from crime.

Guise, s. [Fr. *guise*, G. *weise*] manner, way, wise, dress.

Gulf, s. [Fr. *golfe*, It. *golfo*, Gr. *kolpos*, a bay] an arm of the sea, bay.

Gun, s. [E. *gyne, engyne*, L. *ingenium*; or from *gunner*, Fr. *guigneur, guigner*, to aim, to wink] a tube for discharging missiles.

Gunner, s. [E. *gun*; or, Fr. *guigneur, guigner*, to aim] one who shoots with a gun.

Gusty, adj. [E. *gust, gush*] stormy.

Gyges, s., King of Lydia in Asia, founder of the dynasty of the Mermnadæ, B.C. 716-678.

Habit, s. [Fr. *habit*, L. *habitus, habere*] custom, practice, use, a dress.

Habitual, adj. [Fr. *habituel*, L. *habitus, habere*] usual, accustomed.

Hail, v. [E. *hagol*] to fall as hail, to patter in drops, to fall thickly. *Hailed.*

Hail, interj. [E. *hal, heal*] be of good health.

Hair, s. [E. *hær*] a threadlike process growing on the skin of animals. Adj. *hairy.*

Half, s., one of two equal parts.

Halifax, George Savile, Earl and Marquis of Halifax, minister of Charles II. from 1679, and of James II. and William III. Died 1695.

Hall, s. [E. *heal*] a covered place, a court-yard, a large room, entrance-chamber.

Halter, s. [Du. *halfter, helft*, a handle] a head-rope for holding horses, a rope for hanging.

Hammer, v. [E. *hamor*, from the sound] to beat, to beat into shape, contrive. *Hammered.*

Hammer, s., an instrument for beating.

Hand, s., the end of the arm below the wrist.

Handle, s. [E. *hand*] that which is held.

Handsome, adj. [E. *hand, sam*] handy, convenient, becoming, beautiful.

Hang, v. [E. *hangian*] to fasten on high,· suspend. *Hung* or *hanged*; hung or hanged.

Hannibal, s., a famous Carthaginian general, who spent most of his life in fighting against the Romans. Born B.C. 246; died of poison in Bithynia, B.C. 183.

Haply, adv. [E. *happily*, W. *hap*] by chance.

Happen, v. [E. *hap*] to come by luck, befall. *Happened.*

Happy, adj. [E. *hap*] having good hap, lucky, fortunate, joyous. Subs. *happiness.*

Harbour, s. [E. *herbergh; here*, army, *beorgan*, to protect] shelter, a port for ships.

Hard, adj., strong, close, difficult to pierce. Adv. *hardly.*

Harden, v. [E. *hard*] to make hard, become hard. *Hardened.*

Hare, s. [E. *hara*] a wild animal.

Hark, interj., imperative mood of *hearken.*

Harm, s., evil, damage, injury.

Harold, s., son of Godwine Earl of the West Saxons, was chosen to be King of England, to succeed Edward the Confessor, on Jan. 6, 1066. Killed in the battle of Senlac, or Hastings, October 14, 1066.

Harpoon, s. [Fr. *harpon, harper*, O. H. G. *harfan*, to seize] a barbed iron for spearing fish.

Harsh, adj. [E. *harsk, hask*] rough, hard, severe.

Hart, s. [E. *heorot*] the horned animal, a stag, the male of the deer.

Harvest, s. [E. *hærfest*] autumn-time, the time of gathering crops, fruit, produce.

Haste, s. [O. Fr. *haster*] speed, hurry. Adj. *hasty*.

Hasten, v. [E. *haste*] to hurry, urge, speed. *Hastened*.

Hastings, s., a town on the south coast of Sussex, a settlement of Danes or Northmen.

Hat, s., a covering for the head.

Hatchet, s. [Fr. *hachette*, *hacher*, O. H. G. *hacco*] a small instrument for hacking, a small axe.

Hate, v., to dislike, detest. *Hated*.

Hate, s., dislike, hostility.

Hatred, s. [E. *hate*] the feeling of hate.

Haunch, s. [Fr. *hanche*, G. *ancha*, the flank] the bend of the thigh, hip.

Haunt, s. [Fr. *hanter*, Sw. *hämta*, to take home; or Breton, *hent*, a path] a place much frequented.

Have, v., see page 76.

Haven, s. [E. *hafen*] a harbour, port.

Haw, s. [E. *haga*, hedge] a hedge, a place hedged, thorns, the berry of the thorn.

Hawk, s. [E. *hafoc*] a bird of prey, a falcon.

Haze, s. [E. *has*, hoarse, thick] mist, thick vapour.

He, pron., see page 53.

Head, s. [E. *heafod*] the top of the body, chief, principal.

Headland, s., a cape, a promontory.

Health, s. [E. *heal*] soundness, a right condition of body. Adj. *healthy*.

Heap, s. [E. *heave*] a mass, pile, collection.

Hear, v. [E. *hyran*] to catch with the ear, listen. *Heard*.

Hearer, s., one who hears.

Hearken, v. [E. *hear*] to listen attentively. *Hearkened*.

Heart, s. [E. *heorte*] the organ of circulation of blood, centre, seat of passions, courage. Adj. *hearty*.

Hearth, s. [E. *heorth*, ground, earth] part of the floor made of earth, fireside, home.

Heat, s., warmth, warm temperature. excitement.

Heat, v., to make hot, to warm. *Heated*.

Heath, s. [E. *hæth*] waste, open country, the plant that grows on the open land.

Heathen, s. [E. *heath*] livers on the open, wild, land. As these were the last to remain pagans when others became Christians, therefore *heathen* became equal to pagan, unbeliever.

Heave, v. [E. *hefan*] to lift, raise, throw. *Heaved*.

Heave, s., a throw.

Heaven, s. [E. *heofon*, *hefan*, to heave] that which is heaved, the sky above the earth. Adj. *heavenly*.

Heavy, s. [E. *hefig*, *hefan*] what is heaved, what is heaved with difficulty.

Hebrew, adj., belonging to the race descended from Heber, Jewish, Israelite.

Hector, s., son of Priam, a leader of the Trojans in the famous story of the Siege of Troja by the Greeks, slain by Achilles.

Heed, s., watch, care, attention.

Heifer, s. [E. *heafor*] a young cow.

Height, s. [E. *high*, *hedh*] tallness, distance up, an eminence.

Heighten, v. [E. *high*] to make higher, raise. *Heightened*.

Hellenes, s., the people of Hellas or Greece, the Greeks.

Helmet, s. [dim. of E. *helm*, *hélan*, to cover] a covering for the head, head-armour.

Help, v., to aid, assist, take care of. *Helped*. (The forms *holp*, *holpen*, are not now used.)

Help, s., aid, assistance. Adj. *helpful*, *helpless*.

Helve, s. [E. *helf*] a handle.

Hem, s., a border, edge of a robe.

Hen, s., a female bird, the female of the domestic fowl.
Hence, adv., see page 82.
Herald, s. [O. Fr. *hérauld*, Teut. *haren*, to shout, Scand. *haro*] one who carries messages between armies, one who makes proclamation.
Herb, s. [Fr. *herbe*, L. *herba*, grass] a plant, grass.
Herbage, s. [Fr. *herbage*, *herbe*] a collection of herbs, pasture, grass.
Herd, s. [E. *heordan*, to hoard] a drove of animals kept together, a number of animals, one who watches animals.
Here, adv., see page 82.
Hêrê, s., the chief goddess of the Greeks, wife of Zeus.
Heritage, s. [Fr. *héritage*, *hériter*, L. *hereditare*, *heres*, an heir] what comes to the heir, inheritance.
Hero, s. [Gr. *heros*] a brave man, a famous man. Adj. *heroic*.
Herself, see page 54.
Hew, v. [E. *heawan*] to cut, hack, chop wood. *Hewed, hewn* or *hewed*.
Hide, s. [E. *hýd*] skin, covering.
Hide, v., to cover, conceal. *Hid, hidden*.
High, adj. [E. *heah*] lofty, raised, tall. Adv. *highly*.
Hill, s., a high mass of land, rising ground.
Hillock, s. [dim. of E. *hill*] a small hill.
Himself, see page 54.
Hind, s., a female deer.
Hinge, s. [E. *hang*] the hook on which a door hangs, a joint.
Hint, s., a whisper, suggestion.
Hip, s., the thigh, flank.
Hip, s., the fruit of the rose.
Hiss, v. [from the sound] to make a sound through the teeth like that of the letter S, used to express disgust. *Hissed*.
Historian, s. [E. *history*] a writer of history.

History, s. [L. *historia*, Gr. *historein*, to investigate] a relation of events, the story of past time. Adj. *historic, historical*.
Hit, v. [E. *hettan*, to pursue] to find, come upon, strike. *Hit, hit*.
Hither, adv. [E. *hider*, *he*, this] to this time, or place.
Hitherto, adv., to hither, to this time.
Hive, s. [E. *hyfe*] a swarm of bees, a basket or box in which a swarm of bees is kept.
Ho, interj., calling attention.
Hoarse, adj. [E. *hás*] rough, harsh, with a rough voice.
Hoary, adj. [E. *hoar, hár*] gray-haired, gray, white.
Hold, v. [E. *healdan*] to keep, occupy. *Held, held* or *holden*.
Hold, s. [E. *hole, hollow*] the hollow of a ship.
Hollow, adj. [E. *hole*] having a hole, like a hole, empty, unsubstantial.
Hollow, v., to make hollow, to empty. *Hollowed*.
Holster, s. [E. *heolster, helan,* to cover] a covering, a case for pistols.
Holy, adj. [E. *halig, hal*, whole] whole, pure, sacred.
Home, s. [E. *ham*, a village] dwelling, house, native-place.
Homer, s., a famous Greek poet.
Homestead, s. [E. *home, stead*, a place] dwelling-place, farm-house.
Homeward, adv., in the direction of *home*.
Honest, adj. [L. *honestus*, honourable] upright, just, true.
Honey, s. [E. *hunig*] sweet juice collected by bees.
Honey-suckle, s. [E. *honey, suck*] a climbing plant containing much honey.
Honour, s. [L. *honorem*] esteem, respect, dignity.
Honour, v. [Fr. *honorer*, L. *hon-*

T

orare, honor] to esteem, respect. *Honoured.*

Hoof, s. [E. *hóf*] horn on the foot of animals, foot.

Hook, s. [E. *hóc*] a bend, crook, anything curved.

Hoop, s. [E. *hóp*] a ring, a round band.

Hoot, v. [from the sound] to cry like an owl. *Hooted.*

Hope, v. [E. *hopian*] to expect, expect with pleasure, look anxiously for. *Hoped.*

Hope, s., expectation, expectation of good. Adj. *hopeless.*

Horizon, s. [Fr. and L. *horizon,* Gr. *horizein, horos,* a bound] the boundary of earth and sky.

Horizontal, adj. [E. *horizon*] like the horizon, level.

Horn, s., a hard substance growing from the heads of animals.

Horrible, adj. [Fr. *horrible,* L. *horribilis, horrere,* to shrink] fearful, dreadful.

Horror, s. [L. *horror, horrere*] dread, fear, terror.

Hospitable, adj. [L. *hospitabilis, hospes,* a host] entertaining strangers, kind.

Host, s. [Fr. *hoste,* L. *hospitem, hospes*] an entertainer, inn-keeper.

Hostile, adj. [Fr. *hostile,* L. *hostilis, hostis,* an enemy] behaving like an enemy, opposing, unfriendly.

Hot, adj. [E. *heat*] having heat, ardent, fiery.

Hound, s. [E. *hund*] a dog, a dog kept for hunting.

Hounslow, s., a heath near London on which a camp was formed at the time of the Spanish Armada, and again in the reign of King James II.

Hour, s. [L. *hora*] a space of time equal to sixty minutes; one twenty-fourth of a day.

House, s. [E. *hús*] a building, a dwelling-place, a family.

Household, s. [E. *house, hold*] persons living in the same house, a family.

How, adv. [E. *hu,* interrog. pron.] in what manner.

However, adv., in whatever manner.

Howl, v. [from the sound] to cry as a dog, yell, whine. *Howled.*

Hue, s. [E. *hiew, heawan,* to show] appearance, colour.

Huge, adj. [Du. *hoog,* high] large, bulky, immense.

Hull, s. [E. *hole, hollow*] the frame of a ship, the ship's body without any fittings.

Hum, v. [from the sound] to make a booming, buzzing, sound. *Hummed.*

Human, adj. [L. *humanus, hominem, homo,* a man], belonging to mankind, like a man.

Humanity, s. [Fr. *humanité,* L. *humanitatem, humanus, homo*] kindliness; behaviour of a man not of a brute, human nature.

Humble, adj. [Fr. *humble,* L. *humilis, humus,* the ground] lowly, submissive, meek.

Humble-bee, s. [E. *hum*] the humming bee.

Humility, s. [Fr. *humilité,* L. *humilitatem, humilis*] lowliness.

Humour, s. [Fr. *humeur,* L. *humorem,* moisture] moisture, state of mind, disposition (which was supposed to depend on the bodily moisture).

Hundred, adj. [E. *hund*] ten times ten.

Hunger, s., want of food, longing.

Hunger, v., to long for food, desire, crave. *Hungered.*

Hunt, v. [E. *hund,* a dog] to follow with hounds, pursue *Hunted.*

Hunter, s., one who hunts.

Hurl, v. [from the sound] to throw with a whirring sound. *Hurled.*

Hurry, v. [from the sound] to whirl, throw violently, urge, hasten. *Hurried.*

GLOSSARY.

Husband, s. [E. *hús*, house, *bonda*, owner, *búa*, to dwell] master of the house, a married man.

Husbandry, s. [E. *husband*] the business of the owner of a house, farming, careful management, thrift.

Hut, s., a cabin, a small house.

Huzza, interj., expressing joy.

Hyads, s. [L. *Hyades*, Gr. *huades*, *huein*, to rain] the rainers, a group of seven stars in the head of the constellation Taurus.

Hymn, s. [L. *hymnus*, Gr. *humnos*] a song, a religious song.

Hymeneal, adj. [L. and Gr. *Hymen*, the god of marriage] belonging to marriage.

Ice, s. [E. *ís*] frozen water, frozen fluid.

Ida, s., a mountain in the Troad, or district famous as the scene of the siege of Troja, on the western coast of Asia.

Idea, s. [L. *idea*, Gr. *idea*, *idein*, to see] an image seen by the mind, representation, opinion.

Identity, s. [Fr. *identité*, L. *identitatem*, *idem*] sameness.

Idiot, s. [Fr. *idiot*, L. *idiota*, Gr. *idiotes*, a private person] a man unskilled in business, unfit for business, a fool.

Idle, adj. [E. *ídel*] empty, unemployed, lazy. Adv. *idly*.

If, conj. [E. *gif*] expressing doubt.

Igneous, adj. [L. *igneus*, *ignis*, fire] fiery, produced by fire.

Ignoble, adj. [Fr. *ignoble*, L. *ignobilis*, *in*, *nobilis*] not noble, low-born, mean.

Ignominy, s. [L. *ignominia*, *in*, *nomen*, a name] loss of name, infamy, disgrace.

Ill, adj. [contraction of *yfel*, evil] evil, bad, wicked.

Illuminate, v. [L. *illuminatus*, *in*, *lumen*, a light] to enlighten, adorn with pictures. *Illuminated*.

Im-, see **In-**.

Image, s. [Fr. *image*, L. *imaginem*] a copy, representation, statue.

Imagination, s. [L. *imaginationem*, *imago*] power of forming images in the mind, fancy.

Imagine, v. [Fr. *imaginer*, L. *imago*] to form an image in the mind, fancy, think. *Imagined*.

Immediate, adj. [Fr. *immédiat*, L. *in*, *medius*] with nothing in the midst, at once. Adv. *immediately*.

Immense, adj. [L. *in*, *mensus*, *metiri*, to measure] not measured, enormous, very large.

Immerse, v. [L. *immersus*, *in*, *mergere*, to dip] to place in water, dip. *Immersed*.

Imminent, adj. [L. *imminentem*, *in*, *minere*] threatening, close at hand.

Immix, v. [E. *in*, *mix*] to mix in. *Immixed*.

Immortality, s. [Fr. *immortalité*, L. *immortalitatem*, *in*, *mortalis*, *mors*, death] freedom from death, endless life.

Immoveable, adj. [*in*, not; *moveable*].

Impart, v. [*in*, Fr. *partir*, L. *partiri*, *pars*] to give a share, give. *Imparted*.

Impatience, s. [*in*, not; *patience*].

Impatient, adj. [*in*, not; *patient*].

Impeach, v. [Fr. *empêcher*, It. *impacciare*, L. *impedicare*, *pes*, a foot] to entangle in a charge, accuse of treason. *Impeached*.

Impediment, s. [L. *impedimentum*, *impedire*, *pes*] a thing in the way of the feet, hindrance.

Implore, v. [Fr. *implorer*, L. *implorare*] to beg, entreat. *Implored*.

Import, v. [Fr. *importer*, L. *in*, *portare*] to bring in. *Imported*.

Important, adj. [Fr. *important*, L. *in*, *portantem*, *portare*, to bring] bringing in something new, making a difference, of great weight.

Impose, v. [Fr. *imposer*, L. *in, pausare*] to lay on, cheat. *Imposed.*
Impossible, adj. [*in*, not; *possible*].
Impregnate, v. [L. *in, praegnatus, nasci*] to make pregnant, fill one thing with the qualities of another. *Impregnated.*
Imprison, v. [E. *in, prison*] to place in prison. *Imprisoned.*
Improve, v. [*in*, O. Fr. *prover*, L. *probare*] to make better, become better. *Improved.*
Impute, v. [Fr. *imputer*, L. *in, putare*, to think] to reckon as belonging to, ascribe. *Imputed.*
In, prep., expressing presence.
In-, a prefix, meaning (1) *in*; (2) *not*.
Inarticulate, adj. [L. *in*, not; *articulatus, artus*, a limb] not jointed, spoken indistinctly.
Inbred, adj. [E. *in, bred*] natural.
Incessant, adj. [Fr. *incessant*, L. *in, cessantem, cessare*, to stop] unceasing, continuous.
Inch, s. [L. *uncia*] one-twelfth of a foot.
Inchcape, s. [Gael. *ynys*, an island, *cape*, L. *caput*, a head], the name of a rock off the east coast of Scotland.
Incisor, s. [L. *incisor, incisus, in, caedere*, to cut] a cutter, front-tooth.
Incline, v. [Fr. *incliner*, L. *inclinare*] to bend, slope, be disposed, tend. *Inclined.*
Inclose, v. [*in, close*]. See Close.
Incorrect, adj. [*in*, not, *correct*, L. *correctus, corrigere*, to make straight] not right, wrong.
Increase, v. [L. *increscere*] to grow, become greater, make greater. *Increased.*
Increase, s., growth.
Incredible, adj. [*in*, not, *credible*, L. *credibilis, credere*, to believe] not worthy of belief, monstrous.
Incumbrance, s. [E. *in, cumber*] a hindrance, load.
Indeed, adv. [E. *in, deed, do*] truly.

India, s., the Persian form of the Sanscrit word *sindhu*, a river, which passed into Greek and Latin as the name of the great southern peninsula of Asia.
Indicate, v. [L. *in, dicatus, dicare*] to point out, show. *Indicated.*
Indifferent, adj. [Fr. *indifferent*, L. *in*, not, *differentem, differre*, to alter] not making a difference, unconcerned, impartial, careless.
Indignation, s. [L. *indignationem, in, dignari*, not to think worthy] anger, wrath.
Indignity, s. [Fr. *indignité*, L. *in, dignitatem, dignus*, worthy] insult, unworthy treatment.
Individual, s. [Fr. *individuel*, L. *in*, not, *dividuus, dividere*] a person.
Indulge, v. [L. *indulgere, dulcis*, sweet] to treat kindly, please. *Indulged.*
Inequality, s. [*in*, not, *equality*].
Inevitable, adj. [Fr. *inévitable*, L. *in, e, vitabilis, vitare*, to avoid] unavoidable. Adv. *inevitably.*
Infant, adj. [L. *infans, in*, not, *fari*, to speak] unable to speak, a young child.
Infantry, s. [Fr. *infanterie*, Sp. *infanteria, infanta*, a servant] foot-soldiers, the attendants of knights.
Inference, s. [L. *inferentia, in, ferre*, to bring] deduction, consequence.
Inferior, adj. [L. *inferior, infra*, below] lower, worse.
Infinite, adj. [L. *in, finitus, finire*, to end] unbounded, endless, immense.
Infirm, adj. [L. *in, firmus*] not strong, weak.
Infirmary, s. [Fr. *infirmerie*, L. *in, firmus*, strong] a place for the infirm, hospital.
Influence, s. [Fr. *influence*, L. *influentia, in, fluere*, to flow] sway, power, authority.
Inform, v. [Fr. *informer*, L. *in,*

formare, forma, shape] to put into shape, to tell, acquaint. *Informed.*

Ingratitude, s. [L. *in, gratitudinem, gratus*, thankful] thanklessness, unthankfulness.

Inhabit, v. [L. *in, habitare*, to dwell] to occupy, dwell in. *Inhabited.*

Inhabitant, s. [L. *inhabitantem, habitare*] a dweller.

Inheritance, s. [*inherit*, L. *in, haeres*, an heir] a thing inherited.

Injure, v. [Fr. *injurier*, L. *injuriari, in, jus*, right] to treat with injustice, harm, wrong. *Injured.*

Injury, s. [L. *injuria, in, jus,*] injustice, wrong, harm. Adj. *injurious.*

Innocent, adj. [L. *innocentem, in, nocere*, to hurt] not doing harm, guiltless.

Innumerable, adj. [L. *innumerabilis, in, numerare, numerus*] that cannot be numbered, countless.

Inquire, v. [L. *inquirere, in, quaerere*, to seek into] to seek, ask. *Inquired.*

Inquiry, s. [E. *inquire*] a seeking, question.

Insect, s. [Fr. *insecte*, L. *insectum, in, secare*, to cut] a small animal, as a wasp or fly, whose body appears divided into sections or portions.

Inside, s. [E. *in, side*] the part within.

Insight, s. [E. *in, sight*] power of looking into a thing, a deep view.

Insist, v. [Fr. *insister*, L. *insistere*] to press, be urgent. *Insisted.*

Inspire, v. [Fr. *inspirer*, L. *in, spirare*, to breathe] to breathe a spirit into, encourage. *Inspired.*

Instance, s. [Fr. *instance*, L. *instantia, in, stare*] urging, an example.

Instance, v., to mention as an example. *Instanced.*

Instant, adj. [Fr. *instant*, L. *instantem, in, stare*] pressing, urgent. Adv. *instantly.*

Instantaneous, adj. [L. *instantaneus, in, stare*] done in an instant.

Instead, adv. [E. *in, stead*] in place.

Instruction, s. [L. *instructionem, instructus, in, struere*, to build] building of the mind, teaching.

Instrument, s. [L. *instrumentum, in, struere*] a tool, means of doing anything.

Insult, s. [Fr. *insulte*, L. *insultum, in, salire*, to trample] affront.

Intelligence, s. [Fr. *intelligence*, L. *intelligentia, intelligere*] understanding, sense, information.

Intense, adj. [L. *intensus, in, tendere*, to stretch] strained, vehement, eager. Subs. *intensity.*

Intent, adj. [L. *intentus, in, tendere*] eager, attentive. Subs. the thing intended, purpose.

Interference, s. [L. *interferentia, interferre*] coming between, interposition, meddling.

Interior, adj. [L. *interior, inter*, inside] inner, inland.

Intermission, s. [L. *intermissionem, missus, mittere*, to send] interval, rest, interruption.

Interrupt, v. [L. *interruptus, rumpere*, to break] to break in upon, divide. *Interrupted.*

Interval, s. [L. *inter, vallum*, space between the ramparts] a space, rest, remission.

Intervention, s. [L. *interventionem, ventus, venire*] coming between, interference.

Interweave, v. [L. *inter*, E. *weave*] to weave together, mingle. *Interwove* or *interweaved, interwoven* or *interweaved.*

Into, prep., expressing entrance.

Invade, v. [L. *invadere*, to enter] to enter with hostile purpose. *Invaded.*

Investigate, v. [L. *investigatus, vestigare*, track] to trace, search into, examine. *Investigated.*

Invincible, adj. [Fr. *invincible*, L. *vincere*, to conquer] unconquerable.
Invisible, adj. [Fr. *invisible*, L. *visibilis, videre*] unable to be seen, out of sight.
Invite, v. [Fr. *inviter*, L. *invitare*] to call, summon, attract, tempt. *Invited.*
Ireland, s., an island off the western coast of Britain. Adj. *Irish.*
Iron, s. [E. *iren, isen*] metal, a hard dark-coloured metal. Adj. *iron*, made of iron, hard, strong, lasting.
Irradiate, v. [L. *in, radiatus, radiare, radius*, a ray] to cast rays upon, to light. *Irradiated.*
Irrigation, s. [L. *irrigationem, irrigatus, rigare*, to water] watering of land.
Irritate, v. [L. *irritatus, irritare*] to anger, excite. *Irritated.*
Isaac, s., son of Abraham and Sarah, a patriarch of the Hebrews.
Isis, s., a goddess of the ancient Egyptians.
Island, s. [E. *igland, eóland, ea*, water, the *s* having arisen from confusion with *isle, insula*] waterland, land surrounded by water. Subs. *islander*.
Isle, s. [O. Fr. *isle*, L. *insula*] an island.
Israel, s. [Hebrew *Isar, el*, prince of God] a name of Jacob, son of Isaac and Rebekah; the nation descended from Israel.
Issue, s. [Fr. *issue, issu*, O. Fr. *issir*, L. *exire*, to go forth] outlet, offspring, children.
Issue, v., to come forth. *Issued.*
Italy, s., the southernmost peninsula of Europe, projecting into the middle of the Mediterranean Sea. Adj. *Italian.*
Ivy, s. [E. *ifig*] an evergreen creeping plant which clothes walls and trees.

Jack-boots, s. [*jack*, a rough coat of mail] boots protecting the upper part of the leg.
Jacket, s. [E. *jack*, Fr. *jaquette, jaque*, a coat worn by the French peasants in the 14th cent.] a small coat.
Jacob, s., son of Isaac and Rebekah, a patriarch of the Hebrews.
Jag, v., to notch, cut into teeth, roughen. *Jagged.*
James, s. [O. Fr. *Jaquemes*, L. *Jacobus*] King of England, James II of England and VII of Scotland, son of Charles I, reigned 1685-1688, died at St. Germains in France, 1701.
Japan, s., a large island off the eastern coast of Asia.
Jason, s., a Greek hero, son of Æson, leader of the Argonauts, who sailed from Iolkos in Thessaly, in the ship Argo, to fetch the golden fleece from Æa, or Colchis, in the far East, ruled by Æaetes, son of the Sun-God.
Javelin, s. [Fr. *javeline*] a small spear, a dart.
Jaw, s. [E. *chaw, chew*] the bones which hold the teeth, mouth.
Jebus, s., the ancient name of Jerusalem.
Jericho, s., a town of Canaan near the western bank of the Jordan.
Jerk, s., a sudden stroke.
Jerusalem-artichoke, s. [It. *girasole, girare*, to turn, *al sole*, to the sun] the sun-flower artichoke, a vegetable whose root tastes like the artichoke.
Jest, s. [E. *gest*, Fr. *geste*, a story, L. *gestum*, a deed, *gerere*] a story, laughable story, joke.
Jesus, s. [Gr. *Iesous*, Heb. *Joshua*] a saviour, the Saviour of man.
Jet, s. [O. Fr. *jaiet*, L. *gagates, Gagas* in Lycia] a black mineral, originally obtained from a river in Lycia.
Jew, s. [Fr. *juif*, L. *Judaeus*] a man of Judæa, Hebrew.
Jewel, s. [O. Fr. *jouel*, L. *jocale*] a precious stone, treasure.

GLOSSARY.

Join, v. [Fr. *joindre,* L. *jungere*] to unite, annex. *Joined.*
Joiner, s., one who joins, a carpenter.
Joint, v. [Fr. *joint,* O. Fr. *joinct,* L. *junctum, jungere*] a joining, seam, hinge.
Jolly, adj. [Fr. *joli,* Scand. *jol = yule,* the winter feast] festive, happy, joyous.
Joshua, s., son of Nun, the great leader of Israel into Canaan, the successor of Moses.
Journey, s. [Fr. *journée, jour,* L. *diurnus, dies,* a day] a day's march, travel.
Jove, s. [L. *Jovem*] Jupiter, the god of day, the chief god of the Romans.
Joy, s. [Fr. *joie,* It. *gioia,* L *gaudium*] delight, happiness. Adj. *joyful, joyous.*
Judæa, s., the land of Judah, the southern part of Canaan.
Judgment, s. [Fr. *jugement, juge,* L. *judicem, judex,* a judge] act of judging, decision, doom.
Jump, s., a leap, spring.
June, s. [Fr. *juin,* L. *Junius*] the sixth month.
Jury, s. [Fr. *juré, jurer,* L. *jurata, jurare,* to swear] a body of men sworn to give judgment justly.
Just, adj. [Fr. *juste,* L. *justus, jus,* law] upright, honest, fair, exact. Adv. *just,* exactly, almost exactly, very nearly.
Justice, s. [Fr. *justice,* L. *justitia, jus*] lawfulness, right, a magistrate.
Justify, v. [Fr. *justifier,* L. *justificare, justum, facere*] to make just, excuse, vindicate. *Justified.*
Jutting, adj. [E. *jut, jet,* Fr. *jeter,* O. Fr. *jecter,* L. *jactare,* to throw] projecting, shooting out.

Keel, s. [E. *ceol,* Scand. *kiölr,* a ship] a vessel, the bottom of a vessel, the great timber on which a ship's ribs are supported.

Keen, adj. [E. *céne*] sharp, eager, acute.
Keep, v. [E. *cepan,* to watch] to observe, take care of, hold. *Kept.*
Key, s. [E. *caeg*] an instrument for shutting and opening locks.
Kill, v. [E. *cwellan*] to smother, slay, put to death. *Killed.*
Kind, s. [E. *kin, cyn, cennan,* to beget] family, race, sort.
Kind, adj. behaving like one of the same family, loving, gentle. Adv. *kindly.*
Kindle, v. [E. *candle,* L. *candela, candere,* to shine] to light up, set on fire. *Kindled.*
Kindred, s. [E. *kinrede, cyn, rædan,* state] kinship, relationship, relations.
Kine, see Cow.
King, s. [E. *cyning,* father] the father of a people, ruler, monarch.
Kiss, v., to touch with the lips *Kissed.*
Kitchen, s. [E. *cycene,* L. *coquina, coquere,* to cook] a cooking-place, room for cooking.
Knee, s. [E. *cneow*] the chief joint of the leg, an angle like a bent leg.
Kneel, v. [E. *knee*] to fall upon the knees. *Kneeled* or *knelt.*
Knife, s. [E. *cnif*] a nipping, cutting, instrument.
Knight, s. [E. *cniht,* a servant] the king's servant, a gentleman ranking below a noble.
Knit, v. [E. *cnittan*] to unite, tie together. *Knitted* or *knit.*
Knot, s. [E. *cnotta, knit*] a thing knitted, a lump.
Know, v. [E. *cnáwan*] to hold in the mind, apprehend, perceive clearly, understand. *Knew, known.*
Knowledge, s. [E. *knowleche, know, lece, lác,* sport, condition] state of knowing, information, learning.
Kronos, s., an ancient god among the Greeks; in later days the name was explained to mean Time, and

he was accounted the father of Zeus the supreme god.

Labour, s. [L. *laborem*] toil, work.

Labour, v., to toil, work, to be in difficulty. *Laboured.*

Labourer, s., one who labours, a workman.

Lacedemonian, s., an inhabitant of Lacedæmon, a city of Laconia.

Lack, v., to be in want, to want, fail. *Lacked.*

Laconia, s., a district in the south of the Peloponnesus, in Greece.

Lad, s., a boy, youth.

Lade, v. [E. *hladan*] to heap upon, weigh, oppress, load. *Laded, laden* or *laded.*

Lady, s. [E. *hlœfdige = hláfweardige*, fem. of *hláfweard*, the loaf keeper, lord] mistress of a house, wife, gentlewoman.

Lair, s. [E. *layer, lay*] the lying place of a wild beast, a den.

Lake, s. [Fr. *lac*, L. *lacus*] a small inland sea.

Lamb, s., a young sheep.

Lament, v. [Fr. *lamenter*, L. *lamentari*] to cry, wail, mourn. *Lamented.*

Lamp, s. [Fr. *lampe*, L. and Gr. *lampas*, a torch] a vessel containing a light, a light.

Lance, s. [Fr. *lance*, L. *lancea*] a spear, a long pointed weapon used by some horse soldiers.

Land, s., earth, ground, a country. Adj. *landless.*

Land, v., to come to land, to come to shore, to disembark. *Landed.*

Lane, s. [variation of E. *lawn*] an open space between hedges.

Language, s. [Fr. *langage, langue*, L. *lingua*, a tongue] speech, tongue.

Languid, adj. [L. *languidus*] weak, feeble, listless.

Languish, v. [Fr. *languissant, languir*, L. *languere*] to grow weak, to be weak, to fail. *Languished.*

Lantern, s. [Fr. *lanterne*, L. *lanterna*, a lamp] a case containing a light, portable lamp.

Lap, v., to lick, drink like a dog. *Lapped.*

Lapse, s., [Fr. *lapse*, L. *lapsus, labi*, to glide] a passing, slip.

Large, adj. [Fr. *large*, L. *largus*] big, great.

Lark, s. [E. *laverock, laferc*] the little singer, a bird noted for singing in the open sky.

Last, adj., see page 51.

Late, adj., slow, behind the time, past, see page 51.

Latin, adj. [L. *Latinus*] belonging to the people of Latium, Roman.

Latitude, s. [Fr. *latitude*, L. *latitudinem, latus*, broad] breadth, liberty, distance from the equator.

Laugh, v. [E. *hlihan*, from the sound] to make a noise expressing mirth, or joy. *Laughed.*

Laugher, s. [E. *laugh*] one who laughs.

Laughter, s. [E. *laugh*] the sound of laughing.

Launch, v. [Fr. *lancer, lance*] to throw as a lance, let slip. *Launched.*

Law, s. [E. *lag, lecgan*, to lay down] rule, statute, order. Adj. *lawful.*

Lawn, s. [W. *llan*] an open space, an open piece of grass.

Lay, v. [E. *lecgan*] to cause to lie, place, put down. *Laid, laid.*

Lazy, adj. [E. *leas, loose;* or Fr. *las*, L. *lassus*] idle, sluggish.

Lea, s. [E. *leag*, pasture] land laid in grass, pasture, meadow.

Lead, s., a metal of dull bluish colour.

Lead, v. [E. *lædan, lad*, a way] to guide upon the way, direct, help. *Led, led.*

Leaf, s., the flat part of a plant, a page, part of a table.

Leafage, s. [E. *leaf*] leaves, foliage.

League, s. [L. L. *leuga*, Gael.

leag, a stone] a measure of distance, three miles; **League-long**, stretching three miles.
Leaguer, s. [E. *league*, Fr. *ligue*, L. *ligare*, to bind] one who joins a league, an ally.
Lean, v. [E. *hlynian*] to bend, incline, slope. *Leaned* or *leant*.
Leap, v. [E. *hleápan*] to spring, jump, bound. *Leaped* or *leapt*.
Leap, s., a spring, jump.
Learn, v. [E. *leornian*, *læran*, to teach] to teach, gain knowledge. *Learned* or *learnt*.
Least, see page 51.
Leather, s. [E. *lether*] dressed skin, tanned hide.
Leave, v. [E. *læfan*] to go away from, forsake. *Left*.
Leave, s. [E. *leaf*, *lýfan*, to allow] permission, liberty.
Leaven, s. [Fr. *levain*, *lever*, L. *levare*, to raise] yeast which makes dough rise.
Lebanon, s., a range of mountains in the north of Canaan.
Ledge, s. [E. *lecgan*, to lay] a flat strip, shelf, rim.
Left, adj. [E. *lift*, from same root as *light*] the lighter or weaker hand, opposite to right.
Leg, s., the limb on which animals stand.
Legend, s. [Fr. *legende*, L. *legenda*, *legere*, to read] a story to be read, a story, an unlikely story, an old story resting on little foundation.
Legion, s. [Fr. *legion*, L. *legionem*, *legere*, to enrol] a body of Roman soldiers, a body of soldiers, a very large number.
Leisure, s. [Fr. *loisir*, L. *licere*, to be allowed] permission, liberty, freedom from work, rest.
Lend, v. [E. *lænan*] to let for hire, give on condition of repayment. *Lent*.
Length, s. [E. *long*] extent longwise.
Leopard, s. [Fr. *léopard*, Gr. *leon*, *pardos*] the lion-pard, a spotted animal of the tiger family.
Lesbos, s., an island in the Ægean sea, off the coast of Æolis in Asia Minor.
Less, see page 51.
Lessen, v. [E. *less*] to make less, make smaller, diminish. *Lessened*.
Lest, conj. [E. *less*, *least*] that the less, that not.
Let, v. [E. *lætan*] to loose, leave alone, allow, permit. *Let*, *let*.
Let, v. [E. *lettan*] to put a stop to, hinder, prevent. *Let*, *let*.
Let, s., a hindrance.
Letter, s. [L. *litera*] a mark representing a sound, an epistle.
Level, s. [E. *læfel*, L. *libella*, *libra*, a balance] a plummet, line, rule.
Level, adj., smoothed by a level, even, horizontal.
Level, v., to make even, smooth. *Levelled*.
Lever, s. [Fr. *levier*, *lever*, L. *levare*, to raise] a lifter, an instrument for raising weights.
Liberal, adj. [L. *liberalis*, *liber* free] free-handed, generous, open.
Liberality, s. [Fr. *liberalité*, L. *liberalitatem*, *liber*] generosity, bounty, largeness of mind.
Liberty, s. [Fr. *liberté*, L. *libertatem*, *liber*] freedom.
Library, s. [L. *librarium*, *liber*, a book] a place for books, a collection of books.
Lichen, s. [L. *lichen*, Gr. *leichen*] cryptogamic, or flowerless, vegetation growing on trees or stones.
Lick, v. [E. *liccian*] to touch with the tongue, lap. *Licked*.
Lie, v. [E. *leogan*, *lyge*, a lie] to say what is untrue, tell a falsehood. *Lied*.
Life, s., being, existence.
Lift, v. [E. *hlifian*] to raise, elevate, carry away. *Lifted* or *lift*.
Light, s. [E. *leoht*, *lig*] a thin shining fluid, day, brightness.
Light, adj., not heavy, lively, active. Adv. *lightly*.

Light, v., to give light to, kindle, set fire to. *Lighted* or *lit*.
Lighten, v., to make light, illuminate; free from trouble. *Lightened*.
Lighthouse, s., a tower with light to direct sailors at sea.
Lightning, s. [E. *lighten*] a flash of light after thunder.
Like, adj. [E. *lic*, a body] of same form, similar. Adv. *likely*.
Like, v., to compare, approve, be pleased with. *Liked*.
Liken, v. [E. *like*] to make like, compare. *Likened*.
Likewise, adv., in like wise, in similar manner, also.
Limb, s. [E. *lim*] a joint, branch.
Lime, s. [E. *lim*] sticky matter, viscous juice of young twigs, calcareous earth used as cement in building.
Limit, s. [Fr. *limite*, L. *limitem*, *limes*, a path] a boundary, end.
Line, s. [L. *linea*, *linum*, flax] a thin cord, a long stroke, a row.
Line, v., to place a row alongside of, cover the inside of. *Lined*.
Linen, s. [Fr. *linon*, *lin*, L. *linum*, flax] cloth made of flax.
Linger, v. [E. *long*] to stay long, delay, dawdle. *Lingered*.
Linnet, s. [Fr. *linotte*, L. *linum*] the flax-finch, a finch which feeds much on flaxseed.
Lion, s. [Fr. *lion*, L. *leonem*, *leo*] a large quadruped closely allied to the cat.
Lip, s. [E. *lippe*, *lap*] that which laps, the border of the mouth, edge.
Liquefy, v. [Fr. *liquéfier*, L. *liquefacere*] to make fluid, melt. *Liquefied*.
Liquid, adj. [L. *liquidus*] flowing, fluid.
Literature, s. [L. *literatura*, *litera*, a letter, *linere*] the science of letters, books, writings.
Little, adj., small. See page 51.
Live, v. [E. *lybban*, *lif*] to be, exist, have life, dwell. *Lived*.

Live, adj. [E. *life*] having life, alive, active.
Lively, adj., like a person alive, active, vigorous. Subs. *liveliness*.
Living, s., means of keeping life, income.
Lo, interj., oh, ah, see, behold [a combination of *la*, and *loc*, see.]
Load, v., [E. *hlad*, a load] to heap on, pile, lade. *Loaded*, *loaded* or *loaden*.
Lock, s. [E. *lócan*, to fasten] a fastening, a place shut in.
Lofty, adj. [E. *loft*, *lift*, the air] airy, high, haughty. Subs. *loftiness*.
Log, s., a lumpy piece of wood, anything heavy and unshapen.
Logic, s. [L. *logica*, Gr. *logike*, *logos*, reason] the science of reasoning, reason.
Loin, s. [Fr. *longe*, L. *lumbea*, *lumbus*] a band of flesh along the back; **Loins**, the lower part of the back.
Loiter, v., to idle, go slowly, dawdle. *Loitered*.
Lombardy, s., the land of the *Longo-bardi*, or longbeards; a district in the north of Italy, under the southern slopes of the Alps.
London, s., a city on the river Thames, capital of England.
Lonely, adj. [E. *alone*] alone, unfrequented, solitary.
Long, adj., extended, outspread, not short.
Long, v., to desire earnestly. *Longed*.
Look, v. [E. *lócian*] to fix the eye, spy, seem. *Looked*.
Loom, s. [F. *loma*] a tool, instrument; instrument for weaving.
Loose, adj, [E. *leas*, weak] slack, free, untied, immoral.
Loose, v., to set free, untie. *Loosed*.
Lord, s. [E. *hláf*, loaf, *weard*, warder] master, employer, a nobleman. Adj. *lordly*.

Lordship, s. [E. *lord, ship*] state of being a lord, a lord's land, a lord.

Lose, v. [E. *leas*] to let go free, miss, waste. *Lost.*

Loss, s. [E. *los, leas*] losing, thing lost, waste, injury, harm.

Loth, adj. [E. *loath, lath,* hateful] sorry, reluctant, disliking.

Loud, adj. [E. *hlud,* a sound] sounding, noisy.

Love, s. [E. *luf*] fondness, affection.

Love, v. [E. *lufian, luf*] to be pleased with, desire, be fond of. *Loved.*

Lovely, adj. [E. *love*] fit to be loved, beautiful.

Lover, s., one who loves.

Low, adj. [E. *lecgan,* to lay] laid, far down, mean, common.

Lower, v. [E. *low*] to put down, degrade, sink, let down. *Lowered.*

Lowly, adj. [E. *low*] humble, meek, unassuming.

Lucifer, s. [L. *lucem, lux,* light, *ferre,* to bring] the morning star, a name given to Satan.

Luck, s. [G. *glück*] fortune, chance, good fortune. Adj. *luckless,* unfortunate.

Lump, s., an unshapen piece, mass, heap.

Lung, s., the organ of breathing.

Lurid, adj.[L.*luridus*] pale, gloomy, stormy.

Luscious, adj. [E. *lushious, lush*] rich, very sweet.

Lustre, s. [Fr. *lustre,* L. *lustrare, lucere,* to shine] light, brightness, splendour.

Lute, s. [O.Fr. *luth, leut,* Arab. *el úd*] a stringed musical instrument, like a small harp.

Luxury, s. [L. *luxuria,* rankness] excess, extravagance, self-indulgence.

Lydia, s., a district in the centre of the west coast of Asia, a woman's name. Adj. *Lydian.*

Lyonnesse, s., a district famous in the romances as the scene of many of King Arthur's deeds, represented as west of Cornwall, now submerged by the sea.

Lyre, s. [Fr. *lyre,* L. and Gr. *lyra*] a harp.

Mackerel, s. [O. Fr. *maquerel,* It. *maccarello,* L. *macula,* a spot] a fish marked with blotches of dark colour.

Mad, adj., excited, furious, insane.

Magistrate, s. [L. *magistratus, magister*] a public officer, an inferior judge.

Magnificent, adj.[L.*magnificentem, magnus, facere*] acting grandly, splendid, noble, grand.

Magnitude, s. [L. *magnitudinem, magnus*] greatness, importance.

Magpie, s. [*Mag,* Margaret, *pie;* Fr. *pie,* L. *pica,* a daw] the long-tailed pie, a bird of the crow family, of variegated plumage. *Pica Caudata.*

Maid, s. [E. *magð,* a child] a child, a female child, girl.

Maiden, s. [E. *maid*] a young girl.

Mail, s. [Fr. *maille,* L. *macula,* a mesh] armour formed of chain-work or net-work, armour. Adj. *mailed,* clad in mail.

Main, s. [E. *mægn, magan,* to be able] strength, greatness. Adj. *main,* great, chief, the chief sea.

Maintain, v. [Fr. *maintenir.* L. *manus, tenere*] to hold, keep, support. *Maintained.*

Maintenance, s. [Fr. *maintenant, maintenir*] support, means of living.

Maize, s. [Sp. *maiz,* Haitian, *mahiz*] Indian corn.

Majesty, s. [Fr. *majesté,* L. *majestatem, major, magnus,* great] grandeur, dignity, the title of a king. Adj. *majestic.*

Make, v. [E. *macian,* from root of *magan,* to be able] to form, create, cause. *Made.*

Malefactor, s. [L. *malefactor, malum, facere*] an evil-doer, criminal.

Malice, s. [Fr. *malice*, L. *malitia*, *malus*, bad] ill-will, spite, enmity.

Mammalia, s. pl. [L. *mammalis*, *mamma*, a breast] animals that suckle their young.

Man, s., a male human being, mankind. Adj. *manful*, brave.

Manage, v. [Fr. *manège*, It. *maneggio*, L. *manus*, a hand] to take in hand, govern, guide. *Managed*.

Mangle, v., to tear to pieces, cut, destroy. *Mangled*.

Manhood, s. [E. *man*, *had* = state] state of being a man, prime of life in man.

Manifestation, s. [L. *manifestationem*, *manifestus*, clear] opening, disclosure, making plain, show.

Manifold, adj. [E. *many*] of many folds, numerous.

Mankind, s. [E. *man*, *kind*] the race of man, men.

Manner, s. [Fr. *manière*, It. *maniero*, L. *manus*, a hand] way of handling, mode, plan.

Many, adj. [E. *manig*] numerous, not few.

Map, s. [L. *mappa*, a cloth, hence *Mappa-mundi*, a drawing of the earth on a cloth] a drawing of the earth's surface, a plan.

Marble, s. [Fr. *marbre*, L. *marmorem*, *marmor*, a bright surface] limestone bearing a good polish.

March, s. [L. *Martius*, *Mars*] the third month, called by the Latins after Mars, their God of War.

March, v. [Fr. *marcher*, to beat with the feet, L. L. *marcare*, *marcus*, a hammer] to tramp, to move as soldiers.

Margate, s., a town on the coast of Kent.

Margin, s. [It. *margine*, L. *marginem*, *margo*] an edge, rim.

Marine, adj. [Fr. *marine*, L. *marinus*, *mare*, the sea] belonging to the sea. Subs. *mariner*, a sailor.

Mark, s. [E. *mearc*] a sign, trace, proof.

Mark, v., to sign, note, note with the eyes, perceive. *Marked*.

Market, s. [Fr. *marché*, L. *mercatus*, *merx*, commerce] a place for traffic, a place of public sale.

Marriage, s. [Fr. *mariage*, *marier*, L. *maritare*, *maritus*, a husband] a wedding.

Mars, s., the name of the God of War among the Latins.

Marsh, s. [E. *mersc*, *mere*, water] wet land, bog, a fen.

Mart, s., contraction of **Market**.

Marvel, s. [Fr. *merveille*, L. *mirabilia*, *mirari*, to wonder] a wonder. Adj. *marvellous*.

Marvel, v., to wonder, be astonished. *Marvelled*.

Mary, s., Queen of England, daughter of Henry VIII and Catharine of Arragon; reigned 1553-1558; married Philip II of Spain.

Masculine, adj. [L. *masculinus*, *mas*, male] male, like a man, strong.

Mass, s. [L. *massa*] a lump, heap, large quantity. Adj. *massive*, *massy*.

Massacre, s. [Fr. *massacre*, G. *metzger*, a butcher, L. *macellarius*, a butcher] a butchery, slaughter, carnage.

Massena, s., a French general, under Napoleon I, who was in command at Busaco, 1810, and before the lines of Torres Vedras in Portugal.

Mast, s. [E. *mæst*] a pole on which the ship's rigging is fastened.

Master, s. [O.Fr. *maistre*, L. *magister*, *major*, greater] a teacher, employer, lord, a man in authority.

Masterful, adj., full of authority as a master, strong.

Match, s. [softened form of E. *make*] a thing of the same make, a mate, mating.

Mate, s. [softened form of E. *make*] an equal, comrade, companion.

Material, adj. [L. *materialis*, *materia*] of matter, substantial, solid, important.

Mathematics, s. pl. [Fr. *mathé-*

matiques, L. *mathematica*, Gr. *mathema*, learning] the science of numbers.

Matted, adj. [E. *mat*, L. *matta*, a tuft of rush] bunched, plaited together, thick.

Matter, s. [E. *matere*, Fr. *matière*, L. *materia*] substance, cause, importance.

Matter, v., to be of importance. *Mattered.*

May, v. [E. *magan*, to be able]. See pages 75, 77.

Mead, s. [E. *medu*] a drink made of fermented honey.

Mead, s. [E. *mæd, mawan*, to mow] mown land, grass-land.

Meadow, s. [E. *mædewe, mæd*] a small mead, a field of grass-land.

Meal, s. [E. *mæl*] a piece, bit, a portion of food.

Mean, adj. [E. *gemæne*, common] common, low, poor, base. Subs. *meanness.*

Mean, v. [E. *mænan*, to have in mind] to think, intend, have in mind. *Meant.*

Means, s. pl. [E. *mean*, Fr. *moyen*, L. *medianus, medius*, middle] that which comes between as a help, instrument, opportunities, income.

Meanwhile, adv. [E. *mean*, Fr. *moyen*, middle, E. *while*] between the time.

Measure, s. [Fr. *mesure*, L. *mensura, mensus, metiri*] extent marked out, extent, space, degree, metre.

Measure, v., to estimate extent, to mark, stretch. *Measured.*

Meat, s. [E. *mete*] food, flesh, animal food.

Mecheln, s., a town in the province of Antwerp in Belgium, also *Mechlin*, and *Malines*.

Mede, s., a man of Media, a country in Asia.

Mediocrity, s. [Fr. *mediocrité*, L. *mediocritatem, mediocris, medius*] middling condition, neither very good nor very bad.

Meet, v. [E. *metan*] to come against, encounter, assemble. *Met, met.*

Meet, adj. [E. *mete*] measured, fitted, suitable.

Melancholy, s. [L. *melancolia*, Gr. *melas*, black, *chole*, bile] having black bile, gloomy, low-spirited.

Mellow, adj., soft, ripe.

Melody, s. [Fr. *mélodie*, L. and Gr. *melodia*, Gr. *melos, ode*] sweet music, symmetrical succession of parts, an air in music.

Melon, s. [Fr. *melon*, L. *melonem*, Gr. *melon*, an apple] a large round fruit allied to the cucumber.

Melt, v. [E. *meltan*] to make liquid, become liquid, waste. *Melted, molten* or *melted.*

Member, s. [Fr. *membre*, L. *membrum*] a limb, part of a body.

Memory, s. [L. *memoria*] the power of keeping knowledge, recollection.

Mental, adj. [L. *mentem, mens*, mind] belonging to the mind.

Mention, v. [L. *mentionem, mentio*, a reminding] to notice, speak of, name. *Mentioned.*

Merchant, s. [Fr. *marchant*, L. *mercantem, mercari*, to trade] a trader, a wholesale trader.

Mercy, s. [Fr. *merci*, L. *mercedem, merces*, reward] favour, thanks, pity. Adj. *merciful.*

Mere, adj. [L. *merus*, unmixed] pure, unmixed, simple. Adv. *merely.*

Mermaid, s. [E. *mere*, sea, *maid*] a sea-maiden, a fabulous creature half woman half fish dwelling in the sea.

Merry, adj. [E. *mirig*] sportive, joking, lively.

Message, s. [Fr. *message*, L. *missaticum, missus, mittere*] a word sent, communication sent, errand.

Messenger, s. [E. *messager, message*] one sent on a message.

Metallic, adj. [E. *metal*, L. *metalla*] of metal, like metal.

Metheglin, s. [E. *mead*] a drink made of honey and water.

Methinks, see **Think.**

Mexican, adj., belonging to Mexico, a country in the south of North America, Spanish colony and possession from A.D. 1519 till 1821.

Mid, adj., between two ends, middle.

Middle, adj. [E. *middel*, *mid*] equally distant from two ends, central. Subs. the centre.

Middling, adj. [E. *middle*] of middle quality or size.

Midnight, s., the middle of the night, twelve o'clock.

Midship, s., the middle of the ship.

Midst, adj. [E. *middest*, *mid*], see page 51.

Might, s. [E. *might*, *may*] strength, power, ability. Adj. *mighty*.

Mile, s. [E. *mil*, L. *mille* (passuum), a thousand paces] a measure of distance; an English mile is 1760 yards.

Military, adj. [L. *militaris*, *miles*, a soldier] belonging to soldiers, war-like, like a soldier.

Milk, s. [E. *meolc*] a white liquid coming from the breasts of female mammals, white juice, white sap.

Mill, s. [E. *myln*] a place for grinding, a place for grinding corn.

Miller, s. [E. *mill*] one who keeps a mill, a corn-grinder.

Mind, s., that which thinks, the understanding, intention.

Mind, v., to call to mind, to have in mind, intend, care for, attend to. *Minded.*

Mine, s., a pit or excavation from which ore, or coal, or stones, are dug.

Minister, s. [L. *minister*, *minus*, less] a servant, attendant, clergyman.

Minstrel, s. [O. Fr. *menestrel*, L. *ministerellus*, *minister*] a workman, artist, musician, singer. Subs. *minstrelsy*, song.

Mint, s. [E. *mynet*, L. *moneta*, Juno the Adviser, in whose temple coin was struck at Rome] a place where money is coined.

Minute, adj. [Fr. *minute*, L. *minutus*, *minuere*, to lessen] very small.

Miracle, s. [Fr. *miracle*, L. *miraculum*, *mirari*, to wonder] a wonder, a portent.

Mirage, s. [Fr. *mirage*, *miroir*, *mirer*] an illusion by which things are seen in the air as if reflected in a mirror.

Mirth, s. [from root of E. *merry*] gladness, joy, laughter.

Mischief, s. [O. Fr. *meschef*, L. *minus*, *caput*] misfortune, loss, harm.

Misdemeanour, s. [E. *mis*, *demean*, Fr. *démener*, *mener*, L. *minare*] ill behaviour, a crime.

Misenum, s., a promontory and town at the end of the northern arm of the Bay of Naples.

Miserable, adj. [Fr. *misérable*, L. *miserabilis*, *miser*] wretched, poor.

Misery, s. [L. *miseria*, *miser*] wretchedness, ill-fortune, grief.

Miss, v.. to fail in hitting, err from, lose, want. *Missed.*

Mist, s., darkness, thickness, thick vapour, small rain. Adj. *misty*.

Mistress, s. [O. Fr. *maistresse*, fem. of *maistre*, L. *magister*, master] the female head of the family, a woman who rules.

Mitigate, v. [L. *mitigatus*, *mitigare* *mitis*, mild] to render mild, soften. *Mitigated.*

Mix, v. [E. *miscan*, L. *miscere*] to mingle, join into one mass, confuse. *Mixed.*

Moab, s., the name of a tribe living near the east of the Dead Sea, said to be descended from a son of Lot.

Moan, v., to make low murmuring

sound with the lips, to lament, whine. *Moaned.*

Mob, s. [L. *mobile*, the fickle (crowd)] a crowd, tumultuous meeting, tumult.

Mock, v., to make a sound with the mouth, to jibe, jeer, ridicule. *Mocked.*

Moderate, adj. [L. *moderatus, modus*, a measure] measured, temperate, restrained. Adv. *moderately.*

Moderation, s. [L. *moderationem, modus*] temperance, fairness, calmness.

Modern, adj. [L. *modernus, modo*, now] of the present time, late, new.

Moil, v. [Fr. *mouiller*, L. *molliare, mollis*, soft] to weary oneself with labour, to work. *Moiled.*

Molar, adj. [L. *molaris, mola*, a mill] grinding, a double tooth.

Mole, s. [Fr. *mole*, L. *molem, moles*, a mass] a mass of earth, pier, a breakwater.

Moment, s. [Fr. *moment*, L. *momentum, movere*, to move] importance, the time in which one can move, the smallest division of time, one-sixtieth of a minute. Adj. *momentary.*

Monarch, s. [Gr. *monarchos, monos*, alone, *archon*, a chief] one who rules alone, a sovereign.

Money, s. [Fr. *monnaie*, L. *moneta*, see **Mint**] stamped metal, coin, anything used as a standard of exchange.

Monkey, s. [It. *monicchio, monna*, an old woman, *madonna*, mistress] an ape, a mischievous person full of tricks.

Monotonous, adj. [E. *monotone*, Gr. *monos*, alone, *tonos*, a note] in one note, unchanging, dull, tedious.

Monster, s. [Fr. *monstre*, L. *monstrum, monere*, to warn] a warning, portent, a thing uncommon, a thing larger than usual. Adj. *monstrous.*

Month, s. [E. *mônáth, mona*, the moon] a revolution of the moon, twenty-eight days, one of the twelve divisions of the year. Adj. *monthly.*

Monument, s. [L. *monumentum, monere*, to warn] a memorial.

Mood, s. [E. *mod*, mind] disposition, temper.

Mood, s. [L. *modus*, manner] a manner of inflexion showing the manner in which the action expressed by the verb is presented.

Moon, s. [E. *mona*, the measurer] a planet revolving round the earth, one planet revolving round another.

Moor, s. [Fr. *maure*, L. and Gr. *mauros*, black] dark inhabitants of Mauretania in North Africa; Saracen, Arabian.

Moral, adj. [L. *moralis, mores, mos*, manners] belonging to conduct, of good conduct, virtuous.

More, adj. [E. *máre, má*] greater, see page 51.

Moreover, adv., further, in addition.

Morning, s. [E. *morn, morgen*] the dawn of day, the early hours.

Morrow, s. [E. *morwe, morgen*] morning, the coming morning, next day; *to-morrow*, at, or, on the morning coming.

Morsel, s. [Fr. *morcel*, L. *morsellum, morsus, mordere*, to bite] a bite, bit, piece.

Mortal, adj. [L. *mortalis, mortem, mors*, death] deadly, giving death, subject to death.

Moses, s., the leader of Israel out of Egypt to the borders of Canaan.

Most, adj., greatest, see page 51.

Mother, s. [E. *modor*, from root *ma*, producer] a female parent.

Motion, s [L. *motionem, motus, movere*] a movement. Adj. *motionless.*

Motive, s. [L. *motivus, motus, movere*] moving power, inducement.

Mouldy, adj. [E. *mould*, earth] covered with mould, decaying.

Mount, s. [E. *munt*, L. *montem*,

mons, a mountain] high projecting ground, a high hill.

Mountain, s. [Fr. *montagne*, L. *montanus, mons*] ground rising high above the neighbouring land.

Mount, v. [Fr. *monter, mont*, a mountain] to go up, rise, get on a horse. *Mounted.*

Mourn, v. [E. *murnan*] to murmur, moan, grieve, lament. *Mourned.*

Mouse, s. [E. *mus*] a small animal of the class rodentia.

Mouth, s. [E. *muth*] the chewer, the opening of the jaws, the opening of the face by which an animal eats.

Mouth, v., to speak with much use of the mouth. *Mouthed.*

Move, v. [Fr. *mouvoir*, L. *movere*] to change position, alter. *Moved.*

Move, s., a change of place, change.

Movement, s. [Fr. *mouvement*, L. *movere*] a move, change.

Much, adj. [E. *moche*, softened form of *mycel*] of great quantity. See page 51.

Muffle, v. [Fr. *mouffler*, L. L. *muffula*] to cover the mouth, cover, wrap closely. *Muffled.*

Mule, s. [L. *mulus*] a cross-bred animal bred from the horse and ass, an obstinate person.

Multiply, v. [Fr. *multiplier*, L. *multus, plicare*, to fold] to increase many times. *Multiplied.*

Multitude, s. [L. *multitudinem, multus*, many] a very large number, crowd.

Murder, s. [E. *morthor*] wilful killing of a man.

Murder, v., to kill wilfully, destroy. *Murdered.*

Murmur, s. [L. *murmur*] a soft low sound as of a gentle wind in trees, or bubbling water, &c.

Murmur, v., to make a humming sound, to be discontented. *Murmured.*

Music, s. [Fr. *musique*, L. *musica*, Gr. *mousike, mousa*] the art of song, the science of harmony.

Musician, s. [Fr. *musicien*] one who knows music, a player of music.

Musk, s., a perfume got from the musk-deer of Nepaul.

Must, v., see page 75.

Muster, v. [O. Fr. *mustrer, monstrer*, L. *monstrare*, to show] to assemble for inspection, collect, gather. *Mustered.*

Mute, adj. [Fr. *mute*, L. *mutus*] silent, dumb, making no sound but a murmur through the lips.

Mutter, v. [root *mu*, from sound of the lips] to keep making a murmuring sound. *Muttered.*

Myriad, s. [Fr. *myriade*, Gr. *murias*] ten thousand, a countless number.

Myself, pron., see page 54.

Mystery, s. [L. *mysteria*, Gr. *musterion*] a thing hidden, a secret, a thing unexplainable. Adj. *mysterious.*

Nail, s [E. *nægel*] a claw at the end of the fingers and toes, a spike of wood or metal.

Nail, v., to fasten by nails. *Nailed.*

Naked, adj., bare, uncovered, unclothed.

Name, s. [E. *nama*, from the root *gna*, know] that by which a thing is known, title, reputation.

Nape, s. [E. *cnæp*, a knop, knob] the top of the head, top.

Napkin, s. [E. *hnoppa*, the nap or flock of cloth] a small cloth.

Napoleon, a Corsican who became Emperor of France, born at Ajaccio, A.D. 1769, died at St. Helena, A.D. 1821.

Narrow, adj. [E. *nearwe, near*] of little breadth, close.

Narrow, v., to make narrow, contract. *Narrowed.*

Nation, s. [L. *nationem, natus, nasci*, to be born] a race of people. Adj. *national.*

Native, adj. [L. *nativus, natus, nasci*] born in the place.

Naturalise, v. [E. *natural*] to make natural, to give the rights of a native. *Naturalised*.

Nature, s. [L. *natura, natus, nasci*] birth, the order of the world, what comes by birth, disposition. Adj. *natural*.

Nay, adv., no.

Near, adj. [E. *neah*] see page 51.

Neat, adj. [Fr. *net*, L. *nitidus, nitere*, to shine] clean, tidy, pure.

Nebo, s., a mountain in Palestine, near the river Jordan.

Necessary, adj. [L. *necessarius*] needful.

Necessity, s. [Fr. *nécessité*, L. *necessitatem*] need, obligation.

Neck, s. [E. *hnecca, hnigan*, to bend] part of the body between the head and shoulders.

Necklace, s. [E. *neck*, Fr. *lacer*, to fasten, L. *laqueare*] a neck-ornament of beads, &c.; on a string.

Need, s. [E. *nead, ne*, not, *eath*, ease], want, poverty, necessity.

Need, v., to want, require. *Needed*.

Needle, s. [E. *nædl*, G. *nadel*, *nähen*, to sew, *nagan*, to prick] a sharp instrument for sewing.

Needs, adv. [gen. case of E. *need*] of necessity.

Neglect, v. [L. *neglectus, negligere*] to be careless about, leave undone. *Neglected*.

Negro, s. [Sp. *negro*, L. *nigrum, niger*, black] a black man, the black African race.

Neighbour, s. [E. *neh*, nigh, *gebur*, dweller] a near dweller, one who lives near.

Neighbourhood, s. [corruption of E. *neighbour-rede*] the state of being neighbours, the surrounding district.

Neither, conj. [E. *nather, ne, œgther*] not either.

Nereid, s. [Gr. *nereides, nereus*, a water-god, *neros*, wet] a water-nymph.

Nerve, s. [L. *nervus*] a fibre conveying sensation to the brain, strength, courage.

Nest, s., a home built by birds for their eggs.

Net, v. [from root of E. *knit*] to intertwine with meshes, to catch in a net, snare. *Netted*.

Never, adj. [E. *næfre, ne*, not, *æfre*, ever] not ever, not at any time.

New, adj., fresh, young, recent ;

News, s., a fresh report, intelligence.

Next, adj., see page 51.

Nice, adj. [Fr. *nice*, foolish, L. *nescius*, ignorant] simple, foolishly particular about trifles, refined, pleasing.

Nigh, adj. [E. *neh*, near] near, close at hand, see page 51.

Night, s. [E. *niht*] darkness, time from sunset to sunrise. Adj. *nightly*.

Nightfall, s. [E. *night, fall*] the close of day, beginning of night.

Nightingale, s. [E. *niht, galan*, to sing] the night-singer, a small bird of the Sylviadæ or warblers. *Philomela luscinia*.

Nightrack, s. [E. *night, wreak*] mist and fog and storm driven up at night.

Ninth, adj. [E. *nine*] the ordinal of nine.

Nip, v., to pinch, check, bite. *Nipped* or *nipt*.

Nireus, s., one of the Grecian leaders at the siege of Troja, son of Charops and Aglaia, notable for his personal beauty.

No, adv., of negation.

Nobility, s. [Fr. *nobilité*, L. *nobilitatem, nobilis*] nobleness, rank, the class of peers.

Noble, adj. [Fr. *noble*, L. *nobilis*] honourable, well born, good, a peer.

Nod, v., to move to and fro, shake, bend the head. *Nodded*.

Noise, s. [Fr. *noise*, L. *nausea*,

annoyance] brawl, dispute, loud sound. Adj. *noisy*.

None, adj. [E. *nan, ne,* not, *an,* one] not one, not any.

Noonday, s. [E. *non, noon,* L. *nona,* the ninth hour, i.e. three o'clock] midday, twelve o'clock. The change of meaning from three o'clock to twelve o'clock seems to have arisen from the service, *Nona*, having been transferred from three o'clock to midday.

Nor, conj. [E. *ne,* not, *or*] a disjunctive negative.

Norman, s. [Fr. *Norman*] a Northman, a man of Normandy, of the race of Northmen who overran the west of Neustria about A.D. 912.

Northumberland, s. [E. *north, Humber*] a district of England, once all the land north of the river Humber, now the land north of the river Tyne.

Nose, s., the organ of smell.

Nostril, s. [E. *nosethril, nose, thyrl,* a hole] a hole in the nose.

Not, adv. [E. *ne,* no, *wiht,* a thing] expressing negation.

Notch, s. [softened form of E. *knock*] an indentation, a hollow, cut.

Notch, v., to cut a hollow into, indent. *Notched*.

Note, s. [Fr. *note,* L. *nota*] a mark, remark, comment, short letter.

Note, v., to mark, remark, record. *Noted*.

Nothing, s., no thing.

Notice, s. [Fr. *notice,* L. *notitia, notus*] attention, regard, warning.

Notice, v., to pay attention to, regard, remark. *Noticed*.

Notion, s. [L. *notionem, notus*] opinion, belief, idea.

Notwithstanding, adv. [E. *not, withstand*] without opposing, yet.

Nought, adj. [E. *ne,* no, *wiht*] nothing.

Nourishment, s. [Fr. *nourrir,* L. *nutrire*] nourishing, food.

Nova Zembla, s., New Land, an island at the extreme north of Europe, belonging to Russia.

Now, adv., at this time.

Nowise, adv. [E. *no, wise,* a manner] in no way, not at all.

Noxious, adj. [L. *noxius, noxa, nocere*] harmful, hurtful, evil.

Nudge, v., to push gently with the fist or elbow. *Nudged*.

Number, s. [Fr. *nombre,* L. *numerus*] a unit, more than one, a group, several, many.

Numerous, adj. [L. *numerosus, numerus*] consisting of a large number.

Nurse, s. [Fr. *nourrice,* L. *nutricem, nutrix, nutrire*] one who nourishes a child, a woman who takes care of children.

Nut, s. [E. *hnut*] a fruit like a small hard ball, the fruit of the hazel.

Nymph, s. [L. *nympha,* Gr. *numphe*] a fabulous maiden inhabiting the sea, rivers, mountains, &c.; a maiden.

Oak, s. [E. *æc*] a tree of the genus Quercus, famous for the hardness of its wood; strength, endurance.

Oar, s. [E. *ar, erian,* to plough] the ploughshare of the water; a pole with end flattened for rowing.

Oat, s. [E. *etan, eat*] food, a kind of corn.

Oatmeal, s., meal made from oats.

Obdurate, adj. [L. *obduratus, durare, durus,* hard] hardened, stern, unyielding.

Obedient, adj. [L. *obedientem, obedire*] obeying, carrying out orders, submissive. Subs. *obedience*.

Obey, v. [Fr. *obéir,* L. *obedire*] to submit to orders, listen to commands, yield. *Obeyed*.

Object, s. [L. *objectus, ob, jacere,*

to throw] a thing in the way, purpose, end.
Objection, s. [L. *objectionem, ob, jacere*] opposition.
Oblige, v. [Fr. *obliger*, L. *ob, ligare*] to bind, force, compel. *Obliged*.
Obscure, adj. [L. *obscurus*, dark] hidden, dark, unknown, abstruse.
Observant, adj. [L. *observantem, observare*, to watch] watching, watchful, careful.
Observation, s. [L. *observationem, ob, servare*] watching, attention.
Observe, v. [L. *ob, servare*] to watch, attend to, remark, say. *Observed*.
Obstruct, v. [L. *obstructus, ob, struere*, to build] to hinder, block. *Obstructed*.
Obtain, v. [Fr. *obtenir*, L. *ob, tenere*] to gain, get, gain credence. *Obtained*.
Obvious, adj. [L. *obvius, via*, a path] in the path, plain, easily seen.
Occasion, s. [L. *occasionem, occasum, ob, cadere*, to fall] something happening, opportunity, time. Adj. *occasional*; Adv. *occasionally*.
Occupation, s. [L. *occupationem, ob, capere*] business, employment.
Occupy, v. [Fr. *occuper*, L. *occupare, ob, capere*] to hold, employ. *Occupied*.
Occur, v. [L. *occurrere, ob, currere*, to run] to happen, to meet. *Occurred*.
Ocean, s. [Fr. *océan*, L. *oceanus*, Gr. *okeanos*] the great body of water on the earth's surface, the largest division of water.
Odd, adj., not even, out of the common, strange.
Odour, s. [Fr. *odeur*, L. *odorem*] a smell, a sweet smell.
Odysseus, s., the hero of Homer's poem the Odyssey, king of the island of Ithaka.

Of, prep., expressing separation, or possession.
Off, adv. prep. [E. *of*] from, away.
Offa, s., king of the Mercians, from A.D. 755 to 794, from whom Offa's dyke from the Wye to the Dee took its name.
Offence, s. [Fr. *offense*, L. *offensare, offendere*, to hurt] harm, hurt, anger, displeasure.
Offer, v. [L. *offerre, ob, ferre*] to bring to, present, try. *Offered*.
Office, s. [Fr. *office*, L. *officium*] business, duty, place of business.
Officer, s., one in office.
Oft, Often, adv., many times.
Oh, interj., expressing surprise.
Oil, s. [L. *oleum*] juice of the olive, liquid grease.
Old, Olden, adj. [E. *eald*, Goth. *elan*, to bring up] grown up, past the prime of life, ancient.
Olive, s. [L. *oliva*] a fruit-bearing tree which grows on the coasts of the Mediterranean Sea.
Omit, v. [L. *omittere, mittere*, to send] to leave out, pass over. *Omitted*.
On, prep. and adv.
Once, adv. [E. *ones, one*] at one time.
One, adj. [E. *an*] single.
Onion, s. [Fr. *oignon*, L. *unionem*] a strong-smelling bulbous plant.
Only, adj. and adv. [E. *an, lic*] one-like, alone, not more than one.
Onward, adv. [E. *on*] forward, further.
Open, adj. [E. *up*] lifted up, uncovered, unfenced, plain, public, free.
Open, v., to uncover, unlock, make plain, make public. *Opened*.
Opinion, s. [L. *opinionem*] belief, thought.
Oppose, v. [Fr. *opposer*, L. *ob, pausare*] to put in the way, obstruct, hinder. *Opposed*.
Opposite, adj. [L. *oppositus, ob,*

ponere] standing in the way, over against.

Opposition, s. [L. *oppositionem*] hostility, resistance, hindrance.

Oppress, v. [L. *oppressus, ob, premere*] to press upon, weigh down, treat harshly. *Oppressed.*

Oppression, s. [L. *oppressionem*] harsh treatment, tyranny, injustice.

Oppressor, s. [E. *oppress*] one who oppresses.

Orange, s. [Fr. *orange*, L. L. *aurantia*, It. *arancio*, Venet. *naranza*, Ar. *naranj*] a yellow fruit brought from the East to the lands round the Mediterranean Sea.

Orator, s. [L. *orator*] a public speaker, one who speaks well.

Orchard, s. [E. *wort*, a root, *geard*] a yard for roots, a garden, an enclosure containing fruit-trees, an apple-garden.

Order, s. [Fr. *ordre*, L. *ordinem, ordo*] arrangement, a rank, line, command.

Order, v., to arrange, command. *Ordered.*

Ordinary, adj. [L. *ordinarius, ordo*] according to the usual order, usual, common.

Ore, s., a vein of metal in the rock, metal in the state in which it is found.

Organ, s. [L. *organa*, Gr. *organon*, an instrument, *ergon*, a work] an instrument, a musical instrument.

Origin, s. [Fr. *origine*, L. *originem, origo*] source, beginning. Adj. *original;* Adv. *originally.*

Ornament, s. [L. *ornamentum, ornare*, to adorn] a decoration. Adj. *ornamental.*

Orphan, s. [L. *orphanus*, Gr. *orphanos*] one who has lost father and mother.

Osier, s. [Fr. *osier*, Gr. *oisos*, a willow] the water-willow.

Other, adj., the second, different.

Ought. See **Owe**, page 75.

Our, pron. See page 55.

Out, adv., away, off.

Outcast, s., one *cast out.*

Outshine, v. [E. *shine*] to surpass. *Outshined.*

Outskirt, s. [E. *skirt*] the outer border, edge.

Outwork, s. [E. *work*] an advanced fort, defence.

Over, adv. prep. [E. *ofer, ufera, ufan*] above, more than.

Overboard, adj. [E. *board*] over the side of a ship, in the water.

Overcome, v. [E. *come*] to surpass, conquer, beat. *Overcame, overcome.*

Overlay, v. [E. *lay*] to spread over, cover. *Overlaid.*

Overlook, v. [E. *look*] to look over, to attend to, watch, pass the eyes over, miss, neglect. *Overlooked.*

Overthrow, v. [E. *throw*] to throw over, upset, defeat. *Overthrew, overthrown.*

Overtire, v. [E. *tire*] to tire too much. *Overtired.*

Overwhelm, v. [E. *whelm*] to cover over, swallow up, destroy. *Overwhelmed.*

Owe, v. [E. *agan*, to *own*, of which *owe* is a form] to have for another, to have to pay. *Ought* or *owed*, see page 75.

Owl, s. [E. *hule*, from the bird's note] a bird which flies by night, and has a howling screeching note.

Own, v. [E. *agan*] to possess, claim as a possession, admit. *Owned.*

Own, adj., owned, possessed, peculiar property.

Ox, s. [E. *oxa*] the male of the cow. Pl. *oxen.*

Pace, s. [Fr. *pas*, L. *passus*] a step.

Paddle, v. [E. *paddle*, dim. of *spade*] to use a paddle, to propel with a small oar, to dabble in water. *Paddled.*

Pageant, s. [E. *pagyn*, L. *pagina, pangere*, to fasten] an exhibition, a show.

Pain, s. [Fr. *peine*, L. *poena*, penalty] suffering, distress, punishment. Adj. *painless*, free from pain.

Paint, v. [Fr. *peint, peindre*, L. *pingere*] to colour, represent, draw, describe. *Painted.*

Pair, s. [Fr. *paire*, L. *par*, equal] two equal things, a couple.

Palace, s. [Fr. *palais*, L. *palatium*] the name of the Domus Aurea, or Golden House, built by the Emperor Nero at Rome, on the hill Palatinus, sacred to the deity Pales; a royal house, a grand building.

Palate, s. [L. *palatum*] the roof of the mouth, that which tastes, relish.

Pale, adj. [Fr. *pale*, L. *pallidus*] wan, whitish, colourless.

Palestine, s. [*Philistine*] a long strip of coast, on the east of the Mediterranean Sea, also called Canaan. It had the name Palestine from the Philistines, or 'strangers' from Crete, who held much of the coast district.

Pallas, s., a name of the Grecian goddess Athene.

Palm, s. [Fr. *palme*, L. *palma*] the inside of the hand, a tree with a broad leaf like the palm of the hand, a sign of victory, a prize.

Pang, s. [E. *pyngan*, to prick] sharp grief, pain, sorrow.

Panther, s. [L. *panthera*, Gr. *panther*] a spotted beast of the cat family.

Papist, s. [L. *papa*, pope] a name given to the followers of the Pope.

Paradise, s. [L. *paradisus*, Gr. *paradeisos*, an Eastern word meaning a park] the garden of Eden, heaven.

Parallel, adj. [Gr. *parallelos, para,*

allelon] alongside of one another; a line in the same plane, and running in the same direction as another, and in all parts equally distant from it.

Parent, s. [Fr. *parent*, L. *parentem, parens, parere*, to produce] the producer, father or mother.

Paris, s., son of Priam, king of Troja, who, by carrying off Helen, wife of Menelaus, was the cause of the Trojan war.

Parish, s. [Fr. *paroche*, L. *parochia*, Gr. *paroikia, oikia*, a house] an ecclesiastical district, a district under one clergyman in charge.

Parliament, s. [Fr. *parlement, parler*, to speak] the meeting of the advisers of the king, the House of Lords and House of Commons.

Parlour, s. [Fr. *parloir, parler*] the conversation-room, sitting-room, the ordinary business room of a house.

Parsimonious, adj. [E. *parsimony*, L. *parsimonia, parcere*, to spare] sparing, niggardly.

Parsley, s. [E. *persely, peterselige*, L. *petroselinum*, Gr. *petroselinon*, rock plant] a plant with crisp bright green leaves.

Parsnep, s. [L. *pastinaca, pastinum, napus*, a root] a plant with a long root like a white carrot.

Part, s. [L. *partem, pars*] a piece, share, portion.

Part, v., to divide, share, go away. *Parted.*

Partake, v. [Fr. *partager, partage*, L. *partem, pars*] to share, take part in. *Partook, partaken* (as if from E. *part, take*).

Partial, adj. [Fr. *partial*, L. *partialis, pars*] favouring one part, one-sided, having to do with a part, not equally distributed.

Particular, adj. [L. *particularis, pars*] having care for each little part, exact, careful.

Partridge, s. [E. *pertrich,* Fr. *perdrix,* L. *perdicem*] a gallinaceous bird. *Perdix cinerea.*

Party, s. [Fr. *parti, partir,* L. *partiri, pars*] a division, company, faction, assembly.

Pass, v. [Fr. *passer,* L. *passus,* a step] to walk by, go beyond. *Passed* or *past.*

Pass, s., a narrow way, defile, permission to pass.

Passage, s. [Fr. *passage, passer,* L. *passus*] going, course, journey, way, road.

Passion, s. [Fr. *passion,* L. *passionem, passus, pati,* to suffer] suffering, rage, anger.

Passionate, adj. [L. *passionatus*] given to passion, easily enraged.

Passive, adj. [L. *passivus, passus, pati*] suffering, enduring.

Pastoral, adj. [L. *pastoralis, pastor,* a shepherd] belonging to shepherds, belonging to flocks, country.

Pasture, s. [L. *pastura, pastus, pascere,* to feed] grazing-land, feeding.

Pat, v., to strike gently. *Patted.*

Path, s. [E. *pæd*] a way, road. Adj. *pathless.*

Patience, s. [Fr. *patience,* L. *patientia, pati*] endurance.

Patient, adj. [Fr. *patient,* L. *patientem, pati*] enduring, long-suffering.

Patrician, adj. [L. *patricianus, patricius, pater*] belonging to the Roman patres or noble families, noble.

Patroclos, s., a Greek hero, son of Menœtios, comrade of Achilles, slain at Troja by Hector.

Patron, s. [L. *patronus, pater,* a father] one who acts like a father, protector, helper.

Pattern, s. [Fr. *patron,* L. *patronus, pater*] a master, example, model.

Pause, s. [Fr. *pause,* L. *pausa,* Gr. *pausis, pauein,* to stop] a stop, cessation, rest.

Pause, v., to stop, cease, rest. *Paused.*

Pave, v. [Fr. *paver.* L. *pavire*] to lay with stones. *Paved.*

Pavement, s. [Fr. *pavement,* L. *pavimentum, pavire*] a floor laid with stones, a pathway.

Paw, s., an animal's foot.

Pay, v. [Fr. *payer,* L. *pacare,* to pacify] to satisfy, to satisfy with money, hand money to.

Pea, s. [mistaken sing. from E. *peas,* Fr. *pois,* L. *pisum*] a leguminous plant. Old form, sing. *pise, pese*; pl. *piosan, pesen, peason, peses*; modern form, sing. *pea,* pl. *peas, pease.*

Peace, s. [E. *pes,* Fr. *paix,* L. *pacem, pax*] quiet, freedom from war, rest.

Peach, s. [Fr. *pêche,* O. Fr. *pesche,* L. *persicum,* Persian] a fruit tree brought from Persia to Italy.

Peak, s. [Gael. *pic*] a point, pointed mountain.

Peal, v., to sound loudly, resound, bellow. *Pealed.*

Pear, s. [L. *pirum*] a fruit tree, the fruit of the tree.

Pearl, s. [Fr. *perle,* It. *perla,* L. *pirula,* dim. of *pirum,* a pear] a small round gem found in shell-fish.

Peasant, s. [Fr. *paysan, pays,* L. *pagensis, pagus,* a village] a villager, rustic.

Pebble, s., a small rounded stone.

Peculiar, adj. [L. *peculiaris, peculium,* property, *pecus,* cattle] private, belonging to oneself, special, uncommon. Subs. *peculiarity.*

Peer, v. [Fr. *paroir,* L. *parere,* to come in sight] to appear, to peep forth, to look about carefully. *Peered.*

Peer, s. [Fr. *pair,* L. *par,* equal] an equal, a nobleman, member of the House of Peers.

Peg, s., a pin for fastening.

GLOSSARY.

Peleus, s., a Greek hero, father of Achilles, ruler of the Myrmidons in Thessaly.

Pelion, s., a mountain in the south east of Thessaly.

Pen, s. [L. *penna*, a feather] an instrument for writing.

Penetrate, v. [L. *penetratus, penetrare*] to go into, to go through. *Penetrated.*

Pent, adj. [E. *penned, pen*] shut up, enclosed.

Penthouse, s. [corruption of E. *pentice*, Fr. *appentis*, L. *appendicium, pendere*, to hang] a sloping shed built against a house, an outhouse, hovel.

People, s. [Fr. *peuple*, L. *populus*] a nation, tribe, persons.

Perceive, v. [Fr. *percevoir*, L. *percipere, capere*, to take] to take in thoroughly, understand, see. *Perceived.*

Perch, v. [Fr. *perche*, L. *pertica*, a rod] to alight on a perch or rod, to settle. *Perched.*

Perfect, adj. [L. *perfectus, per, facere*] thoroughly made, finished, complete. Adv. *perfectly.*

Perfection, s. [L. *perfectionem, facere*] completeness.

Perform, v. [L. *per, formare*] to form thoroughly, do, act. *Performed.*

Perfume, s. [Fr. *parfum*, L. *fumus*, smoke] a sweet smell, odour, scent.

Perfume, v., to fill with a sweet odour, scent. *Perfumed.*

Perhaps, adv. [L. *per*, E. *hap*] by chance, possibly, it may chance.

Periander, s., son of Cypselus, ruler, or Tyrant, of Corinth, B.C. 625-585.

Peril, s. [Fr. *péril*, L. *periculum*] danger. Adj. *perilous.*

Period, s. [L. *periodus*, Gr. *peri*, round, *hodos*, a way] a circuit, a fixed time, a completed sentence, a mark at the end of a sentence.

Perpetual, adj. [L. *perpetualis, perpetuus*] everlasting, continuous, never-ending.

Perplexity, s. [L. *perplexitatem, perplexus, plectere*, to weave] difficulty, doubt.

Persian, adj., of Persia, a country in Asia.

Persistence, s. [L. *persistentia, persistere, stare*, to stand] standing to a thing, steadiness, obstinacy.

Person, s. [L. *persona*] a man, or woman, a character. Adj. *personal.*

Personage, s. [Fr. *personnage*, L. *persona*] an important person, a character.

Persuade, v. [L. *per, suadere*, to advise] to convince, influence, advise. *Persuaded.*

Pert, adj., lively, saucy.

Pestilence, s. [L. *pestilentia, pestis*] plague, contagious disease.

Pet, s. [It. *petto*, L. *pectus*, a heart] a favourite child, or animal.

Peterkin, a Dutch name, little *Peter.*

Petrify, v. [Fr. *pétrifier*, L. and Gr. *petra*, a rock, L. *facere*] to make into stone, harden, to astonish. *Petrified.*

Pewter, adj. [O. Fr. *peutre*] a mixture of lead and tin, or of lead and zinc.

Pharaoh, s., a name or title borne by the ancient rulers of Egypt, perhaps meaning King, or from the word Ra, meaning the sun.

Phase, s. [Gr. *phasis, phainein*, to shew] a show, an appearance, form.

Philip, s. [L. *Philippus*, Gr. *Philippos*, lover of horses] King of Macedon, born B.C. 382, began to reign B.C. 359, assassinated by Pausanias B.C. 336.

Philistian, s. [*Philistine*, stranger]. The Philistines were immigrants from Crete into the coast districts of Canaan.

Philological, adj. [Gr. *philos*, a lover, *logos*, a word] belonging to philology, the science of language.

Philosopher, s., one given to the study of philosophy.

Philosophy, s. [Gr. *philos, sophia,* wisdom] love of wisdom, knowledge of causes.

Phœnician, adj., belonging to Phœnicia, a strip of coast on the north of Palestine, washed by the Mediterranean Sea.

Pick, v., to strike with a sharp instrument, to pluck, gather. *Picked.*

Picture, s. [L. *pictura, pictus, pingere,* to paint] a painting, representation, likeness.

Piece, s. [Fr. *pièce*] a small bit, a portion.

Piecemeal, s. [*piece,* E. *meal,* a division] piece by piece, bit by bit, in separate pieces.

Pierce, v. [Fr. *percer,* It. *perciare, pertugiare,* L. *per, tundere*] to make a hole through. *Pierced.*

Pile, s. [Fr. *pile,* L. *pila*] a heap, mass.

Pile, v., to raise in a heap, to heap. *Piled.*

Pilgrim, s. [It. *pelegrino,* L. *peregrinus, per,* over, *ager,* the land] a wanderer, one who goes to visit a shrine in another land.

Pillar, s. [Fr. *pilier,* L. *pila*] a column, post.

Pillow, s., a cushion.

Pincers, s. pl. [E. *pinch*] an instrument for grasping, a nail-drawer, &c., in plural only.

Pinch, v., to catch with the points of the fingers, nip, grip, grasp. *Pinched.*

Pine, s. [L. *pinus*] a fir-tree, a resinous cone-bearing tree.

Pineapple, s. [E. *pine, apple*] a tropical fruit, shaped and marked like the cone of the pine.

Pinion, s. [Fr. *pignon,* L. *penna,* a feather] a wing, the last joint of the wing.

Pious, adj. [L. *pius*] religious, devout, godly.

Pipe, s. [Fr. *pipe,* L. *pipare*] a thin hollow tube used as a musical instrument, a tube for smoking.

Pique, s. [Fr. *piquer*] offence taken, displeasure.

Pique, s. [Fr. *pique,* a point] the point of a saddle.

Pit, s., a hole in the ground, a hole.

Pitch, s. [E. *pic*] a sticky black stuff obtained from the fir-tree.

Pity, s. [Fr. *pitié,* L. *pietatem, pius*] piety, kindness, compassion, mercy. Adj., *piteous,* full of pity, fit for pity; *pitiless,* without pity.

Place, s. [Fr. *place,* L. *platea,* a broad street] an open street, space, position, rank.

Place, v., to put, settle, fix. *Placed.*

Plain, adj. [Fr. *plain,* L. *planus,* even] smooth, level, flat, open. Subs. a level place, flat land.

Plaintive, adj. [Fr. *plaintif,* L. *planctus, plangere,* to wail] complaining, sad, repining.

Plan, s. [Fr. *plan,* L. *planus*] a flat drawing, scheme, arrangement.

Plane, s. [L. *planus*] a flat surface, a tool for making a flat surface.

Plane, v., to make level, flatten, to work with a plane. *Planed.*

Plank, s. [L. *planca*] a flat board.

Plant, s. [L. *planta*] a sprout, a sapling, any vegetable growth.

Plant, v., to set to grow, put into the ground, establish. *Planted.*

Plantation, s. [L. *plantationem, planta*] a place planted, young wood, a colony.

Planter, s., one who plants.

Plate, s. [Fr. *plat,* G. *platt*] a flat dish, a flat piece of metal, worked silver.

Plausible, adj. [Fr. *plausible,* L. *plausibilis, plausus, plaudere,* to cheer] that may be praised, insinuating, specious.

Play, v. [E. *plegan*] to exercise oneself, sport, idle, act in a play, gamble. *Played*.

Play, s., a game, amusement, a drama, tragedy, or comedy.

Player, s., one who plays, an actor in a play.

Plea, s. [O. Fr. *plait*, L. *placitum*, *placere*] an excuse, argument, entreaty, an answer to a charge in a law court.

Plead, v. [Fr. *plaider, plaid*, O. Fr. *plait*, L. *placitum*] to argue a suit at law, urge, discuss, offer as an excuse. *Pled* or *pleaded*.

Pleasant, adj. [Fr. *plaisant, plaisir*, L. *placere*, to please] pleasing, delightful.

Please, v. [Fr. *plaisir*, L. *placere*] to delight, gratify. *Pleased*.

Pleasure, s. [Fr. *plaisir*, L. *placere*] delight, amusement.

Plebeian, adj. [Fr. *plébeien*, L. *plebeius, plebs*, the commons] vulgar, common, low, ill-bred.

Pleiades, s. pl., the seven daughters of Atlas and Pleïone, fabled to have been turned into a group of stars in the constellation Taurus.

Plenty, s. [Fr. *plenté*, L. *plenitatem, plenus*, full] fullness, abundance.

Plight, s. [E. *ply*] condition, state.

Ploughman, s. [E. *plough*] one who ploughs, a tiller of the ground, a rustic.

Plum, s. [Fr. *prune*, L. *prunum*] a stone-fruit.

Plumage, s. [Fr. *plumage*, L. *pluma*, a feather] feathers on a bird.

Plume, s. [Fr. *plume*, L. *pluma*] a feather, a crest of feathers.

Plume, v., to adorn, boast, to think oneself important. *Plumed*.

Plunge, v. [Fr. *plonger*, L. *plumbicare, plumbum*, lead] to fall suddenly, to fall into water, to jump. *Plunged*.

Plunge, s., a jump, rush.

Plutarch, s., a Greek of Chæronea in Bœotia, who wrote lives of eminent men, flourished about the end of the first century.

Plutus, s., God of riches among the Greeks.

Ply, v. [E. *plegan*] to bend, give one's mind to, attend to, work. *Plied*.

Poem, s. [Fr. *poème*, L. *poema*, Gr. *poiema, poiein*, to make] a metrical composition, a composition in verse.

Poet, s. [Fr. *poète*, L. *poeta*, Gr. *poites, poiein*] a writer of verses.

Poetry, s. [Fr. *poéterie, poète*] verse-composition.

Point, s. [Fr. *point*, L. *punctum, pungere*, to prick] a sharp end, dot, stop, moment of time.

Point, v., to sharpen, to aim. *Pointed*.

Poise, v. [Fr. *poiser, poids*, L. *pondus*, a weight] to weigh, balance. *Poised*.

Poison, s. [Fr. *poison*, L. *potionem, potare*, to drink] a deadly draught, venom, anything that corrupts.

Polish, v. [Fr. *polissant, polir*, L. *polire*] to smooth, make glassy. *Polished*.

Polite, adj. [L. *politus, polire*, to polish] polished, gentlemanly, courteous.

Politics, s. pl. [Gr. *politica, polis*, a state] the science of government.

Pomegranate, s. [L. *pomum, granatum, granum*, a seed] a round fruit containing many seeds or grains.

Pomp, s. [Fr. *pompe*, L. *pompa*, Gr. *pompe*] a procession, show, grandeur.

Pool, s. [E. *pol*] a hole containing water, pit, pond.

Poor, adj. [Fr. *pauvre*, L. *pauper*] needy, in want, having little or no money, weak, spiritless.

Popish, adj. [E. *pope*] like a pope,

belonging to the pope, favouring the pope.

Poplar, s. [Fr. *poplier*, L. *populus*] a tree.

Population, s. [E. *populate*, L. *populus*, people] people, the inhabitants of a district.

Populous, s. [L. *populosus, populus*] full of people, abounding with people.

Pork, s. [Fr. *porc*, L. *porcus*, a pig] the flesh of the pig.

Porpoise, s. [E. *porpesse*, It. *porcopesce*, L. *porcus, piscis*] the hogfish, sea-swine, a kind of whale.

Porridge, s. [corruption of E. *pottage*, what is boiled in a *pot*] broth, boiled meat, soup.

Port, s. [L. *portus*] a harbour.

Port, s. [Fr. *port*, L. *portare*, to carry] bearing, carriage, manner.

Port, v., to run a ship to the left, put the helm to larboard. *Ported.*

Portable, adj. [L. *portabilis, portare*] able to be carried, easily carried.

Portion, s. [L. *portionem*] a part, division, share.

Portion, v., to divide, allot in shares. *Portioned.*

Portrait, s. [Fr. *portrait, portraire*, L. *protrahere*, to draw] a drawing, likeness, likeness of a person.

Poseidon, s., the name of the God of the sea among the Greeks.

Position, s. [L. *positionem, positus, ponere*] place, situation, state.

Possess, v. [L. *possessum, possidere, sedere*, to sit] to occupy, own, have. *Possessed.*

Possession, s. [L. *possessionem, possidere*] ownership, a thing owned, property.

Possible, adj. [Fr. *possible*, L. *possibilis, posse*, to be able] able to be done.

Postern, s. [Fr. *posterne*, L. *posterula, post*, behind] a back gate.

Posthumous, adj. [L. *posthumus*

postumus, post, after] late-born, born after the father's death, belonging to a time after death.

Posture, s. [Fr. *posture*, L. *positura, positus, ponere*] position, state, condition, attitude.

Potato, s. [Haitian *batata*] a plant whose tubers are used for food, introduced from Haiti into Europe by the Spaniards.

Potter, s. [E. *pot*] one who makes pots.

Pounce, v. [O. Fr. *ponce*, a claw, L. *pugnus*, a fist] to drop suddenly upon, spring on. *Pounced.*

Pound, v. [E. *punian*] to stamp to powder, to beat small in a mortar. *Pounded.*

Pour, v., to cause to rush, shed forth, drive forth. *Poured.*

Poverty, s. [Fr. *pauvreté*, L. *paupertatem, pauper*] want of money, a needy condition, poorness.

Powder, s. [Fr. *poudre*, O. Fr. *puldre*, L. *pulverem, pulvis*] dust.

Power, s. [Fr. *pouvoir*, O. Fr. *pooir* as from an infinitive, L. L. *potere*, for *posse*] ability, strength. Adj. *powerful.*

Practice, v. [Fr. *practice*, L. *practica*, Gr. *praktike, prassein*, to act] to do often, to have a habit of doing, exercise. *Practised.*

Praise, s. [O. Fr. *preis, prix*, L. *pretium*, value] expression of value, value, honour, glory.

Praise, v., to attribute value, to honour, laud, glorify. *Praised.*

Prance, v. [softened form of E. *prank*] to strut, spring, ride in a showy manner. *Pranced.*

Pray, s. [Fr. *prier*, L. *precari*] to beg, ask earnestly, entreat, entreat God. *Prayed.*

Prayer, s. [Fr. *prière*] an entreaty, request, address to God.

Precious, s. [Fr. *précieux*, L. *pretiosus, pretium*] of great value, valuable, costly.

Precipice, s. [Fr. *précipice*, L. *prae-*

cipitium, praeceps, headlong, *caput*] a steep cliff, a steep descent.

Precipitate, v. [L. *praecipitatus, praeceps*] to throw head-foremost, to hurry. *Precipitated.*

Predecessor, s. [L. *praedecessor, cessus, cedere*, to go] one who has gone before.

Prefer, v. [L. *prae, ferre*] to take before, choose, promote. *Preferred.*

Preferment, s. [E. *prefer*] advancement, promotion, office.

Prejudice, s. [L. *praejudicium, judicare, judex*, a judge] a prejudging, prepossession, bias, narrow-mindedness.

Prelate, s. [L. *praelatus*] one preferred to an office, a bishop.

Preparation, s. [L. *praeparationem, paratus, parare*] readiness, arrangement.

Prepare, v. [L. *prae, parare*] to make ready, arrange. *Prepared.*

Prerogative, s. [L. *praerogativus, rogatus, rogare*, having the right to be asked first] a special privilege.

Presence, s. [Fr. *présence*, L. *praesentia, praesens*] being in sight, mien.

Present, adj. [Fr. *présent*, L. *praesentem, praesens*] at hand, in sight, time now passing, a gift.

Present, v., to set forth, to show, offer, give. *Presented.*

Preserve, v. [L. *prae, servare*] to keep, protect. *Preserved.* Subs. *preservation.*

Preside, v. [L. *praesidere, sedere*] to sit in authority, to be chairman. *Presided.*

Press, v. [Fr. *presser*, L. *pressare, premere*] to crush, squeeze, urge. *Pressed.*

Presume, v. [L. *praesumere*] to take upon oneself, take for granted, suppose. *Presumed.*

Presumptuous, adj. [L. *praesumptuosus, sumptus, sumere*, to take] full of presumption, taking too much on self, overbearing, overbold.

Pretend, v. [L. *prae, tendere*, to hold out before as a cloak] to offer a pretext, feign, affect. *Pretended.*

Pretty, adj. [E. *pratty, præte*] pleasing, beautiful, tasteful.

Prevail, v. [L. *prae, valere*] to overcome, succeed, gain advantage. *Prevailed.*

Prevent, v. [L. *prae, ventus, venire*] to come before, come in the way of, hinder, obstruct. *Prevented.*

Prey, s. [Fr. *proie*, L. *praeda*] booty, spoil, plunder.

Priam, s., the king of Troja at the time of the siege celebrated by Homer.

Price, s. [Fr. *prix*, L. *pretium*] value, value in money.

Prick, v. [E. *prica*, a point] to run a point into, to goad, spur. *Pricked.*

Prickly, adj., covered with prickles.

Pride, s., haughtiness, self-esteem.

Priest, s. [E. *preost*, L. *presbyter*, Gr. *presbuteros*, an elder] one who officiates in the service of God, a fully ordained minister of the Christian Church.

Primate, s. [L. *primatem, primus*, first] the first officer in the church.

Prince, s. [Fr. *prince*, L. *principem, primus, capere*] a chief ruler, the son of a king.

Principal, adj. [L. *principalis, princeps*] chief, most important.

Principle, s. [L. *principalis*] the chief point, first truth, law.

Prison, s. [Fr. *prison*, L. *prensionem, prensus, prendere*, to catch] a place of confinement, jail.

Private, adj. [L. *privatus, privus*, single] apart, by oneself, retired, secret, not engaged in public business.

Prize, s. [Fr. *prise, pris*, L. *prensus*,

prendere] a capture, booty, a reward.

Probable, adj. [Fr. *probable*, L. *probabilis*, *probare*, to prove] able to be proved, likely. Subs. *probability*.

Proceed, v. [L. *pro*, *cedere*] to go forward, go on, advance. *Proceeded*.

Produce, v. [L. *pro*, *ducere*] to draw out, bring forth, lengthen. *Produced*.

Product, s. [L. *productus*, *ducere*] a thing brought forth, result, fruit.

Profession, s. [L. *professionem*, *pro*, *fessus*, *fateri*, to confess] statement, declaration, business, occupation.

Profit, s. [Fr. *profit*, L. *profectus*, *facere*] gain, earnings, benefit.

Profit, v., to get gain, benefit. *Profited*.

Progress, s.[L. *progressus*, *gradior*, *gradus*, a step] advance, movement forward.

Project, v. [L. *projectus*, *jacere*] to put forward, plan, scheme. *Projected*.

Projection, s. [L. *projectionem*, *projectus*, *jacere*, to throw] a thing thrown forward, something jutting out, a design.

Prolong, v. [L. *prolongare*, *longus*] to lengthen, delay. *Prolonged*.

Prominent, adj. [L. *prominentem*, *prominens*, *minere*, to threaten] jutting forth, standing out, conspicuous.

Promise, s. [L. *promissum*, *mittere*, to send] an engagement, offer, agreement.

Promise, v., to engage, agree, offer to give at a later time. *Promised*.

Promontory, s. [L. *promontorium*, *montem*, *mons*] high land standing out into the sea, a cape, headland.

Promote, v. [L. *promotus*, *motus*, *movere*] to move forward, advance, assist. *Promoted*.

Pronounce, v. [Fr. *prononcer*, L. *pronuntiare*, *nuntius*, a messenger] to tell openly, declare, say publicly. *Pronounced*.

Proof, s. [E. *prove*] a proving, test, experiment showing truth.

Propensity, s. [L. *propensitatem*, *pensum*, *pendere*, to hang] inclination, tendency, liking.

Proper, adj. [Fr. *propre*, L. *proprium*] one's own, belonging to oneself, suitable, fitting.

Prophet, s. [L. *propheta*, Gr. *prophetes*, *pro*, *phemi*, to speak] one who speaks forth, one who speaks before, one who predicts.

Proportion, s. [L. *proportionem*, *portio*, a part] relation of one thing to another.

Propose, v. [Fr. *proposer*, L. *pro*, *pausare*] to put forward, offer. *Proposed*.

Prospect, s. [L. *prospectus*, *prospicere*] view, thing viewed, scene.

Prosper, v. [L. *prosperus*] to succeed, get on well, thrive. *Prospered*. Subs. *prosperity*.

Prostrate, adj. [L. *prostratus*, *sternere*, to lay low] laid low, overthrown.

Protection, s. [L. *protectionem*, *tectus*, *tegere*, to cover] covering, guard, guardianship.

Protract, v. [L. *protractus*, *trahere*, to draw] to draw out, prolong, delay. *Protracted*.

Proud, adj. [E. *prute*] haughty, full of pride, overbearing.

Prove, v. [Fr. *prover*, L. *probare*] to try, examine, test. *Proved*, *proved* or *proven*.

Proverbial, adj. [E. *proverb*, Fr. *proverbe*, L. *pro*, *verbum*] belonging to proverbs, common as a proverb.

Provide, v. L. *pro*, *videre*] to look out for, take care, see to. *Provided*.

Providential, adj. [E. *providence*, L. *providentia, pro, videre,* to see] done by providence.

Province, s. [Fr. *province*, L. *provincia*] a division of a country, a rural district.

Provision, s. [L. *provisionem, visus, videre*] looking forward, care, a thing provided, food provided.

Provocation, s. [L. *provocationem, vocatus, vocare,* to call] a challenge, a thing that rouses anger.

Prow, s. [Fr. *proue*, Sp. *proa*, L. *prora, pro*] the forepart of a vessel, bow.

Prudent, adj. [Fr. *prudent*, L. *prudentem, providens, videre*] foreseeing, careful, thoughtful.

Public, adj. [L. *publicus, populus*] belonging to the people, open, free to all.

Publish, v. [E. *public*] to make public, make known to all men. *Published.*

Pull, v. [form of E. *pill, peel*] to pluck, strip, tug, draw. *Pulled.*

Pulse, s. [Fr. *pouls,* L. *pulsus, pellere,* to beat] a beating, the throbbing of the blood, passing through the arteries.

Pumice, s. [L. *pumicem, pumex*] an ash sent forth from volcanos.

Punishment, s. [E. *punish*, Fr. *punir*, L. *punire*] penalty, pain for wrong-doing.

Pup, s. [E. *puppy*, Fr. *poupée*, L. *pupata, pupus*, a small boy] a small animal, a young dog.

Purple, adj. [E. *purpur*, L. *purpura*, Gr. *porphura*] a dark bluish red colour.

Purpose, s. [Fr. *purpos*, L. *pro, pausare*] an end, aim, intention.

Purring, s. [*purr* from the sound] a sound made by a cat.

Pursue, v. [Fr. *poursuivre*, L. *prosequere, sequi*] to follow up, chase. *Pursued.*

Pursuit, s. [Fr. *poursuit*] pursuing, a chase.

Pursuivant, s. [Fr. *poursuivant, poursuivre*] a follower, attendant upon a herald.

Push, v. [Fr. *pousser*, O. Fr. *polser*, L. *pulsare, pellere*] to strike, thrust, press outwards. *Pushed.*

Put, v., to push, drive, place. *Put* or *putted.*

Pyramid, s. [Fr. *pyramide*, L. and Gr. *pyramida, pyramis*] a large Egyptian building, a solid building with sides triangular meeting in an apex or point.

Quality, s. [L. *qualitatem, qualis*] nature, sort, kind.

Quantity, s. [L. *quantitatem, quantus*] amount, greatness, size.

Quarry, s. [O. Fr. *quarrière*, L. *quadraria, quadrum*, a square, *quatuor*, four] a place for squaring stone, a place where stone is dug or worked.

Quarterdeck, s., the deck on a ship's quarter, i.e., aft of the mainmast.

Quay, s. [Fr. *quai*, E. *key*] 'a space on the shore compacted by beams and planks as it were by keys,' a wharf.

Queen, s. [E. *cwen,* mother, woman] the wife of a king, a woman ruling as sovereign.

Quest, s. [O. Fr. *queste*, L. *quaestus, quaerere*] a search, seeking, pursuit.

Question, s. [L. *quaestionem, quaerere*] enquiry, investigation.

Quick, adj. [E. *cwic*] alive, lively, nimble, speedy, soon.

Quiet, adj. [L. *quietus, quies,* rest] resting, silent, calm.

Quit, v. [Fr. *quitter*, L. *quietare, quietus*] to satisfy, leave satisfied, leave, discharged, acquit. *Quitted.*

Quite, adv. [E. *quiet*] fully, absolutely, discharged from any condition.

Quiver, s. [Fr. *couvrir,* to cover] a case for arrows.

Quiver, v., to shake, tremble. *Quivered.*

Quoth, v. [E. *cwaethan* to speak] defective, used in the phrases only *quoth* I, *quoth* he, or she, or they; said I, said he, &c.

Race, s. [Fr. *race*, Teut. *reiza*, a line] a line, family stock, breed.

Race, v. [E. *race, raes,* a rush, current] to run fast, contend in running, to cause to contend. *Raced.*

Racer, s., one who *races,* a racehorse.

Radiance, s. [L. *radiantia, radiare, radius,* a ray] brightness, brilliancy.

Radish, s. [Fr. *radis,* L. *radicem, radix,* a root] a plant of which the root is eaten.

Raft, s., a float made of spars of wood.

Rag, s., a piece broken, or torn, a torn piece of cloth.

Ragged, adj. [E. *hracod*] torn, in rags, worn into holes.

Rage, s. [Fr. *rage,* L. *rabiem, rabies*] fury, anger, madness.

Raiment, s. [E. *arrayment,* array, O. Fr. *arroi,* It. *arredare*] clothing, garments.

Rain, s. [E. *reine, regen*] wet, drops falling from clouds.

Rain, v., to fall in drops. *Rained.*

Raise, v. [E. *rise*] to cause to rise, lift, take up. *Raised.*

Rally, v. [Fr. *rallier,* L. *re, alligare,* to bind afresh to] to reassemble beaten troops, to recover. *Rallied.*

Range, v. [Fr. *ranger, rang,* Teut. *rank, hring,* a row] to set in a row, dispose, move about in succession, wander. *Ranged.*

Range, s., wandering, stretch, reach.

Rank, s., a row, arrangement, order, grade, position.

Rap, v., to strike a sharp blow, knock, tap. *Rapped.*

Rapid, adj. [L. *rapidus, rapere,* to snatch] hurrying, quick, swift. Subs. *rapidity.*

Rare, adj. [Fr. *rare* L. *rarus*] scattered, scarce, uncommon, thin.

Rash, adj. [Danish, *rask,* akin to E. *race,* a rush] eager, rushing, violent, wild, thoughtless.

Rather, adj. [E. *rathe,*early] sooner, more willingly; *rathe, rather, rathest.*

Rational, adj. [L. *rationalis, ratio*] reasonable, sensible.

Raven, s. [E. *hraefn,* the shouter] a large black bird, of the crow family, with a hoarse croaking note.

Ray, s. [Fr. *rai,* L. *radius,* a staff] a line of light, a sunbeam.

Reach, v., to stretch, extend. *Reached (raught).*

Read, v. [E. *rædan,* to advise, speak] to interpret, explain what is written, study. *Read.*

Ready, adj. [E. *ræd*] plain, straight, prepared, ordered, prompt. Subs. *readiness.*

Real, adj. [L. *realis, res*] actual, true, genuine. Adv. *really;* Subs. *reality.*

Realize, v. [Fr. *réaliser,* L. *realis, res,* a thing] to make real, bring before one as real, turn into money. *Realized.*

Realm, s. [O. Fr. *realme,* L. *regalimen, regalis, regis, rex,* a king] the land ruled by a king, kingdom.

Reap, v. [E. *ripan*] to pluck, gather harvest, to cut corn with a sickle, to get as fruit. *Reaped.*

Rear, s. [Fr. *rière,* L. *retro,* behind] what is behind, the back.

Reason, s. [Fr. *raison,* L. *rationem, ratus, reri,* to think] motive, cause, the faculty of judging, sound judgment.

Rebel, s. [L. *re, bellare*] one who fights against authority.

Rebellion, s. [L. *rebellionem, re, bellare*] resistance to authority, revolt against the government.

GLOSSARY. 303

Recall, v. [L. *re*, E. *call*] to call back. *Recalled.*
Receive, v. [Fr. *recevoir*, L. *recipere, re, capere*] to take back, get, obtain, accept. *Received.*
Recent, adj. [L. *recentem, recens*] fresh, new, late.
Reckon, v. [E. *recan*, to say] to count, consider, think. *Reckoned.*
Recognise, v. [Fr. *reconnaissant, reconnaître*, L. *re, cognoscere, noscere*] to know again, to know at sight. *Recognised.*
Recoil, v. [Fr. *reculer, cul*, a bottom] to rebound, start back, shrink. *Recoiled.*
Recollection, s. [E. *recollect*, L. *re, collectus, colligere*] gathering again in the mind, calling to mind, remembrance.
Recompense, s. [Fr. *récompense*, L. *re, cum, pensare*, to weigh] a return, reward, payment for service.
Recover, v. [Fr. *recouvrir*, L. *recuperare*] to regain, get again. *Recovered.*
Recumbent, adj. [L. *recumbentem, cumbens, cumbere*, to lie] lying at full length.
Recur, v. [L. *re, currere*] to happen again, come again, go again. *Recurred.*
Red, adj., of the colour of blood.
Redeem, v. [L. *redimere, re, emere*, to buy] to buy back, ransom, free by paying a price. *Redeemed.*
Reduce, v. [L. *re, ducere*] to bring back, bring into subjection, bring down, diminish. *Reduced.*
Reed, s. [E. *hreod*] a coarse water plant akin to the grasses, the stalk of wheat and other grain-producing plants. Adj. *reedy.*
Reef, s. [E. *riff*, Icel. *hrifa*, a rake] a jagged ridge of rocks.
Re-establish, v., to establish again. See **Establish.**
Reference, s. [E. *refer*] referring, allusion.

Refinement, s. [E. *refine, fine*] refining, purity, grace, delicacy.
Refit, v., to fit again. See **Fit.**
Reflect, v. [L. *re, flectere*, to bend back] to throw back, throw light back, to turn the mind back, think. *Reflected.*
Refrain, v. [Fr. *refréner*, L. *re, frenare, frenum*, a bit] to hold back, forbear, abstain. *Refrained.*
Refresh, v. [*re*, E. *fresh*] to make fresh again, restore. *Refreshed.*
Refuge, s. [Fr. *refuge*, L. *refugium, fugere*, to flee] a shelter, protection, safe place.
Refulgent, adj. [L. *refulgentem, re, fulgere*, to shine] shining brightly, gleaming.
Refuse, v. [Fr. *refuser*, L. *refutare*] to say no, decline, reject. *Refused.*
Regard, v. [Fr. *regarder, garder*] to look at, attend to. *Regarded.*
Regiment, s. [L. *regimentum, regere*, to rule] government, a division of the English army under command of a colonel.
Region, s. [Fr. *région*, L. *regionem*] a district, territory.
Reign, v. [Fr. *règne*, L. *regnum, regere*] to rule as a king, to be in power. *Reigned.*
Reject, v. [L. *rejectus, rejicere, jacere*] to cast back, refuse, decline. *Rejected.*
Rejoice, v. [Fr. *réjouir, joie*. See **Joy**] to feel joy, be glad, gladden. *Rejoiced.*
Rejoin, v. [*re, join*] to join again, to answer. *Rejoined.*
Relate, v. [L. *re, latus*] to bring back, tell, narrate, to refer. *Related.*
Relation, s. [L. *relationem, latus*] reference, narration, connection.
Relaxation, s. [L. *relaxationem, laxatus, laxare*, to loosen] loosening, ease, leisure.
Relent, v. [Fr. *ralentir*, L. *re, lentus*,

slow] to yield, soften, cease to be angry. *Relented*.

Relief, s. [Fr. *relief, relever*, L. *re, levare*] aid, help, assistance.

Relieve, v. [Fr. *relever*, L. *re, levare*] to lift, help, case, lighten trouble. *Relieved*.

Religion, s. [L. *religionem, re, ligare*, to bind] service to God, worship of God, piety.

Remain, v. [L. *re, manere*] to stay, wait, last. *Remained*.

Remains, s. pl., things remaining, a dead body.

Remarkable, adj. [E. *remark, mark*] worthy of notice, out of the common.

Remember, v. [Fr. *remembrer*, L. *re, memorare, memor*] to recall to mind, to have in mind. *Remembered*.

Remnant, s. [Fr. *remenant*, L. *re, manentem, manere*] that which remains, what is left.

Remote, adj. [L. *remotus, movere*, moved away, distant, far off.

Remove, v. [L. *re, movere*] to move back, put away. *Removed*.

Rend, v., to tear asunder, tear to pieces. *Rended* or *rent*.

Render, v. [Fr. *rendre*, L. *reddere, dare*] to give back, give up, give what is due. *Rendered*.

Renew, v. [*re*, E. *new*] to make new. See **New**. *Renewed*.

Renowned, adj. [E. *renown, renome*; Fr. *renom*, L. *re, nomen*, a name] having a great name, famous.

Rent, s. [Fr. *rente*, L. L. *rendita*, L. *redditus, reddere*] yield, profit, income, profit on land or houses.

Repair, v. [Fr. *réparer*, L. *re, parare*] to refit, mend, renew. *Repaired*.

Repeat, v. [Fr. *répéter*, L. *re, petere*] to seek again, go over again. *Repeated*.

Reply, v. [Fr. *réplier*, L. *re, plicare*, to fold] to return answer. *Replied*.

Report, v. [L. *re, portare*] to bring back answer, relate, tell. *Reported*.

Repose, v. [Fr. *réposer*, L. *re, pausare*] to rest, be quiet. *Reposed*.

Represent, v. [L. *repraesentare*. See **Present**] to stand in place of, show. *Represented*. Subs. *representation*.

Reprove, v. [Fr. *réprouver*, L. *re, probare*] to chide, find fault with, blame. *Reproved*.

Republic, s. [Fr. *république*, L. *res, publica*. See **Public**] a form of government in which power is in the hands of the people or their representatives.

Request, s. [L. *re, quaestus, quaesitus, quaerere*] an entreaty, desire, prayer.

Require, v. [L. *requirere, quaerere*] to ask, demand, want, need. *Required*.

Resemble, v. [Fr. *resembler*, L. *simulare, similis*, like] to be like. *Resembled*.

Reserve, v. [L. *reservare*] to keep back. *Reserved*. Adj. *reserved*, cautious, quiet.

Reside, v. [L. *residere, sedere*, to settle] to live, dwell. *Resided*.

Resignation, s. [L. *re, signare, signum*] signing away, giving up, patience, endurance, calmness.

Resin, s. [L. *resina*] an inflammable sap which flows from the fir-tree.

Resist, v. [L. *re, sistere, stare*, to stand] to stand out against, oppose. *Resisted*.

Resistance, s. [E. *resist*] withstanding, opposition.

Resolute, adj. [L. *re, solutus, solvere*] resolved, determined, of firm purpose.

Resolve, v. [L. *resolvere*] to determine. *Resolved*.

Resource, s. [Fr. *ressource, source*,

GLOSSARY.   305

sourdre, L. *surgere*] supply, plan, resources, means, money.

Respect, v. [L. *respectare*, *respicere*] to look upon, regard, honour. *Respected*.

Respective, adj. [L. *respectivus*, *respectus*] relating to each separately.

Rest, s., quiet, repose, leisure. Adj. *restless*.

Rest, s. [L. *restare*, to remain] what remains, all that is over.

Restrain, v. [Fr. *restraindre*, L. *re*, *stringere*] to keep in bounds, hold back. *Restrained*.

Restraint, s. [E. *restrain*] loss of liberty, hindrance, check.

Retain, v. [Fr. *rétenir*, L. *re*, *tenere*] to hold back, keep, employ. *Retained*.

Retire, v. [Fr. *retirer*] to go back, leave, go into a quiet place. *Retired*.

Retreat, s. [Fr. *rétraite*, L. *retracta*, *tractus*, *trahere*] a withdrawal, retirement, falling back of troops, place of safety.

Return, v. [E. *re*, *turn*] to come back, go back, give back. *Returned*.

Revelry, s. [E. *revel*, Fr. *révéler*, L. *rebellare*] riot, riotous feasting.

Revenge, v. [Fr. *revenger*, L. *re*, *vindicare*, to claim] to punish in return for an injury, retaliate. *Revenged*.

Reverence, s. [Fr. *révérence*, L. *reverentia*, *vereri*, to respect] respectful fear, respect, honour.

Reverend, adj. [L. *reverendus*, *vereri*] fit to be respected.

Reverent, adj. [L. *reverentem*, *vereri*] showing respect, humble.

Revolve, v. [L. *re*, *volvere*, to roll] to roll round, to turn over in the mind, think upon. *Revolved*.

Reward, v. [L. *re*, Fr. *guerdon*, Teut. *widerlon*, recompense] to repay, recompense, give a prize to. *Rewarded*.

Rhetoric, s. [Gr. *rhetorike*, *rhetor*, a speaker] the art of speaking like an orator, oratory.

Rhone, a river of France, rising in the mountains of Switzerland, flowing west and south, and emptying itself into the Gulf of Lyons.

Rib, s., one of the bones proceeding from the backbone and enclosing the chest, a side beam of a ship's framework.

Rice, s. [Fr. *riz*, It. *riso*, Gr. *oruza*, Arab. *aruz*] a grain cultivated in warm climates.

Rich, adj. [E. *rice*] powerful, wealthy, having great possessions, fruitful.

Richness, s. [E. *rich*] fertility, fruitfulness, abundance.

Ride, v., to sway, move up and down, be carried, sit on a horse. *Rode*, *ridden*.

Rider, s., one who rides, a horseman.

Ridge, s. [E. *hrycg*, the back] a back, a line upheaved, bank.

Right, adj. [E. *riht*] straight, just, true, proper. Adv. *rightly*.

Right, v., to set right, put straight, do justice to. *Righted*.

Righteous, adj. [corruption of E. *rightwise*] upright, just.

Rill, s., a small trickling stream, a little brook.

Rim, s. [E. *rind*] edge, border.

Ring, s. [E. *hring*] a circle, round, circular ornament.

Ring, v. [E. *hringan*] to tingle, tinkle as bells, sound, to make a bell sound. *Rang*, *rung*.

Riot, s. [Fr. *rioter*, to brawl] a brawl, tumult, noise.

Rioter, s., one who riots.

Ripe, adj. [E. *rip*, harvest] fit for harvest, mature, ready, of full age.

Ripen, v. [E. *ripe*] to grow ripe, to make ripe. *Ripened*.

x

Ripple, s., a very small wave, wavy motion of the surface of water.
Ripple, v., to form little waves, curl into waves like running water. *Rippled*.
Rise, v. [E. *risan*] to move upward, get up, ascend, begin. *Rose, risen*.
Risk, s. [Fr. *risque*, Sp. *risco*, a rock] danger, hazard.
River, s. [Fr. *rivière*, L. *riparia*, L. *ripa*, a bank, with meaning as if from L. *rivus*, a stream] a stream of water.
Rivulet, s. [Fr. *rivule*, L. *rivulus*, *rivus*] a small river, a little stream.
Road, s. [E. *rad*, a riding] a place for riding, a highway, path.
Roan, adj. [*Rouen*, in Normandy] a Rouen horse, reddish, as the common colour of Rouen horses.
Roar, v. [from the sound] to make a loud noise, bellow. *Roared*.
Roast, v. [G. *rost*, a grate, a gridiron] to cook on a gridiron, to cook before a grate, to dry, to heat. *Roasted*.
Rob, v. [O. Fr. *rober*, G. *rauben*, to reave, plunder] to plunder, spoil, take by force, steal. *Robbed*.
Robe, s. [Fr. *robe*, It. *roba*, spoil, G. *rauben*, to strip] a garment, a dress, a long trailing garment.
Robust, adj. [L. *robustus, robur*, strength] strong, stout, vigorous.
Rock, s., a rough broken mass of stone, firmly fixed lump of stone, a defence. Adj. *rocky*.
Rocket, s. [It. *rocchetto*, a distaff, a short piece of stick] a firework discharged into the air attached to a stick.
Rod, s., a stick, staff, pole.
Roe, s. [E. *ra*] a small kind of deer.
Rogue, s. [Fr. *rogue*] a vagabond, knave, dishonest person.
Roll, v. [Fr. *rouler*, L. *rotulare*, *rota*, a wheel] to go round, turn over, to rattle along. *Rolled*.
Roller, s., that which rolls, a cylinder for levelling ground.
Rome, s., a famous city on the river Tiber in Italy.
Romance, s. [*Roumanisch, Romanus, Roma*] a fiction, a story, so called from being first written in one or other of the Romance languages—that is, the languages which have sprung from the modification of the ancient Italian speech.
Roof, s. [E. *hrof*] the covering of a house, a covering.
Rook, s. [E. *hroc*] the croaker, a bird of the crow family, the gregarious crow.
Room, s., space, extent, a place, space enclosed, chamber.
Roost, s. [E. *hrost*] a pole, or perch, on which fowls sleep.
Root, s., the part of a plant which grows down into the earth, the bottom, cause, original form.
Rope, s. [E. *ræp*] a twisted line, a thick cord.
Rose, s. [L. *rosa*] a flowering plant, the colour pink the usual colour of the rose flower. Adj. *rosy*.
Rosemary, s. [E. *rosemaryne*, L. *ros marinus*, sea dew] an aromatic evergreen plant.
Rot, v., to decay, become putrid, corrupt. *Rotted*.
Rote, s. [L. *rota*, a wheel] by *rote*, by heart, as a mechanical exercise, careless of sense.
Rough, adj. [E. *hruh*, hairy] rugged, uneven, harsh, unpolished.
Round, adj. [Fr. *rond*, L. *rotundus, rota*, a wheel] circular, like a globe.
Round, prep., on all sides, about.
Roundhead, s., a nickname given to the Puritans, or supporters of the Parliament, during the Civil War in the reign of Charles I,

from their cutting their hair close and showing rounded heads.

Rouse, v. [E. *raise*] to stir up, lift, wake, excite. *Roused*.

Rout, s. [Fr. *route*, L. *rupta*] a tumult, uproar, noisy assembly, crowd.

Rove, v. [Du. *rooven*, to rob] to sail as a pirate, wander at sea, wander. *Roved*.

Row, s. [E. *rawa*] a line, rank, a number of persons or things in a line.

Row, v., to move a boat with oars. *Rowed*.

Royal, adj. [Fr. *royal*, L. *regalem*, *regis*, *rex*, a king] kingly, belonging to a king, splendid.

Royalty, s. [Fr. *royaulté*, L. *regalitatem*, *regalis*, *rex*] the condition of being king, kingly state, majesty.

Ruby, s. [Fr. *rubis*, L. *rubeus*] red colour, a red precious stone.

Rudder, s. [E. *rother*, *row*] an oar at the stern by which the vessel or boat is steered, an instrument for steering.

Rude, adj. [Fr. *rude*, L. *rudis*] rough, uncultivated, ill-mannered.

Ruffle, v. [E. *ruff*] to crumple, crease, disorder, tumble, disturb. *Ruffled*.

Rugged, adj. [E. *rug*, *rough*] shaggy, ragged, rough.

Ruin, s. [L. *ruina*, *ruere*, to fall] a falling to destruction, overthrow, decay.

Ruinous, adj. [L. *ruinosus*, *ruina*] full of ruin, destructive, decayed.

Rule, s. [O. Fr. *reule*, Fr. *regle*, L. *regula*, *regere*] that which governs, a law, standard, maxim.

Rule, v., to govern, regulate, manage. *Ruled*.

Ruler, s., one who rules.

Rumour, s. [L. *rumorem*] a report, story.

Run, v., to go quickly, flow. *Ran*, *run*.

Rush, v. [E. *hreosan*] to move violently, move with violent sound. *Rushed*.

Rush, s. [E. *risce*] a plant with straight rounded stalks without leaves, growing in damp ground, which rustles and rattles in the wind.

Sable, s. [Fr. *sable*, Polish *sobal*; an animal of the weasel family found in cold climates, especially Siberia, valued for its dark fur; dark colour.

Sacred, adj. [E. *sacre*, to hallow, Fr. *sacrer*, L. *sacrare*, *sacer*] hallowed, set apart for holy purposes, consecrated, holy.

Sacrifice, s. [L. *sacrificium*, *sacrum*, *facere*] a thing devoted to God, an offering, a thing given up for another's sake, loss.

Sad, adj. [E. *set*, *settan*, to settle] settled, serious, solemn, downcast, mournful.

Saddle, s. [E. *set*, *seat*] a seat for placing on a horse's back, the part of the back on which the saddle is placed.

Safe, adj. [Fr. *sauf*, L. *salvus*] secure, free from danger, unhurt. Subs. *safety*.

Sail, s. [E. *segel*] a sheet of canvas by means of which a vessel is driven by the wind, a voyage in a sailing vessel.

Sailor, s., one who sails, a seaman.

Saint, s. [L. *sanctus*, holy] a holy man, a person canonized.

Sake, s. [E. *sac*, *sacu*, a dispute] a cause, purpose, regard.

Salad, s. [Fr. *salade*, It. *salata*, *sal*, salt] a mess of herbs seasoned, lettuce, &c., seasoned with salt, vinegar, &c.

Salutary, adj. [L. *salutarius*, *salus*, health] healthful, beneficial.

Salute, v. [L. *salutare*, *salus*] to wish health to, greet, hail, kiss; *Saluted*.

Salvation, s. [L. *salvationem, salvare, salvus*] saving, safety of the soul, safety from sin.

Same, adj., self, equal, exactly like.

Sample, s. [E. *ensample,* Fr. *ensample,* L. *exemplum*] an example, model, specimen.

Samson, s., a famous Israelite hero of the tribe of Dan, son of Manoah, judge.

Samuel, s., a prophet of the Israelites, a Levite, son of Elkanah and Hannah, judge.

Sand, s., fine particles of stone or shell. Adj. *sandy.*

Sandal, s. [L. *sandalium,* Gr. *sandalon, sanis,* a board] a wooden sole, a sole strapped to the foot, worn instead of shoes in Eastern lands.

Sapless, adj. [E. *sap*] without sap, without juice, dry, dead.

Satisfy, v. [L. *satis, facere*] to do enough for, content, please. *Satisfied.*

Sausage, s. [Fr. *saucisse,* It. *salsiccia,* L. *sal,* salt] chopped meat salted and seasoned.

Savage, adj. [O. Fr. *salvage,* L. *silvaticus, silva,* a wood] belonging to the woods, rough, unrefined, coarse, brutal.

Safe, v. [Fr. *sauver,* L. *salvare, salvus*] to make safe, preserve, keep from danger. *Saved.*

Savoy, s., a palace in London, so called from Peter of Savoy who built it.

Saw, s., a cutting tool, formed of a strip of metal with its edge jagged.

Saw, v., to cut with a saw. *Sawed, sawed* or *sawn.*

Saxon, s. [E. *seax,* a short sword] a name given to a people of the Teutonic race, some of whom came from Germany and settled in England in the fifth and sixth centuries.

Say, v. [E. *secgan*] to speak, tell, declare. *Said.*

Scaffold, s. [O. Fr. *eschafaut, escadafaut,* L. L. *scadafaltum, ex, cadafaltum,* It. *catar,* O. H. G. *palco,* planking] a platform, a platform for an execution.

Scale, s., a shell, dish, thin plate, layer.

Scamander, s., a river represented as bounding the Trojan plain on the west.

Scan, v. [Fr. *scander,* L. *scandere,* to climb] to examine closely, count the number of feet in a verse. *Scanned.*

Scape, v., to escape. *Scaped.*

Scarce, adj. [It. *scarso,* L. *excarpsus, ex, carpere,* to pick] rare, uncommon, not plentiful. Subs. *scarcity.*

Scare, v., to frighten, drive away. *Scared.*

Scarlet, adj. [It. *scarlatto,* Pers. *sakarlet*] of a bright-red colour.

Scathe, v. [E. *sceathian*] to damage, hurt, destroy. *Scathed.*

Scatter, v. [hard form of E. *shatter, sceddan,* to divide] to shoot in all directions, throw about, disperse. *Scattered.*

Scaur, s. [E. *scar*] a ravine in a mountain side, a river-bed, place washed by a flow of water.

Scene, s. [Fr. *scène,* L. *scena*] a stage, a place of action, an exhibition, part of a play represented at one view.

Scent, v. [Fr. *sentir,* L. *sentire*] to perceive with the nose, smell, make to smell. *Scented.*

Sceptre, s. [L. *sceptrum,* Gr. *skeptron,* a staff] a king's staff.

Science, s. [Fr. *science,* L. *scientia, sciens, scire,* to know] knowledge, accurate knowledge, knowledge of abstract principles.

Scientific, adj. [Fr. *scientifique,* L. *scientia, facere*] belonging to science, given to science, accurate.

Scissors, s. pl. [L. *scissor, scindere,* to cut] cutters, a tool formed of two cutting blades working on a pin at the middle.

Scoop, v., to empty with a ladle, empty, hollow, dig out. *Scooped.*

Scope, s. [L. *scopus*, Gr. *skopos*, an outlook] aim, drift, intention.

Scorn, s., contempt, derision, ridicule.

Scotland, s., the land of the Scots, the part of Britain north of the river Tweed.

Scourge, s. [Fr. *escourgée*, L. *excorrigiata, corrigia, corium*, leather] a leathern whip, a cat-o'-nine tails.

Scream, s., a sharp cry, shriek.

Scrofula, s. [L. *scrofula, scrofa*, a sow] a disease of the glands thought to be common among swine.

Sculpture, v. [L. *sculptura, sculptus, sculpere*, to carve] to engrave, cut in marble. *Sculptured.*

Scum, s., foam, froth, refuse on the surface of a liquid, dirt.

Scythe, s. [E. *sithe*] a long sickle for mowing grass.

Sea, s., a large body of water, salt-water, the ocean.

Seal, s. [E. *sea*] a mammal living in the sea.

Seal, v. [O. Fr. *seel*, L. *sigillum, signum*] to mark with a seal, confirm. *Sealed.*

Seaman, s., a man who spends his time at sea, a sailor.

Seamanship, s., the business of a seaman, skill in navigation.

Search, v. [O. Fr. *sercher*, Fr. *chercher*, L. *circare, circa*] to go round, seek in every part. *Searched.*

Season, s. [Fr. *saison*, L. *sationem*, sowing time] due time, an opportunity, one of the four divisions of the year.

Season, v., to bring into a fit condition, fit for the taste, give a relish to. *Seasoned.*

Seat, s. [E. *settan*] a thing set; a chair, bench, country-house.

Seat, v. [E. *settan*] to cause to sit, take a seat, place in a seat. *Seated.*

Seaward, adv., towards the sea, out at sea.

Second, adj. [L. *secundus, sequi*, to follow] that which follows the first, the ordinal of two.

Secret, adj. [L. *secretus, secernere*, to separate] hidden, unknown. Subs. secrecy, concealment.

Secular, adj. [L. *secularis, seculum*, an age] belonging to time, worldly, not religious, lay.

Secure, adj. [L. *securus, se, cura*, without care] free from care, safe.

Security, s. [L. *securitatem, securus*] freedom from care, safety.

Sedge, s. [E. *secg*] coarse grass growing in swampy wet land.

Sedge-warbler, s., a small bird, *Salicaria Phragmitis*, of the species Sylviadæ, which frequents patches of reeds or willows, or herbage, in marshes, on the low sides of rivers, or on islands. It comes to this country in April and leaves again in September.

See, v. [E. *seon*] to perceive with the eye, observe, mark. *Saw, seen.*

Seed, s. [E. *sæd, sawan*, to sow] a thing sown.

Seek, v. [E. *sęcan*] to enquire after, search for, ask. *Sought.*

Seem, v. [E. *seman, sam*, same] to fit, appear suitable, appear, look. *Seemed.*

Seethe, v., to boil, cook by boiling. *Seethed, seethed or sodden.*

Seize, v. [Fr. *saisir*, It. *sagire*, Teut. *sazjan*, to set] to give possession of land, to take hold of, grasp. *Seized.*

Seldom, adv. [old ablat. case pl. of E. *seld*, rare] not often, rarely.

Self, adj., one's own. Subs. one's own body.

Selfish, adj. [E. *self*] having care for self, caring overmuch for self.

Sell, v. [E. *sellan*, to transfer] to give for money. *Sold.*

Senate, s. [L. *senatus, senes,* old men] the Roman council of elders; a council, parliament.

Send, v., to make to go, despatch, make to be carried. *Sent.*

Sense, s. [L. *sensus, sentire,* to feel] the faculty of perceiving objects, reason, good judgment, meaning.

Sensible, adj. [Fr. *sensible,* L. *sensibilis, sensus*] rational, of sound judgment, prudent.

Sentence, s. [Fr. *sentence,* L. *sententia, sentire*] thought, thought put into words, judgment, form of expression.

Sentiment, s. [Fr. *sentiment,* L. *sentire*] feeling, sensibility, a maxim.

Separate, v. [L. *separatus, se, parare*] to part, divide, mark off. *Separated.*

Sepulchre, [L. *sepulcrum, sepelire,* to bury] a burial place, tomb, grave.

Series, s. [L. *series, serere,* to join] a connected line, order, sequence.

Serious, adj. [L. *seriosus, serius*] sad, severe, solemn, grave.

Sermon, s. [L. *sermonem*] a discourse, a religious discourse.

Serpent, s. [Fr. *serpent,* L. *serpentem, serpens, serpere,* to glide] a reptile without legs, which moves itself by the muscular power belonging to the joints of the spinal column. Adj. *serpentine.*

Servant, s. [Fr. *servant, servir,* L. *servire*] one who serves.

Serve, v. [Fr. *servir,* L. *servire*] to work for, attend, help, suit. *Served.*

Service, s. [Fr. *service,* L. *servitium, servire*] the position of a servant, duty of a servant, employment, aid, benefit.

Servitude, s. [Fr. *servitude,* L. *servitudinem, servus*] service, serfdom, slavery.

Set, v. [E. *settan*] to seat, fix, appoint. *Set, set.*

Set, s., a number of things appointed together, a suit.

Settle, v. [E. *settan, setl,* a seat] to fix in a seat, steady, make certain, finish. *Settled.*

Settlement, s. [E. *settle*] a settling, end, a colony.

Seven, adj. [E. *seofon*] the numeral next after six.

Sever, v. [Fr. *sevrer,* L. *separare*] to cut asunder, divide, part. *Severed.*

Several, adj. [E. *sever*] taken separately, more than one, many, divers.

Severe, adj. [Fr. *sévère,* L. *severus*] grave, solemn, harsh, morose.

Sex, s. [L. *sexus*] the distinction between male and female.

Shadow, s. [E. *shade, sceadu, sceaddan,* to divide] a covering, a dark covering caused by the interception of light, shelter.

Shaft, s. [E. *sceafan,* to shave] a stalk, rod, arrow, pole.

Shake, v. [E. *scacan*] to move quickly, tremble, make to tremble, totter. *Shook, shaken.*

Shall, v. [E. *scal,* to be bound] see page 74.

Shallow, adj. [E. *shelve*] shelving, not deep, superficial.

Shame, s. [E. *sceame*] modesty, reproach, disgrace. Adj. *shameful,* full of disgrace.

Shape, v. [E. *sceafan,* to shave] to form, fashion, mould. *Shaped.*

Shape, s., form, figure.

Share, s. [E. *scearan,* to cut] a division, part, portion.

Sharp, adj. [E. *scearp*] cutting, edged, clever.

Shatter, v. [soft form of E. *scatter, sceotan,* to shoot] to shed, shoot, throw about, disperse. *Shattered.*

Shed, v. [E. *sceadan,* to divide] to cut into pieces, throw, let drop as water, pour. *Shed.*

Sheen, s. [E. *shine*] brightness, gleam, beauty.

Sheep, s. [E. *scæp*] a woolbearing animal, a foolish person.

Sheet, s. [E. *schet, sceat, sceotan,* to shoot] that which is shot or spread out, a broad piece, a sail, the rope that fastens a sail.

Shell, s. [softened form of E. *scel, scale*] a thin hard covering, framework, a hollow iron ball filled with combustibles.

Shelter, v. [E. *shield*] to cover, protect, defend, guard. *Sheltered.*

Shelter, s., a covering, protection, defence.

Shepherd, s. [E. *sheep, herd*] one who herds sheep.

Shield, s. [E. *scyld*] a covering, defence, a piece of armour to defend the body, worn on the left arm, a buckler.

Shift, s. [E. *scyftan,* to divide] a change, an artifice, plan.

Shine, v. [E. *scinan*] to send forth light, to beam, gleam, to be conspicuous. *Shone* or *shined; shone* or *shined.*

Shingle, s., coarse gravel, pebbles on the shore. Adj. *shingly.*

Ship, s. [E. *scip,* from root of *scoop*] a boat or vessel for seagoing, a threemasted vessel with yards on each mast.

Shipwreck, s. [E. *ship, wrack*] the destruction of a ship, loss of a ship.

Shirt, s. [soft form of E. *skirt, sceort,* short] a short garment, an inner garment worn by men.

Shoal, s. [E. *sceol*] a large number of fish, a multitude.

Shock, s. [E. *shake*] a collision, violent blow, sudden astonishment.

Shoe, s., a covering for the foot.

Shoot, v., to dart, discharge with force, hit, send forth shoots, grow. *Shot, shot.*

Shop, s., a place where things are sold.

Shore, s. [E. *score, sciran,* to divide] that which divides, the edge of the land, coast.

Short, adj. [E. *sceort*] not long, brief, scanty.

Shorten, v., to make short. *Shortened.*

Shot, s. [E. *shoot*] a thing discharged, a missile, a pellet for use in a gun.

Shoulder, s. [E. *sculder, scyld, shield*] the broad top of the arm, the broad upper joint of an animal's foreleg.

Shoulder, v., to push with the shoulder, take upon the shoulder. *Shouldered.*

Shout, s. [from the sound] a loud cry, a cry of joy.

Shout, v., to cry aloud. *Shouted.*

Show, Shew, v. [E. *sceawian*] to place in sight, exhibit, teach, explain, guide. *Showed* or *shewed; shown* or *shewn* or *showed* or *shewed.*

Shower, s. [E. *schowre, scur*] a fall of rain or hail, an abundant fall. Adj. *showery.*

Shriek, v. [form of E. *screech*] to make a shrill sound, scream. *Shrieked.*

Shrill, adj., piercing, sharp, high-pitched.

Shroud, s. [E. *scrydan,* to clothe] a covering, clothing, garment, garment for a dead body.

Shrub, s. [softened form of E. *scrub, scrob*] a dwarfed tree, a bush.

Shudder, v., to shiver, tremble, quiver. *Shuddered.*

Shut, v. [form of E. *shoot*] to push, close, fasten. *Shut, shut.*

Shuttle, s. [E. *sceathel,* the shooter] an instrument for shooting the thread of the woof between the threads of the warp.

Sicily, s., an island in the Mediterranean, south of Italy.

Sick, adj. [E. *seoc*] feeble, ill, weary, disgusted.

Sickle, s. [E. *sicel,* L. *secula, secare,* to cut] a reaping-hook.

Side, s., the edge, margin, part, party.

Sideways, adv., towards one side with one side in front.

Siege, s. [Fr. *siège, siéger,* L. *sediare, sedere*] a sitting down before a town, blockade.

Sigh, s. [from the sound] a deep breathing, a sob.

Sight, s. [E. *gesiht,* seen; *seon,* to see] a thing seen, spectacle, power of seeing, vision. Adj. *sighted,* seen, caught sight of.

Sign, s. [Fr. *signe,* L. *signum*] a mark, proof, notice.

Signal, s. [Fr. *signal,* L. *signale, signum*] a sign at a distance, notice, message given by signs.

Signal, v., to give notice by signal. *Signalled.*

Silence, s. [Fr. *silence,* L. *silentium, silere*] quiet, stillness, absence of noise.

Silent, adj. [L. *silentem, silere*] calm, quiet, taciturn.

Silenus, s., the most famous of the Satyrs, the constant companion of Bacchus.

Silk, s. [E. *seolc,* L. *sericum, seres,* the Chinese] a fine thread produced by a caterpillar, introduced into Europe from China.

Silver, s. [E. *seolfer*] a white metal, money.

Similar, adj. [Fr. *similaire,* L. *similis*] like, of like kind.

Simois, s., a river represented as being on the eastern side of the plain of Troja.

Simple, adj. [Fr. *simple,* L. *simplicem, simplex, plica,* a fold] onefold, uniform, single, plain, unaffected, silly.

Since, adv. [E. *sithens, sith*] after then, thenceforth, because.

Sincere, adj. [Fr. *sincére,* L. *sincerus*] pure, unadulterated, true, real.

Sinew, s. [E. *sinu*] a muscle, tendon.

Sinful, adj. [E. *sin*] full of sin, wicked, base, guilty.

Sing, v., to utter musical sounds, chant. *Sang, sung.*

Singer, s., one who sings.

Single, adj. [L. *singulus*] one, alone, separate. Adv. *singly.*

Singular, adj. [L. *singularis, singulus*] alone, unusual, uncommon.

Sink, v. [E. *sincan*] to fall to the bottom, set, go down, to cause to go down. *Sank, sunk.*

Sir, s. [Fr. *sire,* L. *senior, senex,* old] a title of respect, a title belonging to baronets and knights.

Sire, s. [Fr. *sire,* see **Sir**] a title used in addressing a king, father, the male parent of an animal.

Sister, s. [E. *sweostor*] daughter of the same parents.

Sit, v. [E. *sittan*] to rest on the haunches, rest, remain, stay in a seat, brood upon eggs. *Sat, sat.*

Situation, s. [E. *situate,* L. *situatus, situs*] position, place, state.

Sixty, adj. [E. *six, tig*] ten times six.

Size, s. [corruption of *assize,* Fr. *assise,* L. L. *assisa,* a settlement, L. *ad sedere*] a settlement, regulation, regulated form, proper form, form, bigness.

Skeleton, s. [G. *skeleton,* a dried body, mummy; *skellein,* to dry] the dried fleshless bones of an animal.

Skill, s. [E. *scylan,* to divide] power of distinguishing, discernment, knowledge. Adj. *skilful.*

Skim, v. [E. *scum*] to take off scum, move lightly over the surface, to touch gently. *Skimmed.*

Skin, s. [E. *scin*] outer covering, hide, rind, bark.

Skulk, v., to hide away, sneak, slink off. *Skulked.*

Skull, s. [E. *scel*] the shell of bone that contains the brain, the head.

Sky, s. [E. *scua,* a shade] the clouds, the vault of heaven.

Slack, adj. [E. *sleac*] loose, not tight, flapping, faint, feeble.

Slave, s. [*Slave*, the name of the race inhabiting most of Eastern Europe, from which the Teutons made captives] a captive in bondage, a bond-servant, a drudge.

Slay, v. [E. *slean*] to smite to death, kill, destroy. *Slew, slain*.

Sledge, s. [E. *sled, slide*] a sliding car, a car without wheels used to glide over the snow.

Sleep, v. [E. *slæp*] to repose, rest, slumber, to be inactive, to be dead. *Slept*.

Sleepy, adj. [E. *sleep*] inclined to sleep, lazy, torpid, indolent.

Slender, adj., thin, slim, spare, slight.

Slide, v., to slip, glide, glide on ice. *Slided* or *slid*.

Slim, adj., thin, slight.

Slip, v., to glide, fall, make a mistake, escape. *Slipped* or *slipt*.

Sloe, s., a small wild plum, the fruit of the blackthorn.

Slope, s. [E. *slip*] an incline, land inclining downwards.

Slow, s., dull, inactive, indolent, lazy.

Sluice, s. [Fr. *escluse*, L. L. *sclusa, exclusa*, L. *excludere*, to shut off] a trap-door shutting off and regulating the supply of water, a floodgate.

Small, adj., little, not large, trivial, trifling.

Smallish, adj., rather small, somewhat small.

Smell, v., to give forth odour, affect the nose, to perceive with the nose. *Smelled* or *smelt*.

Smile, v., to laugh gently, look pleased. *Smiled*.

Smite, v., to strike, beat. *Smote, smitten*.

Smith, s. [E. *smitan*, to smite] the smiter, one who works metals, an artificer.

Smoke, s. [E. *smeoc, smec*] vapour from fire, darkness, fog.

Smooth, adj. [E. *smethe, smeate*, beaten, *smitan*, to beat] beaten, not rough, even, soft, pliable, complaisant.

Smoulder, v. [E. *moulder*] to fall away into dust, die away into ashes, burn low. *Smouldered*.

Snail, s. [E. *snael, snagel, snican*, to creep] a creeping mollusc, or soft-bodied creature, living in a univalve shell.

Snake, s. [E. *snaca, snican*, to creep] a reptile of the serpent order.

Snarl, v., to growl like a dog. *Snarled*.

Snatch, v. [softened form of E. *snack*] to snap at, seize hurriedly. *Snatched*.

Snatch, s., a hurried seizing, a short time.

Sneeze, v. [E. *niesan* from the sound] to send air out violently through the nose. *Sneezed*.

Sniff, v. [from the sound] to draw air through the nose. *Sniffed*.

Snip, v. [E. *nip*] to cut suddenly, cut with a pair of blades, slip. *Snipped* or *snipt*.

Snore, v. [from the sound] to breathe hard through the nose in sleep. *Snored*.

Snow, s., wet of the atmosphere frozen into soft white flakes. Adj. *snowy*.

So, adv. [E. *swa*] thus, in this way, as.

Soak, v. [E. *suck*] to make to suck, drench, steep, to suck in. *Soaked*.

Sob, s. [from the sound] a violent sigh, a tearful sigh.

Sober, adj. [Fr. *sobre*, L. *sobrius, se, ebrius*, not drunk] not drunk, temperate, serious, calm.

Society, s. [Fr. *société*, L. *societatem, socius*] persons united for a common object, a community.

Socket, s. [dim. of E. *sock*] a small hollow into which a thing is fastened, as a foot into a sock.

Soft, adj., not hard, yielding, tender, delicate, malleable. Subs. *softness*.

Soil, s. [Fr. *soile*, L. *solum*] ground, foundation, earth, mould.

Soil, v., to make dirty, stain, tarnish. *Soiled.*

Sojourn, v. [Fr. *séjourner*, L. *sub*, *diurnare*, *dies*, a day] to stay a short time, remain. *Sojourned.*

Soldier, s. [O. Fr. *souldier*, L. *solidarius*, *solidus*, a piece of money] a mercenary, one who fights for pay, one who fights.

Sole, adj. [Fr. *sol*, L. *solus*] alone, only, single.

Solemn, adj. [L. *solemnis*] belonging to religious festivals, serious, grave. Subs. *solemnity.*

Solemnise, v. [E. *solemn*] to celebrate, to make solemn. *Solemnised.*

Solid, adj. [L. *solidus*] dense, firm, compact, strong.

Solitary, adj. [L. *solitarius*, *solus*] lonely, alone, living alone, without companions.

Solitude, s. [L. *solitudinem*, *solus*] loneliness, a lonely place.

Solution, s. [L. *solutionem*, *solutus*, *solvere*] dissolving, separation, explanation.

Some, adj. [E. *sum*] an indefinite quantity.

Son, s. [E. *sunu*] a male child, a male descendant.

Song, s. [E. *sing*] what is sung, a ballad, melody, birds' notes, a trifle.

Soon, adv. [E. *sona*] in a short time.

Soothe, v., to lull, calm. *Soothed.*

Sore, s. [E. *sar*, a wound] a wound, an ulcer.

Sorrow, s. [E. *sorwe*, *sorg*] care, grief, anxiety.

Sorry, adj. [E. *sarig*, *sar*] wounded, pained, grieved, sorrowful.

Sort, s. [Fr. *sorte*, L. *sortem*, *sors*, a lot] a number, class, kind, manner.

Sortable, adj., able to be sorted.

Sound, adj. [E. *sund*, *gesund*] hale, entire, unbroken.

Sound, s. [E. *soun*, L. *sonus*] noise, tone, report.

Sound, v. [E. *sounen*, L. *sonare*] to make a noise, to cause to make a noise. *Sounded.*

Source, s. [Fr. *source*, *sourdre*, L. *surgere*, to rise] origin, spring.

South, s. [E. *sud*, *sun*] turned towards the sun, the position of the mid-day sun as seen by Northern people. Adj. *southern.*

Sovereign, adj. [O. Fr. *soverayn*, It. *sovrano*, L. *superanus*, *superus*, *supra*, above] possessing power above all others, ruling supreme.

Space, s. [Fr. *espace*, L. *spatium*] room, extent.

Spacious, adj. [L. *spatiosus*, *spatium*] roomy, extensive, large.

Spain, s. [L. *Hispania*] the south-western peninsula of Europe.

Spaniard, s., a man of Spain.

Spare, v. [E. *sparian*] to use carefully, refrain from using, save, let go. *Spared.*

Spare, adj. [E. *spær*] thin, scanty.

Spark, s., a particle of fire, small light.

Sparkle, v. [E. *spark*] to throw out sparks, shine brightly, glimmer, twinkle. *Sparkled.*

Sparrow, s. [E. *sparwe*, *spearwe*, *spear*] a bird with a strong straight pointed beak, like a spearhead, of the family Conirostres, *Passer domesticus*; also a bird of the family Dentirostres, *Accentor modularis.*

Spartan, adj. [L. *Spartanus*, *Sparta*] belonging to Sparta, a town of Laconia, in the Peloponnesus; stern, hard.

Speak, v. [E. *spæcan*, *sprecan*] to give forth words, talk, say. *Spoke* or *spake*; *spoken.*

Speaker, s., one who speaks.

Spear, s. [E. *spar*] a rod, a pointed pole, a lance.

Special, s. [L. *specialis*, *species*] of a certain kind, peculiar, particular.

Species, s. [L. *species*] appearance, form, kind, a class of things of the same appearance.

Specimen, s. [L. *specimen, specere*, to look at] a sample, pattern.

Speck, s., a spot, small mark.

Spectacle, s. [L. *spectaculum, spectare*] a thing to be seen, sight, show, representation. *Spectacles*, glasses to aid the sight.

Speculation, s. [L. *speculationem, speculari*] careful view, thoughtful consideration, theory.

Speech, s. [E. *speak, spæce*] language, mode of talk, a discourse.

Speed, v., to go well, prosper, succeed, hasten. *Speeded*.

Speed, s., success, diligence, haste. Adj. *speedy*.

Spend, v. [L. *expendere*, to weigh out] to pay away money, consume. *Spent*.

Spherical, adj. [E. *sphere*] like a sphere, round, globular.

Spice, s. [O. Fr. *espice*, L. *species*, kinds, kinds of produce] special kinds of produce, aromatic wares, fragrant fruits, &c., drugs.

Spigot, s., [E. *spike*] a spike to stop the vent of a cask.

Spin, v., to twist into thread, twirl quickly, draw out to a great length. *Span* or *spun*; *spun*.

Spirit, s. [L. *spiritus, spirare*, to breathe] breath, life, energy, courage, a ghost. Adj. *spirited*, bold.

Spite, s. [O. Fr. *despit*, L. *despectus, de, specere*, to look down upon] envy, malice, annoyance. *In spite of*, notwithstanding.

Splendid, adj. [L. *splendidus, splendere*] shining, bright, magnificent, showy.

Spoil, v. [O. Fr. *(de)spouiller*, L. *spoliare*, to strip] to rob, strip, plunder, damage. *Spoiled* or *spoilt*.

Spoil, s., plunder, pillage, booty.

Spoon, s. [E. *spon*, a chip of wood] an implement ending in a small bowl for dipping liquid.

Spot, s. [E. *spit*] a speck, blot, dot, mark. Adj. *spotted*.

Spray, s. [E. *sprengan*, to sprinkle] particles of water driven by the wind, foam-flakes.

Spread, v. [E. *sprytan*] to scatter, extend, diffuse, stretch. *Spread*.

Spring, v., to bound, leap, burst forth, arise, grow. *Sprang, sprung*.

Spring, s., a leap, bursting forth, the bursting growing time of the year, a source, fountain.

Sprout, v. [E. *sprytan*] to shoot forth, grow, send out shoots. *Sprouted*.

Spume, s. [L. *spuma*] foam, froth, scum.

Spur, v. [E. *spura*, a footmark] to press with the heel, goad, urge, incite. *Spurred*.

Squall, s. [E. *squeal*] a rushing wind, a sudden blast of wind.

Square, adj. [O. Fr. *esquarre*, It. *squadra*, L. *quadratus, quadrare, quatuor*, four] having four sides equal and four right angles.

Squeal, v. [from the sound] a shriek, wild cry, scream. *Squealed*.

Squib, s., a firework consisting of a tube filled with powder, &c.

Staff, s. [E. *stæf*] a stick, pole, prop, stake.

Stag, s., a male, a male deer.

Stage, s. [O. Fr. *estage*, L. *staticum, status, stare*] a standing, platform, resting-place on a journey, distance between two resting-places.

Stagger, v., to reel, fall about, hesitate, doubt. *Staggered*.

Stair, s. [E. *stæger, stigan*, to go up] a ladder, number of steps, a step.

Stake, s., a post stuck into the ground; *at stake*, pledged, risked.

Stake, v., to fasten with a stake, to risk, wager. *Staked*.

Stalwart, adj. [E. *stælwyrthe*, worthy of the post, *stæl*, station, *wyrthe*, worthy] serviceable, brave, strong.

Stand, v., to stop, stay, be still, keep one's ground, endure. *Stood.*

Stand, s., a place, post, resistance.

Standard, s. [E. *stand*] a fixed rule, a flag erected.

Star, s. [E. *steorra*] the strewer of light, a bright body in the heaven.

Stare, v. [E. *starr*, stiff] to look fixedly, fix the eyes upon. *Stared.*

Starling, s. [dim. of *stearn*, *stær*] a bird of dark speckled plumage, *Sturnus vulgaris.*

Start, v., to move suddenly, begin to move, begin. *Started.*

Startle, v. [freq. of E. *start*] to cause to start, frighten, excite. *Startled.*

Starve, v. [E. *steorfan*, to die, *stærf*, stiff] to die of hunger, suffer hunger, to kill by hunger. *Starved.*

State, s. [L. *status*, *stare*, to stand] standing, position, condition, rank.

Statue, s. [L. *statua*, *statuere*, *stare*] an image, sculptured figure.

Stature, s. [L. *statura*, *stare*] the standing height of a body.

Staunch, adj. [E. *stanch*, O. Fr. *estancher*, L. *stagnare*, *stagnum*, standing water] steady, firm, true, unflinching.

Stay, v., to remain, stop, wait, continue. *Stayed* or *staid.*

Stead, s., a standing-place, a place, room.

Steadfast, adj., steady, firm, unyielding, stable.

Steady, adj. [E. *stead*] firm, fixed, stable.

Steady, v., to make firm, fasten, fix. *Steadied.*

Steed, s., a horse.

Steel, s. [E. *styl.* Ger. *stachel*, a point, akin to the root of *stick*] edge-metal, because steel at first would be too valuable to be used for more than the edges of weapons; carbonized iron.

Steep, adj., abrupt, precipitous, inclining abruptly.

Steeple, s. [E. *steep*] a church-tower, belfry, tower ending in a spire.

Steer, v. [E. *steoran*, *styran*, to stir] to move, guide, guide a ship. *Steered.*

Stem, s. [E. *stema*] the trunk of a tree, stalk, that which sends out shoots.

Stem, v., to stop, resist, check. *Stemmed.*

Step, s., a stamp, a setting down the foot, pace, movement.

Step, v., to set down the foot, tread, move forward. *Stepped* or *stept.*

Sterile, adj. [L. *sterilis*] barren, unfruitful, unproductive.

Stern, adj., troubled, severe, hard, austere.

Stern, s. [E. *steer*] the steerage place, hinder part of a vessel.

Stick, s. [E. *sticca*, *sticcian*, to stab] a pointed piece of wood, staff, rod.

Stick, v., to stab, pierce, fasten in, adhere, be in difficulty. *Stuck, stuck.*

Still, adj., calm, unmoving, quiet, resting. Subs. *stillness.*

Sting, v. [E. *stick*] to pierce, pain, hurt the feelings. *Stang* or *stung, stung.*

Stir, v., to move, rouse, bustle about. *Stirred.*

Stir, s., disturbance, bustle, commotion.

Stirrup, s. [E. *stige*, *ræp*, stepping rope, *stigan*, to step] a strap for mounting on horseback, a ring for the rider's foot.

Stock, s. [E. *stick*] a stump fixed in the ground, a tree-trunk, stem or origin from which a family grows.

Stond, s., stop, hindrance, obstacle.

Stone, s. [E. *stán*] hardened earth or mineral.

Stool, s. [E. *stol*] a bench, a seat without a back, a small seat.

Stoop, v. [E. *steep*] to bend, fall forwards, incline. *Stooped.*
Stop, v., to close, hinder, impede, stay, remain. *Stopped* or *stopt.*
Store, v. [O. Fr. *estorer*, L. *instaurare*, to provide] to provide, furnish, lay up, take care of. *Stored.*
Store, s. [O. Fr. *estoire, estorer*] provision, stock, a place for stores.
Storm, s. [E. *stir*] a violent wind, tempest, rush of wind and rain, tumult. Adj. *stormy.*
Story, s. [O. Fr. *estore*, Fr. *histoire*, L. and Gr. *historia*, an enquiry] a narrative of events, tale, fiction, lie.
Stout, adj., bold, stubborn, undaunted, powerful, of full body.
Straddle, v. [freq. of E. *stride*] to open the legs widely, stride far, stand with the legs far apart. *Straddled.*
Straight, adj. [E. *streht, streccan,* to stretch] outstretched, direct.
Straightway, adv., in a straight way, instantly, directly, at once.
Strain, v. [O. Fr. *estreindre*, L. *stringere*] to draw tight, overstretch, wring, filter. *Strained.*
Strain, s., a violent stretch, injury caused by overstretching, wrench.
Strait, adj. [E. *streyt*, O.Fr. *estreit*, L. *strictus, stringere*] stretched, strict, narrow. Subs. a narrow passage of sea.
Strand, s., an edge of the sea, beach, shore.
Strange, adj. [O. Fr. *estrange*, L. *extraneus, extra,* out] foreign, out of the common, odd.
Stranger, s., one who is strange, a foreigner, an unknown person.
Strap, s., a band, tie, fastening.
Stray, v. [O. Fr. *estrayer*, L. *extrarius, extra,* outside] to go outside, wander, lose the way. *Strayed.*
Streak, s. [E. *strike*] a stroke, stripe, line.
Stream, s., a flow, flowing water, a streak of light.

Street, s. [L. *strata*, a levelled way] a paved road, a road in a town.
Strength, s. [E. *strong*] power, force, vigour.
Stretch, v. [E. *streccan*] to draw tight, draw out, extend, lengthen. *Stretched.*
Strew, v. [E. *streowian*] to scatter, spread, sprinkle, shed. *Strewed, strewed* or *strewn.*
Strict, adj. [L. *strictus, stringere*] exact, particular, severe.
Stride, v., to walk with long steps, to step far. *Strode, stridden.*
Stride, s., a long step.
Strife, s. [E. *strith*] a struggle, contest, quarrel, contention.
Strike, v., to smite, hit, deal a blow to, stamp. *Struck, stricken* or *struck.*
Stripling, s. [dim. of E. *strip*] a scion, young shoot, youth, boy.
Strive, v. [E. *strife*] to struggle, contend, work hard. *Strove, striven.*
Stroke, s. [E. *strike*] a blow.
Strong, adj., powerful, able, firm, enduring.
Strongbow, s., Richard de Clare, Earl of Strigul or Chepstow, a Norman who invaded Ireland to assist Dermot of Leinster to recover his power, in the reign of Henry II, 1170.
Structure, s. [L. *structura, structus, struere,* to build] mode of building, a pile of buildings.
Struggle, v., to strive violently, contend, labour hard. *Struggled.*
Struggle, s., a violent effort, contest.
Stubble, s. [E. *stub*] the stumps after corn has been cut, land off which corn has been cut.
Stubborn, adj. [E. *stub;* or *stydeboren, styde,* firm, *bora,* a supporter] firm, immoveable, obstinate, unyielding.
Student, s. [L. *studentem, studens, studere*] one who studies, a reader, scholar, learner.
Study, v. [O. Fr. *estudier*, L. *stu-*

dere] to attend to, examine, read carefully. *Studied.*

Study, s., attention, application of the mind, subject of learning, a room given to study.

Stuff, s. [G. *stoff*] that which fills, furniture, goods, material.

Stumpy, adj. [E. *stump*] like a stump, short, thickset.

Stun, v., to stupefy by sound, stupefy, astonish, surprise. *Stunned.*

Sturdy, adj. [O. Fr. *estourdi, estourdir*, It. *stordire*, L. *extorpidire, torpidus*] strong, vigorous, stout.

Subdue, v. [Fr. *-duire*, L. *sub, ducere*, to draw under] to bring under one's power, overcome, conquer. *Subdued.*

Subject, adj. [L. *subjectus, subjicere, jacere*] placed under, serving, inferior, liable.

Subject, v., to overcome, make to serve, make liable to. *Subjected.*

Submit, v. [L. *submittere*] to send under, yield, give way, give in. *Submitted.*

Subsequent, adj. [L. *sub, sequentem, sequens, sequi*, to follow] following, coming later.

Subsist, v. [L. *sub, sistere*, to stay] to exist, remain, live. *Subsisted.*

Substance, s. [Fr. *substance*, L. *substantia, stare*] that which is under, foundation, reality, body, essence.

Subtle, adj. [Fr. *subtil*, L. *subtilis, texilis, texere* to weave] fine-drawn, cunning, clever, artful.

Succeed, v. [L. *succedere*, to come up] to come on, follow, advance, prosper. *Succeeded.*

Success, s. [L. *successus, succedere*] prosperity, gain. Adj. *successful.*

Successive, adj. [L. *successivus, succedere*] following in order.

Successor, s. [L. *successor, succedere*] one who comes after.

Such, adj. [E. *swilc, swa-lic*, so like] of this sort, of that sort, so.

Suck, v., to draw in with the mouth, draw in. *Sucked.*

Sudden, adj. [Fr. *soudain*, O. Fr. *soubdain*, L. *subitaneus, subitus, sub-ire*] coming secretly, unexpected, swift.

Suffer, v. [L. *sufferre*] to bear, endure, be in pain. *Suffered.*

Suffice, v. [L. *sufficere, facere*, to be enough. *Sufficed.*

Sufficient, adj. [L. *sufficientem, sufficiens*] enough, competent, fit.

Suffocate, v. [L. *suffocatus, focare, fauces*, the throat] to strangle, choke, stifle. *Suffocated.*

Suggest, v. [L. *suggestus, sub, gerere*, to bring] to bring up into the mind, insinuate, hint. *Suggested.*

Suggestion, s. [L. *suggestionem, gestus, gerere*] a hint, proposal.

Suicide, s. [L. *sui, cida, caedere*, to kill] a slayer of himself, self-murder.

Suit, s. [Fr. *suit, suivre*, L. *sequere* for *sequi*, to follow] a following, an action at law, prosecution, set of things following one arrangement.

Suit, v., to follow in order, fit, agree. *Suited.*

Suitable, adj. [E. *suit*] fitting, proper.

Sullen, adj. [E. *soleine*, L. *solus*, alone] unsociable, gloomy, morose.

Sulphur, s. [L. L. *sulphur*, L. *sulfur*] brimstone, a yellow mineral very inflammable.

Sultan, s., prince, a ruler, the ruler of the Ottoman race settled in Turkey.

Summary, s. [L. *summarius, summa*] a statement of the chief points, a short account.

Summer, s., the warm season.

Summit, s. [L. *summitas, summus*, highest, *supremus, supra*] the highest point, top.

Sun, s., the planet that lights the earth by day. Adj. *sunny*, bright, warmed by the sun, cheerful.

Superhuman, adj. [L. *super*, above, *humanus*] more than human.

Superior, adj. [L. *superior*, higher,

supra] above, better, more important.

Superiority, s., better condition, advantage.

Supper, s. [Fr. *souper, soupe*, G. *suppe*] a meal at which soup was usual, the last meal at night.

Supply, v. [Fr. *supplier*, L. *supplere*, to fill up]-to provide, furnish. *Supplied.*

Support, v. [L. *supportare*, to carry up] to uphold, bear, endure, assist. *Supported.*

Suppose, v. [Fr. *supposer*, L. *sub, pausare*] to lay down, assume, think. *Supposed.*

Suppress, v. [L. *suppressus, premere*] to press down, overcome, crush. *Suppressed.*

Supreme, adj. [L. *supremus, supra*] uppermost, most powerful, having absolute power.

Sure, adj. [Fr. *sûr*, O. Fr. *seür*, L. *securus*] safe, secure, trustworthy, confident.

Surf, s., the foaming broken water on the sea-shore.

Surface, s. [Fr. *surface*, L. *superficies, facies*] the upper face, flat top, top.

Surge, v. [L. *surgere*] to rise, bubble up, boil as waves, toss to and fro. *Surged.*

Surgeon, s. [E. *surgen*, Fr. *surgien, chirurgien*, L. *chirurgus*, Gr. *cheirourgos, cheir*, a hand, *ergein*, to work]. an operator, one who cures diseases by operating upon the diseased part.

Surpass, v. [Fr. *surpasser*, L. *super, passus*] to step beyond, exceed, go too far. *Surpassed.*

Surprise, v. [Fr. *surprise*, L. *super, prensus, prendere*, to catch] to catch suddenly, astonish. *Surprised.*

Surrender, v. [Fr. *surrendre*. L. *reddere*] to give over, yield a fortified place. *Surrendered.*

Surround, v. [Fr. *sur, round*] to enclose, encompass, encircle. *Surrounded.*

Survey, v. [O. Fr. *surveoir*, L. *super, videre*, to see] to look over, look out upon, inspect. *Surveyed.*

Suspicion, s. [L. *suspicionem, sub, specere*, to look] conjecture, distrust, doubt.

Sustain, v. [L. *sustinere, sub, tenere*] to hold up, endure, bear. *Sustained.*

Swallow, s. [E. *swalewe*] a migratory bird of the family of the Hirundinidæ, *Hirundo rustica*.

Swallow, v. [E. *swelgan*] to take through the throat, devour, take in as food. *Swallowed.*

Swarm, v., to cluster, throng, gather in a crowd. *Swarmed.*

Swathe, s., the grass cut by one stroke of the scythe, the path cut by the mower.

Sway, v., to wave to and fro, swing, incline, influence, govern. *Swayed.*

Swear, v. [E. *swerian*, from root of *wahr*, true, sure] to take oath, affirm, declare solemnly. *Swore* or *sware, sworn.*

Sweat, s. [E. *swat*] wet from the skin, moisture, toil producing sweat.

Sweep, v., to brush, wipe, clear away, range over a distance. *Swept.*

Sweep, s., range, extent of a stroke, compass, a curve.

Sweeten, v. [E. *sweet*] to make sweet. *Sweetened.*

Sweetness, s. [E. *sweet*] the condition of being sweet, pleasantness.

Swift, adj. [E. *swifan*, to move quickly] quick, fleet, rapid.

Swim, v., to move to and fro, float, move on the surface of water. *Swam, swum.*

Swine, s., the pig (sing. and pl., but now mostly used in plural).

Swing, v., to move to and fro, wave, vibrate, brandish. *Swung.*

Sword, s. [E. *sweord, ward*] a

weapon for cutting and thrusting, a long knife.

Syllable, s. [L. *syllaba,* Gr. *sullabe, sun, labein,* to take together] letters making a complete sound when taken together.

Syracusan, adj., belonging to Syracuse, a city on the south-east coast of Sicily, a Greek colony, founded, about B.C. 734, by Corinthian settlers.

Syrian, adj., belonging to Syria, a country bordering on the east coast of the Mediterranean sea.

Table, s. [Fr. *table,* L. *tabula,* a plank] a board, a piece of furniture with a surface of flat board.

Table-land, s., a broad expanse of flat land far above sea-level.

Tablet, s. [dim. of E. *table*] a small table, a small flat surface for writing.

Tactics, s. [Gr. *taktika, tassein,* to arrange] rules for arranging troops, the science of marshalling forces, plans.

Tænarus, s., the ancient name of the southernmost headland of Greece, now Matapan.

Tail, s. [E.*tægel*] the last vertebræ of an animal's back-bone hanging beyond the body, that which is behind, the end.

Tailor, s. [Fr. *tailleur, tailler,* L. L. *taleare,* to cut] a cutter, one who makes clothes.

Take, v. [E. *tacan*] to seize, capture, lay hold on, accept, receive. *Took, taken.*

Tale, s. [E. *tellan,* to count] a reckoning, number, account, story.

Talent, s. [L. *talentum,* Gr.*talanton*] a weight of money, natural ability.

Talk, v. [E. *tell*] to speak, continue speaking, converse. *Talked.*

Talk, s., conversation, discourse, idle words.

Tall, adj., high, of great stature.

Tallow, s. [E. *talwe, telg, telgan,* to smear] fat, grease, animal fat.

Tame, adj., subdued, mild, gentle, domesticated.

Tangle, v., to interweave, twist together, confuse, muddle. *Tangled.*

Taper, s., a small wax candle.

Tar, s., a dark resinous sap of pine trees.

Tarentum, s., a city on the northeast coast of the gulf of Taranto, in the south of Italy, a colony founded by Greeks from Laconia, about B.C. 708.

Target, s. [dim. of E. *targe,* Fr. *targe,* Scand. *targa*] a shield, buckler, a round mark for shooting.

Tarn, s., a small lake, a mountain lake.

Task, s. [O. Fr. *tasque,* L. *tasca, taxa, taxare,* to fix] a fixed burden, work set to be done.

Taste, v. [O. Fr. *taster,* L. *taxitare, taxare,* to handle, *tangere,* to touch] to touch with the tongue, perceive a flavour, eat a little, have a flavour. *Tasted.*

Taste, s., flavour, relish, choice, nice power of discrimination, delicacy. Adj. *tasteless.*

Teach, v. [E. *tæcan,* to show] to show, instruct, direct, inform. *Taught.*

Team, s. [E. *tyman,* to produce] a string of horses, two or more animals drawing a plough or carriage.

Tear, s. [E. *tær*] a drop from the eye, liquid secreted by a gland of the eye.

Tear, v. [E. *teran*] to rend, break, separate, destroy. *Tore* or *tare, torn.*

Tell, v. [E. *tellan*] to count, reckon, speak, inform, say. *Told.*

Temper, s. [L. *temperare,* to moderate] moderation, calmness, condition of mind.

Temperate, adj. [L. *temperatus*] moderate, sober, calm.

Tempest, s. [O. Fr. *tempeste*, L. *tempestas*] a storm.

Temple, s. [L. *templum*] a building for religious services, the holy building at Jerusalem, the Templars' Inn in London.

Temple, s. [Fr. *temple*, L. *tempora*] the side of the forehead.

Temporal, adj. [L. *temporalis*, *tempus*, time] belonging to time, worldly, passing, unspiritual.

Tempt, v. [O. Fr. *tempter*, L. *temptare*] to try, allure, urge to evil. *Tempted.*

Ten, see page 51.

Tend, v. [L. *tendere*, to stretch] to incline. *Tended.*

Tender, adj. [Fr. *tendre*, L. *tenerum*, *tener*] gentle, soft, mild.

Tender, v. [Fr. *tendre*, L. *tendere*, to reach] to stretch out, offer, make a proposal. *Tendered.*

Tendril, s. [O. Fr. *tendrillon*, *tendron*, L. *tenere*, to hold] the young shoot of a climbing plant, slender shoot of a vine.

Tenement, s. [L. *tenementum*, *tenere*] the holding of a tenant, land with buildings, a building.

Tent, s. [Fr. *tente*, L. *tenta*, *tendere*, to stretch] canvas stretched on poles, a canvas hut.

Tenth, the ordinal of ten.

Term, s. [Fr. *terme*, Gr. *terma*, a bound] an end, a limit.

Terminal, adj. [L. *terminalis*, *terminus*, an end] growing at the end, happening every term.

Terrace, s. [E. *terrasse*, Fr. *terrasse*, It. *terrazza*, *terra*, earth] an open walk of earth or rubble, a raised walk.

Terrible, adj. [L. *terribilis*, *terrere*, to frighten] frightening, dreadful.

Terrify, v. [Fr. *terrifier*, L. *terrere*, *facere*] to frighten, alarm. *Terrified.*

Terror, s. [L. *terror*] dread, fright, alarm.

Test, s. [Fr. *test*, L. *testa*, a crucible in which metals were assayed] an assaying of metals, examination, trial.

Thames, s. [*Temse, Tamese*] a river which rises in the Cotswolds in Gloucestershire, and flows past London into the North Sea.

Than, conj., expressing comparison [E. *then, thaene*, neut. accus. of the demonstrative pronoun].

Thane, s. [E. *thegen*, a man] a servant, the king's servant, a nobleman.

Thank, v., to express good will, be grateful. *Thanked.*

Thanks, s., pl. expression of gratitude.

That, see pages 54, 55.

Thaw, v. [akin to E. *dew*] to melt, dissolve, cause to melt. *Thawed.*

The, see pages, 55, 58.

Their, see page 55.

Then, adv., at that time.

Thence, adv., see page 82.

There, adv., see page 82.

Thick, adj. [E. *thic*] close, compact, solid, stout.

Thicket, s. [dim. of E. *thick*] a thickly set plantation, a close wood.

Thigh, s., the upper part of the leg, from the body to the knee.

Thin, adj., outstretched, slender, lean, sparse.

Thine, see page 53.

Thing, s., any object of sense or of thought.

Think, v. [E. *thincan*] to use the mind, judge, consider, contemplate. *Thought.*

Third, see page 52.

Thirst, s., dryness, want of water, desire of drink. Adj. *thirsty.*

Thirteen, adj. [E. *three, ten*] the cardinal next after twelve, three and ten.

Thirty, adj. [E. *thryttig, three, ten*] three times ten.

This, see page 55.

Thistle, s., a prickly plant.

Y

Thither, adv., to that place.
Thong, s., a strap of leather.
Thorny, adj. [E. *thorn*] full of thorns, prickly.
Thou, see page 53.
Though, conj. [E. *theah, that*] on that condition, allowing that, yet.
Thought, s. [E. *think*] what one thinks, thinking, reasoning, a judgment of the mind.
Thousand, adj. and s. [E. *thusend*, compare Mœso-Goth. *taihuns, hund*, a hundred] ten times a hundred.
Thread, s. [E. *thrawan*, to twist (to *throw* silk)] a twisted line, yarn, cord, twisted cotton.
Threat, s., menace, promise of evil, denunciation of punishment.
Threaten, v. [E. *threat, threatnian*] to menace, promise punishment, reprove. *Threatened.*
Three, see page 51.
Throat, s. [E. *throte*] the gullet, front of the neck.
Throne, s., [Fr. *throne*, L. *thronus*, Gr. *thronos*, a seat] a king's seat, the office or position of king.
Throng, s. [E. *thringan*, to press] a press, multitude, crowd.
Throng, v., to press, crowd, close in on every side. *Thronged.*
Through, prep. [E. *thurh*] across, over, from one side to another, by means of.
Throughout, prep., entirely through, all through.
Throw, v. [E. *thrawan*] to twist, hurl, cast, heave. *Threw, thrown.*
Thrush, s., a small bird of the family *Merulidæ.*
Thrust, v., to put forth with an effort, push, shove. *Thrust, thrust.*
Thumb, s. [E. *thuma*] the thick finger, the finger that faces the others.
Thunder, s. [E. *thunor*] a rumbling sound in the air caused by the discharge of electricity. Adj. *thunderous.*

Thunder, v., to cause thunder, sound loudly as thunder, roar. *Thundered.*
Thus, adv. [E. *this*] in this way, so.
Thwart, adj. [E. *thweorh*] across, transverse, crossing.
Thyme, s. [L. *thymus*, Gr. *thumos, thuein*] a sweet-smelling herb.
Tide, s., time, the time when the sea ebbs and flows, the ebb and flow of the sea.
Tidings, s. pl. [E. *tidan*, to betide] events, news.
Tie, v., to bind, draw tight, fasten. *Tied.*
Tier, s., a row, rank, row of seats.
Tiger, s. [Fr. *tigre*, L. *tigris*] a striped beast of prey of the genus *Felis.*
Tight, adj. [E. *tie*] close, fastened, staunch.
Tigris, s., a river which rises in the mountains of Armenia, flows south-eastwards almost parallel to the Euphrates, into which at last it falls.
Till, adv., prep. [E. *til*, an end] to the end of, to the time of.
Timber, s., building stuff, wood, a large beam of wood.
Time, s. [E. *tima*] season, period, course of events.
Timorous, adj. [L. *timorosus, timor*, fear] fearful, timid, shrinking.
Tin, s. [Fr. *étain*, O. Fr. *estain*, L. *stannum*] a white malleable metal.
Tint, v. [Fr. *teint, teindre*, L. *tingere*, to stain] to colour, dye, tinge, to give a slight colour. *Tinted.*
Tip, s. [E. *top*] a little top, small end.
Tire, v. [E. *tear*] to weary, vex, fret. *Tired.*
Tissue, s. [Fr. *tissu*, p. part. of *tistre*, L. *texere*, to weave] woven stuff, texture, a series.
Tobacco, s. [Sp. *tobaco*, Haitian, *tambaku*, a pipe] a narcotic herb which the Spanish found in use

among the people of the West Indies, who smoked it through pipes made of clay.

To-day, s. [corruption of *the day*] this day.

Together, adv. [E. *togædere, gather*] gathered into one, in company.

Toil, s. [E. *tiola, till*] work, labour, weariness.

Token, s. [E. *tacn*] a mark, sign, remembrance.

Toll, v., to sound a bell, to sound, strike. *Tolled.*

To-morrow, s. [E. *to, morrow*] the morning coming next.

Tone, s. [Fr. *ton*, L. *tonus*] sound, quality of sound.

Tongue, s. [E. *tunge*] a fleshy organ in the mouth used for licking, and tasting, and by man for speaking.

Topmost, adj. [E. *top*] uppermost.

Too, adv., enclitic, [E. *to*] in addition, over, moreover.

Tool, s. [E. *tol*] a thing to work with, an instrument.

Tooth, s. [E. *toth*] a small bone set in the jaw, used for eating, a tooth-like prong or projection. Pl. *teeth.*

Top, s., uppermost part, summit, head, surface.

Torch, s. [Fr. *torche*, It. *torcia*, L. *torta, torquere*, to twist] a light of twisted tow or rope tarred.

Torpid, adj. [L. *torpidus, torpere*] sluggish, slow.

Torrent, s. [Fr. *torrent*, L. *torrentem, torrere*] a boiling stream, a rushing river, a rushing shower.

Tortoise, s. [E. *tortuce*, It. *tortesa*, L. *tortus, torquere*] a reptile which has its body enclosed between two shields of bone or shell, with openings for the head, the tail, the legs, so called from its twisted crooked legs.

Toss, v., to jerk, throw, heave about. *Tossed.*

Total, adj. [L. *totalis, totus*] whole, entire, complete.

Totter, v., to stumble, walk feebly, tremble greatly. *Tottered.*

Touch, v. [Fr. *touche*, It. *toccare*, Old Ger. *zuccón*] to take, handle, reach with the fingers, influence, affect. *Touched.*

Tough, adj. [E. *toh, teon*, to tug] able to bear tugging, strong, firm.

Tow, v. [E. *teohan*, to pull] to tug, draw a boat or ship. *Towed.*

Towards, adv., prep. [E. *to, wards*] tending to, reaching near.

Tower, s. [L. *turrim, turris*] a high building, tall fortress.

Tower, v., to rise high into the air. *Towered.*

Town, s. [E. *tun, tynan*, to hedge] an enclosure, a farm enclosure, a collection of houses, an inhabited place having markets.

Trace, s. [Fr. *trace, tracer*, L. *tractiare, trahere*, to draw] a track, mark, sign.

Trace, v., to follow the track, follow by observing marks, draw. *Traced.*

Track, s. [L. *tracta, trahere*] a trace, a mark, footprint, impression, a road traced out. Adj. *trackless.*

Tract, s. [L. *tractus, trahere*] an extensive piece of land, district.

Trade, s. [E. *tredan*, to go] a way of life, a course of business, business, commerce.

Traffic, v. [It. *trafficare*, L. *trans, facere*] to travel for trade, to trade, buy and sell. *Trafficked.*

Tragedy, s. [Fr. *tragédie*, L. *tragoedia*, Gr. *tragodia*] poetry representing serious action in dramatic form.

Train, s. [Fr. *trainer*, L. L. *trahinare*, L. *trahere*] what is drawn, a series, a trailing line.

Traitor, s. [Fr. *traitre*, L. *traditor, tradere*] a betrayer, one who commits treason.

Tramp, v., to walk, walk with a

heavy tread, wander over the country. *Tramped.*

Trample, v. [freq. of E. *tramp*] to tread down, break down with the feet, insult. *Trampled.*

Transcendent, adj. [L. *transcendentem, transcendere, trans, scandere,* to climb] surpassing, eminent.

Transit, s. [L. *transitus, trans, ire,* to go across] crossing, passage.

Transporting, adj. [E. *transport,* L. *transportare*] carrying away, carrying away with joy, delightful.

Trash, s., useless matter, refuse, rubbish.

Travel, s. [Fr.*travail,* L.*trabaculum,* a break, *trabem*] toil, labour of journeying, journey, a tour.

Travel, v., to move from place to place, journey. *Travelled.* Subs. *traveller.*

Treachery, s. [E. *trechour,* O. Fr. *trachor,* L. *traditorem, tradere,* to betray] treason, falseness, faithlessness.

Tread, v. [E. *tredan*] to set down the foot, step. *Trod* or *trode, trodden.*

Treadle, s. [E. *tread*] part of a machine on which the foot treads in working.

Treasure, s. [Fr. *trésor,* L. *thesaurus,* Gr. *thesauros*] a store of wealth, riches, valuables.

Treat, v. [Fr. *traiter,* L. *tractare*] to handle, deal with, attend to. *Treated.*

Treatment, s. [Fr. *traitement, traiter*] mode of handling, management.

Treble, adj. [Fr. *treble,* L. *triplicem, triplex*] threefold.

Tree, s. [E. *treow*] a large plant with woody stem.

Tremble, v. [Fr. *trembler,* L. *tremulare, tremere*] to shiver, quake with fear. *Trembled.*

Tremulous, adj. [L. *tremulus, tremere*] trembling, quivering, shaking.

Trench, s. [O. Fr. *trencher,* Fr. *trancher,* to cut] a cutting, ditch.

Trial, s. [E. *try*] an attempt, examination, trouble.

Tribute, s. [L. *tributum*] a tax, amount of money levied.

Trickle, v., to roll in small quantity, flow in a little stream. *Trickled.*

Trim, adj., ordered, well arranged, neat.

Trim, v., to set in order, steady, arrange, make neat. *Trimmed.*

Triumph, s. [L. *triumphus*] victory, pomp, celebration of victory.

Triumphant, adj. [L. *triumphantem, triumphare*] victorious, boasting.

Troop, s. [Fr. *troupe*] a crowd, number, body of horse.

Tropics, s. [Gr. *tropica, trepein,* to turn] the zones or circles reaching to 23° 28′ N. and S. of the equator, from which points the sun turns again towards the equator.

Trot, v. [Fr. *trotter,* L. *tolutare, tolutim,* lifting the foot] to move fast, run. *Trotted.*

Trouble, v. [Fr. *troubler,* L. *turbulare, turba,* a crowd] to disturb, confuse, perplex. *Troubled.*

Trousers, s., pl. [Fr. *trousses, troussers,* It. *torciare,* L. *torquere*] short tucked breeches, breeches.

True, adj. [E. *treowe*] firm, settled, honest, upright.

Trumpet, s. [Fr. *trompette, trompe*] a wind instrument of music, a horn.

Trunk, s. [Fr. *tronc,* L. *truncus*] a stem, body, large box.

Truss, s. [Fr. *trousser,* O. Fr. *torser,* It. *torciare,* L. *torquere,* to twist] a bundle, a pack.

Trust, s., faith, confidence, a charge.

Trust, v. [E. *treowe*] to confide, believe, give over into charge. *Trusted.*

Truth, s. [E. *true*] what is true, agreement with fact, honour.

Try, v. [Fr. *trier,* It. *tritare,* L. *tritus, terere,* to rub] to test, sift, examine, endeavour. *Tried.*

Tub, s., a wooden vessel, small cask.

Tug, v. [E. *teogan*] to pull hard, drag, tow. *Tugged.*
Tumble, v. [E. *tumbian*] to fall, roll over. *Tumbled.*
Tumult, s. [L. *tumultus, tumere*, to swell] riot, commotion.
Tune, s. [E. *tone*] sound, melody, harmony, order.
Tunic, s. [L. *tunica*] a robe, frock, an under garment, a coat.
Turban, s. [It. *turbante*, Pers. *dulbend*] a covering for the head, made of a long cloth folded.
Turf, s., the surface of grass land, a piece of dried peat. Pl. *turves*, dried peat.
Turkey, s., a large gallinaceous fowl, supposed at one time to come from Turkey, really introduced into Europe from America.
Turn, v. [L. *tornare*] to shape in a lathe, revolve, twist, change about. *Turned.*
Turnip, s. [E. *turn*, rounded, E. *næpe*, L. *napus*, a root] a large round root.
Turret, s. [Fr. *tourette*, dim. of *tour*, L. *turris*] a small tower, a small tower forming part of another building.
Twain, adj. [E. *twegen*, old masc. form] two.
Twenty, adj. [E. *twegen, tig*, two tens] twice ten.
Twice, see page 52.
Twilight, s. [E. *two, light*] between the lights, the time after the sunlight has faded, and before the artificial light is lighted, faint light, obscurity.
Twin, s. [E. *twegen*, two] one of two born at a birth.
Twine, v. [E. *twin, two*] to double, twist, wind round, climb round.
Two, adj. [E. *twa*] one and one.
Typical, adj. [E. *type*, Gr. *tupos*] belonging to a type, figurative, standing as a model.
Tyrannical, adj. [E. *tyranny*] acting as a tyrant, oppressive, cruel.

Tyranny, s. [Fr. *tyrannie*, L. and Gr. *turannis*] the government of a tyrant, oppression, injustice, cruelty.
Tyrant, s. [Fr. *tyrant*, L. *tyrannus*, Gr. *turannos*] an absolute ruler, an unlawful ruler, an unjust or cruel ruler.

Ultimate, adj. [L. *ultimatus, ultimus*, last] last, latest.
Umbrella, s. [It. *ombrella, ombre*, L. *umbra*, shade] a shelter, a protection from sunshine or rain.
Un- in composition has the force of *not*, as, *unknown, not* known, *unhappy, not* happy; the derivation of such compounded words is to be found under the simple forms.
Unable, adj., not able.
Unanimous, adj. [L. *unanimus, unus, animus*] of one mind, agreeing.
Unapt, adj., not apt.
Unawares, adv., not aware, suddenly.
Uncle, s. [Fr. *oncle*, L. *avunculus*] father's brother or mother's brother.
Under, adv., prep., below, beneath.
Underneath, adv., prep., below, beneath.
Understand, v., to stand under, to know, perceive, take in. *Understood.*
Undertake, v., to take under one's power, enter upon, engage in. *Undertook, undertaken.*
Unflinching, adj. [E. *flinch, flicker, fly*] not shrinking, firm, steadfast.
Unfurl, v. [E. *furl*] to unwrap a sail, let loose, spread. *Unfurled.*
Unite, v. [L. *unitus, unire, unus*, one] to make one, join into one, join closely. *United.*
University, s. [L. *universitatem, unus*] a corporate body, a corporate body which undertakes higher education.
Unless, conj. [E. *on, less*] if not.

Unsavoury, adj. [E. *savoury, savour*, Fr. *saveur*, L. *saporem*, taste] not tasty, unpleasing to the taste, nasty.

Until, adv., prep. [E. *on, till*] till, to the time when.

Up, adv., prep., on, upon, over, on high, aloft.

Uphold, v. [E. *hold*] to hold on high, sustain, help, support. *Upheld, upheld* or *upholden*.

Upland, s., high land, land on hill-country, or on the mountain side.

Upon, prep., on.

Upper, adj. [E. *up*] more up, higher, superior.

Upraised, adj., raised up. See **Raise**.

Upright, adj., right, straight, erect.

Uproar, s. [G. *aufruhr*] disturbance, confusion, noise.

Upset, v., to set up what is down, overturn, overthrow, disturb. *Upset*.

Upward, adv., towards a higher place.

Urchin, s. [E. *urchone*, Fr. *hérisson*, L. *ericionem, ericius*] a hedgehog, a child.

Urge, v. [L. *urgere*] to drive, press forward, incite. *Urged*.

Use, s. [L. *usus*] purpose, employment, enjoyment, benefit. Adj. *useful*; Subs. *usefulness*.

Usual, adj. [L. *usualis, usus*] often used, common, frequent. Adv. *usually*.

Utmost, adj. [superlative of E. *ut*, out] outmost, to the farthest degree.

Utter, adj. [comparative of E. *ut*] outer, extreme.

Utter, v. [E. *ut*, out] to send forth, publish, speak. *Uttered*.

Vague, adj. [Fr. *vague*, L. *vagus*, wandering] unfixed, unsettled, uncertain.

Vain, adj. [Fr. *vain*, L. *vanus*, empty] useless, unreal, empty-headed, conceited.

Vale, s. [Fr. *val*, L. *vallem, vallis*] a glen, low ground between hills, a valley.

Valet, s. [Fr. *valet, vaslet*, dim. of vassal, W. *gwasawl, gwas*, a servant, a boy] a man servant, a confidential servant.

Valiant, adj. [Fr. *vaillant*, L. *valentem, valere*, to be strong] strong, bold, brave.

Valley, s. [Fr. *vallée, val*, L. *vallis*] a glen, vale.

Valour, s. [Fr. *valeur*, L. *valorem, valere*] strength, bravery, courage.

Value, s. [Fr. *valu, valoir*, L. *valere*] worth, estimation, price, cost of production.

Value, v., to estimate, esteem, prize. *Valued*.

Van, s. [Fr. *avant*, L. *ab, ante*, before] the front, front division of an army.

Vanish, v. [O. Fr. *vanir*, L. *vanescere, vanus*, empty] to pass away and leave a place empty, disappear.

Vapour, s. [L. *vaporem*] steam, water in the atmosphere, gas generated by heat.

Variegate, v. [L. *variegatus, varius, agere*] to make varied, diversify, mark in different ways. *Variegated*.

Variety, s. [Fr. *varieté*, L. *varietatem, varius*] unlikeness, difference, change.

Various, adj. [L. *varius*] unlike, different, several.

Vary, v. [Fr. *varier*, L. *variare, varius*] to change, be unlike, alter. *Varied*.

Vast, adj. [Fr. *vaste*, L. *vastus*] very large, immense, huge.

Vegetable, adj. [L. *vegetabilis, vegere*, to grow] growing. Subs., plant used for food.

Vengeance, s. [Fr. *vengeance, venger*, L. *vindicare*] retribution, punishment in return for an injury, fierce punishment.

Venice, s., a city of Italy built on the

GLOSSARY. 327

lagoons on the northern coast of the Adriatic sea, founded A.D. 452.

Venture, v. [corruption of *aventure*, L. *ad*, *venturus*, *venire*, to come] to chance, risk, dare. *Ventured*.

Verdure, s. [Fr. *verdure*, *verd*, L. *viridis*, *virere*, to be green] greenness, rich growth.

Verse, s. [Fr. *vers*, L. *versus*, *vertere*, to turn] a line of poetry, poetry, language in metre.

Very, adj. [Fr. *vrai*, L. *veracem*, *verus*, true] true, real, in great measure, greatly.

Vessel, s. [O. Fr. *vaissel*, L. *vascellum*, *vas*, a cup] a bowl, anything which holds liquid, a ship.

Vestment, s. [L. *vestimentum*, *vestis*] a garment, robe.

Vesuvius, s., a volcano (3932 ft.) in Campania in Italy, near the shore of the bay of Naples.

Viands, s. pl. [Fr. *viande*, L. *vivenda*, *vivere*, to live] victuals, food, provisions.

Vice, s. [Fr. *vice*, L. *vitium*] fault, wickedness, a breach of morals.

Vicinage, s. [Fr. *voisinage*, L. *vicinus*, a neighbour] the neighbourhood.

Victim, s. [L. *victima*] a thing offered in sacrifice, an offering, an injured person.

Victory, s. [L. *victoria*, *victor*, *vincere*, to conquer] success in battle, superiority, conquest. Adj. *victorious*.

Victuals, s. pl. [Fr. *vitaille*, L. *victualia*, *victus*, *vivere*] food, provisions.

View, s. [Fr. *vue*, *voir*, L. *videre*, to see] a seeing, thing seen, prospect, scene.

View, v., to look over, see, examine. *Viewed*.

Vigour, s. [L. *vigorem*, *vigere*, to flourish] strength, force, energy. Adj. *vigorous*.

Village, s. [Fr. *village*, L. *villati-*

cum, *villa*, a country-seat] a collection of houses in the country, a small collection of houses without a municipal authority.

Vine, s. [L. *vinum*] a climbing plant which bears grapes.

Vineyard, s. [E. *vine*, *yard*] a garden of vines.

Violence, s. [Fr. *violence*, L. *violentia*, *violare*, *vis*, force] great force, wrongful, force, outrage.

Violent, adj. [Fr. *violent*, L. *violentus*] using excessive force, outrageous.

Violet, s. [Fr. *violette*, dimin. of L. *viola*] a plant producing a flower, usually of a purple shade.

Virgin, s. [L. *virginem*, *virgo*] a maiden, young woman.

Virginia, s., a state in North America, so called in honour of Queen Elizabeth, the virgin queen, in whose reign a number of Englishmen founded a colony there, in the year 1587.

Virtue, s. [Fr. *vertu*, L. *virtutem*, *virtus*, manliness; *vir*, a man] excellence, goodness, a form of moral goodness.

Visible, adj. [L. *visibilis*, *visus*, *videre*, to see] that may be seen, manifest to the eye.

Visit, v. [Fr. *visiter*, L. *visitare*, *visere*, *videre*] to go to see, call upon. *Visited*.

Visit, s., a going to see, call.

Vivacity, s. [L. *vivacitatem*, *vivax*, *vivere*, to live] liveliness, animation, brightness.

Vivify, v. [Fr. *vivifier*, L. *vivus*, *facere*] to make alive, enliven, animate, quicken. *Vivified*.

Vociferate, v. [L. *vociferatus*, *vociferari*, *vocem*, *ferre*, to carry the voice] to call loudly, shout, scream. *Vociferated*.

Voice, s. [Fr. *voix*, L. *vocem*, *vox*] sound from the mouth, tone, speech.

Volcanic, adj. [Fr. *volcanique*, *volcan*, L. *vulcanus*] of a volcano, caused by a volcano, caused by the influence of subterranean fires.

Volcano, s. [It. *volcano*, L. *vulcanus*, the god of fire] a mountain which gives forth flame.

Volume, s. [Fr. *volume*. L. *volumen, volvere*, to roll] a roll, a book, anything which issues in a full rolling manner, as smoke.

Vote, v. [L. *votum, vovere*, to vow] to express a desire, to elect, declare choice of a candidate at an election. *Voted.*

Vow, s. [Fr. *vœu*, L. *votum, vovere*] a desire, promise to God, promise.

Vow, v., to promise solemnly. *Vowed.*

Voyage, s. [Fr. *voyage*, It. *viaggio*, L. *viaticum, via*, a way] wayfaring, a journey, a journey by water.

Vulgar, adj. [L. *vulgaris, vulgus*, the common people] common, ordinary, low, base, ill-mannered.

Vulture, s. [L. *vultur*] a large bird of prey found chiefly in the tropical countries of the old and new worlds.

Wade, v., to walk through water, get through a thing with difficulty. *Waded.*

Waist, s. [W. *gwasg*] the part of the body which is squeezed in, the middle.

Waistcoat, s. [E. *waist, coat*] a coat, or covering for the waist, an under coat.

Wait, v. [O. Fr. *guaiter, waiter*, G. *wahten*, to watch] to observe, look out, expect, remain. *Waited.*

Wake, v. [E. *wacan*] to watch, to rise from sleep, rouse from sleep, sleep, stir. *Woke or waked, waked.*

Wake, s., a watching, watching over the dead, funeral.

Walk, v. [E. *wealcan*, to roll] to go on foot, move forwards, live. *Walked.*

Walk, s., mode of walking, gait, distance walked, ground laid out for walking.

Wall, s. [L. *vallum*, a rampart] a bank-rampart, fence of stone.

Wallet, s., a bag, travellers' bag, pouch.

Walnut, s. [E. *weal, hnut*, the foreign nut] the Italian nut.

Walsingham, s. [E. *home* of the *Wælsings*] a town in Norfolk, where was a shrine of the Virgin Mary, very famous in the days of pilgrimages.

Wander, v. [freq. of E. *wend*] to go about, go to and fro, ramble, stray. *Wandered.*

Want, v. [E. *wan*, loss, absence] to feel the absence of, miss, desire, covet. *Wanted.*

Want, s., poverty, need, scarcity.

Wanton, adj. [E. *wan*, ill; *towen, teon*, to lead] unrestrained, loose, licentious.

War, s., strife, contest, contention.

Warble, v., to trill as a bird, quaver, sing sweetly. *Warbled.*

Warble, s., a bird's song, trill, song.

Warlike, adj. [E. *war*] suiting war, soldierly, hostile, fierce.

Warm, adj., rather hot, eager. Subs. *warmth*.

Wary, adj. [E. *ware*] cautious, careful, on the watch.

Wash, v. [E. *wæsc*] to cover with water, overflow, splash, clean with water. *Washed.*

Wasp, s., a stinging insect, of a bright yellow colour marked with black somewhat like a bee.

Waste, v. [E. *westan*] to destroy, spoil, spend fruitlessly. *Wasted.*

Waste, s., barren land, misuse, barren expenditure.

Watch, v. [softened form of E. *wake*] to be awake, guard, look at. *Watched.*

Watch, s., attention, a guard, time of keeping guard, an instrument for marking the passage of time. Adj. *watchful*, attentive.

Watcher, s., one who watches.

Water, s. [E. *wæter*] a fluid composed of hydrogen and oxygen, the fluid composing the sea, rivers, &c., a sea. Adj. *watery.*

Waterspout, s., a moving column of water.

Wattles, s., pl. [E. *wæth*, a swathe] twigs, osiers.

Wave, s., moving water, a billow, surge, unevenness, a surging line.

Wave, v., [E. *wæg*] to move up and down, vibrate, brandish. *Waved.*

Waver, v. [E. *wave*] to move unsteadily, shake, totter, hesitate. *Wavered.*

Wax, s., a yellow stuff made by bees, any viscid substance resembling beeswax. Adj. *waxen.*

Way, s., [E. *weg*] a going, path, passage, direction, mode.

Weak, adj. [E. *wac*] soft, yielding, feeble, infirm.

Weaken, v., to make weak, grow weak. *Weakened.*

Wealth, s. [E. *weal*] prosperity, welfare, riches. Adj. *wealthy.*

Weapon, s. [E. *wæpen*] an instrument of war, tool.

Wear, v. [E. *werian*] to bear on the body, put on, endure, waste by endurance, consume by use. *Wore, worn.*

Weary, adj. [E. *werig, wear*] worn, consumed, tired out.

Weary, v., to tire, fatigue. *Wearied.*

Weather, s. [E. *weder*] the state of the wind, state of the atmosphere.

Weave, v. [E. *wave*] to move to and fro, move a shuttle to and fro, make cloth in a loom, intertwine. *Wove, woven.*

Wed, v. [E. *wed*, a pledge] to pledge, engage in marriage, marry. *Wedded* or *wed.*

Wedding, s. [E. *wed*] a marriage.

Weed, s. [E. *weod*] a herb, useless plant.

Week, s. [E. *weoc*] a period of seven days.

Weep, v. [E. *wepan*] to lament, shed tears, cry. *Wept.*

Weigh, v. [E. *wegan, wag*] to raise in a balance, examine in a balance, raise, ponder in mind. *Weighed.*

Weight, s. [E. *weigh*] heaviness found by weighing, gravity, importance.

Welcome, adj. [E. *well, come*] received gladly, acceptable.

Welcome, v., to say welcome to, receive gladly. *Welcomed.*

Well, adj., good, in good health, proper. Adv. *well*, rightly.

Wend, v. [E. *wendan*] to go, turn, walk. *Wended* or *went.*

West, s., the place of sunset, the countries lying in the direction of sunset. Adj. *western;* Adv. *westwards.*

Wet, adj., watery, moist, damp.

Whale, s. [E. *bwal*] a name given to an order of Mammals, a large mammal living in the sea.

Wharf, s. [E. *hwarf*, G. *werpen*, to cast up] a raised bank by the waterside, a raised yard for lading and unlading ships.

What, see page 56.

Whatever, see page 56.

Whatsoever, see page 56.

Wheat, s. [E. *hwæte*, the white] a species of grass producing a large ear of grains giving white flour, the staple food of England.

Wheel, v. [E. *hweol*, a circle] to circle, to turn on wheels, convey on wheels, turn. *Wheeled.*

Wheeze, v., to breathe noisily, breathe with a hissing or gurgling sound. *Wheezed.*

When, adv. [E. *hwæne*, acc. case of *hwá*, interr. pron.] at what time.

Whence, adv. [E. *whenes, when*] from when, from what time or place, expressing motion from.

Where, adv. [E. *hwær, hwá*] at what place, expressing rest.

Whereby, see page 56.

Wherefore, see page 56.

Whereof, see page 56.

Whereunto, see page 56.
Whereupon, see page 56.
Wherever, see page 56.
Wherewith, see page 56.
Whether, see page 56.
Whetstone, s. [E. *whet, hwæt*, sharp, *stone*] a stone for sharpening tools.
Which, see page 56.
While, s. [E. *hwil*] time, leisure. Adv. during the time that.
Whilst, adv. [E. *whiles*, gen. case of *while*] during the time that.
Whip, s. [E. *hweop*] an instrument for lashing or driving, consisting of a handle and a lash, a stick for whipping.
Whisper, v. [E. *hwisprian*] to speak with a low voice. *Whispered.*
Whisper, s., a low voice, soft utterance.
Whit, s. [E. *wiht*, a creature] a thing, piece, bit.
White, adj. [E. *hwit*] shining, showing no colour, pure, clean.
Whitehall, s., the hall of a royal palace in London, so called because it was built of white stone.
Whither, adv. [E. *hwider, hwá*] to what place, expressing motion towards.
Who, see page 56.
Whole, adj. [E. *hal*] hale, sound, complete, entire. Adv. *wholly*, entirely.
Wholesome, adj. [E. *whole, sam*] healthy, healthful, sound.
Whoop, v. [E. *wop*, a cry] to shout with a high-pitched tone, cry aloud, shout. *Whooped.*
Why, adv. [E. *hwy*, instrumental case of *hwá*] for what reason.
Wicked, adj. [E. *wikke, wican*, to be weak] poor, mean, wrong, evil, faulty, ungodly.
Wide, adj., broad, extended, ample, spacious.
Wield, v. [E. *wealdan*] to use, manage, rule. *Wielded.*
Wife, s., a married woman.

Wild, adj., wandering, untamed, uncivilised, rash.
Wilderness, s. [E. *wilder, wild*] a wild uncultivated place, desert.
Will, s. [E. *willa*] the power of choice, volition, desire, intention, purpose.
Will, v., to resolve, determine, purpose, pp. *willing, willed* or *would*: also, auxiliary verb, see page 74.
William, s., Duke of Normandy, son of Robert the Devil, born 1027, crowned King of England 1066, died 1087.
Willow, s. [E. *welig*, W. *helig*] a tree of the genus *salix*, with long slender branches.
Win, v. [E. *winnan*] to gain, get, conquer, earn. *Won.*
Wind, s., that which blows, air moving.
Wind, v. [E. *windan*] to twist, wrap round, turn, screw. *Wound.*
Window, s. [E. *wind, edge*, an eye] an opening for 'wind, an opening in a wall to let in air and light.
Wine, s. [L. *vinum*] fermented juice of grapes.
Wing, s., the limb of a bird by which it flies, a side limb, side of an army.
Wing, v., to furnish with wings, fly with wings, wound in the wing. *Winged.*
Winter, s., the cold season of the year.
Wisdom, s. [E. *wise*] the condition of being wise, knowledge, prudence.
Wise, adj., sensible, learned, prudent, knowing.
Wish, v. [E. *wiscan*] to long for, desire. *Wished.*
Wistful, adj. [E. *wisht*, ill *wished*] full of trouble, anxious.
Wit, s. [E. *witan*, to know] knowledge, insight, humour. Adj. *witty.*

Wit, v. defective, to know: Present, I *wot*, he *wot*; Past, I *wist*. *To wit*, to know, that is to say.
With, prep., against, towards, near, by.
Withdraw, v. [E. *with*, against] to draw back, go away, retire. *Withdrew, withdrawn.*
Wither, v., to dry up, shrivel, fade. *Withered.*
Within, prep., inside.
Without, prep., outside, beyond, not with.
Withstand, v. [E. *with*, against] to stand against, oppose, resist. *Withstood.*
Witness, v. [E. *witan*, to know] to state one's knowledge, bear testimony, affirm. See **Wit.**
Woe, s. [E. *wa*] grief, misfortune, great sorrow.
Wolf, s. [E. *wulf*] a carnivorous animal of the same family as the dog.
Woman, s. [E. *wif, man*] female of man.
Wonder, s. [E. *wundor*] astonishment, surprise, a thing producing surprise, a marvel, anything uncommon. Adj. *wondrous.*
Wonder, v. [E. *wundrian*] to feel surprise, be astonished. *Wondered.*
Wont, v., defect. [pp. of *wone*, to dwell, E. *wunian*] accustomed.
Wood, s. [E. *wudu*] trees, a collection of trees, substance of trees, timber.
Woodland, s., land covered with wood.
Wool, s., the shaggy hair of sheep, fleece. Adj. *woolly.*
Word, s., one or more letters having a complete meaning.
Work, s. [E. *weorc*] labour, toil, business, employment.
Work, v., to labour, toil, make. *Wrought* or *worked.*
Workmanship, s. [E. *work, man*] the business of a workman, handicraft, execution, finish.

World, s. [E. *weorold, wer*, man, *old*, age, the age of man] lifetime, the age, universe, the earth and all upon it.
Worry, v., to strangle, tease, disturb, fret. *Worried.*
Worse, adj. [E. *wyr*] more evil, more sick, see page 51.
Worship, v. [E. *worth, ship*, a worthy condition] to hold in esteem, honour, reverence. *Worshipped.*
Worshipper, s., one who worships.
Worst, adj. [E. *wyrst*] most evil, see page 51.
Worth, s., price, value, honour, esteem; Adjectives, *worth*, equal in value, *worthy*, deserving honour, estimable, *worthless*, of no value.
Wot, v. See **Wit.**
Wound, s. [E. *wund*] hurt, cut, injury.
Wound, v., to cut, injure, hurt, give pain to. *Wounded.*
Wrangle, v. to quarrel, hold a noisy dispute. *Wrangled.*
Wrath, s. [from root of E. *writhe*] anger, rage, fury.
Wreath, s. [E. *writhe*] a twist, garland of leaves or flowers.
Wreathe, v. [E. *wreath, writhe*] to twist, entwine, encircle. *Wreathed.*
Wreck, s. [E. *wræc*] breaking, crash, ruin, destruction.
Wretched, adj. [E. *wretch*, soft form of E. *wræcca*, an exile, *wreak*] miserable, unhappy, wicked.
Write, v., to trace, draw letters, express in letters, compose. *Wrote* or *writ, written* or *writ.*
Writer, s., one who writes.
Wrong, adj. [E. *wring*] wrung out of course, twisted, unjust.
Wrong, v., to injure, harm, treat unjustly. *Wronged.*
Wrought. See **Work.**

Yard, s. [E. *geard*] a rod, a rod three feet long, an enclosure, a court.

Yawn, s., a gaping, opening of the mouth from fatigue or drowsiness.
Year, s. [E. *gear*] a period of time consisting of 365 days.
Yell, v., to scream, cry aloud, howl. *Yelled*.
Yellow, adj. [E. *gelewe*, from root of *gall*, *gold*] of a bright gold colour.
Yes, adv. of assent, aye.
Yet, adv., still, again, besides; conj. however.
Yield, v. [E. *gildan*] to pay, give up, restore, submit. *Yielded*.
Yoke, s., a wooden framework to fasten oxen for drawing, a badge of slavery.
Yon, Yonder, pron. [E. *geond*] that at a distance. Adv. at a distance.
Yore, s. [E. *geara*] olden time.
Young, adj. [E. *geong*] new, not long born.
Youngster, s. [E. *young*] a lad, boy.
Your, see page 53.
Youth, s. [E. *young*] young age, early life, a person in early life.
Yule, s. [E. *geol*, the merry time] Christmas-tide, Christmas feast.

Zealous, adj. [E. *zeal*, L. *zelus*, Gr. *zelos*] eager, vehement.
Zenith, s. [Sp. *zenit*, Ar. *semt*, the (head) region] the part of heaven just overhead, greatest height.
Zincalo, s., the Spanish name for a gipsy. Pl. *zincali*.

www.ingramcontent.com/pod-product-compliance
Lightning Source LLC
Chambersburg PA
CBHW030004240426
43672CB00007B/823